Education for Liberation

Education
for
Liberation

The American Missionary Association
and African Americans,
1890 to the Civil Rights Movement

Joe M. Richardson and Maxine D. Jones

The University of Alabama Press
Tuscaloosa

Typeface: Bembo

∞

The paper on which this book is printed meets the minimum requirements of
American National Standard for Information Sciences-Permanence of Paper for
Printed Library Materials, ANSI Z39.48-1984.

Library of Congress Cataloging-in-Publication Data

Richardson, Joe Martin.
    Education for liberation : the American Missionary Association and African Americans,
1890 to the Civil Rights Movement / Joe M. Richardson and Maxine D. Jones.
        p.   cm.
    Rev. ed. of: Christian reconstruction.
    Includes bibliographical references (p.   ) and index.
    ISBN 978-0-8173-1657-0 (cloth : alk. paper) — ISBN 978-0-8173-8245-2 (electronic)
1. American Missionary Association—History—19th century. 2. American Missionary
Association—History—20th century. I. Jones, Maxine Deloris. II. Richardson, Joe Martin.
Christian reconstruction. III. Title.
    BV2360.A8R54 2009
    266′.02208996073—dc22
                                                                            2008050470

To Pat, Leslie, and Joseph
and to the memory of
James "Skeeter" McDonald, Arthur Carl Jones,
Robert "Bo" Bennett, and Willie Bowles

Contents

Illustrations

Preface

The Confederate shelling of Fort Sumter had barely penetrated northern consciousness when the American Missionary Association (AMA) exulted that the war had opened a grand field for missionary labor. Organized in New York as a nonsectarian anti-slavery society in 1846, it quickly focused on relief and education for slaves fleeing Confederate lines.[1] In September 1861, it sent agents to Fortress Monroe, Virginia, and its teachers tracked the Union Army so closely that roaring cannons occasionally interrupted classes, and killed at least one teacher.[2] The number of AMA teachers and missionaries assisting freedmen in the South increased from 250 in 1864 to 320 in 1865 and to 532 in 1868. In addition, the association provided much needed relief for black refugees, insisted on equal pay for black soldiers, attempted to help freedmen acquire land, demanded civil and political rights for former slaves, established scores of schools and colleges, and lobbied for a system of free public education for all southern youth. AMA supporters were motivated by religion, patriotism, and a sense of fairness, and an equal, educated, moral, industrious black citizenry was their goal.

Equality before the law was "the gospel rule," the AMA concluded, and the country's "political salvation" depended upon its implementation. It enthusiastically supported the Fourteenth and Fifteenth Amendments, and initially believed that they would provide equality before the law and substantial black political clout. Education, improved morals, and economic success, the AMA hoped, would result in white Americans' acceptance and recognition of blacks. Association officials were bitterly disappointed that by the mid-1870s violence, fraud, and declining northern interest in black welfare allowed southern whites to make a mockery of the amendments and relegate their former slaves to a politically powerless, economically dependent, segregated class.[3]

Not surprisingly, the AMA sometimes failed to live up to its own lofty ideals. After Democrats drove black and white Republicans from office in southern states, a few members speculated whether blacks had been given the ballot too quickly. Even these skeptics, however, argued that educated black men should have equal voting rights. Others failed to recognize the vitality and richness of black culture and institutions and were slow to accept black insistence upon self-determination. Teachers and agents were too often paternalistic and racially prejudiced. The AMA occasionally stumbled; its members frequently disagreed on the proper course of action; it sometimes may have erred on the side of caution. Yet it never wavered from its claim that blacks were equal in God's sight, that any "backwardness" was created by circumstances rather than inherent inferiority, and that blacks should and could eventually become equal citizens. It came far closer to full recognition of black ability, humanity, and aspirations than most nineteenth- and twentieth-century white Americans, and even after the disappointment of Reconstruction it consistently and eloquently pleaded for equal protection of black life, liberty, and property. Milton Hurst, a student and later professor at the association's Talladega College in Talladega, Alabama, said the AMA "provided an experience that could only be dreamed of, wished for, longed for. It was an experience of hope in the midst of despair, of trust for a future beyond the present history, of daring to dream that you are not held by your circumstances." The AMA had its shortcomings, but Hurst did not exaggerate. Thousands of young black men and women shared his view.[4]

During the tragic decades after Reconstruction, the period of this study, the AMA consistently opposed disfranchisement, vigorously condemned lynching, and challenged segregation laws in court. At the 1901 annual meeting, it spoke of "unjust legislation by which Negroes are disfranchised and ignorant white men are allowed to vote," and decried recent attacks on black "manhood and citizenship." AMA member Joseph Cook of Boston urged the AMA to "Educate, Evangelize, Enfranchise" and denounced disfranchisement as "a national peril." "The disfranchisement of ignorance or of moral worthlessness is not to be deprecated," Washington Gladden told the association in his 1901 presidential address, "but the drawing of the line of political privilege between the ignorant white man and the ignorant black man is a wrong that cannot endure." The AMA demanded that voting requirements "respect the manhood of the Negro and shall apply to white and black, without respect to race, color or previous condition." In 1903, it proclaimed it would "never cease to protest" laws which excluded voters on account of color. When the Georgia legislature considered disfranchisement laws in 1907, the AMA condemned racial demagogues and "low and worthless white registration officers" who disfranchised black men "greatly their superiors in knowledge, manners and morals." In 1911, it declared that "a voteless people is a helpless people" and demanded the enforcement of the Fourteenth and Fifteenth Amendments "which to our reproach and disgrace, remain . . . a 'dead letter' in the state books." It claimed that whites who were unwilling to meet blacks fairly in any contest were inferior rather than superior to them. The AMA appealed for black voting rights throughout its lifetime and in the 1960s was helping register black voters.[5]

By the mid-1890s, lynching was probably the primary issue in American race relations and the AMA played a prominent role. In 1895, Washington Gladden, then association vice president, and perhaps the most prominent advocate of social Christianity at the time, praised the organization for its long record of condemning lynching and racial violence. That same year, the association called lynching a "disgrace to our civilization," which proved perpetrators unfit for citizenship and also revealed "a shameful moral cowardice and indifference" of southern whites who failed to protest. It labeled a 1911 Coatesville, Pennsylvania, lynching as "The Ineffaceable Disgrace of Coatesville" and, in 1913, pointed out that by late summer at least thirteen blacks had been lynched and not one had been accused of sexual assault which whites often used as an excuse for violence. The AMA lamented "the atrocious massacre" of African Americans in East St. Louis, Illinois, in 1917, and in 1919 quoted an American soldier who said if the allies really wanted to punish the former German Kaiser they should clip his hair, blacken his face, and send him to the southern United States. The AMA consistently supported attempts to secure federal anti-lynching legislation, and sent a representative to the hearing of the Costigan-Wagner Anti-Lynching Bill in 1935. In 1937 and 1938 it appropriated $200 and $700 to the NAACP's anti-lynching program.[6]

The AMA challenged segregation laws in court, and regretted the increasing racial restrictions and prejudice in both North and South. It ridiculed Mississippi's segregation of street cars in 1901 and castigated President Woodrow Wilson for segregating federal facilities in Washington. Such segregation was "un-Christian, unmanly and Un-American," the *American Missionary,* the AMA's periodical, declared in 1914. The color line in the capital, the journal added, was "an anachronism as well as an insult to the innate sense of justice of the American people." All Americans should take an "interest in the removal from them of every vestige of the degradation of slavery." While most barbs were aimed at the South, the AMA frequently exposed northern prejudice. It said in 1913 that the posturing of racial demagogues might be no more important in allowing segregation and discrimination than the "indifference of the men of influence, culture, scholarship and Christian profession, North and South, who do not help remove this blight from our national life." In 1928, corresponding secretary Fred L. Brownlee rebuked northern colleges that had established racial quotas. The AMA retained interracial faculties in its southern colleges and began student exchanges with northern white schools long before the 1954 Brown decision which it worked for and celebrated. The AMA's ultimate aim, as it declared in 1936, was a "casteless society."[7]

Association officers commended President Theodore Roosevelt for sharing lunch with Booker T. Washington in 1901, but sternly criticized his unjust treatment of black soldiers in the Brownsville, Texas, affair in 1906.[8] In the same year it suggested that there were really no distinctive races, that all humans were varieties of the same race. It held AMA annual meetings only in cities where hotels entertained black delegates, and it supported the National Association for the Advancement of Colored People and other organizations created to improve the position of black Americans. When the Niagara Movement was being organized in 1905, it received limited national press, but the AMA recognized it and urged African Americans to "fight to the last ditch" and exhaust every legitimate means to gain their rights.[9] It reproached author Thomas Dixon's low appeal to racial prejudice in *The Leopard's Spots: A Romance of the White Man's Burden, 1865–1900* (1903) and *The Clansman: A Historical Romance of the Ku Klux Klan* (1905), and criticized as hateful, outrageous, and misleading *The Birth of a Nation,* a motion picture based on Dixon's racist writings which, historian John Hope Franklin claimed, "did more than any other single thing to nurture and promote the myth of black domination and debauchery during Reconstruction."[10]

The *American Missionary* publicized W. E. B. Du Bois's investigation of discrimination of black soldiers during World War I, and gloried in blacks' "new sense of self esteem and new consciousness of their constitutional rights."[11] After the "Red Summer" of 1919, AMA president Rev. Nehemiah Boynton excoriated the craven white cowards who inflicted pain and injustice upon black citizens. At its 1919 annual meeting the AMA deplored the "recrudescence of race prejudice, race hatred, and race discrimination in its fiercest and most passionate forms" and declared it was the association's "historic duty to take up with new emphasis and a burning zeal a constructive program for the remedy of these evils." The next year the AMA called for federal intervention on behalf of African Americans. Any government that compelled its citizens to bear arms in the country's defense, the *American Missionary* declared, "must by the same token have the power to protect them. A nation which proposes a democratic program for the weak and oppressed peoples of the world should inaugurate the same program at home."[12] The AMA constantly attacked economic discrimination which frequently prevented even educated blacks from securing meaningful jobs. Its protests against discrimination often included other disadvantaged races; for instance, it established schools for American Indians and for Chinese children in California, it built schools and a hospital in Puerto Rico, and it opposed the Immigration Act of 1924 which excluded Asians.[13] Northern racists did not escape AMA censure. As will be seen, northern white prejudice and indifference to black welfare affected the AMA's fund collecting efforts after 1900, and many of the 1919 "Red Summer" riots were outside the South. The AMA noted with sadness that when Dr. O. H. Sweet of Detroit, who had purchased a home in a white neighborhood, was arrested for protecting his home from a white mob in 1925, not a single white church came to his aid, and that black admission to northern colleges was becoming more difficult.[14] The association supported the Scottsboro Boys from the beginning. In 1933 the *American Missionary* proclaimed the defendants' innocence and criticized the lack of blacks on the jury and "the open and flagrant and unabashed violation of the constitutional guarantees of Negro rights." The following year the AMA administrative committee expressed "profound sympathy" with those who were "earnestly striving to secure an adequate and just verdict" for the "boys." It authorized corresponding secretary Fred L. Brownlee and black Alabama teacher Marion Cuthbert to do whatever they deemed "best in the use of the good name and offices of the Association to further the course of justice in the case." It made several appropriations to the American Scottsboro Committee.[15]

The AMA's aim was equality for African Americans in every way. It recognized in 1890 that alteration of the condition of black southerners would demand extended time and herculean effort. The failed Reconstruction experiment had proved that there were no immediate and simple solutions, and that allies in the struggle would be scarce. Longtime AMA member Amory Bradford warned at the annual meeting that "in all plans we must remember the time-factor. Great objects require long periods for accomplishment. There are a thousand difficulties to overcome." Association members knew of the difficulties, but also agreed with AMA secretary C. J. Ryder. "It is sometimes said that time will settle these monstrous inequalities in the South," Ryder had proclaimed in June 1890, "but time never settles anything. Mischievous forces only increase in power, the longer they are permitted to operate. There must be set in operation beneficent forces in order to make the element of time useful. Agitation is needed, patriotic, prayerful agitation."

The *American Missionary* reiterated that view in 1904. "If we consent now to postponement of justice we consent to a more difficult and more nearly hopeless future. Time hardens and does not soften evils."[16]

The AMA lobbied politicians, wrote books and pamphlets, made speeches, formed committees, and joined organizations established to assist African Americans, but it viewed education as its most effective vehicle for Secretary Ryder's call for agitation, as the best opportunity to gain voting rights, justice, and equality for blacks. Schooling might appear to be a conservative approach, but the AMA's interracial faculties, quality schools, and the vision of equal opportunity and ultimately first-class citizenship for black Americans were clearly radical for the period. Indeed, many southerners, both black and white, viewed the AMA's teaching the liberal arts, citizenship, and equality as revolutionary.[17] At its 1903 annual meeting Washington Gladden declared that the AMA initially had gone South to prepare former slaves for "responsible citizenship," and it would remain until citizenship became a reality. The AMA and its black constituents, in the words of Adam Fairclough, "expected education to serve double duty as a means of advancing both the individual and the race."[18]

After 1890, the association continued its efforts on behalf of black education, and enhanced its common and secondary schools and colleges. It urged publicly supported education and closed its common schools as soon as state alternatives became available and concentrated upon teacher training, secondary schools, and colleges. When southern states began to make greater provisions for black high schools in the 1920s and 1930s, the AMA cooperated with public authorities to transform its many secondary institutions into free public schools. In the late 1930s and '40s, the association expanded its efforts by placing greater emphasis on adult education, creating community centers, and in 1942 it organized a Race Relations Department to deal directly with discrimination and segregation. In the AMA's view, the common and secondary schools, colleges, community centers, and the Race Relations Department served the same interests: education for liberation—liberation from poverty, ignorance, and second-class citizenship.

This book is an attempt to delineate the strengths and weaknesses, successes and failures of the American Missionary Association's struggle to bring blacks into the mainstream of American life from 1890 to the post–World War II era. Common schools, primary-secondary schools, and colleges are treated in separate chapters. Special attention is given to the AMA's efforts to foster public education in the South. From the end of the Civil War it urged southerners to take responsibility for educating its citizens, and it cooperated with public authorities in creating and sustaining public schools when possible. The AMA often merged with or completely gave its school buildings and grounds to public authorities when they agreed to maintain quality education for blacks at public expense, but it also transformed a few of its schools into adult education and community centers, "Houses of Refuge," which taught, among other things, self-reliance, economy, health, farming, cooperation, and citizenship. These centers and the Race Relations Department created in 1942, considered by the AMA as merely extensions of its educational work, are discussed at length. All American Missionary Association institutions and activities were aimed at securing justice, respect, and equality for black Americans.

Acknowledgments

Many people assisted in the preparation of this book. We appreciate the courtesies extended us by the library staffs at Fisk University; Talladega College; Huston-Tillotson College; Dillard University; Florida State University; Howard University; Yale University; Schomburg Center of Research and Black Culture; University of Missouri, St. Louis; University of Texas; Tulane University; and the Library of Congress. We are especially grateful to the Amistad Research Center at Tulane University, an outstanding repository for African American and American Missionary Association history. During the many months we worked there the staff was ever professional, pleasant, and helpful. Brenda B. Square, Director of Archives and Library, sent us several rolls of microfilm through interlibrary loan and granted us permission to use images from the library's large collection of photographs. Christopher Harter assisted in making the selection of pictures both quick and pleasant. Juliette Smith, Talladega College, saved us a trip by graciously checking the accuracy of a citation.

We are especially indebted to the late Clifton H. Johnson, founder and longtime executive director of the Amistad Research Center. Cliff's encouragement, advice, enthusiasm for our project, and knowledge of all facets of the American Missionary Association were invaluable. We thank Clifton H. Johnson, Roderick Dion Waters, Lee Williams, and Titus Brown who read the manuscript and made useful suggestions on both substance and style.

Education for Liberation

1
Common Schools

It was truly heartrending, an Andersonville, Georgia, teacher wrote in 1895, to watch her pupils straggle into the schoolhouse after having walked four or five miles, "their feet protruding from their broken shoes, bringing their baskets of tuition in the way of chickens, eggs, etc. to pay their school bills." Although the AMA generally abandoned its elementary schools as quickly as public alternatives were available and concentrated on secondary, normal, and college education, it had fifty-one "common schools" in 1891. As James D. Anderson points out in *The Education of Blacks in the South, 1860–1935,* public elementary schools became available to a majority of southern black youth only in the first third of the twentieth century.[1]

The association's elementary schools were usually in isolated areas unreached by public education, and often associated with rural churches. Secondary, normal schools, and colleges were essential, the AMA stated in 1893, but elementary rural institutions were also needed "for here are ignorance and destitution. We must not . . . forget the isolated and desolate people in rude homes without schoolhouses and books, ignorant and weak, the prey of those who are stronger." Or, as the AMA stated in 1899, "Whatever charter we have to continue our common schools is in the call to do that which must be done by us or go undone." George C. Burrage, principal of the AMA's Ballard Normal School in Macon, Georgia, visited such a school in 1901. Forty students were in a 20 x 25 log house, heated by a fireplace with a chimney made of mud and sticks. The building was primitive, and the students were ragged, Burrage stated, but they were learning.[2]

Often the AMA assumed responsibility for schools established by its students. Joanna A. Greenlee left a poverty-stricken home in Bainbridge, Georgia, and worked her way through Allen Normal School in Thomasville. Upon graduation in 1896, Greenlee, who had not been "educated out of sympathy with her people," said the AMA approvingly, began teaching in a country school at Duncanville, Georgia. Her ambition was to prepare students for Allen Normal. On opening day in 1900, Greenlee arrived in Thomasville with seven young women and for the next sixteen years Allen was never without some of her pupils. Later she founded a school at Beachton, Georgia, where she became teacher, janitor, Sunday school superintendent, and moral leader of the community. In her home she boarded girls from farther in the country where there were no educational opportunities. The AMA responded to Greenlee's entreaties by assisting with both schools. Sometimes the AMA simply took ungraded public schools and extended their short terms by two to four months.[3]

The AMA's longest lived common school was Cotton Valley in Macon County, Alabama. In 1884, the Woman's Home Missionary Association of Massachusetts organized the school after Booker T. Washington spoke of the many poor black youth in the area lacking educational opportunities. Lillian V. Davis, a young black graduate of Boston High School and the school's first teacher and principal, began classes in a wretched log hut. Davis boarded nearby with Eliza Boyd in a log cabin with only a drape separating her quarters from those of the mother and nine boys who all lived in one room.[4] Davis's first task was to convince the area's sharecropping, illiterate parents that their children should be removed from the fields and entrusted to her care. A visitor to Cotton Valley said he had never seen more "serf-like human beings than the stolid group of tenants gathered at . . . the rude country store." The area appeared not to be fertile ground for a private, tuition school. Davis's initial teaching was not from books. She went into homes of the people; talked, ate, and lived with them; and earned their loyalty and affection. The school grew steadily under her leadership and, importantly, in 1889 she persuaded the AMA to assume responsibility for the institution.[5] When Davis resigned in 1896 she had transformed the original cabin into a three-room school building and had added a log teachers' home. Three young women helped her teach two hundred students in eight grades, and the school had become a community treasure. AMA secretary Augustus F. Beard judged Cotton Valley a "wonderful" school, "not inferior to any school of its kind known to me," and Davis an "exceptional" teacher. When Davis married in Boston, Beard acted as her father and gave her away. As he marched her down the aisle, Beard "was as proud that day as anyone there except the gentleman who was made her husband."[6]

After Davis retired, a series of remarkable black women with a "genius of making much of little, a native faculty for business and an instinct for neatness and order" led Cotton Valley. In 1900 three Fisk University graduates assisted principal Carrie Alexander. Most Cotton Valley teachers after 1900

Fig. 1. Principal Julia Johnson and students at Cotton Valley School (Courtesy of Amistad Research Center, Tulane University, New Orleans, Louisiana)

were normal school or college trained, including Gertrude Ella Boyd, granddaughter of the woman who first boarded Lillian Davis. Boyd attended Cotton Valley, earned a scholarship to Fisk, graduated from the normal department in 1905, and returned to teach others. Boyd, whose picture revealed a lovely, refined young woman, hoped her appointment would encourage other young girls to pursue education. Indeed, several Cotton Valley graduates continued their training. Three students who completed the eighth grade in 1904 went to Talladega College. Student enrollment remained high. In 1905 there were 229 students, many of whom walked as far as five miles "through the woods and field, over hills and creeks." An additional seventeen students who lived too distant to commute boarded in a cottage near the teachers' home. They brought food from home and prepared their own meals. Most parents, though illiterate, wanted better for their children, but for a few education was secondary. When in 1911 a teacher urged a mother to send her second-grade daughter to school, she refused because her child could earn sixty cents a day picking cotton.[7]

The AMA also opened a school at Mound Bayou, Mississippi, the all-black community established by Isaiah T. Montgomery, former slave of Jefferson Davis's brother Joseph, and the only black delegate to the Mississippi constitutional convention of 1890 which effectively disfranchised African Americans. Montgomery and Ben Green donated a school plot in 1892, and the AMA erected a building and sent two teachers. In 1899, Rev. B. F. Ousley, whose father Ben had been a Joseph Davis slave, became principal of the school and gradually built it into the Mound Bayou Normal Institute. The association sponsored the school until 1918 when it transferred it to the Episcopal Diocese of Mississippi.[8]

By 1902 the AMA common schools had decreased to thirty, and Secretary Beard reiterated that elementary education was not the association's major thrust. "Our larger interest . . . continues to be chiefly to prepare Christian teachers to meet the increasing demand of the public schools both in rural communities and in towns." In the same report, Beard wrote of the pathetic "struggles of parents to pay the trifling tuition" of the common schools and of the "unabated interest of both parents and children to get away from the thralldom of ignorance and the helplessness which goes with it." The AMA emphasized post-elementary training, and was already operating at a deficit, but Beard often responded to direct pleas from those completely devoid of educational opportunities. In 1902 he persuaded the AMA executive committee to support institutions in Alabama, Louisiana, and Georgia taught by AMA graduates at not more than $400 each. In 1905 Beard claimed that fully one-half of black school-age children in the South got no schooling at all.[9]

Generally the AMA favored coeducation, but two of its elementary schools, Girl's Industrial School (later Almeda Gardner Industrial School) at Moorhead, Mississippi, and Mount Herman Seminary, near Clinton, Mississippi, were for females. In 1892 Chester H. Pond, who founded Moorhead thirty miles east of Greenville, donated a ten-acre school site. The AMA constructed a $3,000 building on the land, but lacked money for current expenses. It appointed Miss Sarah L. Emerson principal and asked her to open the school with whatever funds she could solicit, and the Girl's Industrial School was born. The school was in a virtual forest with cane growing a dozen feet high in the yard. The only bare space was a footpath leading to the town a quarter of a mile distant. Emerson felled the trees, cleared the cane, planted fruit trees and grass, and soon had a meticulously maintained lawn enclosed by a white picket fence. The school was noted for its beautiful yard and thriving vegetable garden.[10]

Blacks were in a majority in Moorhead and, according to a teacher, "had the fewest rights and the least consideration." Men and women alike worked in cotton production. Emerson concluded that girls were the most needy, and her aim became to provide character and industrial training to females age seven to fifteen. An elderly black neighbor called the school the "House of Principle." Emerson added a boarding department which in 1902 housed sixty girls who lived beyond walking distance. The teachers took in, reared, and even adopted homeless children. This school probably took this type of service further than any other AMA institution.[11] Each boarder gave one hour daily to household work including cooking, sewing, and laundry. A 1909 visitor was favorably impressed with the clean, modestly dressed girls with their "bright expectant" faces and their admirable work ethic. Each morning one group "set to rights" the bedrooms and parlors, while another scoured the dining tables and reset them for the next meal. In the afternoon others did laundry and cleaned classrooms. Each girl ironed her own clothes after which a supervisor inspected them for rips, tears, or missing buttons. If necessary, the clothes were sent to the repair room under the supervision of the sewing teacher. Students also worked in the yard, weeded the garden, and helped preserve fruits and vegetables. Teachers were not preparing students to become domestics. They simply taught household chores they assumed all women should know. Despite the emphasis on cleaning, sewing, cooking, and good work habits, the school was industrial in name only. It offered a "thorough common English" education, and those who could were encouraged to continue their training elsewhere. Although there were pupils as old as fifteen most of them were in the first four grades.[12]

Sarah A. Dickey, the founder and first principal of Mount Herman Seminary, deeded the school to the AMA upon her death in 1905. At that time it had five teachers, eighty-one students, and dormitory space for forty-five. In 1907, AMA secretary H. Paul Douglass found the school "beautifully situated" though buildings were "somewhat in disrepair." The students were well behaved and "directly from a needy class," he added. "I confess," Douglass continued, "that these small girls schools seem valuable to me, even though they are relatively expensive." The AMA believed that young black women were pivotal in race elevation. Most black teachers were women, and they also nurtured the family, were important church leaders, and served as the major transmitter of culture and values. In defense of the more expensive female boarding schools, Douglass wrote that there was "a very real and urgent" moral threat to black girls "at the hands, primarily of white men, but also from men of their own race." The more refined the girl, the "more constant and insidious the attack," Douglass continued. "No social tradition protects her virtue; no social obloquy punishes its despoiler." The Women's Christian Temperance Union and others agreed with Douglass. Though the WCTU was not noted for friendliness to blacks, its anti-rape campaign in the 1890s was aimed, in part, at protecting black girls. Martha Schofield, a Quaker who directed a black school in South Carolina, said the WCTU knew who the enemy was. Schofield criticized respectable white men "who led colored school girls from the path of virtue." There were no "young lives in America that had as much to contend with as the *young* colored women" who were never safe from white men. She urged white women to uplift their men.[13] The AMA's female schools concentrated on strengthening character and preparing young women to become virtuous wives, mothers, teachers, and community leaders. Teachers inculcated truthfulness, gentleness, self-control, self-respect, sexual purity, and interest in education in their students, and urged them to become "leaders of righteousness" in their communities and homes.[14]

Whether housed in a log cabin or in a modest frame building, the AMA common schools, unlike public schools for African Americans, tended to have well-trained teachers. In 1920, seventy percent of the instructors in black public elementary schools in Georgia and Alabama had less than an eighth-grade education, but AMA schools were likely to have normal- and college-trained teachers even at the turn of the century. Most of them came from AMA institutions. In 1888, Anna Richardson, an Atlanta University graduate, founded Lamson School in Marshallville, Georgia, the only black school in that rural county. In 1897, it had two teachers from Atlanta University, one each from Fisk University and Talladega College, and one from Avery Normal Institute. In 1900, three recent Fisk University graduates taught at Cotton Valley. Joanna Greenlee began teaching after graduation from Allen Normal, but for years she spent summers continuing her education at Fisk University.[15]

Teachers in AMA rural schools were overwhelmingly black. Parents often preferred teachers of their race if they were competent, and blacks more than whites were willing to go to isolated areas, "carrying into darkened homes and to darkened hearts the light of their knowledge and character." Moreover, the AMA assumed that blacks could safely go where northern whites could not. Southern whites saw northern white teachers as a threat to segregation, and black subordination. Unfortunately, being black did not guarantee safety for teachers. On August 30, 1903, two white men ambushed Laforest A. Planving, founder and principal of Ponte Coupee Industrial and High School in Oscar, Louisiana, and committed an "unprovoked and cruel murder." Whites had earlier warned Planving, who left a widow and three small children, to leave town and had fired shots into his school and home. AMA president Washington Gladden asked the Louisiana governor to investigate the murder, and declared that no one was safe with "the wild beast" of lynching running loose. Gladden added that the association "stood for perfect equality for the Negro before the law, and behind the law; we stand for his rights as a citizen; we stand for his opportunity to be a man among men—not a menial among Lords, not an inferior among superiors, but a self-respecting, self-directed, self-reliant American man." Teaching such ideas was dangerous in Oscar, Louisiana, and other areas of the South. The AMA sent Rev. Alfred Lawless, a Straight University graduate, to replace the murdered principal. When Lawless reopened the school in January 1904 a white man fired into the building almost striking him. Lawless complained to the local constable who advised him to leave. White hostility eventually forced Lawless to abandon the school. Few rural schools were completely insulated from white violence. In 1907, an unidentified teacher wrote that "a mob of white men hunted down a Negro in the woods near the school, then . . . tied him to a tree and riddled him with bullets." Students clearly heard the fury of the guns and the mob's shouts.[16]

Although teachers in the rural schools were usually black, a few had white and racially mixed faculties. A 1914 U.S. Bureau of Education survey of black schools described Almeda Gardner Industrial as "a small, well-managed elementary" school with six white women teachers, all of whom were effective and graduates of reputable institutions. At Mount Herman Seminary four women, one black and three white, taught seventy-eight girls. "All the teachers have had training in good schools." The AMA tried to maintain interracial staffs in its colleges and city institutions, but to find mixed faculties in black, rural Mississippi elementary schools was astonishing. Even decades later southern whites often demanded that black youth acquire the "right kind of knowledge imparted by the right kind of teachers."[17]

At the turn of the twentieth century the AMA's black teachers tended to be young while the white rural teachers, with few exceptions, were single, older women, some of whom had been with the AMA since the 1870s and 1880s. According to Lura Beam who became an AMA teacher in 1908 and assistant superintendent of education in 1911, these white women "were shellacked in duty and eaten by sacrifice, but somehow when they communicated with the young, the faith and ambition of their generation were transplanted in full bloom." They accepted their isolation from white society and devoted their lives to black children. Rural students often had to go away to attend even seventh and eighth grades, and these dedicated teachers urged the better ones to do so. They "roused him, made him do extra work, called on his parents and persuaded them to let him go away to school," Beam said. Such teachers arranged departures, used their own meager resources to purchase clothes or train tickets, and begged books, clothing, and scholarship aid from the North.[18]

White teachers rarely gained the "spontaneous confidence" of black students. "The gulf dug by the white men between the two races" had become too wide, a white teacher wrote in 1909, and parents trained children to distrust whites. However, oppression had made blacks keen judges of character. "They know the difference between assumed and true friendliness, and real kindness will win them," she added. Although many people spoke of black youth as being docile, Ida F. Hubbard, principal of the Slater Training School in Knoxville, Tennessee, said it was not true with her students. She found "a certain independence of thought and action" which feared control as tending toward slavery. Insincere whites did not last long in black schools, but if the community was convinced that white teachers were genuine the black families were grateful, loved their schools, and contributed generously.[19]

Whatever their age or color, the early teachers were overworked, poorly paid, and often ostracized by whites. They taught the children, visited parents, recruited students, organized and directed Sunday schools, planted gardens, trimmed or swept the yard, cut firewood, maintained the school building, and in boarding schools, supervised dormitories. The teachers' home at Cotton Valley boasted a built-in sideboard constructed by a female teacher who also laid the front walk out of brick fragments. Rev. George W. Moore, black AMA field missionary, said Cotton Valley was "the one bright spot in the lives" of the many poor blacks in the area. In addition to their school duties the young teachers taught Sunday school, sponsored a Christian Endeavor Society, organized after-school sewing classes for both students and mothers, and directed a literary society and a singing school. On Friday afternoon they held a "mother's meeting" at which they discussed housekeeping and child rearing. They urged neighbors to improve farming methods and to grow more food. The school had its own demonstration field of corn and a truck garden, in part to supply food for themselves and students, but also to show farmers the advantages of fertilizer and scientific farming. People looked to them for advice, medicine, used clothing, and help in many ways. It was a "veritable social settlement," Moore exclaimed. They did all this for twenty dollars a month and room and board.[20] In 1891, the AMA executive committee announced, "this being a missionary work, deriving its support from the . . . poor as well as the rich, the salaries cannot be high, and in each grade of work the sum paid cannot exceed a moderate support." Some older teachers received as little as twenty-five dollars a month as late as 1920. The AMA usually paid transportation to and from the South, along with room and board for teachers.[21]

Cotton Valley teachers were not satisfied with simply teaching improved agricultural methods. They strongly encouraged parents to save their meager funds and buy land of their own. Only a few were able to do so, but Principal

Etta M. Cottin (1908–13) not only collected enough money from northern friends to buy a small farm for the school (it now had forty-three acres), she also assisted five nearby families in purchasing and subdividing a two-hundred-acre plantation. A good teacher and excellent disciplinarian, Cottin was popular in the community. She visited parents, delivered Thanksgiving baskets to the poor, and solicited clothing for the needy. While AMA officials generally approved Cottin's activities, they worried that too much help created dependency. They concluded that she "weakened the community financially by too much giving."[22]

Cottin's best efforts could not protect tenants from the climate and ravages of the sharecrop system. Surrounding farmers had an unusually difficult time in 1916–17. Soon after crops were planted heavy rains destroyed most of the cotton. Merchants withdrew credit, leaving tenants without money or food. Croppers "hustled around" to find potatoes, corn, and peanuts to eat during the summer months and hoped for better luck in the fall. Unfortunately, merchants and landlords, in order to recoup their losses, seized cows, hogs, and foodstuffs, again leaving tenants without food. Many faced the winter with "neither pork fat nor meal." Children went to school hungry, half-clad, and barefoot. The *American Missionary* claimed that the famine was so great some parents gave their children away rather than watch them starve.[23]

By the early 1900s poor salaries and isolation made it difficult for the AMA to keep efficient and dedicated teachers in some of its rural schools. In 1916, only fifty percent of its several hundred teachers had been with the AMA for three years. Convinced that inadequate pay was a major reason for the constant turnover, the AMA increased salaries by forty dollars a year effective October 1917, but they were still low.[24] Rural seclusion may have been more important than poor salaries in the dismal teacher retention rate. The AMA could not keep a stable teaching force at Cotton Valley in the 1920s because "it comes pretty close to being nowhere." Young women reared and educated in the North often found the rural South depressing, and even southern-born teachers were sometimes reluctant to return to their impoverished neighborhoods after spending several years in AMA colleges in Atlanta, New Orleans, and Nashville.[25]

During World War II when jobs were more widely available, the AMA experienced even greater difficulty in keeping sympathetic teachers in the rural South, and parents, at least at Cotton Valley, noticed the difference. "They come down here from New York and they don't associate," one declared. They failed to visit homes and attend local churches. "They ain't been a single time . . . and if they are going to work with the people they have to know them." They were "mighty fussy teachers," said one mother. "They just bribe the children and they so overbearing." Another whose son and daughter were paddled stated, "they is quick to get malicetry in them. They whips them pretty bad." Most parents approved spanking, but they were hurt and angry when teachers called them poor and backward and shunned community activities. The AMA generally selected understanding and sensitive personnel, but critical parents were correct about some of the teachers. Four of six Cotton Valley teachers in 1946 had bachelor degrees and one had a master's in social work, and they often knew little of extreme poverty and rural life. They found parents backward and immoral, and the children poor, hungry, dirty, and superstitious. Mrs. Marjorie Ball gave stars for cleanliness and personally bathed some of her pupils. Teachers were appalled when students told them that parents and friends had been hexed, that drinking bluing and rubbing turpentine on the body could prevent conception, and that root or witch doctors were effective.[26]

Mrs. Evelyn Black complained that her students had too little food and shabby clothes, but most of her seventh- and eighth-grade girls could afford to dip snuff. Some teachers complained that the children knew far too much about sex. A second grader wrote the slang terms for male and female genitalia on his desk, "and he was just snickering." His disgusted teacher, Mrs. Lorene Hastings, was not surprised. The children "couldn't help but learn all kinds of bad things," she stated, when they lived with as many as eighteen in three rooms. Scandalized teachers apparently overlooked the many families and students with high moral standards. Student interviews at Cotton Valley School revealed that their ideal male-female relationship was marriage. Fourteen-year-old Willola Anderson, who was determined to protect herself from sexual predators, feared white more than black men. She walked to school and when she reached the main road "sometimes white mens and Colored be there meddling." Whites offered her rides and one day tried to force her into a car. "White men get after us often, they got my sister-in-law," Willola said. "Ain't nothing my daddy can do but tell us always to have our brother carry us when we go somewhere."[27]

Although they were black, some teachers showed little appreciation for rural culture and limited patience with students. Hastings declared that when her first graders got "nasty and impudent" she spanked them even though she ordinarily did not believe in such punishment. "But some of them, I have to straighten out," she added; "you have to whip them, or else they will whip you." At a time when musicologists were praising black folk music, teacher Elinor Foster complained that she was unsuccessfully trying to raise the students' musical standards. They sang only "the sorrow songs and the blues." The teachers could hardly wait for the school year to end so they could go home. Cotton Valley was fortunate, however, to have a series of dedicated principals. Alice B. Donaldson remained more than two decades, but teachers often stayed only one year. In 1944–45, every single teacher except the principal was new. The young women at Cotton Valley had at least each other for companionship and could occasionally make the thirteen-mile trip to Tuskegee. In many rural schools there was only one teacher and no nearby towns. On the other hand, some of those who remained the longest were in the most rural areas. Anna Richardson taught at Lamson for twenty-six years. Only death prevented a longer tenure. Joanna Greenlee taught in two small, rural Georgia schools from 1896 until her death in 1915. Greenlee and Richardson, unlike the above-mentioned women, became a part of the communities in which they lived.[28]

The Cotton Valley teachers were correct that some students were poor and backward. Those in the common schools were among the most disadvantaged in the country, often children of sharecroppers or farm laborers. At Nixburg, Alabama, the parents were all farmers, and most of them were of the "one gallus" type, teacher John R. Savage wrote. Many of the people, including women, wore shoes "only in the heart of the winter." Inadequate clothing, illness, and the need to work affected school attendance. In 1925, the AMA commissioned black sociologist E. Franklin Frazier, director of the Atlanta University School of Social Work, to survey the Cotton Valley area. In some ways the district had changed little since Lillian Davis's arrival in 1884. Most residents were tenant farmers, lacking capital "even to the extent of food." The few landowners were more secure than tenants, but their land tended to be infertile. Farm laborers were the lowest stratus. "Because of their ignorance and lack of incentive," Frazier concluded, their lot was little above that "of their forbears during slavery."[29]

In December 1936, Myrtle W. Knight, Cotton Valley principal, wrote that some students could not attend classes until the corn and peas were picked, cane stripped and syrup made, sweet potatoes dug and buried, and peanuts picked and stacked. Some would still be enrolling after Christmas. As late as 1946, Cotton Valley teacher Lorene Hastings said that by March most of her second grade "will drop out to plow." Of an enrollment of twenty-nine, as many as twenty-four had been out plowing at one time. Some parents considered school "a luxury, fine for the young ones too tender for hoeing, and a good place for the older ones to go once the crop was in." Poverty was omnipresent. A 1947 study of eighty-three families in Cotton Valley revealed that one family generally had no breakfast, twenty-five skipped lunch, and twenty-one ordinarily had no supper. Often children went to school without breakfast, and only sporadically brought lunch. One student regularly received her first and only meal at 7 p.m. Since students missed so often, many were older than normal for their grade. In 1936 first- and second-grade teacher Dorothy P. Childs taught students ranging in age from five to sixteen. AMA Director of Schools Ruth Morton spoke in 1949 of "over-age, maladjusted" students. Still, hundreds of poor, disadvantaged students completed the common schools and eventually went to high school and college. Among former Cotton Valley students in 1938 was a college president, M. Lafayette Harris of Philander Smith College in Little Rock, Arkansas; numerous teachers and ministers; and a prosperous dentist. Countless others who were limited to elementary grades learned to read, write, and cipher, which, the AMA hoped, enhanced the quality of their lives and helped them protect their interests against rapacious whites.[30]

Despite their poverty, students helped pay teachers. All of the common schools charged tuition, though the parents at Cotton Valley were so poor that the AMA initially suspended its policy of requiring a minimal fee. Later it assessed each student ten cents a month and slowly raised the cost to one dollar. Tuition charges were necessary, Secretary Beard explained, to stimulate self-reliance and self-respect. In 1914, students paid $223 in tuition and fees at Cotton Valley, $570 at Mount Herman Seminary, and $260.16 at Gardner Industrial.[31] Students at Cuthbert, Georgia, paid in potatoes, chickens, eggs, and "anything else that could be bartered for education." Another Georgia teacher said she longed to cook the food that hungry students brought in and feed them, but "I know the only way to make them self-reliant and keep them from the spirit of mendicancy is to require them to pay." A boy in Hillsborough, North Carolina, was school janitor through the week and a bootblack on Saturday to earn money for tuition. Some families brought butter or firewood, or did odd jobs around the school. Many of the female students were weekend laundresses and could frequently "be seen 'toting' the baskets of laundry" upon their heads. Schools were relatively lenient with those who simply could not pay. In 1925, only about half of the Cotton Valley students paid tuition in either money or produce. Frazier thought that a few parents saw the school as a philanthropic enterprise supported by rich Yankees who were more able to give than these parents were able to pay.[32]

The curriculum at the common schools evolved with the times and changing constituency. In 1912 Lura Beam said instruction in the first six grades was "fairly orthodox" except for a greater emphasis on Bible stories and quotations. The AMA taught love of country, though after Reconstruction blacks were barred from citizenship and the government did little to educate or protect them. Students daily pledged allegiance to the flag and sang the national anthem. Early in life blacks understood how "unreasoning and unreasonable" race prejudice was. "It is the meanest thing in our country," the AMA lamented in 1908, yet children of no race could "outvie them in heartiness" when black children saluted the flag or sang "My Country 'Tis of Thee."[33] Cotton Valley stressed the three R's, cleanliness, neatness, self-respect, and racial pride. Black materials were used in class when appropriate. All the common schools featured public closing exercises, which allowed proud students to display their learning and pleased parents who had sacrificed to keep their children in school. Cotton Valley's 1908 closing exercises featured "A Morning with [Paul Laurence] Dunbar." Teacher Millie Belle Davis said "the children could have given it in the old way" even if Dunbar had written in standard English. "The greatest fun about it," Davis stated, "was the way in which the pieces were rendered. An old Methodist minister could never have given out his hymns to common meter any better."[34]

Instruction was not limited to the classroom, especially in the schools that had boarding departments. The school atmosphere was often dramatically different from the students' outside world. "The skies fell" on the tardy child, Beam recalled, "the one who let a piece of paper flutter on campus, the one who did not sweep under beds. Unnatural demands for order, cleanliness, and punctuality stalked like wolves in waiting." Bible study and daily devotionals were an integral part of instruction. "Christian education is an essential lever in the uplift of ignorant and impoverished people," the *American Missionary* proclaimed in 1893.[35] Occasionally, ministers were brought in to preach to students. Many teachers were uncomfortable with active soul-seeking, but nearly all were zealously pious and advocated a rigid code of personal conduct. They severely condemned lying, drinking alcohol, smoking, gambling, and profanity. In 1898 the AMA stated that the common denominator of all of its schools was "the one supreme purpose to bring souls to Christ and into His life." A decade later it reminded its teachers to impress upon students their dual obligation of "uplifting and saving" the race. "They must be willing to listen to the voice of Christ calling them" to devote themselves to God and racial betterment. Leadership and service were emphasized even in common schools. AMA officers saw racial uplift as a religious duty for both themselves and students in its schools. Students must not separate themselves from fellow blacks, but go back into the community and assist others. Although the AMA emphasized religion, Beam said, its schools "were deeply religious only in the sense of teaching brotherhood. Their strength was in respect for the individual and the fostering of personality."[36]

The number of common schools declined to sixteen by 1905, then climbed back to twenty-three in 1907. In some of these schools the AMA cooperated with both the Anna T. Jeanes Foundation, created in 1907 to assist in educating rural blacks, and public school officials. For example, the AMA had a church in Wadsworth, North Carolina. Its building was the schoolhouse for the four-month public school term which the AMA extended an additional four months as a mission school. But a better structure was badly needed. By 1910 parents had raised $100, the county contributed $200, and the Jeanes Foundation added $200 for a new schoolhouse. This had happened before "not once or twice," the AMA claimed. The association still had twenty-three common schools in 1910, mainly in Georgia and North Carolina. It believed these schools had assisted its rural churches there and had stimulated interest in improving public education.[37]

Wherever the school, teachers urged their better students to go on to higher grades. Miss Mary E. Wilcox of Andersonville, Georgia, insisted that she and her colleagues made their students "hungry to know more" and sent them on to AMA normal schools and colleges which had upper grades. The Hillsborough, North Carolina, school building had two floors. The first floor took pupils through the fourth grade. The best of those completing the fourth grade were sent to the second floor and taught arithmetic, geography, and grammar until they were ready to transfer to a graded school. Of the twenty recent graduates of Cotton Valley in 1925, six were in college and five went away to high school.[38]

In 1920, the AMA claimed four common schools, now sometimes called opportunity schools, and by 1930 only Cotton Valley remained. The common schools disappeared for two reasons. Some became public schools and others were upgraded. Strieby school in the foothills of the Blue Ridge Mountains in North Carolina was an example of upgrading. In 1905 the community led by Talladegan Reverend O. W. Hawkins, pastor and principal, erected a larger building with the intent to transform its institution from common school into a graded and normal school. Local blacks donated four thousand feet of lumber, nails, and other material, and were doing the construction themselves. The AMA promised only forty dollars for school furniture. Mound Bayou grew into a normal school. Similar things happened with other elementary institutions.[39]

More often the AMA discontinued its schools when public alternatives became available. It had always insisted that the state was obligated to provide education for black youth, and it encouraged county boards to take over or supplant its schools. Mount Herman Seminary was closed in 1924 because the development of area public schools made an elementary boarding school impractical. In the same year the AMA considered terminating the Girl's Industrial School, but concluded that it exerted too great a positive influence in the area. It decided rather to add the ninth grade and perhaps become a high school, but in 1930 it also was closed. Despite the AMA's enthusiasm for public education, it was occasionally reluctant to discontinue its institutions because public schools nearly always had much shorter terms and less qualified faculty. For the same reasons parents often begged the AMA to retain its schools.[40]

The AMA refused to close Cotton Valley because county school authorities would not replace it and because there remained "a crying need" for a community work among a "hard working, unfortunate people." The school became an example of the AMA community or functional education emphasis to be discussed later. In 1937, secretary Fred L. Brownlee asked the Macon County school superintendent for assistance. The superintendent replied that he could not give money to private schools. When Brownlee inquired what he would do if the AMA closed Cotton Valley, the superintendent said he would probably establish a one-teacher school for five months. Brownlee asked him to pay one teacher and her students could attend free. The superintendent agreed and later added another teacher. By 1945, the county paid four teachers for eight months and allowed some children to ride the school bus. In 1950 the county rejected an AMA proposal to deed it twenty-five acres in return for building a new consolidated school. The AMA and county continued to operate Cotton Valley jointly until fire destroyed it in 1961. The AMA transferred its property to the Macon County Board of Education and thus closed its last purely elementary school.[41] In the meantime, the AMA had provided at least some education to thousands of children who otherwise would have been totally neglected.

2

Normal and Secondary Schools

"Our general policy has been to prepare the race to save the race," Secretary Beard proclaimed in 1896. As early as the Civil War, the AMA had concluded that preparing black teachers and leaders was essential to racial uplift and eventual black inclusion into the American mainstream. No organization could adequately supply the educational needs of former slaves. It could most economically and effectively reach the masses by "multiplying teachers from the race for the race." Moreover, the AMA declared, "every race coming out of darkness into light must have its own teachers and preachers." Each group must "work out its own salvation," but the AMA could "introduce the leaven for their rising" by training young teachers and leaders to "begin and continue the long and hard work of race self-advancement." Blacks should aspire to the highest education available, the AMA affirmed, and they deserved well-educated instructors, but few were immediately prepared for college, and in the meantime thousands of black children were without teachers of any sort. The AMA set out to remedy the frightful teacher shortage, and at the same time prepare students for college. Teacher training became one of the association's most significant and empowering educational gifts to African Americans because it enabled them to become their own educators. By the end of Reconstruction, AMA common schools began to decline in number and its graded, normal, and secondary schools increased. Of course the secondary schools and even colleges contained elementary grades for many years.[1]

The AMA and other organizations created normal and secondary schools for blacks because the southern states would not. Anderson in *The Education of Blacks in the South* illustrated white reluctance to support black education. As late as 1915, black public schools going beyond the sixth grade were scarce, separate, and uniformly inferior in plant and equipment. AMA secretary H. Paul Douglass understated the case in 1909 when he said the concept of the state furnishing free secondary education to all was "imperfectly rooted in the South." In 1900, eighty percent of black normal graduates and seventy-five percent of black secondary students were in private schools. In 1912, Wilmington, North Carolina, had only two public graded schools, neither of which went beyond grade six. Macon and Bibb County, Georgia, contained approximately 10,000 school-age black children in 1914, and only three public schools completing the sixth grade. Neither Georgia, Mississippi, South Carolina, Louisiana, nor North Carolina had a public four-year high school for African Americans in 1916, and as late as the mid-1920s New Orleans, Charleston, Atlanta, and Memphis offered only three years of secondary education for black youth. In 1930, ninety-seven percent of black children in Georgia schools were in elementary classes.[2] The AMA never fully implemented its initial plan of establishing a "school of higher grade" in each major southern population center, but in late 1867 it offered normal training in five cities, and created new normal and secondary institutions as it could afford them. By 1893, it had twenty-nine normal schools with 1,091 students. The number of normal students rose to almost 2,000 in 1907. The association's colleges also had normal departments. In 1908, the AMA began identifying former normal schools as secondary schools, but continued to train its students for both teaching and college.[3]

AMA normal and secondary schools were scattered throughout the South, but initially its most effective pre-college teacher training institutions were in cities. Among the best known were Emerson Institute in Mobile; Gregory Institute in Wilmington, North Carolina; LeMoyne in Memphis; Beach Institute in Savannah; Avery Normal Institute in Charleston; and Ballard Normal School in Macon, Georgia.[4] The latter two have attracted book-length studies.[5] These schools taught primary as well as advanced students, and at the outset a majority of pupils were in lower grades. Of the thousands who attended Avery between 1872 and 1905, only 552 graduated. In 1909, Ballard graduated only twenty-one students, eighteen females and three males, but clearly met its stated purpose of preparing its graduates to teach and attend college. Sixteen of the women accepted teaching positions, and two of the men began their higher education. Of Emerson's 379 students in 1909, only 52 were in secondary classes. As time passed more students in the lower grades went to high school. Just as the AMA's secondary institutions became feeder schools for its colleges, its secondary schools "raised up" their own advanced students.[6]

While the city schools tended to enjoy better facilities, more teachers, and better prepared students, small-town schools made significant contributions to the growing corps of black teachers and college students. When asked in

1962 to account for his academic success, Dr. William Childs Curtis credited that "fine AMA school" Lincoln in tiny Marion, Alabama, which his parents had attended. In a study of black scholars, Horace Mann Bond concluded that the nature of the family was of first importance and the nature of the secondary school next in producing scholars. Using that criteria Bond judged Lincoln School in Marion "to have been the best predominantly Negro secondary school this country has ever known." Bond theorized that Lincoln and other AMA secondary schools were pipelines to AMA colleges. Additionally, they provided hundreds of African American teachers for southern public schools. Coretta Scott King was one of many luminaries who graduated from Lincoln School. Mrs. King stated that Lincoln's "brave and dedicated" faculty, and its "strong tradition of service to humanity" helped prepare her for life with Martin Luther King Jr. As a young girl, Coretta Scott worked on her father's truck farm and hired herself to local cotton farmers to earn money to help pay tuition at Lincoln. Her father once boasted that she could pick up to three hundred pounds of cotton daily. Trinity School in Athens, Alabama, was scarcely less important to its constituents than Lincoln. It was the only available opportunity for post-elementary education for local blacks until the 1950s.[7]

The rural schools also made a contribution.[8] Gloucester Agricultural and Industrial School (most often referred to as Gloucester Normal School in AMA literature) in Cappahosic, Virginia, and Fessenden Academy in Martin, Florida, under the leadership of black principals William G. Price and John L. Wiley, both to be discussed later, produced hundreds of community leaders, teachers, and college students. Dorchester Academy in poor, sparsely populated Liberty County, Georgia, graduated its initial class in 1896, reputedly the first class of any race to graduate from high school in the county. By 1908, Dorchester had male and female dormitories, and twelve teachers instructed 250 students.[9] Faculty and students proved AMA secretary H. Paul Douglass wrong when he said of Dorchester in 1907, "It isn't and can't be one of the highest grade in results. Its constituency is too near Africa." Dorchester furnished most of the teachers in Liberty County for decades, and it sent many graduates to college.[10]

Allen Normal School—transferred to Thomasville, Georgia, in 1886 after Quitman, Georgia, whites cheered as it burned to the ground—was the association's only secondary boarding school for girls. The AMA justified the expense of a single-sex school with the same argument used in support of Mount Herman Seminary discussed in chapter 1. Though boys were later admitted as day students, Allen's major goal was training women to become teachers, society and community leaders, church workers, and homemakers.

Fig. 2. Lincoln School seniors, 1927 (Courtesy of Amistad Research Center, Tulane University, New Orleans, Louisiana)

In 1905–6, females outnumbered males 142 to 35 in grades two through twelve. Only in the first grade did boys nearly equal girls. In its first years many Allen students became teachers after the seventh and eighth grades. By 1910 greater numbers remained for normal training, and a decade later many were completing twelve grades and going to college. In 1925 Allen graduated ten secondary students, "all of them splendid girls with considerable ability."[11]

Wherever the school, there was an abundance of pupils. The slaves' fervent desire for education upon freedom had hardly abated by 1890. While there were few examples of children and grandparents studying side by side as immediately after emancipation, northern teachers were often astonished and touched by black eagerness for education and the willingness to sacrifice for it. Literally thousands of black students labored in white homes, did laundry, taught during summers, picked cotton, and performed chores at school to pay tuition. In 1904, George B. Hurd, principal of Beach Institute in Savannah, Georgia, declared there were still many eager students who were willing to work for tuition, and who would rather attend class than take a day's vacation. Raymond G. Von Tobel moved from Connecticut to Ballard in 1907 with no knowledge of black experience or culture. "It was not long," he wrote seventeen years later, "before I became intimately associated with these Colored boys and girls and soon learned something of their aspirations, their hopes for the future and, above all, the tremendous sacrifices" many of them made in order to attend Ballard. Students frequently denied "themselves the necessities of life" to save school expenses. Clara Standish, a Lincoln Academy teacher at Kings Mountain, North Carolina, stated that "the zeal which some of them show in getting an education strikes a newcomer forcibly." Two brothers in Perry County, Alabama, worked during the summer, and in the spring of 1891 each paid their father seven dollars to hire help so they could complete the academic year at Lincoln School in Marion. A teacher at Brewer Normal in Greenwood, South Carolina, found herself "stirred" in school work as never before. "The boys and girls realize their needs, they want to improve themselves. They face with courageous optimism, entirely new to me, obstacles that would be the despair of their more favored white brother and sister of the North." A black Burrell teacher said of her students in 1925, "It is their burning enthusiasm with their love of knowledge, their never-waning eagerness to learn—to know the facts of life which manifests itself still after two months of hard work that grips me—that makes me glad that I have come." In 1930, Von Tobel told of a senior from a poor, large farm family slated to graduate in the spring "literally through her own unaided efforts." She earned board by serving in private homes and paid tuition by working on campus. Beulah Rucker was an example of the difficulty of attending school. Born to a sharecropping family in Banks County, Georgia, on April 4, 1888, she began school in a black church five miles from home in 1893. After the sixth grade her parents sent her to Athens to enroll in the American Baptist's Jeruel High School. Crop failure a few years later compelled her parents to withdraw her. Beulah studied on her own, occasionally paying a nearby teacher for temporary assistance with difficult problems. Approximately two years after leaving Jeruel High, Rucker entered the AMA's Knox Institute in Athens with no money. She met expenses by cleaning and nursing, and finally in 1909 graduated sixteen years after entering the first grade.[12]

Students' valiant efforts for education included walking long distances to school. Ophelia and Mary Maxwell, high school students at Dorchester Academy, walked more than eight miles to campus. After six hours in the classroom they walked home, helped around the farm, and then, principal J. F. deCastro claimed, they apparently studied because they were always prepared for class. Neither had missed a day in twelve weeks. Louise Golding, a senior, and her ninth-grade sister, Edith, walked sixteen miles round-trip to Dorchester in 1919. In 1920, thirty-five Dorchester students walked fifteen miles daily. Two walked twenty miles, including a path through cypress swamps.[13]

These eager and self-sacrificing students reflected family and community values. Self-improvement and racial uplift were common themes in the black community, and these ideals were repeatedly reinforced at school. The AMA encouraged its students to go back into the community and assist others. Control of their own destiny and protection against whites were also factors. A Louisiana father sent his children to school even though their absence from the farm cost him money. "Leaving learning to your children was better than leaving them a fortune," he declared, "because if you left them even five hundred dollars, some man having more education than they had would come along and cheat them out of it all." Parents' sacrifices for education equaled and often surpassed those made by their children. Henry Hugh Proctor's parents moved from the country to Nashville seeking better education for their family. "My mother said to my father that they had spent their lives working for other people; now they should spend the rest of it working for their children," Proctor recalled. Proctor graduated from Fisk University and Yale. Eula Wellman Dunlap's father heard of Lincoln Academy in Kings Mountain, North Carolina, and moved his entire family there. For a short time father, mother, and two daughters attended classes together. Although her father was compelled to discontinue school to support his family, he qualified to become a teacher by attending night classes. Eula Wellman graduated from high school.[14]

"It is a wonderful experience," Jennie Curtis wrote from Dorchester Academy in 1891, "to see mothers with dignified humility confessing their ignorance and willing to sacrifice all comforts that they may lift their children above the ignorance they so keenly deplore." Teacher Alice Davis marveled at the many mothers who toiled over washtubs from Monday morning until Saturday night, and performed "all kinds of manual labor" to keep their children in Albany Normal School in southwest Georgia. The black population surrounding Dorchester Academy, Principal Fred W. Foster stated, lived primarily on small farms, largely eating on credit while tilling their crops. A majority of parents, though poor and illiterate, "most earnestly" desired better for their offspring, and were "willing to make great sacrifices to attain that end." Since farmwork was done by hand, simply allowing the children to attend school was a loss of labor. "Even the very young are not *too* young to be useful. If too small to 'scare off the birds,' they can tend to the still smaller mite in the house and liberate an older person for field service." Throughout the South many a mother took the plow handles out of her son's hands and tramped the furrow herself so that he might go to school.[15] A woman born in slavery, seven years old when freedom came, raised fourteen children every one of whom went through Dorchester Academy. In 1916 she enrolled five grandchildren which her son left in her care upon his death. This illiterate grandmother vowed that no child of hers was going to grow up without an education. Mary E. Phillips, principal of Lincoln School in Marion, Alabama, once responded to an urgent call to visit an ill woman. The patient, near death in a wretched cabin, told Phillips that she could not die in peace until she knew her son and daughter would be cared for and educated. Phillips agreed to place them in the boarding school and care for them.[16]

Blacks were so determined to educate their children, James D. Anderson claimed, that they accepted double taxation. They paid taxes for public schools, often diverted by authorities primarily to whites, and then were compelled to make personal contributions in order to acquire their own public schools. In a sense black parents were often triple taxed since they usually had to pay tuition to private schools to enjoy education beyond elementary grades. Indeed, tuition schools were too frequently the only option even for primary students. White benevolence certainly did not completely finance AMA schools. Northern donors and legacies were essential, but blacks paid for a significant portion of their education. For the year ending September 30, 1912, students at AMA schools and colleges invested $67,587.07 in tuition. That sum represented "long days of toil at five to ten cents an hour, sacrifice of home comforts—yes, even necessities, that the children might have a chance." But the black community did far more than pay tuition and taxes. African Americans were contributing partners in the AMA's southern work. In Marion, Alabama, they saved Lincoln School in 1897 when the financially struggling AMA in a retrenchment move decided to close it because of its inferior facilities. A Lincoln graduate implored Secretary Beard to reconsider. "For years this school has been the one shining light of Marion for the colored people, and to take it away now, when it is doing its work so well is to take away the one wholesome influence of our people." She promised that the community would assist as far as its scant means allowed. Parents met and pledged $500, plus board of the teachers for the next year. One parent offered eggs, another milk, another vegetables. In the face of such determination, Beard telegraphed that the school would remain open. In the fall of 1897 students contributed more than $100 made picking cotton. Parents, teachers, and students collected $1,000 within six months. In the same year parents at Storrs School in Atlanta assumed "almost the entire responsibility for self-support."[17]

Athens, Alabama, parents and friends helped rebuild Trinity School three times. After repeated threats the Klan burned it in the early 1870s. Blacks, frantic at the possible loss of their school, shared their meager resources and underwrote $2,000 and promised labor to renovate another building. In 1879 the AMA judged this structure unsafe and unworthy of repair, and decided to close the school. Parents offered to make bricks for a new building if the association would remain. That summer they made and burned 60,000 bricks, and the next summer burned a similar size kiln. They lacked proper machinery so resorted to the treading process with one steer tramping all the bricks.[18] A careless workman ignited a fire that burned this building in 1907. The grief of local blacks was "a pathetic sight," Rev. George W. Moore, black AMA field missionary reported, and again they offered to help rebuild. A young girl, shopping for doll clothes when she heard the cry of "fire," saw that it was the school and rushed out and gave her nickel to her teacher for rebuilding. This was only the first money black constituents gave for a better Trinity. In 1913, after a third fire the community again contributed to construction of a new school. The experiences at Lincoln, Storrs, and Trinity were not unique.[19]

White southerners demonstrated considerably less enthusiasm for educating African Americans. Their attitude ranged from tepid support to indifference to active hostility. As Leon Litwack states in *Trouble in Mind: Black Southerners in the Age of Jim Crow,* whites usually opposed slave education and many continued opposition for years after freedom. "Knowledge encouraged independence and free thought. Knowledge opened new vistas, introduced people to a larger world than the local town and county. Knowledge permitted workers to calculate their earnings and expenditures." These were sufficient reasons, Litwack adds, for whites to maintain black illiteracy, or at least to limit the type of education for freedmen and -women. A Louisianan in 1897 assured AMA Secretary Beard that blacks, unable to absorb higher education, should be confined to industrial training. "Let them do what they are made for, and not try to achieve what is beyond their powers." For far too long northern industrialists and philanthropists advocated industrial education for former slaves, but it was prominent southern white educators rather than northern industrialists, who first "emerged as the most influential propagandists for a system of instruction designed to maintain Black subservience."[20]

Lesser southern luminaries made the same argument. William N. Sheats, Florida superintendent of public instruction, complained that too much time and money were squandered "trying to teach them books that ought to be expended in trying to teach them how to make good workmen." In 1904 the

Charleston *News and Courier* proclaimed that most southern whites objected to educating blacks to be citizens. "They want him to be a white man's help, and if he is not willing to occupy a subordinate position in this country, the sooner he leaves it, or the southern part of it at least, the better for all concerned." The *American Missionary* quoted the above statement and added that the *News and Courier* editor might accurately have claimed that "there is also a class that is wholly opposed to any education for the Negro at all." Unfortunately, this class was "just now most in evidence." Wiser southern whites, AMA officials believed, were "greatly hindered in their influence by the bitter tyranny of the dominant public prejudice." Black students were more than familiar with white prejudice and violence. Gregory students and faculty fled during the 1898 Wilmington race riot, and in 1919 a man was lynched near Ballard in Macon. AMA assistant superintendent of education Lura Beam wrote sorrowfully that all black children bore "too heavy a load." At the time a black child began reading and numbers, he also started assimilating his inferior status. "Mentality and spirit were steadily subtracted from him in early life. An experienced adult could watch the change in his manner, and the difference in his thinking showed in the brown eyes." One goal of AMA teachers was to counter that change.[21]

AMA officials sadly recognized that hostility to African Americans seemed to increase at the turn of the century. There were 214 lynchings in the first two years and racial clashes were common. According to historian Ralph E. Luker, Thomas Dixon Jr. was "the foremost apostle of radical white racism" who "spoke for a movement that swept the South and achieved wide influence elsewhere in the nation." His *The Leopard's Spots* (1903) sold 100,000 copies in less than a year and eventually sold more than a million. *The Clansman* (1905), which praised the terrorist Ku Klux Klan and denigrated blacks and sympathetic whites, outsold the first book. The AMA noted in 1906 that "a change for the worse has suddenly set in—a change in the direction of unreason and injustice, of distrust and violence and mutual hate." It viewed "with deep anxiety the evidence of race discord" and lamented "acts of lawless violence which bring disgrace upon our nation." It decried race prejudice and hatred as seen in the "color line," the line that denied brotherhood, disregarded character, defied Christianity, and made "our boasted democracy a cheat and a lie." The *American Missionary* cited the Atlanta Baptist minister A. C. Ward who suggested repeal of the 13th, 14th, and 15th Amendments, and enactment of laws prohibiting black ownership of real estate, and the Methodist parson C. O. James who contended that blacks were inferior and would be protected only if they remained subordinate laborers and socially separate. A white Floridian responding to charges that southern libraries excluded blacks said they were closed "to the low down negro eyes . . . because he is not worthy of an education." Moreover, he continued, "[a]ll the mean crimes, that are done are committed by some educated negro." Political demagogues incessantly attacked black education. In 1910 governor-elect Cole L. Blease of South Carolina proclaimed that the "Almighty" created blacks subordinate and that the greatest mistake whites had ever made was attempting to educate them. Mississippi senator James K. Vardaman in 1913 praised the "grand old time darky," but warned that blacks were being spoiled by a "faulty and sentimental educational system." Southern churches were of no assistance. AMA Secretary Douglass thought that southern church members "fell more deeply the prey to mingled resentment and despair than did the secular educational forces." State educators discriminated, but white churchmen made little effort at all.[22]

Though white teachers were ostracized and the AMA's struggle to educate southern blacks remained a lonely one, some courageous white southerners supported the AMA's efforts. In 1916 Homer M. Stevens, principal of Brewer Normal in Greenwood, South Carolina, denied that all white southerners were radical racists and demagogues. Although the small white class in Greenwood most friendly to African Americans regarded themselves as superior, and rejected social equality, Stevens thought they honestly desired black improvement and took a keen interest in Brewer, and there were other occasional acts of friendship. In 1916 a Knox Institute student wrote principal L. S. Clark that poverty might prevent her return to school. She sent Clark her deceased grandfather's gold watch, valued at $86 when new, which she agreed to sell for $35 to pay school expenses. Clark took it to several Athens, Georgia, jewelers who offered only its value in gold since it did not work. Clark then took the watch to a Jewish merchant and related the student's woes. The merchant asked that the watch be left with him. A few days later, he returned it in working order along with a $40 donation to the student with a note asking that the keepsake watch be returned to its owner.[23]

Despite the widespread outrages against African Americans after World War I, the AMA in the 1920s thought the southern attitude toward education had improved, in part, because the great black northern migration convinced whites that their prosperity depended upon black labor; therefore, they were more amenable to black demands for education. In 1923, the *American Missionary* stated that the better white southerners were "creating a public opinion in respect to race relationships and duties that greatly hearten[s] the AMA in its ministries." Black AMA officials were less optimistic, and sometimes considered white colleagues hopelessly naive. Alfred E. Lawless, black general superintendent of AMA churches, wrote Brownlee in 1921 that "it seems next to impossible to get the Northern white man of high standards to realize the willingness of the Southern white man to take advantage of the Negro." White AMA officials' optimism was tempered by contact with southern whites. In 1924 on a train from Deland to Martin, Florida, Brownlee told his seat mate that he was visiting Fessenden Academy at Martin. "Why educate the nigger?" the man asked, as it unfitted him for his place. He told Brownlee what he "would do personally if a 'nigger' ever aspired to vote or become a member of the legislature, and particularly what he would do" if a black policeman ever tried to arrest him. He flatly denied Brownlee's assertion that blacks were educable, and was appalled when Brownlee admitted to dining with blacks. But a slight change in southern whites' attitude was not entirely wishful thinking. In 1923, the Florence, Alabama, city council appropriated $3,000 for Burrell Normal. And when in 1927 Trinity in Athens, Alabama, needed $27,000 to add a library and laboratory facilities in order to secure state accreditation, Mayor C. W. Sarver promised to raise $7,000 if the AMA gave $20,000. The association agreed, and whites in the community gave about half of the $7,000, while blacks, including Trinity alumni from throughout the country, made up the remainder. Sarver had been friendly to the school for years, but in return he expected "a powerful influence in the school's relationship with the community." Other whites helped as well. By 1936, Trinity secured about thirty-seven percent of its budget locally. Judge James J. Horton Jr., of Scottsboro Trial fame, and an Athens resident, contributed annually.[24] Southern white support for AMA schools was, however, with few exceptions, grudging or nonexistent. Whites were especially dismayed by what they saw as AMA interracialism. Coretta Scott King said whites called the Lincoln School's white faculty radicals and "nigger lovers," and considered the teachers' desegregated housing as scandalous. Despite limited southern white support, AMA schools continued to grow, and black public schools slowly increased in number during the 1920s and 1930s.[25]

Who were the students attending AMA normal and secondary schools? They were unusual simply by virtue of being there. According to the U.S. Bureau of Education, there were only 492 black secondary students in the entire state of Florida in 1916. Because of their history, discrimination, and the general poverty in the South, most black students were poor. They bartered for tuition and school supplies as late as the 1930s. In 1892, Gloucester A & I acquired two cows and a calf in payment for tuition and board, and Dorchester Academy accepted eggs, vegetables, poultry, and wood for fees. Eggs had a fixed value of one cent no matter the prevailing market price. In 1896, board, tuition, and all expenses at Lincoln Academy in Kings Mountain, North Carolina, was $4.50 per month and a majority of the students worked out two-thirds of that. Most of the schools collected "missionary barrels" of clothing from the North as late as the 1920s and sold it to students at small cost. "Nothing is given away," wrote a Chandler School teacher, "for we must not pauperize these poor people." In 1919, Dorchester Academy faculty learned that apparent student lassitude was in reality a lack of proper nutrition. Many children came to school minus breakfast and after hours of hard work. The school initiated a recess for rest and recreation with a bowl of hot soup and bread, or hot chocolate and biscuit, and students came back to class "with ambition and interest rising, eyes brighter, step lighter and a feeling of general good will." Students commonly enrolled late or dropped out to work during meager crop years.[26]

Nearly all schools offered some scholarships, and teachers used their own money and solicited northern churches to aid students. In 1916, only five of the fifty boarders at Lincoln School in Marion, Alabama, paid the full charge. Lincoln principal Mary Phillips decreed in 1924 that any child who walked more than five miles enroll tuition free, that children of large families attend at reduced rates, and that no student "with the right spirit" be rejected because of economic circumstances. Students were no less generous. The AMA emphasized charitable giving, and many students, no matter how impecunious, freely gave their hard-earned pennies and nickels to support their school, missions to American Indians and Africa, and those less fortunate at home. At Thanksgiving in 1893, scores of Ballard students brought money and food—some a single sweet potato—to aid the poor. Students at Gregory Institute always made contributions at Christmas for those in even worse situations. One girl, so destitute she often went hungry at night, struggled in with the only thing she could collect: twenty pounds of firewood to give to the needy. Numerous graduates remained loyal to their schools and assisted those who followed them. In 1914, alumni paid tuition for a half-dozen Allen Normal students. One young woman upon completion of her program selected an indigent, unrelated female and sent her to Allen promising to pay her expenses and clothe her until she graduated. "I cannot repay those who have helped me," the young benefactor said. "I can only pass on the help."[27]

As time passed there were more middle-class students. An Allen Normal teacher wrote in 1926 that too many pupils still worked to remain in school, and specifically noted a ninth grader who took in washing and frequently labored from after school until midnight. Conversely "a few . . . have more money and ride to school in good-looking cars." Historian Edmund L. Drago has concluded that between 1914 and 1936 most Avery Institute students came from "respectable working class families" with steady incomes, but some were extremely poor. In 1905, teacher Mrs. Mary L. Burnell spent an afternoon visiting fifteen families from Emerson Normal in Mobile. Four homes had "every comfort and many refinements and luxuries," including two with "exquisitely kept bathrooms with porcelain tubs." Five other families were in "comfortable circumstances," while the remaining six lived in abject poverty. There were clearly more economic opportunities in Charleston and Mobile than in smaller towns and the country. Widespread poverty and discrimination guaranteed that a majority of AMA students came from poor families even in the 1940s and 1950s. And whatever their economic circumstances, they had to deal with discrimination and fear of white law. In 1914, the AMA executive committee voted to appropriate whatever amount necessary to assure a proper court defense for seven students at Lincoln Academy in Kings Mountain, North Carolina, "who are in danger of the chain gang."[28]

During the immediate post–Civil War era, there were pupils of all ages even in primary schools. By 1900, students were completing studies at the average age at which they began school twenty years previous, which, the AMA declared, emphatically demonstrated the "upward movement of their race." Still, some got a late start, and others were able to attend only sporadically. In 1912, an eighteen-year-old sixth grader worked in a Wilmington, North Carolina, store before and after school to earn board and tuition at Gregory Institute. A thirty-five-year-old minister was in the sixth grade at Lincoln Academy in North Carolina. And in 1921 several Brewer Normal high school students were over twenty-one. Perhaps the record was set by John R. Mallard, a sixty-year-old eighth grader at Dorchester Academy in 1903. Each decade there were fewer older students in AMA high schools.[29]

At the same time that the average student age declined, student quality improved. An 1889 study claimed that Atlanta University students scored higher on state teaching examinations than white University of Georgia students. By 1900, the high schools were enrolling children of alumni. In that year a LeMoyne graduate was handed the same diploma her mother earned twenty years previously, and the 1902 valedictorian at Avery Institute was the son of the 1880 salutatorian. In 1916, Ballard reported many students whose parents were high school or college graduates. According to the *American Missionary* these second-generation students possessed "a mental horizon far wider and more luminous" than their ancestors just out of bondage. Avery students' intellectual liveliness impressed W. E. B. Du Bois when he lectured on campus in 1928. The pre-lecture dinner conversation was replete "with singular cross-currents of religion and art, education and business, compromise and resentment."[30] While more students came from educated families, the majority were disadvantaged. In 1912, Lura Beam described the background of many students as follows: illiterate parents, perhaps ten children in a rented two-room shack, no books in the house, insufficient food "taken at hit or miss intervals." Children contributed three or four hours daily to the washtub and ironing board or work of some kind, she added. John L. Wiley said in 1907 that Fessenden Academy students were "largely from cabin homes without training in the principles and practices of correct living." They left school, he added, with new views and ideas of life which they took to their old homes and to the homes they built for themselves. An Allen Normal teacher was shocked at students who called "each other black hussies, black devils, and niggers." They were from poor, uneducated homes, she added. Schools welcomed superior, middle-class students, but attempted to avoid becoming exclusive. As Mary E. Richards, teacher at Ballard, said, "we want Ballard ever to hold up the same standard and open its doors to all who seek entrance with determination to make of themselves representative students of the school, responding to their instructors' efforts in fitting" them to be powers for good "in their communities and for their race."[31]

In nearly all AMA secondary schools and colleges there were more women than men. Many black fathers vowed to keep their daughters out of domestic service, and thus out of the grasp of white male sexual predators. For this reason John Hope Franklin's maternal grandfather sent all of his female and none of his male children to college. Sharecroppers and small farmers tended to select daughters rather than sons when deciding which children, if any, to send to school for more than a few years. Although all members of the family sometimes labored in the field, there were gender distinctions, and sons could less easily be spared from farmwork. Disfranchisement of black men after 1890 and discrimination that prevented men from securing employment commensurate with their training may also have discouraged some parents from sacrificing to send boys beyond the lower grades. As significant, between 1900 and the 1930s, southern states increased the number of public schools. Greater educational opportunities increased the demand for teachers, and since most teachers were female, African American women were encouraged to enter the field in large numbers.[32]

Numerous students, especially in secondary schools and colleges, were light skinned. In 1907, H. Paul Douglass described Beach Institute students as "*light,* bright, interesting." Of the twelve graduates at Ballard in 1919, nine were considered light skinned, and Lura Beam claimed some Gregory Institute students were fairer than she. Margaret H. Scott who arrived in Marion, Alabama, in 1936 wrote of her students, "Some are quite light and some are as dark as wet soot."[33] In part, because of its sizeable prewar free population, Avery Institute had several fair-complected students. Edmund L. Drago, who has graphically delineated intraracial prejudice in Charleston, suggests that the color line entered Avery. To what degree is uncertain. Some students sincerely believed that light classmates received preferential treatment, while Arthur J. Clement Jr. remembered that class leaders during his time at Avery were "not dark-skinned but 'black.'" Although a few teachers may have favored light-skinned students, and some students brought their parents' views to school, the AMA, a vigorous opponent of the color line, never countenanced intraracial segregation, and neither did most principals. Ann Rheba Cox Davis, daughter of light-skinned Benjamin F. Cox who became principal of Avery Institute in 1914, said her father quietly dismantled Avery's color line, which, of course, was an admission of its existence. "Wherever it was noticeable, caused someone discomfort or denied an opportunity—my father took *firm* steps to effect a change." Cox also discouraged class pretensions at Avery by enforcing a dress code among young women and by selecting teachers "who detested any caste or color line." Drago concludes that Avery Institute "mitigated blatantly exclusive tendencies in its students, including progeny of the antebellum 'free brown' elite." Indeed, Cox may have helped blur the intraracial color line in Charleston at large.[34] Color prejudice was common in the black community, but it never became a serious problem at any AMA secondary school.[35] Some students were even lighter than at Avery.

A few white students had attended early AMA schools, but most vanished after public schools were opened, and when Democrats redeemed southern states they stridently enforced segregation; but Orange Park Normal and Industrial school in Orange Park, Florida, was desegregated. Opened in 1891 with the aim of preparing black teachers, it developed rapidly and by 1894 had a white faculty of ten and a growing reputation for normal training. As it was the only school in the area, a few local whites enrolled their children, and as white confidence grew so did white attendance, which rose to thirty-five in 1894. Unfortunately, Orange Park's reputation and accessibility, which brought white patronage, contributed to its eventual demise. In 1893, William N. Sheats, a strict segregationist and opponent of political rights for blacks, became superintendent of public instruction.[36] When he learned of the Orange Park mixed school, he lobbied for additional legislation to deal with the situation. The Florida constitution banned mixed public schools, but Sheats demanded a law prohibiting any but blacks teaching blacks in any public or private school. He further advised lawmakers to fortify the already existing antimiscegenation statute by making it "a penal offense to teach whites and negroes in the same schools in either public, private or benevolent institutions." He denounced the Orange Park School as "a social and moral blotch" and a "vile encroachment upon our social and moral system." "What can be the ulterior design of these fanatical equalitists," he raged, "unless it be miscegenation?" In May 1895, the Florida legislature enacted a law prohibiting desegregated classes in any school—public, private, or parochial—but failed to deal with whites teaching black children.[37]

On April 6, 1896, authorities arrested and released on bail six white teachers and three white patrons at Orange Park School. Law officers warned that if teachers returned to the classroom they would be arrested daily and new bail would be required each time. The AMA closed the school for the remainder of the term and took the case to court. Sheats seemed to have won a resounding victory over the hated "miscegenationists." Citing the recent U.S. Supreme Court decision *Plessy v. Ferguson,* which accepted a policy of separate but equal, the Jacksonville *Florida Times-Union* ridiculed the AMA's attempt to overthrow the Sheats law. Much to the surprise of Floridians, the Fourth Judicial Circuit Court of Florida on October 21, 1896, quashed the indictment against the teachers and declared the law unconstitutional. Sheats failed to kill the school immediately, but he did it irreparable harm. It continued to operate, but with few white students. The furor over the Sheats law intimidated most white parents, and increased white hostility toward the school. Then in 1906, Clay County opened a school for whites in Orange Park so there was less reason for them to attend the AMA school. Five years later vandals burned the AMA school chapel in what the AMA called "a vicious but unsuccessful attempt to destroy the whole plant." More important, in 1913, at Sheats's urging, the legislature prohibited whites teaching in black schools. The AMA declared the law so "shameful and vicious" it should be challenged in court, but national sentiment made a successful appeal unlikely. In December 1913, the AMA announced that the school had been closed by adverse legislation.[38]

Though they bore the additional burden of race and poverty, black AMA students were not so different than those of other races. Erasmus M. Cravath of Fisk University joked that the greatest problem with black students was that they were so much like whites. When Lura Beam went to Gregory Institute in 1908, she found kids similar to ones she had taught in the North. She held her hand out to a male student one day, and he put a mouse in it. "Pairs of fourteen-year old girls could not look at each other without giggling, and gangling boys hoped someone would trip over their feet in the aisle. The notes, the gum, tardiness, spitballs, and crushes" she remembered from her own school days. "The bright, the bitter, lazy, lovesick, spoiled" were all in her classes. "A few were splendidly gifted," Beam added, "and even the average were intelligent. Their trouble was that books were not a part of their lives,"

and most had to work outside of school. Beam's students were not above chal-
lenging a new, white teacher. Soon after her arrival Beam was keeping study
hall when suddenly a humming noise filled the room. "No face looked up,
no lip parted, no body changed . . . while above them floated this unhuman
dissent of wind in the trees, or surf on the sand." Beam saw the humming as
an "accusing voice." "These fluent harpstrings brought me a defiance. It said
convincingly that I did not know anything; possibly I could not learn." At the
end of his first year teaching Latin and biology at Ballard Normal School in
1919, Lewis H. Mounts said some of his students were unmotivated, but none
were dumb, and most were intelligent, energetic, and hard workers. Northern
white teachers usually thought black students, at least those with similar advantages, compared favorably with whites, but in 1916 Lorena M. Derby said
Allen Normal students in general were rather slow, which she attributed to
poverty and the barrenness of their lives. Derby may have underestimated
them. In 1926–27 the Georgia Department of Education administered a uni-
form grammar test to all state accredited schools. More than half of Allen's
seniors scored above ninety percent. In reporting test results a Georgia newspaper listed Allen as among the top five in scores, but failed to identify it as
a black school. Derby may have misjudged Allen students for another reason.
She was later dismissed because she disliked "colored people and missionary
life."[39]

Whatever their hue, African American students were often cynical about
whites. They were familiar with lynch mobs and with demagogic politicians,
but not with white moderate George W. Cable, who often protested southern
white treatment of blacks.[40] When in 1915 Lura Beam rejoiced that the U.S.
Supreme Court in *Guinn v. United States* declared the grandfather clauses in
Oklahoma and Maryland unconstitutional, students suggested she curb her
enthusiasm as whites would devise a new method. Most did not believe justice available in the South. Though Gregory Institute students were proud
of the local cotton king and "learned people," they claimed to hate the mass
of whites. They were bored with Beam's lecture on the Revolutionary War
until she discussed black Crispus Attucks, and they enjoyed reading about
Frederick Douglass, Paul Laurence Dunbar, Toussaint l'Ouverture, and "our
painter" Henry O. Tanner. While teachers were often in awe of blacks' seeming love of country at a time when they were distinctly second-class citizens,
one of Beam's students would not sing "America." "I'm going to be a man
can't vote; when I can vote I'll sing, 'My country 'tis of thee.'" In 1912 the
American Missionary told of a twenty-year-old at Gregory Institute who had
fled to the swamps with his mother during the Wilmington race riot in 1898

who also refused to sing "America." He explained his silence with a bitter, "I have no country." Students at Gregory Institute took pleasure in pointing out white weaknesses and mistakes, and "resented loudly" white stereotypes. They deplored the fate of American Indians and were unsurprised to learn of the Salem witchcraft trials. Many students were offended that Gregory did not teach Latin as many AMA secondary schools did, and complained that the incidental cooking and carpentry classes were sending them back to slavery. Despite their earned distrust of whites, and their pessimism about a timely amelioration of the black condition, most students here firmly believed that education would improve their future. Beam said the ideal of Gregory students was to go to college and "do something for the race."[41]

Despite the limited number of actual graduates during the early years, AMA secondary schools and colleges joined other benevolent societies in furnishing most of the adequately prepared teachers for southern black public schools prior to World War II. In this way, the AMA filled an important need. In discussing the poor quality of teachers in black public schools from 1900 to 1940, educational historian Michael Fultz writes, "Low levels of preservice preparation among African American teachers was a refrain so often repeated that it approached the level of stereotype."[42] This limited preparation among black instructors made AMA secondary- and college-graduate teachers even more significant, and they literally dominated the areas in which AMA schools were located.[43] Fourteen teachers in Savannah public schools in 1904 were Beach Institute graduates. The secretary of the International Sunday School of the South personally canvassed sixty Georgia counties in 1897 and determined that more than seventy percent of teachers, preachers, and leaders had been educated by the AMA or by those trained in its schools. In 1901 the president and two faculty at the North Carolina State Normal and Industrial College at Greensboro had begun their work in AMA secondary schools. Titus Brown in *Faithful, Firm, and True* concludes that ninety percent of the central Georgia educators in 1920 were Ballardites. Numerous other Ballard graduates had joined the great migration and were teaching in northern cities. Trinity did more than staff surrounding schools. For years it was the only school for blacks in Limestone County, Alabama, but in response to Trinity and black community pressure, officials began establishing primary schools. In the late 1920s the board of education authorized Trinity to oversee its black rural schools. There were fourteen one-teacher schools, fourteen two-teacher schools, and one three-teacher school, none going beyond the sixth grade. Trinity faculty supervised the schools, advised teachers, and took the Trinity influence and spirit into the community. Many secondary graduates attended college and joined the faculty at their former institutions. In 1897, four alumni were teaching at Avery Institute. Eventually a majority of teachers in AMA secondary schools were AMA graduates.[44]

Before 1900, only hundreds of the thousands of AMA-trained teachers actually graduated from normal or high school. In the early years county superintendents hired even fifth and sixth graders who were often teenagers to instruct in rural schools. In 1891, twenty-five students from Meridian, Mississippi's Lincoln School taught in short-term public schools during the summer. More than forty Lincoln Academy students from Kings Mountain, North Carolina, were teaching in the winter of 1902. Indeed, teaching was a major way for pupils to acquire tuition money. Ballard principal George C. Burrage said in 1902 that nearly all graduates taught, "and every winter a number of pupils from grades as far down as fifth go out to earn money for another year's schooling." Allen Normal faculty complained that county commissioners took "even seventh grade girls for teachers, though we object as strenuously as possible." These temporary teachers clearly belonged to the group with "low levels of preservice preparation," but often the choice for these students was either improperly trained teachers or none at all. As Diane Ravitch writes in *The Revisionists Revised: A Critique of the Radical Attack on the Schools,* critics of industrial education and poor black schools missed a significant point. "Blacks were more often oppressed by education they did not receive than by the education they did receive." In later years more teachers were normal and secondary graduates. By 1914, Allen Normal had sent out almost one hundred teachers, and Ballard and Avery had produced many more. In 1934, W. W. Schiffley, assistant state supervisor of Negro schools, said Avery Institute did the best teacher-training work in South Carolina, and similar statements were made about many other AMA schools.[45]

Life was often difficult for AMA graduates who became teachers. As normal and secondary graduates they were generally qualified to teach only in lower grades. Many staffed city schools, except in Charleston where local whites fearing Yankee influence permitted only southern whites in black schools until 1920,[46] but even more graduates taught in small towns and rural areas. In 1925–26, 93.4 percent of black schools in the South were rural, and 82.6 percent were one-teacher schools. When Mamie Garvin Fields took her first teaching job in 1909 in South Carolina, her miserably furnished school contained no blackboard, chalk, or crayons. The only equipment was a roll book and a hand-held bell with which to summon students. In 1916, eighteen-year-old Septima Poinsette Clark, an Avery graduate with only practice-teaching experience, became principal of Promise Land School, an eight-grade, two-teacher school of 132 on Johns Island, South Carolina. Her feet were "horribly frostbitten" during the winter by long walks to school and from hours in the drafty school building heated only by a fireplace. As a Charleston resident, she knew little of the islands, but grew to admire the people she at first considered primitive.[47] Genevieve Nell Ladson, a 1928 Avery graduate, once taught in a barn with paneless windows. She literally built a school by helping saw down trees and nailing planks into place. Despite unfavorable conditions and low pay, uplifting black youth became a lifelong pursuit for most AMA teachers. Ruby Middleton Forsythe graduated from Avery Normal Institute in 1921. She taught at St. Pleasant and in Charleston County until 1938 when she took a position on Pawleys Island, South Carolina, where she labored until her retirement fifty-three years later. Though she taught at Holy Cross Faith Memorial School, the community knew it as "Miss Ruby's School." AMA-trained teachers became combination principal, teacher, and community leader in hundreds and hundreds of rural, village, and city schools and, along with teachers produced by other educational societies, made serious inroads upon southern black illiteracy. Illiteracy among African Americans above age ten decreased from approximately 81 percent in 1870 to 44.5 percent in 1900 and to 16 percent in 1930.[48]

As noted previously, AMA schools counseled their students to go back into black communities, and become race and educational leaders. Stephanie J. Shaw in *What a Woman Ought to Be and to Do: Black Professional Women Workers during the Jim Crow Era* (1996) says the mission schools "reinforced black family and community traditions that encouraged self-confidence, high achievement, leadership development among individuals, and individual service to the larger community." By the time AMA students graduated, she adds, "many of them were already well versed in the ethic of socially responsible individualism and experienced in carrying it out." Beulah Rucker enrolled in Knox Institute with a vision of material prosperity, but by graduation in 1909 she dreamed of starting a school for her largely unschooled brethren, and of uplifting her race though education and religion. She established a school in Gainesville, Georgia, in 1910. Within a year she had created the State Industrial and High School, and by 1920 the school boasted three classroom buildings and three teachers. Later the Rosenwald Fund assisted her in adding a shop and a teachers' home. Rucker taught black children until her death in 1963, but as with many other AMA graduates, she became more than just a teacher. She fought for education, books, clothing, and funds for black children in an area notably stingy with money for black education. She told her pupils that they were equal to anyone, prepared them for work and service, demanded the practice of Christian principles among both her students and the community, advocated property ownership, and according to her biographer, Ann Short Chirhart, "ultimately asserted the dignity of her race during . . . one of the most undignified examples of racism" in American history. Additionally, "she modeled and redefined gender relations by claiming a leader's position in Georgia—a role" that many men black and white opposed, and she "unveiled an expanded gendered role as an advisor and female professional and a deft negotiator of the color line." The AMA always stressed leadership, and Rucker, Clark, Ladson, and Forsythe were only a few of hundreds of AMA graduates who became community leaders.[49]

To the AMA, the struggle for equality meant training not only teachers, but leaders in all areas of endeavor. Whatever profession they selected, students were expected to strive for racial uplift, and they pursued almost every conceivable occupation available to them in a segregated society, including banker, newspaper editor, farmer, artisan, and mortician. In 1922, graduates of Knox Institute in Athens, Georgia, included sixteen teachers, eleven college students, nine college instructors, nine businessmen, five school principals, five physicians, five nurses, three dentists, three farmers, three mail carriers, two seamstresses, two ministers, one composer, one plumber, and one secretary. Among Emerson Institute alumni in 1907 were several physicians, including Dr. Ferdinand F. Stewart, a Harvard Medical School graduate; a missionary to Africa; several ministers; many teachers; and seven postal employees. Alumni of other schools followed occupations that were equally varied.[50]

A school is no better than its faculty, and for the most part AMA secondary schools had devoted and well-trained teachers. A few were removed for moral turpitude, inefficiency, racial prejudice, or, in the case of one white principal, a lack of "fundamental understanding of Negroes," but a majority were at least adequate and many were outstanding.[51] Superior opportunities for education mandated that most of the early high school teachers were white. Though there was considerable turnover among those who found themselves unfitted for a life of isolation and ostracism, many devoted their lives to the education of southern black children. Raymond G. Von Tobel, for example, went to Ballard as a naive twenty-three-year-old in 1907. He became assistant principal in 1908, principal in 1910, and remained at Ballard until his death in an automobile accident in 1935. Although not a stellar administrator, he was an efficient teacher, an exceptional mentor to his charges, and an effective ambassador to the black community. Based on Von Tobel's service, H. S. Barnwell, black district superintendent of AMA churches, described him as "one of God's finest noblemen." In 1906, four AMA teachers had been in the field more than thirty years, and four others twenty-five to thirty-one years. There were more women than men, though the latter tended to be in positions of authority. However, the AMA was in advance of society at large and appointed women leaders of coeducational high schools. Beam boasted that the AMA had several female principals when New York City was fighting women teachers' promotion and their right to marriage. Beam, who as AMA assistant superintendent of education from 1911 to 1919 hired, fired, and supervised teachers, said the AMA was "impartial as to sex on every point except women's salaries." Supply and demand, she claimed, necessitated paying men more.[52]

Women principals included Mary L. Marden, Louise Allyn, and Mary E. Phillips, all of whom supervised some male faculty. Marden spent thirty-three years with the AMA and in 1921 became principal of Allen Normal where she brought the school up to the highest state certification. Allyn, described by AMA secretary George L. Cady as "one of the wisest and most winsome" AMA workers, was principal of Trinity in Athens, Alabama, from 1909 to 1940. She rebuilt the school destroyed by fire early in her administration, was instrumental in securing free black public schools for grades one through six, negotiated with city officials for greater support, and led Trinity to its rank as a high school by the Southern Association of Colleges and Secondary Schools.[53]

Mary Phillips went to Marion, Alabama, in 1896 just as the AMA threatened to close Lincoln School. Under her leadership Lincoln grew from a feeble school in shabby quarters to one with twelve grades, twenty-six teachers, several sturdy buildings, and almost six hundred students. She spent summers in the North collecting funds for the school. In 1901, when the first brick building was being constructed on campus, workers struck for higher wages leaving a half-finished structure. Phillips, absent when the strike occurred, returned and told students she had no additional money but had recently learned to lay brick. She would teach them and they could continue their lessons while mixing cement and plying a trowel. The line at which Phillips and students took over construction of Van Wagen Hall was "still faintly visible" forty-five years later. Phillips was principal, teacher, purchasing agent, maintenance supervisor, den mother, and defender of black rights. In 1907, H. Paul Douglass remarked, "There is only one Miss Phillips, and we're killing her." She was suffering partial paralysis, and several teachers had "protested earnestly about the great burden she carries." She was in the process of completing a new girls' dormitory when she died on March 2, 1927. Phillips, described by Beam as aggressive, assertive, and exceptional in the classroom, was an independent, determined woman who did what she thought best for Lincoln even in defiance of AMA officials. Secretary Douglass, a sometimes hot-tempered and bellicose man, once vigorously scolded her for disregarding his instructions, but admitted that she would not change and that giving way to her would put the "work in good shape for the year." A 1934 Lincoln graduate, Richard Moore, remembered her as "a tough customer. . . . We feared her—not as somebody who was going to . . . hurt us," but "as a top teacher, a top principal, who was a strict disciplinarian, and who really knew how to run a school." Moore was in the fifth grade when the principal died. Had he been older he probably would have recalled her with even more respect and less fear. When she was seventy, Phillips married her childhood sweetheart who had broken their engagement when she went south to teach. Though local whites were generally hostile to Phillips, her value to the state was belatedly recognized in 1988 when she was inducted into the Alabama Women's Hall of Fame. Beam has claimed that northern white women teachers often became timid and retiring in the face of southern white hostility and contempt, and seldom left the boundaries of campus. Yet her assessment was inaccurate for Mary Phillips and many other AMA female teachers. They raised funds, conducted school business, interacted with merchants, and pressured public officials as fearlessly and effectively as males.[54]

There were many male principals and teachers, but women were most prominent in the classroom. By 1920 they tended to be of two types. Most exciting to students were the young, sophisticated women, both black and white, who wore the latest styles and knew the popular songs. Margaret H. Allison, a Wheaton College graduate, was only twenty-one when she became teacher of science and pedagogy at Allen Normal in 1928. She was attractive, a "fine type" in the words of one AMA official, and an excellent teacher. The other group was what AMA assistant superintendent of education Lura Beam called the "white old-timers," who were usually single (though AMA superintendent of education Douglass sometimes hired married women), devoted, and often more isolated from the white community. These older teachers urged the better students to go to college, badgered their parents to keep them in school, and frequently begged scholarships for them. Many used their own small pay to assist students. They were also occasionally quarrelsome, self-righteous (one attempted to get a principal fired for swearing), resentful of authority, and doubtful whether younger teachers were always properly dedicated.[55]

Some white teachers were tainted by paternalism and assumptions of cultural superiority, but most believed that any shortcomings on the part of blacks resulted from circumstances rather than innate weakness, and most genuinely cared for their students and strove for eventual equality.[56] Katherine M.

Rowley, an 1899 Oberlin College graduate, wrote from Trinity School in Athens, Alabama, in 1901, "This year finds me again in the Sunny Southland, laboring against the cause of disfranchisement of the Colored race. The work is profitable and fascinating, and I am glad to be here." Ina Hopkins Lewis of Dorchester Academy represented the views of many when she stated in 1917, "They need so much these little black folk; clothing, feeding, teaching, training and not least of all loving." Congregational minister J. Taylor Stanley became a boarder at Lincoln School in Marion, Alabama, at age nine in 1907. It was a new experience, he remembered, "to be associated with and taught by white persons, to be respected by them and when I was the most homesick, to be lifted to their laps and given reassurance of tenderness and love and of belonging." Horace Mann Bond attended Talladega College's Drewry High School where the ability and friendliness of white teachers impressed him. His favorable view of whites was not reinforced when he went to Lincoln University in Pennsylvania. Lincoln's faculty members "were socially aloof" and "less predisposed than were AMA affiliated schools to pursue an agenda of black equality in America."[57]

Vanessa Siddle Walker in *Their Highest Potential: An African American School Community in the Segregated South* notes the importance of parent-teacher interaction, and of teachers and principals caring whether students succeeded and demanding they try. Her positive findings about the Caswell County Training School in North Carolina could apply to almost every AMA secondary school. Most AMA long-term faculty, old or young, black or white, cared deeply about students and gloried in their successes and mourned their failures. The misfits and racially insensitive tended not to remain long. Ballard Normal provides a useful example. In preparation for a 1980 reunion, Raymond J. Pitts submitted a questionnaire to Ballard alumni asking the three things that most impressed them about the school. The central theme of the 203 who answered was that teachers were excellent and had a lasting impact. Respondent after respondent gave some variation of the reply of Lillian Roundtree Ford, class of 1932, who remembered "the concern that teachers had about scholastic achievement of students," the "dedication of teachers," "the concern of teachers re: students' needs financially, academically or emotionally." Another said the faculty taught "with love and patience," and "every student was made to feel special." Ruth Howard Davis, class of 1938, remembered "the feeling of being a person of worth and that something worthwhile was expected of me." White teachers' concern "made me know that someone cared even though we were living deep in segregation." Many thought that the faculty taught students "to aspire for something higher." A

1935 graduate wrote that she could "never forget the 'distance' that the faculty members went to assist pupils in their personal as well as their academic lives."[58]

Teachers visited students' homes, took them to school activities, and urged them to go to college. Sarah Calhoun McClendis, class of 1941, said it would have been impossible for her to attend so many school events except for teachers who constantly drove students to activities and home again. Black science teacher Birtill T. Barrow gave her a ride to the prom, and teacher Louis H. Mounts once drove McClendis and four others all the way to Savannah because they wanted to see the ocean. They saw it only at a distance since whites refused to let them on the beach. Officials told Mounts, who was white, that he could go closer, but "he told them 'no thanks,' we are all together." Student Charles M. Killens called Mounts "a most unforgettable character." In Killens's mind, he added, Mounts "was a minor deity." Novelist John O. Killens said Mounts was an "honest and compassionate man, a man with a commitment. He was committed, not just to teach the books, but to open up the world around us." Mounts held Hi-Y Club meetings at his house and took students on hikes, to wiener roasts, and bird-watching. Killens said he and others traveled all over Georgia to conventions in Mounts's Model T Ford. When students talked of aspirations for middle-class careers, Mounts always stressed "service to the people." In 1938, an honors student admitted to Talladega failed to receive necessary financial aid. Mounts personally "guaranteed Miss [Annie Ruth] Cornelius her college opportunity, without reference to what the college might give in work aid." Hundreds of teachers were as dedicated and generous as Mounts. Moreover, they instilled racial pride in their black students. Though the principal and many instructors were white, student John O. Killens said Ballard "gave [him] a sense of history as an Afro-American." The school sang the Negro national anthem, "Lift Every Voice and Sing," a James Weldon Johnson poem set to music by his brother J. Rosamond Johnson; taught about Frederick Douglass, Harriet Tubman, and other notable African Americans; celebrated Negro History Week; and brought in scholars and entertainers who gave dramatic readings from black authors.[59]

Students from other schools expressed similar positive views about their instructors. Evelyn Sanders, a 1925 graduate of Lincoln School in Marion, Alabama, said the school "helped me to know ... that all white people weren't like these that I lived with all my life down here." Teachers "were kind; they were considerate; you heard no racial slurs." Juanita Hatch, who graduated in 1938, remembered, "We were motivated to not be fearful or afraid of anybody. . . . [Y]ou stood up for whatever you thought was good and [the teachers] stood beside you." An Alabama State College friend accused Jesse Billingsley, a 1941 Lincoln graduate, of lying when Billingsley said he had danced with a white teacher at his senior prom. Lincoln "was integrated, and integration wasn't anything new to us," Billingsley declared. "It was just a different world." Jean Childs, of Lincoln School's class of 1950—and later the wife of black activist, politician, and ambassador to the United Nations Andrew Young—stated that she was "steeped in black culture.... So we cultivated an appreciation of ourselves in the midst of segregation." Her school, church, and family, who had attended Lincoln since the Reconstruction era, all taught her she was inferior to no one. There is little doubt that "the values of equality, courage and faith that Lincoln instilled in its students" contributed to the activism in Perry County, Alabama, during the civil rights movement.[60]

Despite their devotion to students and belief in black equality, some teachers had difficulty overcoming feelings of cultural superiority. In 1929, Fred L. Brownlee challenged AMA supporters as well as teachers to confront the following questions: "Are you as ready to work *with* people as you have been zealous in working *for* them?" "As a disciple of Jesus, are you as free as He was from racial and class prejudices?" "Do you really believe in the actual fellowship of *all* the members of the human race?" And finally, "Are you a purveyor of a 'superior' culture or do you consider it a composite produced by the best in customs and experiences of all races, nations, and classes?" Sympathy and meaning well were not enough, Brownlee said. To labor in AMA institutions one must truly believe in black equality.[61]

By the late 1870s black teachers were common in AMA primary schools, but fewer taught in upper grades. The AMA had many black teachers, Secretary Beard claimed in 1890, "but as a rule their rooms and teaching are quite inferior." Moreover, he added, blacks favored white instructors. Actually Beard's statement reflected the views of only a minority of African Americans. They appreciated white teachers who had the right spirit, but if qualifications were equal, many parents preferred teachers of their own race. Three years later Beard told the AMA executive committee that he recognized the need for black teachers, but thought most were not yet up to white standards and demanded less of students. Nevertheless, he added, "there is a place—which is to enlarge constantly—for schools of fair grade with colored teachers." He now admitted that there was growing pressure to commit AMA schools to black educators. Southern whites disliked northern white teachers, and while blacks still accepted white teachers they were "more restive under these than is for their good." Though politically powerless, blacks could and did pressure the AMA to employ more black teachers, and sometimes forced the resignation of principals of whom they disapproved. The AMA officers encouraged black empowerment and agency, but were not always happy when it was used against them. Some of Beard's white principals disagreed with him about the efficiency of black teachers. Ida F. Hubbard of Slater Training School in Knoxville hired an accomplished Fisk graduate who inspired students and was "of inestimable value." Another factor influencing Beard in favor of white teachers was unrelated to effective instruction. The AMA annually struggled to balance the budget, and white teachers who wrote and visited their northern churches and communities were a major source of donations. He feared that the loss of white teachers would "cut our schools away from the touch of our Northern churches and benevolences." As late as 1933, Beard wrote then AMA secretary Fred L. Brownlee that replacing whites with educated blacks "was most wise and the very thing to do," yet it severed the connection between white teachers and their communities in the North. Teachers played a major role in maintaining the dwindling northern interest in AMA work.[62]

As opportunities for advanced education and experience increased for blacks, so did black faculty at secondary schools. Indeed, the number of both principals and teachers grew swiftly. By 1900, six normal and high schools had black principals with all-black staffs. Four years later, twelve normal and high schools were directed by African Americans. Assertive black men were unwelcome in the white South, so circumspection and restraint were essential characteristics for these educators.[63] Outstanding early black principals included L. S. Clark, William G. Price, and John L. Wiley, all of whom transformed primary schools into successful secondary institutions. In 1897, Clark took direction of a one-room graded school in Athens, Georgia; added normal classes; and by 1921 Knox Institute was the first black high school to be accredited by the University of Georgia Accrediting Commission. Clark retired in 1927.[64] William G. Price, a graduate of both Hampton Institute and the State Normal School in Westfield, Massachusetts, and a Harvard summer school student, became principal at Gloucester Agricultural and Industrial School in Cappahosic, Virginia, in 1900. With AMA assistance he built an efficient high school; greatly expanded campus buildings; acquired a 148-acre experimental school farm; organized the Gloucester Land, Loan, and Building Association to help members buy homes; and taught improved farming methods to both black and white neighbors. Price was always frugal with AMA money. School-raised hams were served for dinner. The next day beans were cooked with the leftover ham skin, fat, and bones added for seasoning. The bones were then ground for chicken feed. In 1909, H. Paul Douglass declared that Gloucester County contained "probably the best housed" black rural community in America. This was partially due, he believed, to Price, Gloucester A & I, its model farm, and the Land, Loan, and Building Association which by 1921 had disbursed $44,646 and had $5,000 in the treasury. Gloucester also furnished many teachers, produced local farm leaders, and sent numerous students to college. Though his was an "agricultural" school, Price stressed academics first. His biographer said that despite his background at Hampton, an industrial school, Price "shaped a curriculum for his students of which W. E. B. Du Bois would have approved." Douglass wrote in 1910 that Price had "the most up to date and compelling selected text books in the system" and "a tremendously well ordered school." As late as 1920 Gloucester remained the only school above the seventh grade for black children in the area. In fact, Gloucester had twelve grades approximately forty years before Virginia added grade twelve in its black public schools. Price did this in an "area not hospitable to the highest aspirations of African Americans" and at a time when most Virginia whites favored vocational education, if any, for blacks. Price maintained relatively good relations with local whites without sacrificing all personal rights. He acquired land and assisted other African Americans in doing the same; and he, his wife, Carrie, and his sister voted in Gloucester County in 1933.[65]

In 1898, John L. Wiley, a Fisk University alumnus and an attorney, became principal of Fessenden Academy in Martin, Florida. Fessenden, far from AMA's New York headquarters, was seldom visited by AMA officials, and was considered less important than urban schools which had more students and attracted greater attention. Undeterred, the aggressive, energetic Wiley increased enrollment; added grades nine through twelve; built men's and women's dormitories; added thirty-seven acres to campus; helped organize a black-owned bank in Ocala; and secured a $6,500 Carnegie grant which partially funded a library, accommodations for female boarders, a dining hall, and classrooms for domestic science courses. The Carnegie building, designed by an AMA-retained black architect, was constructed entirely by black labor. The plant, valued at $6,000 when Wiley became principal, was appraised at $30,000 in 1912. Wiley's ambition for his school brought him into conflict with Superintendent Douglass, who believed Wiley followed his own inclinations too much and Douglass's orders too little. Douglass admitted that Wiley was an efficient principal, his influence on students excellent, and his ability to get "public money, furnishings and other favors" remarkable. Yet Douglass was agitated by his independence. In 1909, Douglass wrote, "I expect history to repeat itself. Wiley will add to the plant, involving us more or less but getting the greater portion of the money elsewhere." Wiley, he concluded, was "incorrigible." Wiley could be diplomatic, stubborn, and forceful, and he was a master at passive resistance, but no matter how careful he and other black principals had to be in dealing with southern whites, they generally were not obsequious to white AMA officials. In 1913, Wiley refused Douglass's request that he resign. The Wiley-Douglass tension continued until Wiley mysteriously disappeared in 1915. On July 1 he went to Ocala to attend a movie and parked near the Temple Theater. The next morning his car was still there, and Wiley was never seen again. He had drawn no money from the bank, his financial affairs were in order, and his family remained behind. Many local blacks believed he had been murdered. Lura Beam was never certain "that he was not merely taken to a swamp or out to sea." In 1937, an NAACP agent investigating the disappearance of an Ocala resident wrote, "Ocala did something of this kind . . . years ago with one Prof. Wiley, a respectable school teacher." Whatever Wiley's fate, Florida lost a dedicated and effective black educator. It was estimated that by 1912 at least a thousand pupils had gone out from the school "carrying the leaven of their education and training, high ideas and Christian influence."[66]

The success of the above black principals encouraged the appointment of others. In 1903 George N. White, educated at Atlanta University and the University of Chicago, became principal of Burrell Normal in Florence, Alabama. Superintendent Douglass, usually difficult to please, wrote in 1907, "I think we have a jewel in Mr. White. He is bright, energetic, accurate, yet seemingly thoughtful and wise." White, brother of Walter White, later NAACP secretary, struggled to gain local white support without losing black respect. When Thomas Dixon's virulently racist play *The Leopard's Spots* was scheduled to show in Florence, White pointed out the "despicable and inflammatory" nature of the play to the city council, who wired Dixon that it could not be performed in Florence. After Dixon sent out circulars announcing the play anyway, the mayor closed the theater and there was no performance. When White resigned in 1925 to become AMA associate secretary of the Department of Support, the first black appointed to associate secretary, whites and blacks petitioned the AMA to return him to Florence.[67]

The increase of black principals was accompanied by more black teachers. Larger numbers of blacks became teachers and principals because more were properly prepared, because blacks demanded it, because white southerners preferred and sometimes mandated it (Sheats's Law in Florida), because fewer whites were willing to go south to teach black youth, and because AMA officials thought it was the right thing to do. In 1911 the *American Missionary* pointed out the need for more black instructors. "No savior of a race is of an alien race. Heart throbs must be the same." In 1914, the AMA appointed Benjamin F. Cox the first black principal of Avery Normal Institute, its most

Fig. 3. Principal George N. White and male students at Burrell Normal School
(Courtesy of Amistad Research Center, Tulane University, New Orleans, Louisiana)

prized secondary school; the AMA chose Cox in part as a response to South Carolina governor Cole Blease's race baiting and attacks on black education, and also out of fear that the white administration had "become somewhat stale and out of touch with the community." In 1920, the AMA missions committee, at the request of Liberty County black teachers, decided to reorganize Dorchester Academy under black leadership. After two unsuccessful administrations, Elizabeth Moore was appointed Dorchester principal in 1925. Both Avery and Dorchester flourished under black management. Cox turned Avery into an outstanding college prep school, and Moore energized the community; emphasized self-improvement, self-reliance, and pride; and demanded that patrons pay their bills and quit leaning on the school and waiting for things to be done for them. The AMA had always sent male principals, a local Georgia woman stated, and "[t]hey were good men. We liked them all right. But now they sent us a woman principal and she even makes the men work."[68]

By the 1921–22 academic year, black teachers outnumbered whites 286 to 259, and the latter included those teaching in all-white schools in the Appalachians. In 1931, of 560 AMA workers 340 were black, 30 American Indian, 29 Puerto Rican, 5 Spanish-American and Japanese, and 171 white. A few black teachers were poorly trained and mediocre in the classroom, but many were outstanding, including Marion V. Cuthbert, a Boston University graduate who went to Burrell Normal as a French and English teacher in 1920. Upon her arrival she said she "decided to lift the whole colored population of Florence to literary and social heights whereof it little dreamed." She quickly overcame her naivete, but she was a brilliant teacher who learned the culture of her students and inspired them to do more. She became acting principal of Burrell in 1925 and principal in 1926. She resigned in 1927 to become dean of women at Talladega College. Cuthbert had a varied career but never lost sight of her southern brothers and sisters. She was "a pioneer in the study of black women, an advocate of interracial cooperation, and an accomplished writer in several genres." A few other northern African Americans taught in AMA schools, but unsurprisingly most black teachers were southern and many were graduates of AMA colleges. The AMA continued to appoint blacks as directors of secondary schools. By the 1930s, Ballard, Trinity, and Lincoln School in Marion were the only major secondary schools with white principals. Ballard came under black direction in 1937, and Trinity and Lincoln followed in 1943. Beard's initial fear that schools would falter under black leadership was unfounded. In 1925 AMA official Henry Leiper toured the South. "It is noteworthy," he wrote, "that the educational standards in these schools are far higher than the educational standards which it was possible to maintain in the old days where all the instruction was by white teachers."[69]

A majority of the black teachers were women. But of course, the disparity between men and women teachers in primary schools was also great among whites. Teaching was becoming feminized throughout the country, and salaries were so low that men teachers had difficulty supporting families. In 1911, six hundred black men and three thousand black women taught in Georgia's black schools grade one through eleven. By 1930, the number of men had declined to five hundred, and the number of black women teachers had increased to five thousand. In 1890, 1900, and 1910, black teachers comprised respectively forty-four percent, forty-five percent, and forty-five percent of all black professionals, and in the latter year seventy-six percent of black teachers were female. According to Linda Perkins, the nineteenth-century "Cult of True Womanhood" was interpreted for black women in the post–Civil War era to mean education as an avenue for racial uplift, an obliga-

Fig. 4. Avery Normal Institute faculty, ca. 1941 (Courtesy of Amistad Research Center, Tulane University, New Orleans, Louisiana)

tion that the AMA instilled in both female and male students. Moreover, as James L. Leloudis notes in *Schooling the New South,* southern white officials preferred black female teachers with the assumption that they were more pliant and easy to control. Even relatively progressive Nathan C. Newbold, North Carolina state agent of Negro Education, and others who worked with black education "felt more at ease with black women and viewed them as less of a political liability than men."[70] Although the AMA did not fear men, most of its teachers were women, and despite low salaries, teaching for the AMA was a prime job in the early years for black females who had limited employment opportunities. Teaching was a "genteel" position, preferable to domestic jobs, farmwork, and manual labor which was the plight of most black women. As late as 1940, sixty percent of employed black females were domestic servants. If they taught in public schools, monthly salaries were even lower than at AMA institutions, the school term was fewer months, and they were dependent upon sometimes hostile white officials and impoverished parents. In 1929, the average monthly salary for black public school teachers ranged from $66.25 in Florida to $38.24 in Georgia. The AMA established a minimum salary scale for secondary schools in 1920 at $55 per month with room, board, laundry, and travel; $82.50 monthly with room, travel, no board; $90 per month with travel only. The association gradually increased its salaries and uniformly held school for more months than public institutions.[71]

A 1941 survey indicated that the typical 1930s Avery graduate was teaching in South Carolina public schools for less than $10 a week. Schools often operated only five to seven months a year. On the other hand, in 1922 the AMA paid Anna Maria Hansen at Chandler School in Lexington, Kentucky, $65 a month for eight months, including room, board, laundry, and travel. Ruth D. Anderson, with a B.A. from Straight College, taught at Gloucester Institute for $55 a month for ten months, living quarters, board, laundry, and travel in 1926. Most AMA secondary schools provided a comfortable teachers' home with cook, laundress, and housekeeper. Although far better than in most southern black public schools, AMA pay was low and not competitive with northern institutions. The overextended AMA was keenly aware of low salaries and constantly strove to improve them. Fred L. Brownlee complained in 1925, that the "present meager salaries" made it difficult to secure sufficient faculty.[72] The AMA made no racial distinctions in pay, but men, regardless of color, received more. In 1938, Brownlee, at the urging of assistant Ruth A. Morton began to equalize salaries. By September 1941, the starting salary for new teachers, male or female, with a bachelor's degree and state certification, was $900—still low, but equal. By the early 1940s, with successful southern state salary equalization campaigns, the AMA had difficulty matching state salaries and began to lose teachers to public schools.[73]

Despite white opposition, some AMA secondary schools had interracial faculties until the 1940s. LeMoyne began with an all-white faculty, but by 1902 eight of its teachers were AMA graduates. George C. Burrage reported in 1908 that black and white Ballard teachers were "working together in complete and cordial harmony." In 1914, the school's fourteen teachers were equally divided between black and white. Emerson Institute at first had a mixed faculty, became all white, and then in 1899 began adding black teachers again. Teachers at AMA schools shared living quarters except in Mobile. Emerson's first mixed faculty had lived in the same home, but when the faculty desegregated again, Mobile racial codes mandated a separate campus home for blacks. White teachers at all interracial schools visited in students' homes, went to social gatherings with them, attended their churches, and patronized black businesses. Since parents and children were completely socially segregated otherwise, white teachers thought this was valuable interracial work. Margaret H. Scott, who went to Lincoln School in 1936, said the parents of her black students were friendly. Her presence in their community "please[d] them. No other white folks come, you see, except when they want work done. No other white people ever shake hands with them."[74]

Most parents at AMA schools approved interracial faculties. When in 1920 the AMA considered releasing all white teachers at Emerson, black leaders protested. They relished having teachers of their race, but preferred both black and white. They, as the AMA, believed the example was important. Beard reminded Brownlee in 1933 that the AMA must keep "a sprinkling" of white teachers to illustrate its opposition to segregation. Brownlee did not need prompting. He was committed to an interracial faculty as was his black associate secretary from 1930 to 1934, William A. Daniel, who assiduously searched for teachers of both races with distinctive personalities, those who could inspire students and give them more than knowledge found in books. Daniel's successor, Ruth A. Morton, was no less determined. In 1938, Morton wrote that the Lincoln School faculty was almost evenly divided between black and white. They were living together in the dormitory, "eat[ing] at the same tables, and shar[ing] a common life together, thus, in some measure, trying to bring about the type of situation we believe should exist everywhere." Maintaining interracial faculties was testimony to the AMA's belief in desegregation and equality. Most blacks appreciated the principle and the effort, but it had little positive effect on the white South. Not surprisingly, many whites accused the AMA of teaching social equality by example. Brownlee admitted in 1936 that the AMA's interracial work had been largely intramural, that the practice of human brotherhood had been primarily on campus. The last of the interracial secondary schools ended in 1943. By then, all that had white teachers were cooperating with county, city, or state departments of education which demanded an all-black faculty.[75]

The curriculum at the secondary institutions varied from school to school and changed with the times. At first the schools had primary students, too. The first six grades, as mentioned previously, were "fairly orthodox." Teachers tried to prepare the next two grades for high school and to "give all possible strength" to those stopping at the end of the eighth grade. High schools attempted to train teachers and meet community needs. During the early years, most secondary schools offered normal classes and used elementary grades for practice teaching. The city schools also had some vocational classes and college preparatory programs. Nearly all had some industrial component, but in addition to, rather than in lieu of, regular academic work.[76] For example, Burrell School taught sewing to both sexes through the third grade, assuming that boys as well as girls should know how to patch and sew on buttons. Although principal Orishatukeh Faduma of Peabody Academy in Troy, North Carolina, did not allow women to graduate without taking a course in sewing and being proficient cooks, while males learned carpentry and home repairs, literary education came first. The school was interested in producing "men" and "women," not mechanics and cooks. "Sharp tools are produced by sharp minds," Faduma said, "not sharp minds by sharp tools." Faduma was obviously not a poorly educated vocational education advocate. He was known by the black intelligentsia, and in 1899 was invited to join the elitist American Negro Academy, which limited its membership to fifty. AMA president Washington Gladden was alarmed at the emphasis placed on industrial education for African Americans in the early twentieth century. He rejoiced in what Booker T. Washington had done at Tuskegee, but he argued that education for citizenship, leadership, and the professions was also essential. In 1903, Edgar Gardner Murphy, executive secretary of the Southern Education Board (SEB), which supported industrial education and greater cooperation with southern whites, said that discussing black problems was difficult. "If it is to be done at all, it is to be done by a Southern man. I have turned from such men as [AMA president] Washington Gladden and others." For good measure, another SEB official, George Dickerman, accused the AMA of teaching social equality.[77] Clearly, the SEB, an alliance of northern philanthropy and white southerners, considered the AMA a threat to its plans for "practical" education. H. Paul Douglass stated in 1908 that blacks' friends "should welcome all existing interest in his industrial education while profoundly distrusting much of the motive—both northern and southern." Those who wished to be carpenters and brick masons should be so trained, but they also should be taught academic subjects. The *American Missionary* proclaimed in 1910, "no education is truly vocational which does not prepare for life as well as livelihood."[78]

AMA officials never wavered in their determination to make available to blacks the same education whites enjoyed. In its attempt to reach as many students as possible, the association expanded so rapidly at first that many of its schools lacked quality. They had too few teachers, some of whom were more missionaries than competent instructors, and too little equipment. By 1900, more college graduates were being hired and most schools were trying to meet state requirements for secondary schools, though Wiley at Fessenden in 1907 asked to substitute manual training and domestic science for geometry, trigonometry, and Latin. All AMA secondary schools taught music.[79]

H. Paul Douglass, who became the AMA's superintendent of education in 1906 and corresponding secretary in 1910, did much to transform schools from missionary enterprises into regular secondary schools. He was the first professional educator to supervise AMA schools, and he, sometimes ruthlessly, removed well-meaning but inefficient workers and replaced them with younger, better trained teachers. He hired more black college graduates, de-emphasized religion, and modernized the curriculum. Lura Beam has said that in the face of the evolving curriculum after World War I, some of the older teachers "mourned for what they called character education," while younger teachers tried to move the schools toward national standards. Un-der Douglass's administration, the quality of instruction not "only kept pace with the advance in public schools," but in some areas was "an inspiration for such an advance." Most of the schools were short on money and equip-ment, but were far better than the widely scattered public schools for blacks. Brownlee continued the progress, and in the 1920s the schools began to meet accreditation standards.[80]

By 1924, the Georgia Department of Education had accredited Ballard, Allen Normal, and Knox Institute. In the 1920s, Lincoln Academy at Kings Mountain was the first black school to be accredited by North Carolina. Brick School and Palmer Memorial Institute were accredited soon afterward. The Alabama Department of Education certified Lincoln School and Burrell in 1930. AMA schools clearly met the same requirements as white high schools. Even more significant, in 1928 the Southern Association of Colleges and Secondary Schools (SACSS) finally began to certify black institutions.[81] The SACSS rated Burrell Normal, Talladega High, and Tougaloo High as "A" in-stitutions in 1931. Dorchester Academy and Ballard received the same rating in 1934, and the SACSS accredited Lincoln Academy and Avery Institute in 1935. When Avery was accredited, Brownlee pointed out that Charleston did not have a fully accredited high school for whites. There were only fifty-nine accredited black high schools in the entire South in 1934, twenty of which were private. Ten of the accredited public schools were in North Carolina. Tougaloo High was the only accredited black secondary school in Missis-sippi, which had the largest percentage of African Americans of any state; and South Carolina, which had the second highest percentage, had only one accredited black public high school. AMA secondary schools remained in-dispensable for southern black youth.[82]

The schools pursued the dual aims of preparing students for livelihood and life. Work ethic, integrity, thriftiness, personal responsibility, leadership, ra-cial uplift, and good morals were taught in addition to academic subjects. Fes-senden principal John Wiley represented the view of many when he wrote in 1915 that "geometrical proportions, chemistry tables, dead languages . . . are almost futile if students . . . are not trained in Christian character." Dormito-ries, available at most schools, provided an integral part of the training. "Here the green country girl learns to sleep between the sheets," an Allen Normal teacher stated, "and to eat meals regularly and at a table." Allen women were taught a liberal arts curriculum, leadership, racial uplift, proper housework, dignity of labor, self-reliance, and "to cultivate an earnest Christian spirit." They were then to go out and teach others. Instructors lived with boarders and taught by example. Daily chapel, devotional exercises, and Bible study were common, though Wiley at Fessenden was more likely to discuss manners, morals, and "the true aims and purposes of life" than religion. Sexual laxity, gambling, and drinking alcohol were severely condemned.[83]

During the early years some teachers reported religious conversion of students as enthusiastically as advancement in learning. In 1893 Rev. George W. Moore, an African American AMA field missionary, held a ten-day revival at Avery at which more than one hundred students "confessed Christ." An Allen Normal teacher exulted in 1891 that when the year began "every one of the forty boarding students were rejoicing in the blessed hope of sins forgiven." The schools later attached less importance to revivalism, but continued "character education." The primacy of religion in AMA schools was overstated. Indeed, the AMA church constituency frequently criticized the association for giving too little attention to religion and church building. Still, religion remained important. In 1924, the *American Missionary* editorialized, "The mental and moral training that imparts no reverence for the divine authority, and no trust in the divine goodness, cannot fail to be a miserable, one-sided discipline, unfitted to bear the stress and strain of life."[84]

Although the AMA schools demanded academic performance and enforced rigid rules of personal conduct, they were not grim. Allen Normal had a pleasant playground with swings, seesaws, marbles, and softball games. Older students took trips, participated in school clubs, held fund-raisers, and played in the band or on the basketball team. In 1924, a teacher described "happy-faced girls dressed in their bloomer and middies running hither and thither" on the basketball court. Most of the schools had numerous academic and social clubs, and intramural sports. Allen Normal gave public performances, including a senior class play, May Day exercises, and an operetta. Celestina Higgins Bridgeforth, a 1938 graduate of Trinity in Athens, Alabama, said the faculty "instilled into us every aspect of life that they could." In addition to the usual subjects, Bridgeforth added, students enjoyed "bird watching and bonfires, hikes and afternoon teas, private music lessons, poetry readings, Maypole dances, and [the teachers'] own version of Japanese theater." Ballard boasted a band, orchestra, and choir. All schools had athletic teams. In 1924, Ballard played baseball, basketball, and football in a four-team league. Principal Von Tobel thought athletics were valuable not only for physical training and development, but also for "developing a spirit of fair play and true conduct." The baseball team was "a tonic to scholarship and ethics," the Brewer principal asserted, and fostered school spirit and "interscholastic friendliness."[85] Benjamin F. Cox introduced basketball and football at Avery to encourage males to stay in school, and it was one of the few AMA schools at which male-female enrollment was nearly equal. Burrell Normal provided a fair sample of the activities of all schools. In 1934–35, it competed in interscholastic football, baseball, both men's and women's basketball, girls' softball, and men's and women's track and field. It also had intramural basketball, tennis, horseshoe pitching, volleyball, checkers, and table tennis. Burrell participated in a state academic meet, the North Alabama Music Festival, Elks' District Oratorical Contest, TVA Health Week Poster Contest, and it presented several plays. Students published a mimeographed school paper and were active in the Drama Club, the French Club, and other campus organizations. Several other schools had student newspapers, and in the 1920s most added student councils which gave students experience in self-government and policy making.[86]

Black culture was prominent in both classroom and extracurricular activities, especially by the 1920s. As previously noted, students at Ballard Normal and Lincoln School were "steeped" in black culture. Frederick Douglass visited Allen Normal in 1889 to "offer words of encouragement" to students. In 1899 Rev. Henry H. Proctor, well-known black Atlanta minister and leader, gave the commencement address there. When Benjamin F. Cox became principal at Avery Normal Institute, he stressed black history and culture. Between 1916 and 1934 guests, speakers, and artists invited to Avery included contralto Marian Anderson, W. E. B. Du Bois, and Langston Hughes. Cox, who had been a member of the Fisk University Jubilee Singers, lectured on spirituals and brought many members of the Harlem Renaissance to campus. Even rural schools such as Lincoln in Alabama and Gloucester in Virginia enjoyed visiting dignitaries. Langston Hughes gave a lecture reading at Lincoln School in Marion in 1932, and distinguished performers and speakers visiting Gloucester included Marian Anderson, tenor Roland Hayes, violinist Clarence White, and writer James Weldon Johnson. Several schools introduced courses in Negro history, and all celebrated Negro History Week. As early as 1902, literature courses at Gloucester included black authors. Drama clubs and programs gave special attention to black plays, songs, and readings. No doubt the increasing number of black teachers enhanced interest in black issues, but there is little evidence that black principals, with the possible exception of Cox, gave significantly greater attention to black culture than white principals.[87]

One reason the AMA was able to add the staff, laboratory equipment, and

Fig. 5. Ballard High School band, 1941 (Courtesy of Amistad Research Center, Tulane University, New Orleans, Louisiana)

facilities to meet accreditation standards at both its colleges and secondary institutions was because it discontinued some schools and placed more resources in the remaining ones. In 1893, the AMA had 5 "colleges," 29 normal schools, 43 common schools, and 389 teachers. In 1930, it had 5 colleges and secondary schools, 1 junior college, 12 secondary and elementary schools, and 397 faculty and administrators. AMA expenditures in 1890–91 for all its work including churches, schools, and Indian and Chinese missions were $430,355.53. In 1921, the amount spent for blacks alone was $513,000, increasing to $719,000 in 1926. Even accounting for inflation, schools in the 1920s and 1930s were obviously better staffed and equipped.[88] The association strongly believed that education was a public obligation, and transferred its schools to public authorities as soon as they were willing to take responsibility. As will be seen later, H. Paul Douglass was determined to improve AMA institutions, in part by turning as many as possible over to public authorities and concentrating funds on those remaining.[89] The Depression led to the demise of still other schools. AMA receipts plummeted from $1,634,047 in 1927–28 to $695,175 in 1934–35 and to $533,315 in 1937–38.[90]

Though balancing the budget was an annual ordeal and locals were compelled to supply greater support, AMA schools, as indicated by accreditation, grew in quality, equipment, and facilities during the 1920s. The number of students and graduates also increased. High school enrollment at Peabody Academy in Troy, North Carolina, grew from 30 in 1916 to 137 in 1926. Ballard had 284 secondary students in 1927, and graduates increased from 7 in 1900 to 44 in 1930 and to 50 in 1939. Avery graduated 557 students between 1930 and 1940. Of the Avery graduates, 29.6 percent enrolled in college as did a large portion of Ballardites.[91] Unfortunately, progress in the secondary schools was impeded by the Depression. As mentioned previously, AMA income dropped dramatically, and even World War II and increasing employment did little to alleviate the AMA's financial crisis.[92] Between 1931 and 1933 the AMA budget decreased by forty-two percent. Four schools were closed, 119 positions were discontinued, salaries were reduced by fifteen percent, programs were curtailed everywhere, and still in September 1933 the association suffered a $75,000 deficit. It only got worse for several years. Repairs, construction, needed equipment, and book purchases were delayed. Many students could not pay their bills and dropped out. Schools became more dependent on community support at a time when unemployment was rising among their black patrons.[93]

In order to retain students, some schools resorted to the earlier practice of bartering for tuition. Lincoln Academy in Kings Mountain, North Carolina, accepted food, livestock, wood, and labor for tuition. Only a mild winter and a surplus of fruit and vegetables canned during the summer prevented Trinity students from suffering during the winter of 1932. On the positive side, principal Louise Allyn reported, lack of cash had improved the moral and physical health of males because it had almost eliminated smoking. Ballard principal Raymond G. Von Tobel complained in January 1930 that "the financial stress prevalent in Georgia" had reduced enrollment considerably. Still Ballard had 290 students. That number dropped to 168 by the fall of 1932 due to "the severe financial stress which our people are still undergoing." After an initial decline at Dorchester, enrollment increased from 162 in 1931–32 to 236 in 1932–33 when principal Elizabeth Moore announced that food for the dining room would be accepted as tuition. At Lincoln School in Marion, Alabama, the Parent Teachers Association held rallies and fund drives, collecting $108.68 in 1931–32. Nancy Kynard of Lincoln School, from the graduating class of 1935, recalled that she was one of the poor students and could not have survived without the teachers. If a student lacked a presentable coat, Kynard stated, a teacher would take her to the storeroom, find a good coat for twenty-five cents, and allow her to work it out after school hours. The National Youth Administration (NYA), a national program created in 1935 to help youth remain in school through work-study programs, assisted numerous students. In 1935–36, the NYA paid sixty-five Ballard students to build the school's first tennis court and beautify the campus, while fifty-one NYA students at Dorchester maintained the campus and planted flowers and shrubbery.[94]

The AMA survived the 1930s, but the Depression marked a new direction for its secondary schools. Brownlee became more concerned with the colleges, and with race relations. He continued to negotiate with public officials to take over secondary institutions and, influenced by the Danish Folk School, John Dewey, and, perhaps, New Deal activism, Brownlee concluded to redesign the others as "functional" schools, to be discussed in a following chapter. Ballard, Avery, and Lincoln Academy continued their important college preparatory work, and the others continued to graduate high school students, but all were pushed—sometimes against great resistance—to become "community" schools.[95] The secondary schools were among the AMA's greatest contributions to black Americans. They produced thousands of teachers, community and church leaders, businessmen and -women, competent craftsmen and professionals, efficient homemakers, and enlightened farmers, and these schools prepared hundreds for college.

3
Administration and Fund Collecting

The effectiveness of the AMA's educational mission depended on the efficiency of its central administration, which made and implemented policy, hired and supervised staff, and collected money. In 1890, the association's constitution called for a president, several vice presidents, two corresponding secretaries, a treasurer, and an executive committee with corresponding secretaries and treasurer as ex-officio members. The presidents and vice presidents were often honorary, chosen to enhance the AMA's prestige and fund-raising potential.[1] Although presidents were honorary and did not make day-to-day decisions, they could influence the AMA's direction and public image. Washington Gladden, a vice president from 1894 to 1901 and president from 1901 to 1904, was widely known throughout the North as a leading advocate of the Social Gospel, and "the most prominent of social Christianity's evangelical neoabolitionists." From the 1870s he channeled his interest in African Americans through the AMA. In some ways the AMA shaped him more than he influenced it. Initially, he was optimistic about racial progress, but his faith was badly shaken in the 1890s and he began speaking publicly with greater urgency about conditions "not much better than slavery." In 1903 he visited Atlanta, where he personally viewed the experience of black southerners for the first time and finally accepted "the deep roots of racial hatred." He also met W. E. B. Du Bois and read his *Souls of Black Folk*. Thereafter Gladden placed greater emphasis on higher education and political rights. In his 1904 presidential address, he advised other AMA members to read Du Bois's book.[2]

Gladden was succeeded as president in 1904 by Amory H. Bradford, pastor of the First Congregational Church in Montclair, New Jersey, who had avidly supported the AMA since the early 1880s. Bradford was elected moderator of the National Council of Churches in 1903, which gave him a unique opportunity to encourage Congregationalists to support the AMA's efforts for black Americans. In a 1905 speech at the AMA annual meeting, he called segregation "the most insidiously pernicious and unpatriotic" trend in the country. Bradford wrote *My Brother* (1910), which historian Ralph E. Luker has called "one of social gospel's most important critiques of racism." *My Brother* developed the theme that the AMA had long taught: Fatherhood of God and the brotherhood of man. Discrimination based on race, color, or nationality was wicked because all men were made in God's image, and all were sacred. Bradford's creed for the AMA included universal brotherhood and equal opportunity for the best education and culture available. All races had barbaric periods and unworthy individuals, but, as AMA colleges had revealed, all had the potential to excel; in Bradford's words, the AMA believed in "America for all its people and all its people for America." Black minister Henry Hugh Proctor called Bradford "[o]ne of the greatest, wisest, most courageous friends my people ever had." Gladden and many other "key evangelical neoabolitionist spokesmen" were AMA leaders and appealed to values expounded in Bradford's book. These men, Luker says, "dominated the center left of the social gospel's attitude in race relations." Many succeeding AMA presidents were no less concerned with black rights.[3]

The primary AMA governing body was the annual meeting, constituted of all officers and members, which reviewed policies and administration and selected officers. The executive committee of twelve—later fifteen— met monthly in New York and exercised considerable power. Committee members tended to be prominent men from all walks of life. For example, William Hayes Ward, who served more than three decades on the executive committee, was a leading evangelical neoabolitionist, clergyman, Orientalist, and editor-in-chief of the *Independent* from 1896 to 1913. Although the annual meeting rarely reversed an executive committee decision, it could set policy and change composition of the executive committee; and in 1890 it undertook a year-long investigation of complaints that executive officers were sometimes rude to field-workers and allowed too little freedom to local school administrators.[4]

The executive committee was a working body which hired and fired corresponding secretaries, opened and closed schools, disposed of bequeathed estates, and dealt with all appropriations ranging from building a privy at Cotton Valley to buying mules for the Brick Farm in North Carolina.[5] Nevertheless, persuasive corresponding secretaries were a powerful force. There were two corresponding secretaries, one dealing with the fieldwork and the other in charge of promotions and fund collecting, and it was the former who usually wielded the greatest influence. There were three especially forceful secretaries between 1890 and 1950: Augustus Field Beard, H. Paul Douglass, and

Frederick L. Brownlee. Born in Norwalk, Connecticut, on May 11, 1833, Beard was educated at Yale University and Union Theological Seminary. He led several Congregational churches in New England before becoming pastor of American Church in Paris, France, in 1883. While there, a couple who had lost a son came to him for comfort. He suggested they found a memorial university in the son's name, thereby planting the idea of Leland Stanford University. In 1886, the AMA executive committee elected him corresponding secretary, a position he held until 1903 when he became honorary secretary and editor of the *American Missionary*. Beard once said he knew nothing of "Negro education." "All I know is education. The best of it belongs to all races." Beard, though an effective minister, was less openly pious than many AMA members. As a young pastor he "created a flurry by advocating . . . theater-going, dancing and card playing," and he scandalized many teachers by smoking. Once a teacher chided him for violating the AMA rule against smoking and asked him what he would think if he saw her smoking. "If you are thinking about it," he said, "I advise you to start with a cigarette."[6] Although he was guilty initially of blunt correspondence with teachers, Beard learned that the administration needed to know the field-workers and their efforts, and the workers needed to know the administration and to feel that they were more than machines cranking out impersonal correspondence. Beard developed into a sagacious leader who raised school standards and multiplied teachers, schools, and students. Beard was devoted to black freedom but, as already noted, was at first slow to place black teachers in the classroom. He continued to support the AMA after his final retirement from editorship of the *American Missionary* in 1928. At age ninety-six he attended an AMA principals' conference and participated in an impromptu game of baseball, and for his one-hundredth-birthday present he chose a plane ride over Norwalk, Connecticut. He died in 1934 at 101.[7]

Beard was followed by J. W. Cooper, a Yale University and Andover Theological Seminary–trained minister. Cooper served as AMA vice president and on the executive committee for several years before becoming senior corresponding secretary in 1903. "Courteous and generous by nature," and popular with AMA workers, Cooper's most important action may have been appointing H. Paul Douglass as superintendent of education in 1906. When offering him the position, Cooper told Douglass that it was "a shifting time" in education, including a serious, ongoing national debate over the merits of liberal arts and industrial training. Cooper was not an educator, he told Douglass, and the AMA needed someone to take up the "problem from a more theoretical standpoint." Cooper gave Douglass complete charge of the elementary and secondary schools. In 1910, in consideration of his wife's fragile health, Cooper resigned, was reelected vice president, and was succeeded as corresponding secretary by Douglass.[8]

Douglass was pastor of a Congregational church in Springfield, Missouri, and also taught psychology and philosophy at Drury College when Cooper first contacted him. He enjoyed both vocations and for some time had seemed unsure whether he wished to be a full-time minister or an educator. After Cooper offered to appoint him AMA superintendent of education, Douglass wrote his parents that he "could undertake it with real enthusiasm. It would not take me out of the ministry and yet would give me some of the educational and social interests which I like." The racial violence taking place around him also contributed to his decision to accept Cooper's offer. He was outraged when in April 1906 a Springfield mob brutally lynched three black men. After some whites threatened to burn the "Negro quarters" the following day, Douglass rushed there and remained with a "citizens posse" until the state militia arrived. He also fretted over his inability to assist a black member of his congregation secure justice for his family. Douglass's certainty that he could not alter race relations in Springfield, his excitement at the chance to superintend a large educational enterprise, his admiration for the AMA's work, and his general concern for African Americans convinced him to join the AMA. When informing his parents of his new position, he told them, "My years at Springfield have only made me feel more deeply the debt of whites to blacks and while I have few illusions I am not pessimistic. As a student I do not believe that there is any such thing as essential race inferiority but only race diversity." He viewed African Americans "as persons, persons who should enter the American mainstream to be sure, but persons who made their own contributions to it and thus transformed the model of the good and true American." Fair treatment of black people was a Christian duty. Blacks should be allowed the same education as whites, Douglass believed, but they need not become "white." They had the potential to make important cultural contributions of their own. As a graduate of Iowa College and Andover Theological Seminary, with additional study in psychology and pedagogy at Harvard and educational theories at the University of Chicago, Douglass was the first trained educator to lead AMA schools. Douglass was knowledgeable about education, farming, mechanics, and construction and could endlessly quote poetry.[9] His assistant superintendent, Lura Beam, said he could build and sail a boat, construct a house, and design a formal garden.[10]

Douglass was a direct and tough antagonist who made no obeisance to denominational politics and little to the old guard on the executive committee. He continued the AMA tradition of concern for black liberation. Ralph E. Luker claims that Douglass's book *Christian Reconstruction in the*

South (1909) "was the decade's most powerful statement of an evangelical neoabolitionism that helped revive racial reform in the twentieth century." At first many considered Douglass a "dangerous radical" in his dealing with the schools. He viewed superior schools as vehicles for needed racial uplift, and he professionalized and significantly improved those under his control. In the process he wounded many feelings. His temper and impatience often showed in unnecessarily harsh letters to faithful workers. A longtime AMA supporter said he was efficient, "but a bit cold and often seemed to some, I imagine, unfeeling in cutting out deadwood." Initially Beard thought he lacked "warmth of sympathy." George L. Cady, corresponding secretary for promotions (1917–36), said Douglass successfully modernized the schools. He infused "new blood and new ideals into the beautiful missionary spirit and the simpler pedagogical ideals," Cady stated, but "the old regime could not see that their day was passing. Of course, it brought irritation and rebellion." Even in 1935, years after Douglass's time at the AMA, Cady added that many in the AMA did not realize the debt it owed Douglass for "his insight and courage—a genius whose full worth has come to be recognized in these later years." Cady gave Douglass's successor, Brownlee, even more credit for modernizing the schools because he continued Douglass's reforms and was a superior manager of personnel. In late 1918, the executive committee, by this time Douglass's supporter, "reluctantly and with regret" accepted his resignation effective January 1, 1919. Years later, Douglass described his twelve years with the AMA "as the best part of his life."[11]

The executive committee selected Joseph E. McAfee, former secretary of the Presbyterian Board of Home Missions, to replace Douglass and in less than a year invited him to resign, making way for Frederick L. Brownlee, the AMA's longest tenured and, perhaps, most significant leader.[12] Brownlee was born in Columbus, Ohio, in 1883 and earned B.A. and M.A. degrees from Ohio State. After attending Union Theological Seminary, he became pastor of and was ordained in a Columbus Congregational church which Washington Gladden had helped organize. Brownlee read "a decidedly liberal theological paper at his ordination." Although he graduated from seminary, Brownlee was more a teacher than a preacher, and he attended Columbia Teachers College specializing in educational theory and practice and served as director of religious education at two churches before joining the AMA in 1920. Brownlee was enthusiastic, analytical, and genial. An AMA teacher listed ten Brownlee characteristics including "wonderful friend," "wise counselor," "zest for life," "sense of humor," "generous," and "looked for good and found it." A member of the black Central Congregational Church in New Orleans said that when Brownlee visited the church "it was like the good Lord was coming" and the church was always full. Unlike some of the ministers, she added, Brownlee was the "kind of man you could talk to . . . the kind you could tell your troubles to." Most observers commented on his patience and kindness, but one stated, "Those who are misled by his engaging disposition into thinking he can be imposed upon, soon discovered that his gloved hand is capable of vigorous action." LeMoyne College president Hollis Price, who knew Brownlee for thirty years, said he was an innovator. If it was something traditional, Price added, Brownlee figured it was out of date. If it was a new venture he was usually for it. This quality enabled Brownlee to keep pace with educational reform but also occasionally led him into unwise ventures such as trying to force "functional education"—to be discussed later—on some of the colleges in the 1940s.[13] His most significant trait was his patient and persistent pursuit of the long-term goal of black equality.

Brownlee joined the AMA with limited experience with African Americans, but eventually became the least paternalistic, and most aggressive, advocate of equal rights of any AMA secretary. He learned not only from older AMA personnel but from black men and women in the field. Whether it was his age, personality, or the times, blacks were more willing than previously to advise and offer friendly, or even hostile, criticism. Soon after Brownlee became secretary, Alfred E. Lawless, black superintendent of church work, warned him that the AMA was in danger of losing its soul, and its constituency. "Someone must go to the altar," Lawless wrote. "Our grand old A.M.A. must not become salt that has lost its savor, a faithless leader in a day when great faith is needed." Brownlee, Lawless added, must step up and return the association to its former fervor for black rights. He and Lawless became fast friends, as did he and several other black workers. When Brownlee took a black man with him to visit former secretary Beard, the latter remarked that Brownlee associated with his black friend as if he were white, which probably revealed as much about Beard as about his visitor. Once, Brownlee spent a morning with a black Mobile physician freely discussing the racial situation. Brownlee wondered whether blacks were oversensitive, "looking for slights and expecting misunderstandings." "Mr. Brownlee," the physician said, "I don't think I can make you understand. I don't think any white man can understand. But if you could crawl into my skin for just twenty-four hours you would understand." Brownlee could not experience being black, but he did gradually achieve greater enlightenment.[14]

Brownlee accepted Lawless's advice to "go to the altar," and blacks in the AMA responded positively. In 1924, the *Southern News,* published in Atlanta, praised Brownlee's leadership. "His broad, liberal, sane views of the question of race relations, his sympathetic interest in the people among whom he is working, his readiness to acknowledge and encourage native leadership, and his loyalty to the fundamental principles for which the association has stood firm from the beginning of its history eminently fit him for a place of leadership" in AMA work. "The spirit of cooperation and hopefulness which now dominate the Southern work of the A.M.A," the *Southern News* added, "is largely due to the personal attitude of Secretary Brownlee." In 1925, Henry Hugh Proctor, Fisk and Yale graduate and noted pastor of the Atlanta First Congregational Church, responded to a Brownlee article in the *Congregationalist* on the need for black leadership as "the sanest thing I have seen from a white man," but Proctor questioned whether Brownlee reflected the views of his AMA associates. "When our men see white workers co-operating by working in subordinate places there will be new faith in the religion of the white man," Proctor added. Brownlee replied that he had just appointed a black president at Tillotson College and a black principal at Lincoln Academy in North Carolina with no opposition from the executive committee, and he would continue to act on the principle of "appointing the best person available, regardless of color." Brownlee later selected an African American, W. A. Daniel, as his assistant and entrusted him with much of the hiring of teachers and supervising of schools. Daniel graduated from Virginia Union University and then earned a Ph.D. from the University of Chicago. After assisting Monroe W. Work, director of research at Tuskegee, Daniel undertook several independent research projects. His study of black theological seminaries was published in 1925 as *The Education of Negro Ministers.* The AMA hired him as a research associate in 1927, and when Lucy B. Crain resigned as Brownlee's assistant in 1930, Brownlee appointed him his associate executive secretary of the Department of Missions. Daniel spent most of his time in the southern field dealing directly with teachers and principals. Brownlee both depended upon and learned from him.[15] In 1932, Brownlee wrote that "volumes could be written on the errors of working *for* people versus working *with* them," and that developing interracial fellowship "deeper and finer and richer than usual blood ties of family relationships" was possible. Brownlee made occasional mistakes and sometimes may have overestimated the depth and extent of black chauvinism, but he was dedicated to black liberation and worked comfortably and enthusiastically *with* black men and women.[16]

While Beard, Douglass, and Brownlee supervised schools and churches, the corresponding secretaries for promotion, Charles J. Ryder (1895–1917) and George L. Cady (1917–36), took the AMA's case to the public and tried to secure donations and legacies.[17] The association's lifeblood was the money that flowed into its treasury, and there was a constant struggle to raise suf-

Fig. 6. Frederick L. Brownlee and black ministers at Kings Mountain, North Carolina, conference (Courtesy of Amistad Research Center, Tulane University, New Orleans, Louisiana)

ficient funds to support its southern work. Success or failure depended not only upon Ryder's and Cady's efforts, but also upon the country's variable attitude toward blacks, the economy, and the political climate. For example, the depression of 1893 seriously affected revenues. Income dropped from $482,671 in 1891–92 to $357,632 in 1894–95. The *American Missionary,* edited by Beard or corresponding secretaries for promotions, was the association's most important propaganda tool. Its pages were filled with examples of black suffering and discrimination along with inspiring tales of black achievement in the face of seemingly insurmountable odds. Teachers were encouraged to write touching articles about their students, and they consistently solicited money, clothes for students, and educational support from northern friends and family. Corresponding secretaries visited hundreds of churches and communities annually. Massachusetts and Connecticut were the most fertile grounds for collections. In the 1891–92 fiscal year, the former contributed $105,511.31 and the latter $103,814.98. The next largest sums, $39,292.64 and $27,027.60 came from New York and Ohio respectively. Maryland donors gave $66.50. In April 1917, 2,116 individuals and churches contributed to the AMA. Donations ranged from a few cents to hundreds of dollars. Although the AMA was associated with the Congregationalists, who furnished about one-half of AMA income in 1898–99, church contributions declined over the years. Some members were aghast to learn that the AMA supported colleges and music departments, luxuries they could not afford for their own children. Other donors and churches sarcastically designated the AMA as "After Money Again." African Americans used a much more generous soubriquet which reflected their gratitude and affection: "Aunt Mary Ann." Although church support was important, the AMA appealed to all advocates for black rights and protection. In 1904 and again in 1924, the AMA blamed increasing northern racial prejudice for declining revenue. In 1927–28, churches and affiliated organizations furnished only eighteen percent of receipts. Individuals supplied eighteen percent, legacies twenty percent, income from invested funds thirty-four percent, and tuition ten percent.[18]

A major source of funds came from legacies, both large and small. In 1898, the AMA collected $150,660.51 in donations and received $119,530.78 in legacies. In 1916 Mary Strater left her life savings of $1,300 to AMA colleges. Her parents had been born in New Jersey when it was still a slave state. She became a servant in Whitinsville, Massachusetts, at age twelve and remained with the family for seventy-seven years. Other blacks, from North and South, gave generously. Between 1916 and 1930, supporters deeded $2,685,704.70 to the AMA.[19] Two especially large legacies provided much of the AMA income during lean years. In 1888, Daniel Hand of Guilford, Connecticut, transferred securities to the AMA amounting to $1,000,894 to be designated as the Daniel Hand Fund for Colored People.[20] When he died in 1891 he left the AMA another half million dollars. Both the income and some of the growth from the Hand Fund were used, and by 1930 it had provided $2,980,905.54 for black education. In 1930 the Hand Fund income paid eighty-six teachers.[21] Charles M. Hall, founder and partner in the Aluminum Company of America, made the largest grant—more than seven million dollars when the AMA came into full possession of it in 1926. Before making the bequest Hall investigated to be certain that the AMA was not controlled by any ecclesiastical body, and he demanded Hall Fund expenditures be determined by the AMA executive committee only and that no part of his gift should be used for theological instruction. Though the AMA worked in many fields, he clearly intended that it be used for black education.[22] The Hand and Hall Funds plus other AMA investments accounted for 34 percent of the association's income in 1927–28 and 57.3 percent in 1931–32. The percentage of church and individual contributions continued to decline. In

1931–32 black students paid almost as much in tuition, 11.6 percent, as the 14.5 percent provided by churches, and in 1935–36 student tuition and fees accounted for $133,759.79 of the AMA budget. As the AMA stated, considering that its constituency came from the lowest economic brackets and lived under "distressing social handicaps, *what they do to secure some of life's higher values is nothing short of phenomenal.*" Blacks usually generously supported AMA schools.[23]

Despite what many poor southern blacks and some disgruntled northern whites thought, the AMA was never rich. It was always overextended and frequently ended the year in debt—for example, $101,151.66 indebtedness in 1894–95. Nevertheless, its receipts gradually climbed until the Depression. Receipts by the decade were as follows: fiscal year 1890–91, $482,419; 1900–1901, $420,056; 1910–11, $493,184; 1920–21, $947,799; 1930–31, $1,228,567; 1940–41, $567,151. Its total receipts from 1846 to 1946 were $48,158,534. Of course, not all expenditures were for black education. In 1920–21, of the AMA's proposed budget of $670,158, only $292,705 was earmarked for southern schools. The AMA also supported black churches, and missions fields in Puerto Rico, among American Indians, among Chinese in the west, in Hawaii, and in the Southwest. By 1931–32, however, sixty-eight percent of all AMA expenditures was for African Americans.[24]

In the meantime, the AMA was slowly losing some of its independence from the church. There had been some tension from the time the Congregational National Council adopted the association in 1865. Although the AMA established Congregational churches in the South, it maintained its nonsectarian posture to the dismay of many church leaders. More than a few Congregationalists thought the AMA should never have been formed, and attempted to dismantle it. In 1884 a prominent member of the Congregational Home Mission Society (HMS) executive committee publicly declared that the AMA should not exist, and not a single member of the HMS executive committee publicly objected.[25] In 1898, the AMA resisted an attempt to federate the various Congregational mission societies, but was less successful in 1914. Under pressure from the Congregational National Council, the AMA agreed to meet with and accept all delegates to biennial National Council meetings as voting members, which severely diluted its power since the National Council attendees greatly outnumbered AMA members.[26] This agreement also compelled the association to close some of its collecting offices to avoid competing with other Congregational missions, and the *American Missionary* to become the journal for all of the societies. Many AMA members questioned the wisdom of the change, but feared that refusal to "surrender its independence to the Council" might end church financial support. Members resolved at the AMA's 1914 annual meeting that unity must not alter the association's original goal "of brotherhood which unqualifiedly repudiates false distinctions of race and color."[27]

While the AMA's character did not change, unity was financially detrimental. The National Council, which met biennially, gave the AMA limited time to present its cause which affected support and supporters; and council members who helped control the AMA's destiny showed little interest in attending association meetings on alternate years. Any gains in efficiency failed to offset the losses of publicity and money gained at previous annual meetings. The potential consequences, the AMA announced at its 1916 annual meeting, "are such to cause the gravest alarm." As the journal for all societies, the *American Missionary* was also less effective as a publicity device.[28] Not surprisingly, the AMA vigorously objected when in 1924–25 Congregational leaders wished to merge all mission agencies. Despite the 1914 alliance, Congregational promoters still "severely criticized" the AMA for its nondenominational approach to its schools and students. Most of its students were not Congregationalists, and the association made little attempt to proselytize them and did not intend to in the future. They appreciated Congregational support, AMA officials said, but the association was nonsectarian and accepted assistance from all denominations. Moreover, interests of the various societies could not be properly represented by one board, the AMA name was too great an asset to be lost, its work with blacks was unique, and a merger presented legal difficulties as it would violate the trust of those who bequeathed funds to the AMA to be used in perpetuity for blacks.[29]

Despite its courageous stand against a merger, the AMA in 1926 gave up more independence. It revised its constitution which brought "a closer and more vital affiliation" with the Congregational churches. The executive committee, elected by voting members at the annual meeting held with the National Council, was increased from fifteen to thirty-six. This revision at least recognized the importance of women's activities on behalf of the association by decreeing that one-third of the expanded executive committee be female. An administrative committee composed of nine members of the executive committee plus six elected at large now met monthly to transact business. The title of corresponding secretaries was changed to executive secretaries, and the AMA's support department's work was to be done in cooperation with a general promotions department serving all the societies, which limited independent solicitations. Church mission funds were apportioned to various agencies. The AMA's portion was set at 11.6 percent, but was almost immediately dropped to 9 percent, a loss of approximately $65,000 annually. The AMA's share continued to decline, in part because the Hand

and Hall Funds convinced many that the association had less need of additional money than the other societies. Fortunately, the AMA's mission was unchanged. Secretary Brownlee, who opposed the above alterations, wrote in 1935 that no positive results had yet shown themselves since the AMA "voted away its right to conduct its own affairs. What I try to do," he added, "is to keep as sweet as possible while plugging away at the real work of the Association." Brownlee was a superb diplomat and, under the circumstances, secured maximum support for the AMA.[30] In Brownlee's view, even worse was yet to come. The "radical rearrangements" of 1936 almost caused him to resign. Ten years later he wrote that only a "first-hand appreciation" of the magnificent AMA accomplishments before his day and the realization that the task was yet unfinished had kept him "at the wheel since 1936."[31]

The AMA in 1936 became a constituent division of the Board of Home Missions (BHM) of the Congregational Christian Church, or as the AMA 1937 annual report stated, "No longer are we apart from the Congregational and Christian churches, but rather a part of them. Our task is their task and their task is our task."[32] The BHM took over the work and the assets of individual societies. A new administrative position of executive vice president of the Board of Home Missions was created, and Rev. William F. Frazier was appointed to the position. Brownlee wrote Frazier and unity committee members opposing unification on the grounds that BHM members "were quite unfamiliar with basic facts" of AMA activity, those actually engaged with the AMA opposed it, and he feared the association's emphasis on race problems would be de-emphasized. He requested a strong statement in the merger agreement of the AMA's "long-time peculiarly lonely and unpopular work" with black Americans, and made a special plea for the preservation of income from AMA-invested funds for that purpose. The board promised to keep trust funds separate and administer them with "careful consideration of the wishes of their donors and for those particular purposes to which they were intended." The AMA continued to exist as a division, but budget and other decisions required BHM approval.[33]

Brownlee was correct that those most intimately associated with the AMA opposed the new relationship, but since all those who attended the National Council meetings were voting members of the association, the church overruled opponents. Ferdinand Q. Blanchard, who served on the executive committee from 1909 to 1936, resigned. Former secretary McAfee reflected the views of many association members when he wrote Brownlee in 1939, "I note that the Home Mission Board has now swallowed you completely, and the old A.M.A. name is scarcely in evidence. I am far from being a good enough Congregationalist to be tickled over that." In 1941 Fred

McCuistion of the General Education Board reported that Brownlee and director of community schools Ruth Morton feared that the BHM would neglect black education. Morton suspected, he added, that church representatives were "anxious to secure" the ten million dollar AMA endowment "for more ecclesiastical purposes." That did not happen immediately, but the BHM gave the AMA division no special favors as indicated by the increase in field budgets from 1946–47 to 1950–51. The percentage increases were as follows: AMA 6.44 percent, Church Extension and Evangelism Division 161.55 percent, Church Education Division 36.57 percent, and Ministerial Relief 17.37 percent. The apportionment increases for the same period were AMA 11.31 percent, BHM 81.35 percent, Church Extension and Evangelism Division 288.57 percent, Church Education Division 63.76 percent, and Ministerial Relief 29.03 percent. Brownlee complained in 1950 that the executive committee and directors of the BHM were ill informed about the AMA, that they neglected to attend association conferences and seminars, and that most had never visited an AMA institution. Many AMA advocates believed that only Brownlee's determination, strong personality, contacts, and diplomacy fended off further BHM incursions. The BHM acted as the agency corporation for administrative purposes, but as long as Brownlee was there the AMA corporation existed and continued to operate under the provisions of its charter. Apparently many BHM officials were happy when Brownlee was forced to retire in 1950 (Brownlee claimed in 1950 that BHM director William F. Frazier had tried for fifteen years to get rid of him), but some AMA supporters feared that without his presence the BHM would soon completely absorb the AMA.[34]

4

"Houses of Refuge"

Functional Education and Community Centers

By the mid-1930s the AMA had transferred most of its secondary schools to public authorities, and its goal of public education available to all black youth, though not yet accomplished, was approaching reality. Free public education was only one AMA ambition, however. "Stated educationally," Brownlee wrote in 1935, "the primary purpose of the Association is to function through education in assisting Negroes to take their rightful place in a democratic society, which is precisely the same place as that of any other intelligent and honorable citizen, regardless of race or color." That aim was far from complete, and since southern public schools had no intention of uniting "all races in a common society," the AMA could justify retaining a few private institutions. The continuance of "a limited number of 'functional' schools," Brownlee stated, might "serve to hasten the day when racial discrimination" would cease to be. Such schools could serve as "houses of refuge" and as "community centers in which both races may mingle and work, free even from racial consciousness."[1]

In reality, Brownlee expected the remaining schools (Avery Institute, Ballard, Dorchester Academy, Fessenden Academy, Lincoln Academy, Lincoln School, Trinity, and Cotton Valley) to become multipurpose institutions with goals of improving race relations, uplifting the surrounding communities through adult education and cooperatives, altering the traditional methods of teaching and learning, and continuing to prepare their students for college. Soon after his appointment in 1920, Brownlee noticed that while the AMA had successfully taught thousands and thousands of black children, people surrounding campuses lived, for the most part, in primitive, dilapidated, and unhealthy conditions. In *New Day Ascending* (1946), Brownlee charged that the early schools, because "they were more or less missionary compounds in alien territories," frequently became blind to service outside their own walls. Brownlee correctly noted that faculty were often ostracized, tended to avoid hostile whites, and neglected adult education, but he exaggerated the lack of service to and contact with the black community.[2]

The AMA had always been concerned about more than simply education and salvation of former slaves. Indeed, a major justification for both its schools and churches was to help improve conditions under which blacks lived. It regularly hired blacks for campus construction and repair, and encouraged the schools to double as social centers. In 1908, H. Paul Douglass said that nearly "all non-sectarian and non-political gatherings for racial betterment" met on school grounds. Avery Institute, the closest place to "a safe haven" for blacks, was the center of early NAACP activity in Charleston. Civil rights activist Septima Clark recalled that she "first became actively concerned in an organized effort to improve the lot of my fellow Negroes" at Avery. Douglass argued that "no mission school is merely a school: all are definitely intended centers of uplifting influence upon their communities." Interestingly, Douglass was one of the first to use the term "social gospel," which initially generally referred "to a fresh application of the insights of the Christian faith to the pressing problems of the social order," and he was only one of many AMA supporters familiar with the idea. Luker claims that between emancipation and 1910 "so many of the Northern white social gospel prophets were officers and supporters of the American Missionary Association that it may have been the most important vehicle of the social gospel prior to the organization of the Federal Council of Churches in 1909."[3]

Since blacks were banned from the Memphis Public Library, LeMoyne Institute opened its library to them in 1903 and kept evening hours. School officials sought and received city funds, and in 1908 LeMoyne's Crossett Library became the Memphis branch library for blacks. It later sent traveling libraries to rural schools and opened its buildings for meetings of "any organization that has for its aim the good of the people."[4] In 1939 Talladega College set aside two rooms in its library as a community reading room and circulating library. The next year it purchased a one-half-ton Dodge truck equipped to hold seven hundred books and began circulating books throughout Talladega County. Although the forty rural schools served as stopping points, the bookmobile often altered its route to serve individual families. Under the leadership of principal William G. Price a thriving farm community grew up around Gloucester, middle-class housing surrounded Allen Normal, Burrell Normal and Fessenden Academy held annual farmers' conferences, and in 1912 Emerson Institute opened the only playground for black children in Mobile. Almost every AMA school was involved in some type of community service.[5]

AMA institutions also attempted to improve black health. The association in cooperation with black and white citizens built and, in May 1924, opened a twenty-four bed hospital on the Brewer Normal campus in Greenwood, South Carolina.[6] Dr. Pauline Dinkins, a graduate of the Woman's Hospital of Philadelphia, became medical director, and in 1926 the hospital staff treated 751 patients and performed 78 surgeries. In the 1932–33 academic year, physicians delivered 25 babies and performed 166 surgeries.[7] The AMA operated and financed Brewer Hospital until 1934, when it transferred the medical facility to a local board of trustees. The AMA continued to support the hospital and retained membership on the board. The AMA also helped establish the Flint-Goodridge Hospital in New Orleans, and had infirmaries that treated locals as well as students at Talladega and Tougaloo. Cotton Valley School, as all AMA institutions, was concerned about student health, but took its efforts into the Macon County, Alabama, community at large. In the mid-1920s it began providing physicals, inoculations, and general health information. Initially, the school contracted local physicians to make examinations, but in 1939 the Julius Rosenwald Fund, at AMA urging, established a clinic at Cotton Valley. The clinic was in part an attempt to address Macon County's infant and maternity death rates, some of the highest in the country. Before Cotton Valley had its own clinic, in 1936, the school began arranging to transport mothers to Tuskegee for prenatal care, and three years later it persuaded the Rosenwald Fund, which already had a prenatal clinic at Tuskegee, to open one at Cotton Valley. The school hallway became the waiting room. Eight mothers attended the first clinic on September 5, 1939. Later the Children's Bureau in Washington, D.C., stationed a midwife at Cotton Valley to provide prenatal and postnatal care for local mothers. She lived in the teachers' home and operated out of the school.[8] Many other campuses provided limited health services.

Despite these examples, the AMA's impact outside the schools was, as Brownlee claimed, too often limited. In 1925 Brownlee regretfully wrote that Dorchester Academy had helped local youth find "a way up in life, but the way up had always been a way out of Liberty County. We keep failing in our efforts to transform the life and condition of the community." AMA institutions were more than mere schools, Brownlee said. "Literally they had long entwined their roots about the felt and unfelt needs of people groping feebly and blindly for their rightful place in society," but it took the Depression to reveal to most AMA officials that they had done little substantial for those who lived near the schools. Brownlee expected "functional" or community schools to "focus their energies upon the improvement of the total life" of the areas where they were located, and to provide training in conventional subjects plus "elements laden with rich social and religious significance." They should teach students how to make a living locally, and train leaders both among students and adults who would then help improve community health, economy, and quality of life.[9]

The first step in achieving his goals, Brownlee believed, was to change the curriculum and methods of teaching. Too often, he thought, "learning by doing and thinking" gave way "to remembering and forgetting by reciting." He intended to take AMA schools "as far as possible out of competition with customary standardized mass education," and increasingly relate what the schools did "to the elementary things of life rather than pursue [a] course which may too easily tend toward the academic." By 1934 he was "determined to face the practical issue of organizing" the "curriculum around areas of living" rather than the usual courses. Math, English, science, and history, for example, should be arranged around "natural units" such as "earning a living, making a home, keeping well and strong, being an intelligent citizen, making provisions for inexpensive, meaningful recreation and building character." Building personal pride and financial reliance among both students and the community surrounding the schools was also an aim. He wanted to stimulate creativity, and teach the community to self-start. He called this "functional education for effective living." By 1935 Brownlee had persuaded the AMA to develop its schools "increasingly along functional and social lines in keeping with a sane and liberal interpretation of what Jesus meant by the Kingdom of God."[10]

Brownlee's changing views about the role of AMA schools was influenced by John B. Dewey and progressive education (Brownlee was a member of the Progressive Education Association formed in 1919);[11] the Danish Folk School; his own observations; his desire to deal with racial problems; and a concern for economic security, health, and equal rights for blacks. "Personally, I would be inclined to say my position is that of John Dewey," Brownlee stated in 1941. Even though he had never studied with or even met Dewey, Brownlee admired his work.[12] Dewey provided, Brownlee added, "not only the philosophy and educational way to intelligent and high living, individually, but also to the highest and noblest religious aspirations, hopes and achievements." He eagerly accepted Dewey's view that education should be "a process of discovery" rather than "one of instruction and drill," and that students learned by doing. Dewey's argument that "the school should be 'a miniature community, an embryonic society' which would produce" a "worthy, lovely, harmonious" larger society appealed to Brownlee's desire to enhance African Americans' quality of life.[13]

Brownlee was no less influenced by the Danish Folk School, a type of adult education inspired by Nikolai Frederick Severen Grundtvig in Denmark in 1851. A photograph of Grundtvig graced Brownlee's office wall. The Danish Folk School began as a short-term young adult school which "succeeded to a remarkable degree in arousing and enlightening the rural population, and in dignifying and vitalizing the whole content of country life." Brownlee attributed his immediate awakening to the need for adult and community education to Olive Dame Campbell and Marguerite Butler, who, after travel and study in Denmark, established the John C. Campbell Folk School near Brasstown, North Carolina, in 1925 in an attempt to "keep an enlightened, progressive, and contented farming population on the land."[14] The AMA financially supported the school from the beginning, and when he retired in 1950 Brownlee moved to Brasstown. Campbell and Butler operated a traditional school, but also emphasized adult education, local culture, and crafts; founded several cooperatives, which strongly appealed to Brownlee; started clubs for men and women; and established a demonstration farm. It was the John C. Campbell Folk School's effort to train and keep educated youth in the Appalachians that reminded Brownlee that too many Dorchester Academy graduates left their homes to the detriment of the community. Brownlee concluded to abandon standardized mass education and develop "techniques more in keeping with progressive education and not unlike many of the techniques of the Danish Folk School."[15]

In 1935, Brownlee, clearly convinced that something was radically wrong with present educational methods, and unsure how to effect desired change, employed Ruth Morton to help him transform AMA schools into functional, creative community centers. Ever since W. A. Daniel, outstanding black associate executive secretary, left the AMA in October 1934, Brownlee had searched for an assistant familiar with community schools.[16] George N. White, now AMA alumni secretary, met Morton in Chicago and forwarded her resume to Brownlee. After what Brownlee called "a heap of persuasion," Morton agreed to become principal of Lincoln School in Marion, Alabama, in the fall of 1935 in order to study AMA schools and community needs. Born in Missouri, Morton earned a B.A. from the University of Denver, and an M.A. from the University of Chicago, where Dewey had done some of his seminal work. She wrote her master's thesis on the "Religious Significance of a Folk School." She had taught for four years, had been pastor's assistant and director of the community house for Grace Community Church in Denver, and had supervised the children's work of the Central Pennsylvania Conference of Methodists. Her specialty was human relations. A Chicago acquaintance said of her, "She has taught school and knows her educational philosophy—especially Dewey—forwards and backwards. But even more marked is her capacity for counseling people." Her training seemed to make her an ideal choice, and her personality and racial views were as significant. After Morton visited Trinity in 1941, Japanese teacher Tsuyoshi Matsumoto wrote Brownlee that "she was charming and inspiring without being like a representative of a 'bunch of missionaries,' really. (Pardon me for saying this.) After meeting Miss Morton, even I had to change my opinion about the missionaries." As director of community schools she strove to retain an interracial faculty and was perfectly comfortable living and associating with black colleagues. In 1944, Brownlee noted "the exceedingly fine and genuine way in which she has become one with those of another racial group."[17]

Brownlee sent Morton to Marion, Alabama, in 1935 to "start a reorganization of the curriculum around areas of living and to 'awaken, enliven, and enlighten'" community adults along the Danish Folk School lines, and to "build up in general a unique form of educational, social, and religious service to the school." That was a tall order, and though Brownlee claimed in late 1935 that "with rare wisdom, unusual tact and common sense she is making a place for herself," Morton made limited changes her first year. Indeed, she and Brownlee, often with little support from their superiors, spent the next fifteen years experimenting and seeking to perfect community education.[18] Morton only slightly tampered with the curriculum her first year at Lincoln because she wanted to study the school and community before making fundamental changes. However, at the end of the year she reported that Lincoln was "truly an institution of human relations, where personal possibilities are discovered and helped to develop in all sorts of unexpected channels." There was "a new freedom and kinship of interests" between students and faculty, she added, which had been accelerated by a new dining hall that allowed teachers and students to dine together at a common table.[19]

After Morton's year of apprenticeship at Lincoln School, Brownlee asked her to become director of community schools. Although initially reluctant to become principal of Lincoln School a year earlier, she was now so attached to Lincoln that Brownlee had even more difficulty persuading her to accept the larger responsibility of supervising all secondary schools. Morton even detailed reasons why she might not be a good choice. She had often criticized mission societies for "leaning toward drab personalities," Morton wrote Brownlee, and admitted that she herself was not especially personable.[20] She added that she inherited from her mother "a hot tempered, high strung, impetuous, over-emotional, domineering nature." Brownlee was not dissuaded, and in April 1936 the AMA administrative committee elected Morton director of community schools at a salary of $3,300 annually, subject to the prevailing scale of Depression salary reductions. Morton's headquarters remained temporarily at Lincoln School. She filled the dual role of Lincoln principal and director of all community schools until the fall of 1938, when Wilfred Gamble succeeded her at Lincoln.[21]

Actual curricular changes in AMA schools varied. The city schools of Ballard and Avery increased their community activities but resisted any significant alteration in curriculum. Lincoln School at Marion emphasized "the development and careful culture of fine attitudes." Morton reported that the transition from a static curriculum to the type of schools that lived "in and for the community" had been difficult. "Change brings inevitable friction, and natural difficulties in trying out new ideas, and we have had plenty of both." In reality, the major changes were to emphasize community service and the local economy. The elementary grades utilized the school farm and woods "in developing units of activity" while the upper grades featured agriculture and health. Simultaneously, Lincoln continued to prepare its students for college. More important, Lincoln renewed its community service. White librarian Margaret Scott refurbished the library and opened it to the black public. "It positively thrills me," Scott wrote, "for Negro libraries are almost unknown here. . . . Ours will be the only place in the county and many a mile beyond where Negroes can come to read."[22] The school nurse, the only one in Perry County for twenty thousand blacks, served the community as well as the school. She supervised the clinic, visited homes, and worked with local doctors. The agriculture teacher advised farmers on how to improve crops, and the school presented lectures, entertainments, and concerts to the community and served as a meeting place for black clubs, both for youth and adults.[23]

Trinity School in Athens, Alabama, began to change in the fall of 1940 when Brownlee appointed as principal Jay T. Wright, a white M.A. graduate of Teachers College, Columbia University. Dr. Harold Clark of Teachers College claimed that Wright knew more about "a really functional school" than any recent graduate, and Morton soon agreed. Soon after his arrival she proclaimed that Wright "comes closest to actually functionalizing a school program of anyone I know." Wright attempted to teach academic subjects while dealing with practical matters. In September 1940, the sewer backed up and flooded the Trinity school basement. Since Wright had decreed that the entire school study health, the course centered around the sewer issue. One class investigated and discovered that the sewer clogged regularly. They unearthed the sewer where it had previously given trouble and learned that the tile pipe had been punctured by tree roots and had been patched with cement. They tried to determine how much time and money had been expended repairing it. Iron pipe was suggested as a solution, and a student delegation went to Athens to get an estimate. Students then decided to lay new sewer lines under the supervision of a professional plumber. The math class tackled the problem of laying the pipe straight and at the proper slope. As a blowtorch was necessary for melting lead to seal joints, students concluded they needed a shop and tools. Others examined health problems associated with open sewers. Brownlee declared Wright's method of dealing with the problem "a corking good educational" experience. After laying new sewer lines, the students installed showers, and a weekly shower bath became a requirement since students did not have indoor plumbing at home. Not all teachers agreed with Wright's "functional" education. Mary Davis, bewildered by it all and believing the principal would bring the school to ruin, resigned. Wright scathingly remarked that Davis was suffering from menopause.[24]

Teachers untrained in functional education plagued all the schools, but Wright ignored teachers and barged ahead. Trinity instructor John A. Buggs was impressed with Wright, who, he said, was "a person uniquely qualified, by virtue of a wide streak of 'non-conformity' . . . to upset without any qualms or scruples, all that is held holy by the mores that support the traditional secondary school." Brownlee and Morton regretted Wright's lack of tact and his cavalier bookkeeping, but approved the results. In 1942, Morton noted that Wright took "the bull by the horns . . . and autocratically revolutionized the educational procedure at Trinity School." The autocratic procedure was necessary and justified, concluded Morton, who ordinarily demanded more democracy in the schools. Now the problem was to keep the new ways going democratically. The Trinity experiment ended in 1943 when Wright left to accept a deanship at LeMoyne College.[25]

The best documented curricular changes occurred at Fessenden Academy. Fessenden's move toward functional education began in 1938 when Josie B. Sellers, a history and sociology instructor at LeMoyne College, became principal with instructions to "work out ways and means of relating the school to life and life to the school." Sellers had earned a B.A. and an M.A. from Fisk University and a certificate in social work from the Atlanta University School of Social Work. She had no secondary teaching experience—an advantage according to Brownlee, who believed she had the personality, character, ability, and vision to make Fessenden a community school. Sellers hired a vocational agriculture teacher to instruct both students and local adults, developed a demonstration farm, and urged the community to work cooperatively. In November 1940, the senior mathematics class opened the Fessenden Fund and Trust Company with deposits of $2.70 in an effort to make mathematics practical. By March 1941, the bank had twenty-nine stockholders holding fifty-six shares at face value of $14, and had made forty-four loans totaling $25. They also measured, figured the cost of new materials, and replaced the hall ceiling in the women's dormitory. Juniors studied practical geometry by re-roofing the principal's house. They measured the roof, met with a salesman from Ocala, and chose shingles, and the male students put them on. Sellers also introduced a student advisory council, and a student newspaper whose staff was elected by students. In 1939, Morton reported that Sellers was "doing an exceptionally fine piece of work."[26]

Practical application of knowledge at Fessenden was not completely new. For years the school's strong manual arts program under the direction of Wesley E. Walthall had made most campus repairs. In the summer of 1938, at Ruth Morton's request, Walthall transported several Fessenden students to Cotton Valley School in Alabama where they built a six-bedroom, two-bath teachers' home with living room, dining room, fireplace, and basement. One of the young men framed the roof in Walthall's absence. The AMA paid the boys the prevailing wage, from which the students furnished transportation and board. They saved the remainder to meet school expenses the following year.[27]

Fessenden instructors sought to use everyday issues to teach academic subjects, but the curriculum was not seriously revised until John A. Buggs became principal in 1942. The twenty-seven-year-old Buggs, born in Bainbridge, Georgia, earned a B.A. in history at Dillard University and an M.A. in sociology from Fisk University, where he, like Sellers, studied with famed sociologist Charles S. Johnson. In 1941–42, he taught at Trinity School. Principal Jay T. Wright considered him his best teacher and vigorously protested his transfer to Fessenden. Morton and Brownlee worried about Buggs's youth, but a year later Morton wrote that "seldom does a young, inexperienced person grasp a situation and take hold so readily," and in 1949, Brownlee declared Buggs "the best man I have ever met in the field of secondary education and school administration."[28] Buggs's first step in organizing the curriculum was to determine what the school wished to achieve. He and the faculty settled on the following purposes: to prepare students for a vocation, citizenship, home membership, command of subject fields, and profitable use of leisure time; to inculcate Christian character and ethical principles; to develop healthy bodies; and to provide an outlet for self-expression of students and faculty. Two other goals, extremely important to Buggs, related more to the community than the classroom: "To foster group action on community problems," and "to perform our special duty as a Negro institution of helping our students to seek, obtain and discharge faithfully, their full privileges and responsibilities as citizens in the American Democracy."[29] Marion

County, Florida, in which Fessenden was located, became a hotbed of black civil rights and political activity.

Fessenden still taught subject matter, but its aim, rather than teach the usual courses, was to devise "some means whereby the various subject fields could be used to give meaning, purpose, direction and understanding to our efforts to solve some of the problems of living in a world which hourly becomes more complex and difficult to understand, analyze and appreciate." Emphasis centered around four "blocks": health, leisure, work, and community living. The work block included study of economic and human geography, political economics, community economic problems, ecology, "the Negro," problems of minority peoples, cooperatives, credit unions, labor unions, farm organizations, and vocational guidance. Statistics, geography, history, economics, political science, ecology, and rural sociology were especially relevant to the above, but all the traditional subject fields studied the same problems. Nine weeks were set aside for the study of each block. During the year the faculty concluded that some classes—science, for example—gained more from the health block than English or other subjects. Fessenden then instituted a schoolwide seminar in which each subject teacher gave her/his approach to the study of the topic. Since no suitable textbooks were available, films and teacher lesson plans were widely used. After a year's experience, the Fessenden staff determined two major program problems: too little prior planning by individual teachers, and the blocks required clearer definition. All teachers needed to know—in health, for example—the kind of problems they should consider, and what areas they should work on in the general area of health. The same curriculum was used the second year with some refinements. Buggs and the faculty also developed special programs for seniors that would move them toward an occupation or college. The faculty tested and interviewed each senior and fashioned individual programs to provide the required foundation for college, professional school, trade school, or job.[30]

After two years Buggs believed he had made definite progress in introducing the functional program, but he had concerns, including the difficulty of finding faculty with the imagination, the ingenuity, and the requisite breadth of knowledge necessary to implement the curriculum. Suitable teachers remained a major problem. Any progress made in curriculum development, Buggs claimed, was in spite of—not because of—teachers.[31] Other program weaknesses led to a major revision of the curriculum for 1944–45. All subject fields were not fully engaged with the block system. Social science was the only area that found "equal expression" in each block. Several teachers were wedded to their subjects and were dissatisfied with the block idea. Moreover, accrediting associations and colleges preferred traditional fields. More important, Buggs said, while the block system dealt with many issues important for a well-rounded education, numerous world problems were not included in the curriculum as organized. Even though in May 1944 Brownlee designated Fessenden the AMA's "most advanced school in the understanding and practice of . . . functional education," Buggs, after extensive consultation with the faculty, switched from block to a "problem area" system. While all courses dealt with the same issues, the revision was a move back toward teaching traditional subjects. Each summer, faculty participated in a three- to five-week workshop immediately preceding the opening of school to decide on problems to be treated, and to agree on "specific and detailed plans" for each course. New instructors were familiarized with the curriculum, and each developed workbooks to substitute for textbooks. The schoolwide seminars were continued. In addition to regular courses, all students took fine arts and could choose extracurricular activities including dramatics, dancing, photography, music, and journalism. Later, Fessenden added a radio station operated by the drama club and the senior class.[32]

In 1944–45, Buggs also instituted a new student government patterned after that of the United States, with an elected president, house of representatives, and senate, and a court appointed by the president with senate approval. Such a system would teach students the functions of the federal government, Buggs assumed, and if they recognized the necessity of participation in student government, they might carry this attitude into the real political arena. Striving for blacks' equality and inclusion in civil affairs was always a top priority for Buggs. Under Buggs's direction, a student council was responsible for discipline. Only in a democratic form of student government, Buggs believed, would students begin to assume responsibility for their own actions. Rarely, Buggs said, did students take advantage of their authority to discipline each other.[33]

In 1948, Buggs evaluated his functional program and detected both failures and successes. The block system was too restrictive and cumbersome, and no teacher had yet produced a completely satisfactory workbook. On the other hand, he saw many positive results of the "problem area" curriculum. It gave meaning and purpose to facts and theories of various subject fields, it allowed for meaningful and interesting courses which gave students "reasons" to study, it delineated problems that students faced as minorities and gave experience in solving those problems, and it could be "made to consider every aspect of the student's life, and of adult life in a dynamic and meaningful way." The new student government was a significant asset because it made students responsible for their own and their schoolmates' actions, it decreased discipline problems, it taught students the meaning of social responsibility, it gave students actual experience in functions of government, and finally, Buggs hoped, it formed habits of participation in civic affairs. The seminars with the entire student body in attendance were also fruitful. They provided a medium for self-expression and opportunities for students to learn to speak before an audience, they developed rapport between students and faculty, and they placed both students and teachers on the spot before the entire student–faculty body, thus encouraging the instructor and class sponsoring the seminar to perform well. Buggs continued to tweak the curriculum in an effort to best prepare his charges for life and livelihood. In additional to curriculum innovation, during his first two years Buggs put the three-hundred-acre school farm under successful cultivation. Students worked the farm both to learn by doing and to help pay expenses. They also built a dairy barn, graded and beautified the campus, and laid cement walks.[34]

A remarkable number of Fessenden graduates went on to college. In 1944, Brownlee suggested that since Fessenden was no longer needed to provide a free high school (the public system now did that), the AMA continue it as a "non-stereotyped" institution primarily concerned with training students to earn a living in occupations not requiring a college education. Nonetheless, an unusually large proportion of Fessenden's regular high school graduates enrolled in college. Between 1945 and 1948, Fessenden graduated 107 students, 55 of whom entered college. Fifteen enrolled in Florida A&M College; ten at Buggs's alma mater, Dillard University; and the others at seventeen different schools. Why did such an astounding number, a larger percentage than at the more exclusive Avery, go to college? Certainly they were not all middle-class students. Some came from nearby poor farm families, and many of them worked to pay school expenses. Nor were they especially selected to attend Fessenden because of intelligence or academic ability. Fessenden accepted almost anyone who applied. Some transferred there because they were doing poorly in public schools, and parents sent others because they thought a rural boarding school would keep them out of trouble. The changing world, the possibility of better jobs, and veterans who could go to college on the G.I. Bill may have been factors in the number of Fessenden students who entered college. It is also likely that Buggs's "functional" education, which instilled racial pride, self-awareness, personal and social responsibility, hard work, and racial uplift, combined with a faculty and community intensely interested in their success, encouraged Fessenden students to seek higher education.[35]

In the meantime, Brownlee and Morton continued their efforts to decide exactly what they wished the schools to do. Their philosophy of education remained fluid, in part because they were still learning and because functional and community education were different issues and were not always as closely intertwined as Brownlee sometimes seemed to think. In 1937, he acknowledged that Ballard and Avery probably would not appreciably alter their curriculum or aims, but he had great hopes for the rural institutions. He wanted not the old-fashioned Latin school, he stated, but "rather schools where pupils learn by doing and thinking, and above all by living." In somewhat lofty rhetoric, he added that few graduates at any level had gotten "far in the art of living,—gracious living, creative living, religious living, triumphant and joyous living." These schools could go far to remedy that failure by "featuring things . . . men really live by, 'work, play, love and worship.'"[36] But in Brownlee's view the schools must not only serve their pupils but also educate the community. Morton was adamant that schools be dedicated "to making the whole democratic process more effective in the lives of pupils and community leaders." In view of world events, she wrote in 1940 that nothing was more pertinent or rewarding. Morton and Brownlee both recognized the necessity of meeting the needs of both those who intended to go to college and those who did not.[37]

The functional schools attracted considerable favorable notice. D. E. Williams, Florida Superintendent of Negro Schools, was "inspired" by a visit to Fessenden in 1939, and superintendents of Negro education in Alabama and North Carolina were also supportive.[38] In 1940, Thomas Jesse Jones, educational director of the Phelps-Stokes Fund, was so impressed with Brownlee's *Bread and Molasses,* which describes functional education, that he forwarded a copy to Dr. Anson Phelps Stokes. It was significant, Jones wrote Brownlee, that the AMA, "the oldest and in many respects the most effective of the Home Missionary Societies, should at last recognize the importance of Education for Life." At times it appeared that Brownlee and Morton found greater support among outside observers than in their own organization. In 1941, Morton noted that she and Brownlee were "interested in a dynamic philosophy of education," but not everyone "in our organization or on our Board of Directors is in sympathy with our educational point of view."[39] Indeed, as will be seen, only Brownlee's long tenure and influence kept the community centers going.

Morton and Brownlee enjoyed more success in motivating schools—even the urban ones—to increase their community activities than in altering curriculum. As Drago states, despite Ballard's and Avery's "unique contributions," Brownlee and Morton complained that they served their communities less effectively than the rural schools, and suggested that they eventually join the public system or become experimental schools. Although these schools never accepted Brownlee's philosophy of education, they became more community oriented. In 1937, Ballard cooperated in the Red Cross and Community Chest drives, sale of TB seals, and collecting money for flood victims, and the faculty helped equip a Girls' Reserve Club House. Hi-Y and Tri-Y assisted churches in collecting and distributing Christmas baskets, and hosted guest day at Ballard for black elementary schools. The Ballard chorus entertained at community functions and performed each Saturday on WMAZ, a local radio station. In reality, this was less a new emphasis for Ballard than a rededication to its earlier community service. Avery promised "to become a greater force in the lives of local citizens through activities that [would] arouse deeper pupil and community interest." Avery's greatest community service was in the struggle for black equality. It helped force employment for blacks in the Charleston Naval Shipyard during World War II, assisted in obtaining a new USO building for the city, and led the fight to equalize salaries for black and white public school teachers.[40]

Brownlee's greatest success in initiating adult and community education came at Brick Rural Life School in Bricks, North Carolina. Before the founding of Brick Rural Life School in 1934, the AMA had operated Brick Junior College. In 1932 Brownlee petitioned the General Education Board (GEB) for funds to purchase science equipment for the junior college, first established by the AMA as an elementary school in 1895 on a 1,129-acre plantation donated by Julia E. Brick of Brooklyn, New York; and Brownlee also suggested the possibility of Brick becoming a four-year institution. Jackson Davis of the GEB responded that North Carolina was already "over colleged." In a January 1933 interview with Brownlee, Davis reiterated that with its many existing black colleges, North Carolina could "scarcely support a four-year college at Bricks," nor was it needed. Since AMA income had declined precipitously since 1929, and several schools had already been closed, Brownlee investigated whether Brick could be added to the list. There were numerous available colleges, but Brick also operated the only black high school in the region. Brownlee contacted the North Carolina State Department of Education, which pledged to help pay salaries of teachers of a centralized black high school at Bricks if the three counties whose boundaries converged on Bricks would administer it. Brownlee offered to lease Brick buildings and equipment for one dollar, pay partial salaries of several teachers for three years, and assist in buying buses if the counties would operate a free public school.[41] The county superintendents agreed, and Brick was discontinued.[42]

When the school closed, the AMA still held 1,100 acres of land. Brownlee saw an opportunity to implement the Denmark Folk School type of adult education, or, as he said, "A dream was dreamed of resident sharecroppers—student families—being guided under adult democratic processes in agricultural and cultural self-education, at a minimum cost to the Association, and without charity to the sharecroppers." Brownlee's dream was not shared by the AMA executive committee, which was willing, even eager, to sell the plantation and use the proceeds; but as Brownlee wrote years later, "the directors allowed me to play with the idea more or less on my own."[43] The emphasis would be on "health knowledge and care, homemaking, agriculture and farm mechanics, citizenship, wholesome use of leisure and religion." In 1934, the Brick Rural Life School was born.[44] Brownlee's plan called for settling six to eight—later ten—tenant families on up to forty acres, each with cottage and barn, for five years. Since tenants knew more about tenancy than anyone else, he believed, they could work out their own problems. Guidance, provided only when requested, would be on a "self-educating, cooperative basis, and in economic ways calculated to get them on their feet." Classes would be in the fields and the homes. Brownlee expected that at the end of five years the tenant family would have established credit and saved enough money to make a down payment on a farm of their own. If at the end of five years the family was not prepared or disposed to own a farm, they gave way to another family. Each tenant paid eight to ten dollars per acre in rent, with the proceeds to be used for adult education programs designed by tenants themselves. Brownlee was sanguine that given a reasonable chance the tenants were "likely to wake up, show a lively interest in getting ahead," and learn how to solve problems individually and collectively.[45]

The Brick Rural Life School began in earnest in 1936 when Neill A. McLean became director.[46] McLean, a Hampton University graduate with additional study at Cornell University, had taught at Alcorn College, an agricultural school in Mississippi. At Brick, McLean was given land and a house where he could demonstrate scientific farming and be a resource person if asked. He encouraged group study, cooperatives, use of fertilizer, crop rotation and diversification, improving stock, recreation programs, credit unions, garden clubs, and budget management. Tenants were required to keep accounts which McLean audited. During the slack winter season, he opened the former dormitories and held short-term sessions and classes for surrounding farmers as well as the tenants.

Indeed, McLean influenced many nearby farmers and sharecroppers as effectively as those on AMA land. At first tenants were wary of McLean, but he dressed as they did, farmed his land, and gave advice only when asked. His earliest and most effective teaching was by example. Most of the early tenants owned scrub hogs which provided limited pork for their families and almost no cash income. McLean bought blooded Duroc Jersey hogs and raised them while neighbors watched "with concealed interest." The pigs provided meat for McLean's family and cash at the market. Local farmers began to add better stock. A similar thing happened with chickens, and soon surrounding farmers marketed both eggs and hogs. McLean next encouraged farmers to purchase a cow, as he and Brownlee both thought the community consumed too little milk. By 1940, most tenant families had cows and ample supplies of milk and butter. Tenants also began raising wheat to be ground for flour. In 1940, the cost of raising wheat and grinding a barrel of flour was $3.27, as compared to $8 per barrel retail. Some tenants failed, but many succeeded. Most arrived at Brick burdened with debt, children, perhaps a "worked-out" mule, and a wagonload of worn-out furniture. One such family was ready after three years to make a down payment on a farm. In some ways Brownlee found the people's newfound confidence even more impressive than their learned skills: "When they first arrived the husband and wife and all their children were shy and scared. Today they meet everyone with heads erect, shoulders back and talk both readily and intelligently." In 1939, Ruth Morton wrote that "I think we are doing our most significant piece of work" there. "Brick is indeed a 'school' of the people and by the people."[47]

Especially meaningful to Brownlee and McLean was collaboration among community members and the formation of cooperatives. In 1937, Brownlee said, "Honestly we are seeking intelligent ways to be of effective service to rural people whose social life needs to be made more satisfying while at the same time they may gain for themselves economic security. This we believe may best be done according to the philosophy and practice of 'cooperatives.'" Brick's most significant impact may have been to spread cooperatives throughout the state. In 1936, after considerable prodding by McLean, seven community members with seventeen dollars[48] formed a credit union, the first black-managed credit union established under federal charter in North Carolina.[49] At first the credit union grew slowly. Sharecroppers had little money and often declined to deposit what they had because they trusted neither banks nor each other. One day, lightning killed a farmer's cow and mule team. McLean showed tenants the difficulty and expense of borrowing from professional money lenders. Credit union members pooled their resources and made their first loan. Loans were promptly repaid. Members who took loans did not want to embarrass themselves or betray bank partners. Brownlee once asked a member how the credit union decided who got loans. It demanded character, the member responded, and it had lost no money yet. By 1947, the credit union had 385 shareholders with almost $19,000 on deposit and had made loans totaling $50,000. Between 1946 and 1948 the credit union made 252 loans ranging from $24.99 to more than $1,000. Loans included forty for farm supplies, twenty-six for improvements on farms, twenty-two for livestock, sixteen for medical bills, fourteen for financing crops, eighteen for consolidating debts, and ten for children's education. The success of the credit union spawned other cooperative ventures. Ten families pooled resources to purchase a $3,900 tractor and equipment. In 1938, farmers opened a cooperative store, Brick Mutual Exchange, which enabled them to buy fertilizer and other goods at cheaper prices. It did $3,000 of business the first year and grew to $40,000 in 1944. When the store building burned in 1944, the AMA built a new one for $1,200 and rented it to members for $20 a month with the rent going toward the purchase of the building.[50]

McLean strove to develop local leadership to assume responsibilities for the various cooperatives, which, he trusted, would increase independence and entice others to join. Cooperatives were one area other than the church and fraternal organizations where blacks could control their own institutions, and they grew rapidly. The Flower Garden Club planted flowers and shrubs around homes and businesses. A wheat cooperative planted cooperatively and hired a combine to harvest crops. The molasses cooperative grew and ground cane and made molasses. Ten men formed a machinery cooperative in 1940, and purchased a tractor, plow, disc, feed grinder, mowing machine, peanut harvester, and hay bailer.[51] Although local farm families had long preserved their own fruit and vegetables, the Brick cooperative cannery significantly increased the variety and quantity of available food during the winter season. The cannery led to temporary cooperation with and black service to needy whites. White farmers also had a cannery, which "had broken down due to lack of care." They asked if they might use the Brick cannery two days per week. The Brick farmers declined to set aside two days for whites, but invited them to come on any day when they needed to do canning, and wait their turn. "Thus came one of the few interracial ventures in the whole area," Ruth Morton said.[52]

Brownlee claimed in 1939 that cooperatives, McLean, and Brick classes had already wrought noticeable changes in this North Carolina community. Tenants painted and repaired their houses, planted grass and flowerbeds, and improved their home furnishings. One of the most popular winter classes was furniture making. Surrounding farmers, noting the change among Brick tenants, followed suit. Farmers were now more likely to own hogs, cows, chickens, and flourishing gardens. More important, Brownlee thought, was the new community spirit and fellowship. Women sponsored the flower club and shared methods of preserving food and making clothing. The men had meetings every Thursday evening with McLean and the vocational agriculture teacher, out of which grew better farming methods and greater cooperation. By 1944, approximately five hundred Brick residents participated in

Fig. 7. Brick cannery, ca. 1942 (Courtesy of Amistad Research Center, Tulane University, New Orleans, Louisiana)

the cooperatives, and the cooperative message was being sent to surrounding counties. McLean deserved much of the credit for positive change. In 1950, Brownlee said that without McLean Brick Rural Life School "just wouldn't be."[53]

Divan "Big Daddy" Reid's experience illustrated the worth of Brick cooperatives. Just after the turn of the century, Reid bought a small piece of land and a house for $2,000. After twenty-five years, the year Brick Rural Life School began, he still owed $1,600, and had made just enough to pay the

Fig. 8. Brick farm family, 1945 (Courtesy of Amistad Research Center, Tulane University, New Orleans, Louisiana)

merchant who had "furnished" him. Ten years later he had paid for his land; improved his house; bought furniture at $300, young mules for $600, a $360 share in a tractor, and a $75 share of the Brick Mutual Exchange; and had $400 in the credit union. In 1945, he netted approximately $1,000 on his tobacco crop. Part of his financial gain resulted from the difference in his "furnishing bill," which was about $750 in 1935 as compared to $300 in 1945, a savings of $4,500 for ten years made possible by planting a garden and cooperative buying. Big Daddy Reid strongly encouraged surrounding farmers to join cooperatives and take advantage of Brick's winter classes. McLean, who valued Reid's holdings at $9,725 in 1942, declared that Reid "is truly the Honorary Mayor of Brick and Mrs. Reid is a gracious First Lady."[54]

Reid was an exceptional case, but many farmers improved their lot by substituting the credit union for the loan shark, participating in cooperative buying and selling, diversifying crops, raising gardens, and making wiser use of their limited funds. In early 1943, McLean gave the change in net worth between January 1, 1935, and January 1, 1942, for some of the successful Brick residents. These included Richard Garrett, $600 to $5,772.70; Benjamin Forbes, $400 to $1,770; E. E. Bowens, $50 to $1,332. 70; Charlie Adams, $800 to $3,551; and Henry Lyon, $1,500 to $3,353.55. Others who had joined Brick in 1937 and 1938 had done equally well. McLean even credited the cooperative movement with ameliorating white hostility. White businessmen had shown increasing respect and goodwill in response to black self-help efforts, he said.[55]

The farmers' new initiative and cooperation were evident in the way they sought health care. Limited health facilities for African Americans were a nationwide problem, but the issue was especially acute in the rural, segregated South. Brick residents, desirous of public health service, wrote letters, conferred with authorities, and called in a state Department of Public Health representative. The Department of Public Health promised one-half, or $1,200, of the amount needed for a nurse's salary and clinic expenses if residents could raise the rest. Within six weeks, 360 families had contributed. The community raised $600, and the AMA added another $600. The health center opened in 1942, and initiated health education as well as health services. The Brick Health Center's 1944 activities revealed its use to the community. It held monthly clinics for mothers and newborn babies; held weekly clinics for venereal disease treatment; and X-rayed high school students, fifteen of whom showed positive tuberculin reaction. In June, typhoid fever immunization clinics were held throughout surrounding counties in schoolhouses, churches, stores, or any place that a clinic could be set up. The center sponsored group meetings on malaria, screened in several houses, and cleared yards of all bottles and cans that might hold stagnant water. The "Willing Workers Club" met monthly to discuss health issues, especially nutrition, and sought to get more milk in the local diet. Another group supported by the health center concentrated on sanitary improvements of outdoor toilets and open wells. Residents were advised to move toilets away from houses and wells, and those with open wells who used rope and bucket to draw water were urged to brick up wells and add pumps. The nurse made monthly visits to area schools; examined students for general defects; gave needed immunizations; and discussed care of teeth, personal cleanliness, and good nutrition.[56]

Brownlee, convinced that cooperatives were a significant tool for enhancing blacks' quality of life, attempted to spread them throughout the state. In 1945, the AMA joined with the Eastern Carolina Cooperative Council in employing Samuel Rosenberg to advise on the financial and merchandising aspect of cooperative enterprises. The following year the AMA offered to appropriate $50,000 to the North Carolina Council of Credit Unions and

Cooperatives (NCCCUC) if it could raise a like amount elsewhere. When that proved impossible, Brownlee assisted the council in applying for GEB and Rosenwald Fund grants.[57] He informed Jackson Davis of the GEB that major responsibility for the program would rest on the local people who had "already learned much by standing on their own feet and reaching out toward a higher standard of living." The AMA would continue its assistance, Brownlee added, but it would be based "on the principle that this is the people's own movement." In January 1947, Flora M. Rhind visited Brick for the GEB and found "evidence of a rare degree of responsibility on the part of the farmers and their wives for their own well-being and for community improvement." The credit union and the cooperatives were major factors in developing this responsibility, she added, and she believed that Brick School was a logical center for leadership and training for cooperative ventures. Two farmers told her that the credit union was even more important to the community than the church. The GEB and Rosenwald Fund rejected the NCCCUC's grant application, but the Rosenwald Fund gave $5,000 per year for three years to the Brick Center, and the GEB granted $2,200 per year for three years to Brick to pay a teacher of low-cost housing construction.[58]

Brownlee, though dejected by the NCCCUC's inability to gain long-range funding, remained confident that cooperatives were one method of black uplift. "We have hold of some grass-roots stuff here which may have deep and wide significance," he wrote in April 1947. In his view the value of cooperatives was many fold. They not only improved standards of living, but also created initiative, personal responsibility, cooperative living, community spirit, and leadership. The Brick cooperative idea spread far beyond the confines of the AMA plantation and its nearby neighbors. Nathan Pitts, in a study of North Carolina black cooperatives, recognizes Brick's influence in stimulating the movement statewide. In December 1946, the *New York Times* credited Brick Rural Life School with forming a twelve-county cooperative cannery, seven cooperative stores, two poultry associations, a cantaloupe market, two hospital medical associations, a sawmill, a gristmill, a burial association, and credit unions as far away as Chapel Hill. According to the *New York Times,* half of North Carolina's counties were involved in cooperatives largely due to Brick's influence. Ruth Morton claimed in 1947 that seventy-six state credit unions sprang from the Brick credit union, and McLean declared in the same year that the entire state cooperative movement resulted primarily from the Brick Rural Life School's educational programs.[59]

In the meantime, the remaining secondary schools continued their efforts both to educate their students and to serve the community. Obviously, they could not become Brick Rural Life schools. They did not own 1,100-acre plantations, and their first obligation was to train high school youth; but all of them increased community activity. Jay T. Wright had altered the curriculum at Trinity, but his successor, black principal W. Judson King, did far more in the community. He helped organize and build a recreation park with a dining room and a pavilion for Boy Scouts, hauled farmers to the United States Agricultural Experiment Station for short courses, and assisted veterans in getting into school and finding jobs. In 1947, he organized Limestone County's first livestock show for blacks. Twenty farmers from six counties entered eighty animals. Eight participants were 4-H members from Trinity. Occasionally, King became discouraged. In a 1948 Trinity School pamphlet he lamented, "medical care is meager—nothing at all for most of the Negroes. Housing is terrible. Negroes can buy only marginal land which is swampy in rainy seasons. The shadow of the plantation and modern serfdom cast darkness over Negro life. To aspire to better living is an affront to the system." Despite his discouragement, King persisted in trying to improve health, housing, and recreation. He worked for better public schools; showed films on crop rotation, livestock, and small grain farming; sponsored night adult schools in sewing and home management; and secured a state- and county-supported dental clinic on the Trinity campus. He helped obtain an Athens community building, which provided recreation and meeting facilities for African Americans, and by 1950 when the county finally absorbed Trinity, King had added voting rights to his agenda. "I think the citizenship participation is just as significant" as advances in the health program, he wrote in 1950.[60]

Wilfred Gamble, an Ireland-born and Columbia University–educated expert on community planning and cooperative movements, succeeded Morton at Lincoln School in 1938. Little change occurred under Gamble. He established a cooperative garden on the unused school farm to teach better gardening methods, and rented other parcels of land to families for $1.50 per acre in produce. In 1941 the senior class called a community meeting and encouraged adults to elect a chairman and committees to deal with problems facing blacks. Brownlee announced that "we are now in the process of preparing the people to work out their own salvation in the years which lie ahead."[61] Earnest A. Smith, a local black educator, became principal when Gamble was drafted into the Navy in 1943. In a ten-page letter to Smith, Morton stressed the importance of community work and the development of group consciousness. Smith should advise and encourage community activity, she stated, but must never accept office in any local organization. That role belonged to those he was training for leadership. The AMA was negotiating with Perry County to take over the school, and Brownlee planned to have in place when that occurred "an adult and community-service program in the untouched social, economic, political and religious areas of living." In this way, Brownlee said, "the pioneering spirit and services of the A.M.A. will keep marching on down through the years."[62] Smith cooperated with locals to build a swimming pool and to establish summer camps for black youth, but school activities left him little time for effort in rural areas. In 1944, Morton appointed Ralph A. Martin to assume command of community work. Martin helped the community establish a cooperative gristmill and a cooperative store. He was succeeded in 1947 by Samuel C. Adams Jr., whose title was director of the Marion Cooperative Center.[63]

Adams, a Texan trained at Fisk University, had participated in a Fisk survey of Cotton Valley School before going to Marion, so he was familiar with community work. Morton's instructions to Adams were simple: "to increase . . . cooperation among low income groups. That, in a nutshell, is what the American Missionary Association is after." Adams became one of Morton's favorite community workers, but two incidents illustrated the difficulty of creating an aggressive black community program in Perry County. In early 1948, a white overseer on a plantation adjoining a black settlement compelled a sixteen-year-old male to miss school to work for him. A few weeks later when the overseer asked the youth to unload some hay, the latter replied that he wanted to cut wood for his mother first. The overseer accused him of "sassing" and chased him with a shotgun. The young man's family, a mother with five children, was forced to move. Nearby black landowners with vacant houses and in need of help were afraid to permit the family to move on their place, or to befriend them in any way. The next month, Adams met with several black farmers to discuss the possibility of cooperative buying of fertilizer. They opened the meeting with a prayer, explaining to the puzzled Adams that according to "law and the habitual unwritten code in this area—it made the occasion safe in the sight of the law." They were not necessarily beseeching God's blessing on the enterprise, but following the long-standing tradition that religious meetings were about the only safe occasion for multiple black men to congregate in the evening. Naturally such fear made community organizing difficult, Adams told Morton. Even the landowners were not "free." Morton had long been baffled by the practice of opening secular meetings with prayer. "How subtle country folk are in dealing with problems for which they might possibly be persecuted if they are not careful," she wrote. Adams strove mightily to secure better health facilities, improve farming methods, and develop cooperatives until he resigned in 1950 to seek a Ph.D.[64]

The Dorchester Cooperative Center (DCC) in Liberty County, Georgia, most closely resembled Brick, though the areas were substantially different.[65]

A majority of the Brick residents were tenant farmers while many in Liberty County were landowners and, as such, had, unlike sharecroppers, enjoyed "a certain individual freedom all their lives." Unfortunately much of the land was swampy, infertile timberland, and owners were poor. Many lived on farms but worked elsewhere for cash to buy necessities and pay taxes.[66] Wood pulp companies were expanding in Liberty County, and Brownlee feared that if owners failed to learn more efficient farming methods they might lose or sell their land. The cooperative venture was initiated in summer 1937 when Brownlee sent Dorchester Academy principal J. Roosevelt Jenkins, two teachers, and a local minister to Nova Scotia for a two-week class on cooperatives. Upon their return, Jenkins formed study groups to direct community thinking "away from profits . . . towards service to one another through cooperative effort"; and Brownlee required all Dorchester students to study cooperatives. In December 1938, locals formed a credit union which, in March 1939, became the Dorchester Federal Credit Union (DFCU). Within a few months the DFCU had 171 members with assets of more than $2,000. Residents also created a cooperative store, a chicken cooperative, and a producers' cooperative in 1939.[67]

In 1940, the AMA discontinued Dorchester Academy after Liberty County agreed, with AMA assistance, to build a black high school at Riceboro. The AMA then created the DCC and turned its attention directly to the people in the community. Principal Jenkins resigned to work with the National Youth Administration adult school housed on the Dorchester campus, and the AMA appointed Lena Smith to form a committee to carry on the work and oversee the property temporarily. No one seemed surprised that a woman was appointed. There was no local tradition that men were the sole decision makers. In 1946, the president and seven of eleven DFCU officers were women. Claudius Turner, who later became DCC director, thought Liberty County women were more liberated than elsewhere, in part because they as well as men had inherited property. The DFCU operated effectively with local direction. By the end of 1940, it had saved nine homes through loans to pay taxes, assisted a member in buying a timber truck, helped four other lumbermen repair trucks, and made loans to six businesses. The credit union supervised the Dorchester School buildings and grounds and, with AMA permission, rented out the former guest room to visitors to help defray expenses of the DFCU bookkeeper.[68]

In 1943, the AMA sent Claudius Turner, a Knoxville College and Atlanta University graduate, to Dorchester as tentative director of the DCC. While teaching in Howard County, Arkansas, Turner had become interested in Tollette, a community formerly peopled by black landholders who had lost their property and become sharecroppers. In an attempt to help them, he sought to initiate a credit union and encouraged participation in the Farm Security Administration land-buying program, which resulted in angry white officials firing him. Brownlee, upon the recommendation of Charles S. Johnson of Fisk University, sent Turner and family to Dorchester for a three-month trial period. If at the end of that time, Brownlee told Turner, the community came to him for advice and approved of his performance, he could stay. Turner led the DCC for the next seven years, striving to implement the AMA's agenda of "health . . . worthy home membership, adequate vocation, intelligent citizenship, worthy use of leisure time, and high moral character."[69]

As McLean at Brick, Turner endeavored to teach better farming by example. He planted and cultivated crops, raised pigs, ditched swampy areas, and encouraged utilizing better machinery and formation of cooperatives. Most farmers had still used oxen or mules to pull their plows, but in the 1940s they began to see the advantage of tractors. In 1943, some farmers appealed to the AMA to help them buy a tractor. When the association refused, Turner advised them "to do their own thinking and work out their own salvation." They responded by forming the Dorchester Farmers' Cooperative Incorporated, borrowed money from the credit union, and bought a tractor. They also took over the Dorchester Academy gristmill and operated it cooperatively. More acreage was placed under cultivation and more farmers raised food and produce for the market, but many farmers still worked for wages, especially at the nearby military base, Fort Stewart. The DCC also established a cooperative sawmill, and unsuccessfully tried to introduce low-cost concrete block housing. The credit union was the most successful Dorchester cooperative. By 1949, it had loaned more than $51,000 and had helped organize credit unions in at least eleven adjoining counties, and in Savannah. The DFCU's success, Turner declared, encouraged other banks to seek black patronage. The DFCU was not entirely free of problems, however. Members were reluctant to take neighbors and friends to court on the rare occasions they defaulted, and in the late 1940s, the treasurer, a popular local woman, embezzled almost $1,000.[70]

In 1948, when thinking over the strengths and weaknesses of the community centers, Morton correctly claimed, "At Dorchester we have fine leadership in the area of political action, but we are lacking in other ways." Brick, on the other hand, had superb leadership in many areas, but "we need someone who can stretch the people's thinking on social and political issues." McLean's strength was in teaching improved farming and cooperative living, and Turner's aptitude was in civic and political organization, though sometimes the community seemed to be ahead of their leader. Although Georgia blacks voted and held office during Reconstruction, they—as blacks throughout the South—had been effectively disfranchised since the turn of the century by intimidation, fraud, poll tax, and the Democratic Party white primary. The first break came in 1943 when the state abolished the poll tax. Then in 1944, the U.S. Supreme Court in *Smith v. Allwright* asserted that the white primary violated the Fifteenth Amendment. Based on this case, a federal district court in Columbus, Georgia, held in *Primus King v. Chapman et. al Democratic Primary* that black voters could not be excluded in Georgia. Democrats appealed to the Circuit Court of Appeals in New Orleans. Realizing the importance of the case, Turner petitioned the community for money to oppose the appeal. The DCC raised fifty dollars.[71]

While waiting for the appeal, the DCC in a show of pride and strength organized a parade for veterans from Dorchester to the Midway Congregational Church two miles away. Fearing white hostility, Turner was initially reluctant, but the community insisted. Fear kept some veterans away, but one hundred participated, and approximately one thousand African Americans and one hundred whites lined the roadside. The county sheriff, aware that blacks might soon be voting, stopped all cars for the parade which "made the Negroes feel mighty good." Turner described the parade as "beautiful to behold for the marching of the Negro soldiers . . . evoked expressions of Negro pride which could not be expressed in words." Blacks were even more jubilant when the New Orleans court let the Primus King case stand. In Turner's words, a nonviolent revolution began in Liberty County.[72]

The DCC created the Liberty County Citizens Council to encourage and assist people in registering. The DCC taught the Georgia and U.S. constitutions to unregistered black voters in case voter registrars questioned them. Turner himself spent much of his time transporting citizens to the county seat in Hinesville to register. Again, community sentiment may have been ahead of Turner. Black citizens did not want a fight, but they were determined to become voters. There was fear. Turner's life was threatened, and white officials attempted to intimidate black citizens from registering, but by May 1946, 1,100 Liberty County blacks were on the rolls. On July 1, Turner reported that Liberty County had made history as the first Georgia county in modern times to register more blacks than whites—1,800 to 1,500. In the 1946 county election, every candidate the Liberty County Citizens Council endorsed won. In 1948, the race-baiting Herman E. Talmadge won the Georgia governorship, but failed to carry Liberty County.[73]

In the meantime, principal John A. Buggs was stressing civil and political rights at Fessenden Academy. Although Fessenden cultivated a demonstration

Fig. 9. Blacks vote in Liberty County, Georgia, 1947 (Courtesy of
Amistad Research Center, Tulane University, New Orleans, Louisiana)

farm, held classes and institutes for local farmers, and supported cooperatives,
Buggs's greatest community service was in advocating civil rights, encouraging political action, and training veterans. Even before the war ended, Buggs
conceived the idea of helping returning veterans complete high school or
gain technical job skills. At first he received little encouragement. In a February 1945 meeting, the state supervisor of vocational education contemptuously dismissed his plans. Brownlee sympathized, saying that "their kind,

like Hitler, will wake up some day and find out that they are not in favor with God or man." "Meanwhile," Brownlee added, "I'm mighty proud that you are not the kind of person who either can be knocked down, spiritually speaking, or who takes these things lying down." Buggs's persistence, combined with assistance from the AMA and the Postwar Emergency Program, resulted in the construction of a $100,000 technical arts building.[74] By fall of 1947, Fessenden offered courses in commercial dietetics, carpentry, auto mechanics, radio servicing, tailoring, furniture building, business training, and typing to approximately eighty veterans. Several veterans also enrolled in the high school.[75] Unfortunately, Buggs had difficulty securing the vocational division of the State Department of Education's approval that was essential to receive Veterans Administration funds. Morton believed that consent was withheld because of Buggs's political activity. In late February 1948, Buggs traveled to Tallahassee and learned that approval was delayed because the certification officer, who doubted "the Negro school was qualified" to offer the variety of courses listed, had rejected his inspector's recommendation. In March, another inspector, Ben Perloff, visited Fessenden, apologized to Buggs because the program had not already been certified, and recommended that the V.A. make payments to Fessenden retroactive to 11 September 1947. The V.A. quickly approved, and the first check arrived a few days later.[76]

Buggs became active in the battle for civil and political rights almost as soon as he arrived in Florida. He was a charming man who got along well with whites who treated him with respect. Brownlee and Morton were both devoted to him. When Morton was fired from the AMA, to be discussed later, she said Buggs was one of the three AMA people she would remember. He also accommodated southern whites when necessary. When in 1943, his draft board reclassified Buggs 1 A and Brownlee appealed, Buggs reminded Brownlee not to call him Mr. Buggs in the board's presence. He had to "submit to many acts of discourtesy" from ration and other boards, he added, in order to get favorable action for Fessenden. Buggs did not tolerate discourtesy when it could be avoided. He withdrew school funds from the Florida National Bank in Ocala because he found "no pleasure in dealing with an institution which refuses to treat me as a full-grown man," and transferred them to another Ocala bank where he kept his own account.[77] More important was his public struggle for black equality. He was secretary of the Marion County NAACP from 1943 until his departure from Fessenden. Marion County had one of the most active NAACP chapters in Florida, and many members were from the Fessenden area. He was also active in the state NAACP, served as president of the United Civic League, was secretary of the State Progressive

League, and was co-chairman of the State Committee for Equal Educational Opportunity. The *Tampa Bulletin* credited him with adding some five thousand black voters to the Marion County roll between 1944 and 1950. The entire school—faculty and students—participated in several voter registration campaigns. Not surprisingly, most black citizens surrounding Fessenden became registered voters.[78]

Ruth Morton probably exaggerated when she said in 1949 that Fessenden was "the only place in Florida where Negro politicians can meet and plan strategy for getting out the Negro vote." Fessenden never became, as Brownlee dreamed for the community centers, a house of refuge where both races might "mingle and work, free even from racial consciousness"; but it and other centers did provide safe meeting places for black activists. The *Tampa Bulletin* stated that Buggs also joined the fight for better recreation facilities, library services, street improvements, black education, and desegregation. Buggs strongly encouraged student activism, and in 1948 organized a NAACP youth council on campus. The student newspaper editorialized against segregated restaurants and other types of discrimination, and advocated desegregation of state universities. In 1949, Buggs unsuccessfully recommended that Fessenden become an interracial prep school emphasizing freedom. Morton may have been correct when she claimed that Buggs's activism was behind the Department of Education's reluctance to certify his veterans' program.[79]

By 1949, Marion County had a black high school in Ocala with bus service to outlying areas, and the AMA division committee saw little need to retain Fessenden. Local blacks, wishing to keep the school and encouraged by Buggs, campaigned to make Fessenden a public junior college. In 1949 Farris Bryant, a Marion County state legislator, supported such a plan, but it never came to fruition.[80] Buggs blamed state financial hardship, but Morton thought Mary McLeod Bethune, president of Bethune-Cookman College, "an astute politician" whom she much admired, and Superintendent of Negro Schools D. E. Williams, who was on Bethune's board of trustees, thwarted the plan because if Fessenden became a junior college it might draw students who otherwise would attend Bethune-Cookman.[81] In the spring of 1951, Fessenden, the AMA's last secondary school, closed its doors.[82]

In the meantime, there was a question of whether the community centers would continue. Brick and Dorchester survived school closings, but would they outlast Brownlee's retirement in October 1950? In 1949, the community centers had suffered a budget cut, which Morton wrote, "sends chills up and down a person's spine." Brownlee had long battled with the larger Board of Home Missions over community work, and some of its members spoke contemptuously of the AMA's "piddling" community centers. In a 1950 confidential letter, Brownlee wrote that for fifteen years William F. Frazier, executive vice president of the Board of Home Missions, had tried to get rid of him and had stirred opposition to Ruth Morton since she joined the AMA. Brownlee believed Frazier had little interest in the community centers and wished to concentrate on the colleges.[83] In early 1951, the BHM claimed that so many schools had been turned over to public authorities that a director of schools was superfluous, and informed Morton that she was being relieved of her duties as of May 31. The history of the AMA secondary schools and community centers was coming to a close. Morton had been an integral part of all aspects of the AMA administration for two decades. She had helped evaluate, hire, and fire faculty both male and female at all institutions and had given direction to secondary schools, community centers, and the Race Relations Department. Herman Long, director of that department, wrote in March 1951 that he was wounded by the news that Morton was being released. "My recovery has been slow, and I can only say now that I deeply regret that Ruth Morton will not be with us after the present year. I will miss her competence and knowledge of the general AMA programs, as well as her presence and friendly interest in race relations work." Many other AMA workers and friends were similarly saddened by Morton's departure.[84]

The Brick and Dorchester centers survived for a time with lesser support and decreased activity. In 1953, the Brick Rural Life School was merged with the Franklinton Christian Center which was to provide the Congregational Christian Church with an in-service training program, as well as an extension service in agriculture, health, and community cooperatives. The AMA deeded 150 acres to the Franklinton Center and sold the timberland to a paper company and the remainder of the plantation to blacks through the Farm Home Loan Association.[85] The Dorchester Community Center languished but did not completely disappear. In 1953, the AMA proposed—and the Midway Congregational Church and the DCC agreed—to call one man to be both minister and center director. Three years later, the DCC was separated from the AMA and placed under the administrative supervision of the Convention of the South. A program was initiated at the DCC in 1961 which Brownlee and Morton would have heartily approved. The Field Foundation funded a citizenship school directed by Rev. Andrew J. Young to train people from black majority counties with few black registered voters to return to their communities to help people register and vote.[86] Dorothy Cotton, an organizer of citizenship schools, said they were on "a mission to make democracy mean what it is supposed to mean in this country." Activist Septima Poinsette Clark, an Avery graduate, was supervisor of citizenship-school teacher training. The schools emphasized literacy, legal rights, and preparation for voting. Fannie Lou Hamer, intrepid civil rights leader in Mississippi, was a "star pupil." Bernice Johnson Reagon went to Dorchester after being expelled from black Albany State College for her civil rights activities. Reagon continued to struggle for civil rights and later founded the outstanding a cappella women's singing group Sweet Honey in the Rock. By January 1963, citizenship school graduates had helped approximately ten thousand African Americans register to vote in areas where it was extremely difficult. Young directed the program until he resigned in 1964 to become executive secretary of the Southern Christian Leadership Conference. Young believed the citizenship schools were a natural extension of the AMA's historic role.[87] Though most of the staff and students were African American, the citizenship schools at DCC approached Brownlee's initial dream of community centers which might "serve to hasten the day when racial discrimination" would cease to be.[88]

5
"Temptation to Right Doing"
The AMA and Public Schools

AMA leaders always contended that education was a public responsibility, and in 1865 it believed the national crisis sufficiently severe to call for a national system of education to include both freedmen and southern whites. Ignorance spawned crime, pauperism, and even disunion, the AMA argued, and the federal government, in its role of protecting citizens, should create a system of schools to reach every child in the country. Such schools embracing both black and white might "solve many questions now under discussion [African Americans' place in American society], promote the union and loyalty of the states, prevent future rebellions, and tend to consolidate and bless the country." Association officials recognized that a national system of education was unlikely, but saw state-supported education for all as a possibility, especially after congressional Reconstruction acts placed blacks and Republicans in office in southern states. The AMA continued to expand its own schools while vigorously advocating, in the words of secretary Augustus F. Beard, "the result for which we have all been laboring—not simply the immediate education for a few pupils, but the establishment of a permanent school system."[1]

AMA agents and teachers were instrumental in the passage of public school legislation in several states, and two AMA officials, C. Thurston Chase in Florida and Samuel S. Ashley in North Carolina, became superintendents of public instruction. Other teachers became county superintendents of schools. The AMA assisted in establishing a public school system by withdrawing when public funds were available, giving or selling its property to school officials, and sharing expenses with state and local boards. In 1865 it relinquished its Baltimore schools to the Baltimore Association for the Moral and Educational Improvement of Colored People, with the words "If the main object is accomplished, it hardly matters by whom it is done."[2] In 1867, it conveyed its common schools to city officials in Lexington and Louisville,

Kentucky, and soon afterward did the same in Chattanooga, Tennessee. In the early 1870s, the Freedmen's Bureau and AMA transferred their buildings to state and local authorities in Louisiana, and in 1872 the AMA began handing some Georgia schools over to public officials and "launched a concerted campaign to pry from the clenched fist of Democrats" who had taken control of the state as much money as possible for black education.[3] The Reverend Henry M. Turner, a fiery African Methodist Episcopal Church minister and politician, once declared that without the AMA there would be no public system of education for Georgia freedmen, and that if the AMA completely withdrew, black public schools "would be of little value." Turner was partially correct. The association consistently badgered the state to create more black schools, placed as many of its own teachers in the system as possible, and gave land and buildings to city and county boards of education. In addition, local officials sometimes established public schools with black teachers to rid themselves of AMA influence and interracial faculties. Christian education was important to the AMA, but free public education was even more significant.[4]

Unfortunately, by 1877 Democrats had regained control of all ex-Confederate states, and both support for black education and possibilities of cooperation declined dramatically.[5] Still, the AMA continued to advocate free public education and cooperated when and where it could. For years it subsidized as many as twenty public institutions so they could lengthen five-month terms to eight months. After 1900, at least one school was dropped or transferred every year. Retrenchment led to the closing in 1904 of two of the AMA's oldest and largest schools, Storrs in Atlanta, and Slater in Knoxville. They were selected because there were several black colleges in Atlanta with precollege departments and the public system was more advanced in Knoxville than in most of the South. The Atlanta city board of education bought the Storrs property and continued the school. The AMA may also have contributed to the development of white public schools. Few southern counties and cities were willing to permit blacks to have schools superior to those of whites. When the AMA founded Brewer Normal Institute in Greenwood, South Carolina, there was no modern secondary school for whites, but a few years later Greenwood built a fine high school. Brewer Normal's success, Secretary Beard firmly believed, had encouraged whites to demand a better education for their children.[6]

H. Paul Douglass, who became AMA corresponding secretary in 1910, was determined to improve and standardize AMA institutions, in part by reducing the number. He advocated turning schools over to local boards even when the AMA executive committee thought it hasty since public officials, as a rule, provided facilities and teachers inferior to those of the AMA. As public schools became available, Douglass gave up some institutions to them, and as they improved he withdrew the AMA from more. "Clinging to its principle of training for race leadership," the AMA under Douglass's leadership emphasized "intensive rather than extensive methods," and was "more fully committed to quality than quantity." Fewer schools meant more teachers and better facilities for those remaining. Moreover, Douglass claimed, it was important not to permit southern states to neglect their duty, and then to give way when they established schools. In 1919, the AMA executive committee discussed the "unwisdom of retarding the development of public school facilities by needless duplication under A.M.A. auspices."[7]

Between 1906 and 1914, Douglass closed ten normal and graded schools, and discontinued grants to nineteen ungraded schools. In 1918, the AMA withdrew from Albany Normal School in Albany, Georgia, when the state established a normal school for blacks there, and the next year it dropped Beach Institute in Savannah, claiming that it was not the AMA's policy to duplicate the work of public schools when the latter could do the work as well. In truth, Savannah operated an industrial high school which did not prepare students for college. Savannah blacks conducted a school at Beach until they persuaded the city to upgrade its institution. This was one of the rare cases in which the AMA abandoned a high school without a good alternative available or promised. African Americans in Savannah were unhappy with the AMA, but, as Brownlee later wrote, the association stimulated local "patrons to take the football 'over the line'" and demand a better school. The AMA established five renewable scholarships for Savannah students to attend AMA colleges. While the AMA turned schools over to the public when possible, it regretted that positive Christian instruction was typically lost and that the "grade of study" was usually reduced. Despite the association's best efforts, public high schools offering a full four-year course grew slowly. Before 1920, high school education was available to blacks primarily in private schools. Public officials were generally unconcerned and northern philanthropists did not yet "view black secondary education as relevant to its schemes for the social and economic development of the New South."[8]

In 1919, the AMA announced the closing of Chandler in Lexington, Kentucky; Gregory at Wilmington, North Carolina; and Emerson in Mobile, Alabama. It chose these schools because they were in large population centers and public funds and blacks themselves could better provide education than in more isolated areas. Parents complained bitterly that public schools could not and would not provide the quality of AMA institutions, and promised to give greater support. Mobile citizens raised $8,000 to keep Emerson open.

Wilmington and Lexington followed suit, and all three schools were temporarily continued. The AMA provided only $5,000 of Emerson's $15,000 budget in 1923–24.[9] The reprieve was only temporary. In 1920–21, Wilmington blacks supplied one-third of Gregory's budget and pleaded with the local school board for assistance. The board voted to allocate $1,500 to Gregory, but discovered that state law prohibited paying state funds to church-supported institutions. The board then offered to rent AMA buildings and establish a full four-year high school, which was exactly what the AMA wanted and it quickly agreed. The AMA gave the teachers' home to the black Congregational church for use as a social center, and employed a kindergarten teacher and social worker for them. Then in 1923, Lexington, at the urging of African Americans and the AMA, opened a modern high school which equaled Chandler in course offerings. The AMA could not in good conscience appeal for funds to duplicate the new school. It did not completely withdraw from Lexington, however. It established an institutional church and transformed the schoolhouse into a community building with a minister to attend to black "social, moral, cultural, and religious" needs.[10]

Emerson survived with local assistance until 1926. Parents paid school taxes, supplied tuition for their children, and also made special gifts to Emerson. Brownlee visited the Mobile school superintendent and suggested that he appoint and pay some of the teachers and that the AMA and city jointly operate the school. He could not legally comply, the superintendent responded, but he acknowledged that Emerson was a good school highly prized by Mobile blacks, and promised that "the day the A.M.A. lays down the school we will take it up and carry forward the same quality of work." The AMA leased the Emerson campus to Mobile for three years with an option to buy, and in September 1927 it opened under city supervision.[11] As in Savannah, the AMA established five $100 renewable scholarships to enable promising black high school graduates to attend AMA colleges.[12] In almost every instance, patrons opposed transferring schools to local boards. Brownlee, new to AMA work in the early 1920s, quickly learned that blacks were so accustomed to false promises from whites that "they put little stock in them." An alumna in 1921 sent him a letter bordered in black crepe asking that her school not be transferred to the local board. He replied that if the AMA did not think "it was serving the cause of education best and hastening the day when every child would have a free education, it never would let a single school pass from under its control." It was "the right of every child, regardless of race to have an education and it is the duty of the state to provide" it, Brownlee said; he added that AMA schools had taught "many a state that its greatest asset is its children, and many an individual that colored children are as educable as any."

Brownlee was not the only AMA official who worried about discontinuing schools. Assistant superintendent Beam loved AMA work and admired blacks and black culture, but she resigned in 1919 because she could not "face the long drain of turning the high schools over to public instruction. I believed in the policy," she wrote, "but the application was too much for me." Black teachers, as well as parents and students, felt betrayed. They told Beam that the "AMA had once lifted them up. Now it was casting them down. The public school authorities would not care for them as people."[13]

Even though law prohibited the joint AMA-Mobile operation of Emerson, the experience persuaded Brownlee that cooperation with public officials could relieve the AMA's financial burden and encourage southern whites to support black education. He selected Brewer in Greenwood, South Carolina, as a test case. Greenwood whites had not accepted Brewer teachers socially, and there had been little black-white accord until the Brewer principal suggested a hospital for black patients. The AMA and local blacks and whites joined to build a hospital which Brownlee viewed as a stepping-stone toward a public high school. In 1925 he approached the school board and offered Brewer property and equipment free if the board would maintain it as an accredited high school. According to Brownlee, this "temptation to right doing" worked. The school board agreed, and the local paper suddenly printed a complimentary story about the AMA's "provisional services." The board appointed and paid five AMA-recommended teachers, all elementary pupils attended public schools, and high school students were admitted to Brewer free. The AMA paid the principal and other instructors. Enrollment doubled the first year. By 1930, the AMA paid the principal and the board employed most of the teachers. Three years later it voted to appropriate $1,000 to Brewer for 1933–34, $500 for 1934–35, and then cease support. Brewer buildings now needed repairs and the board could secure federal funds if it held title to the property; therefore, in February 1935, the AMA deeded buildings and land to the board on the condition that it maintain a free accredited high school for blacks, and that the property be held in perpetuity for welfare of African Americans.[14]

In 1928, the AMA offered the Montgomery County, North Carolina, board of education free use of Peabody Academy buildings and $4,000 if it would operate the school. The board accepted, and cooperation continued until 1936 when the association sold school property to the board "at a ridiculously low figure," claimed Brownlee, "spread over a period of five years." The AMA made a similar and successful offer to the Athens, Georgia, board if it would maintain Knox Institute as an accredited school. As with Brewer, Peabody and Knox enrollments significantly increased when they became free. Not only did the AMA have greater resources for its other schools, but also more youth were being trained. Brownlee in 1929 described the AMA's policy as "progressive absorption" and "cooperation"—that is, the AMA would transfer schools to local authorities when there was duplication, and wherever it continued its schools it would seek cooperation and financial support from local boards. He hoped a few specialized institutions could be retained indefinitely as prep schools with "the very highest and finest moral and cultural influences," or as "educational hubs in a county-wide school system."[15] Between 1920 and 1930, ten AMA schools—six of them secondary—were absorbed by or were cooperating with county or city systems. The AMA still made annual appropriations to Peabody Academy and Brewer Normal, but they operated as free public schools.[16]

The Depression increased the urgency with which Brownlee and the AMA sought public assistance. Declining revenues and a new black high school in Thomasville, Georgia, persuaded Brownlee that despite the school's excellence, and the many entreaties of black Thomasvillians, Allen Normal could no longer be justified. It closed after the 1933 graduation exercises. The Depression also brought an end to Gloucester A & I in Cappahosic, Virginia. The county and local African Americans had established the Free Gloucester Training School; and while it was far less advanced than William G. Price's institution, it was free, and Gloucester A & I began to lose students. The AMA retired Price in 1932 and closed the school in June 1933.[17] The AMA then began a lengthy negotiation with the Florence, Alabama, city board of education to take charge of Burrell School. The AMA administrative committee instructed Brownlee in 1933 to ask the board to assume "in whole or in part" responsibility for Burrell. Although white citizens in Florence had always been more supportive of Burrell than those in many school towns, the board rejected Brownlee's request. The following year, the administrative committee asked Brownlee to notify the city board that the AMA would conduct Burrell for 1934–35 "with the expectation that a year hence" the city board "may assume responsibility for a free High School for the Negroes of Florence." Brownlee reiterated to AMA officers and supporters in 1934 that missionary societies should not postpone public schools for sectarian reasons, or do for education what states could be persuaded to do, and that the AMA should cooperate "with the state in its progressive assumption of such responsibility," but it appeared in this instance that the administrative committee was not following Brownlee's lead, but was pushing him forward. The board declined the AMA's request.[18]

In April 1935, the AMA offered the board free use of Burrell buildings and equipment and $1,000 to operate an accredited high school in 1935–36.

Again the board refused, but asked the AMA to donate the Burrell property on condition that it always be used for the education of black children. The administrative committee reluctantly agreed to turn over the property if the board pledged to conduct a high school accredited by the state department of education and the Southern Association of Colleges and Secondary Schools. The board refused to furnish such guarantees and announced that it planned to build a new school, but for the coming year there would be no classes for blacks beyond the seventh grade. Obviously, the AMA had misjudged the city's willingness to assume charge of the school, but it was still determined to withdraw. After extended discussion, the committee granted free use of school buildings and $1,700 to a local black "sponsoring committee" to keep the school running. It sent George N. White, the popular black former Burrell principal, to explain the implications of this action, and to encourage the community to petition for a free public high school. The sponsoring committee accepted and conducted "a very satisfactory" school in 1935–36 while keeping pressure on school officials. The city board promised to take over the eighth grade in 1936 and the ninth in 1937. The city added tenth, eleventh, and twelfth grades sooner than expected, and in June 1937 the AMA deeded the Burrell property to the board, and that fall Burrell became a free public school. Unfortunately, public schools seldom maintained the quality of AMA schools, and administrators lacked the AMA's concern for equality and democracy. Both patrons and the AMA were dissatisfied with the results at Burrell. When negotiating with the Athens, Alabama, board in 1949 to take Trinity School, Ruth Morton warned, "Let's not repeat the mistakes that were made" at Florence. Friends of black education had mixed views on the AMA policy of giving up its secondary schools. Edwin R. Embree, president of the Julius Rosenwald Fund, commended Brownlee in 1937 on the AMA's determination to concentrate on "a very small number of colleges and even smaller number of secondary schools," but in the same year black educator Horace Mann Bond complained to Embree that the AMA's assumption that public schools had advanced to a degree that they could satisfactorily take over the work might be false.[19]

Years later Brownlee recalled the difficulties of transferring association institutions to public boards. It was the proper thing to do, he said, and what AMA founders had worked toward, but it was always painful. It was much easier, Brownlee confessed, to make decisions in New York "than on the ground in conference with principals, teachers, parents and patrons." Black parents looked askance at every move toward greater cooperation with public school boards. They could hardly admit that "such a step was even in the right direction." Parents believed their children would suffer, and principals and teachers realized that southern white officials would not accord them the same respect and consideration they received from Brownlee and Morton. All knew they were losing something. When Florence, Alabama, took over Burrell, a white Presbyterian minister and school board member said it was the city's duty to provide an accredited black high school and he would vote for it, but only reluctantly. "There is a quality about your school that is lacking in all our schools, white as well as colored," he said. "We need that quality, but, with the passing of Burrell it will be gone." Burrell meant far more to parents than to the white minister, as Brownlee realized. "It meant a house of freedom, a house of refuge, a house of counsel, a house of prayer. It was as if the bottom had fallen out of the universe," Brownlee wrote, "when 'those who care' passed and 'those who must' took hold." Brownlee, who passionately believed in free public education, had to steel his emotions to make the changes. "Yet it always seemed to me that the goal was right," he remembered, "so I took a long look, drew a long breath, and passed my recommendation with a long document to the A.M.A. committee, and every time the committee vote read like a death sentence to the people." The AMA invariably failed "to carry the people" in its conclusions to close schools. Black patrons clearly understood that they were a disfranchised population lacking the political clout to compel county authorities to treat them fairly.[20]

Brownlee's aim was not simply to shift educational expenses from the AMA to the state, but rather to make secondary education more widely available. He realized that public schools might not maintain AMA quality, but he was also acutely aware that enrollment increased each time an AMA tuition school was merged with or was taken over by public officials. Brownlee knew—even if concerned parents sometimes temporarily forgot—that a majority of blacks were unable to send their children to private schools, and that free public education vastly increased opportunities for black youth. Ruth Morton thought Avery Normal Institute parents selfish for fighting to keep the institution private. As she said in 1943, as long as there was a private school of Avery's caliber, more prosperous parents had little incentive to press for good public schools. "Thus we are not really ministering to a large number of needier people, but to the few in higher income groups." Brownlee and Morton pressured local and state boards for public schools, while at the same time admonishing black citizens to more actively demand their rights.[21]

Unfortunately, while turning schools over to the public was progress in "justice and equal opportunity," and achievement of the AMA principle that the state owed free education to all youth, it violated another AMA principle by strengthening rather than weakening segregation. In every instance interracial faculties were lost. "We are not blind to the fact that progress may tend to root more deeply and securely that which must be uprooted if we really mean to have in America the democracy we profess to believe in and which we are now defending at all costs against outside domination," Brownlee wrote in 1942. In 1942, when Ballard began cooperating with the local board in Macon, Georgia, Brownlee asked if white teacher Louis H. Mounts could remain on the Ballard faculty if the AMA paid his salary. He hoped this might be a way to evade the Georgia law that forbade state money going to a white teacher in a black school, but the board deemed it "inadvisable."[22]

Many school patrons regretted this loss of principle as illustrated in Talladega, Alabama. For years Talladega College's Sessions Elementary and Drewry High School educated community and faculty offspring, both black and white, and served as practice schools for Talladega students. They had both interracial faculties and student bodies. In the mid-1940s, Drewry was still the only place in Talladega County where black youth could graduate high school since county schools went only to the tenth grade. In 1946, Talladega College trustees voted to close the schools not merely to save money but to force the city to shoulder its responsibilities for black education. Brownlee, a trustee as well as AMA executive secretary, and Talladega president Adam D. Beittel approved the decision. The trustees, aware that college faculty and the community would be upset, sent Brownlee to explain the decision. Beittel, absent from campus during Brownlee's visit, returned to find teachers and community members "considerably disturbed and confused." He met with the faculty, who insisted that Sessions' and Drewry's interracial character must be maintained. If they became public schools they would be segregated, which Dean James T. Cater contended would be a "backward step." Since Brownlee knew that many of the most distressed faculty were parents, he unfairly concluded that they were primarily motivated by what "might happen to *their* children."[23]

No doubt the faculty and Cater, who had a son in the seventh grade, were reluctant to send their children to inferior public schools, but most were also firm interracialists who were "quite out of sympathy with the basic philosophy that . . . the support of public education" was "a higher value than the maintenance of a non-segregation policy." In the meantime, President Beittel's negotiations for public funds for Drewry went smoothly until the question of white faculty children arose. When Beittel pleaded with the state superintendent of education to "overlook the very slight violation of the principle of segregation" at Drewry, the superintendent tersely replied that desegregation was illegal. Clearly if Drewry received public funds it must be segregated, and on this basis the Talladega faculty and staff unanimously voted that a segregated Drewry was unacceptable and that "we wish to continue to support our charter which reads that no person shall be denied an education because of race or color." Although sympathetic, Brownlee argued that it was a question of securing the best possible public schools for blacks rather than approving segregation and that public officials would provide first-class facilities only if compelled to do so. Faculty parents were unconvinced, and voted that their children must be educated together, that relinquishing interracial Drewry was too great a sacrifice even if it encouraged better public schools for blacks. Every staff member save one endorsed the parents' resolution. In January 1948, Talladega trustees voted to close Drewry and Sessions at the end of the academic year. The city built a school on AMA-donated land and in the fall of 1948 opened a public twelve-grade school for black children only. The closing of Sessions and Drewry contributed to a campus rift that eventually cost President Beittel, who had sided with the trustees, his job. Not all parents were as adamant about retaining the interracial character of their schools as Talladegans, but it was an important issue at all institutions with mixed faculties.[24]

In the meantime, Brownlee and Morton encouraged cities and counties not yet ready to open high schools at least to establish good elementary schools so the AMA could concentrate its resources on the upper grades. The AMA had transferred many of its common schools to the public system and had always supported the founding of more public schools. It frequently aided and encouraged the building of Rosenwald schools, including in Gastonia County, North Carolina.[25] In 1923, Walter E. Ricks, black principal of the AMA's Lincoln Academy in Kings Mountain, North Carolina, took the initiative in securing the cooperation of the Gastonia County superintendent of education in building a Rosenwald school. The AMA deeded 0.94 acre of land, and since blacks were responsible for much of the cost, Ricks and fellow workers canvassed the community for funds which resulted in the erection of a $12,000 building with six rooms and an auditorium. The county superintendent gave Principal Ricks the keys, saying, "you folks have long proved your ability to conduct schools and care for buildings and I want you to consider this public school a part of the Academy. Look after it and use it as freely as you would use your own buildings." This school, staffed by the AMA but financed by the county, allowed Lincoln Academy primary students to attend a reputable school without tuition, and it relieved Lincoln Academy of their care. This venture led to greater cooperation between Principal Ricks and the local school board, which by 1926 was paying the salaries of two secondary instructors; but it also convinced Brownlee that adequate public common schools could ease the crowding at AMA secondary institutions, and that counties and cities with good primary schools might aspire to add secondary education.[26]

In 1928, the AMA administrative committee voted to end the first six grades at Burrell Normal "in the interest of encouraging the Florence school board to assume full responsibility for the elementary education of Negro children." It dropped grades below seven at Allen Normal in 1930; and in 1933 Marion County, Florida, built an elementary school adjacent to Fessenden Academy on two acres donated by the AMA which operated under Fessenden's direction and served as its practice school. This concluded "the dream of quite a few years" and "meant much to the growth and furtherance of education in this immediate vicinity." Fessenden acquired a bus in 1933 which transported students to both Fessenden and the nearby public elementary school. After years of a combination of AMA pleading and black community pressure, Athens, Alabama, improved its facilities to the point that Brownlee was comfortable in abolishing the primary grades at Trinity School in 1933.[27] Negotiating with Marion, Alabama, officials was more difficult. Despite the tremendous growth of Rosenwald schools in the South—and particularly Alabama—in the 1920s, common schools remained inadequate in Marion and many other areas in the early 1930s. In February 1933, the AMA administrative committee voted to endeavor "to secure for Marion a suitable free primary school" to assume responsibility for the first six grades at Lincoln. When the local board was not forthcoming, the AMA urged blacks to demand better schools and abolished the first three grades at Lincoln, but gave free use of a room to a Lincoln teacher to hold a tuition school. The AMA finally got the board's attention in 1936 when it voted to sell to the board two acres on which to build a primary school for one dollar, and agreed to supplement the salaries of teachers at the projected school for three years. Though the relationship was often tense, this move initiated increased cooperation between the AMA and the Marion school board.[28]

The AMA continued to negotiate with local boards to assist in supporting its high schools. In 1944, Brownlee praised Ruth Morton as "a creative genius in suggesting cooperative ways in which our schools are increasingly placed in the hands of public authorities," but the process was "slow, sometimes hazardous, and seldom very steady." As Brownlee said, the momentum "varied according to the handicaps and traditions of each state." State agents for Negro Education were often more supportive than local superintendents, and county and city superintendents were limited by their boards and their own beliefs. Avery Institute, after years of fierce resistance by its patrons, finally merged with the Charleston city system in 1947 when the younger, more progressive George C. Rogers Sr. replaced an "Old South" superintendent. According to historian Edmund L. Drago, Avery remained an outstanding public high school.[29] In Limestone County, Alabama, superintendent W. A. Owens alienated his board by his chumminess with Trinity School staff and his support for equalization of salaries for black and white teachers. He eventually thought it best to resign and was replaced by a man described by black principal W. Judson King as being "from the 'white Africa' section of the county with all the limitations of that section save a little 'book learning.'" Morton and Brownlee deeply regretted the loss of the sympathetic and able Owens. "How difficult it becomes for a man who even gently sticks out his neck on the subject of justice to Negroes," Brownlee wrote. On the other hand, according to Morton, Perry County, Alabama, superintendent L. G. Walker was "rude and uncouth," insulted black teachers, and "openly campaigned for all so-called white supremacy politicians," but he had "done more for the education of Negro youth in his county than any other superintendent with whom we are working."[30] Walker attempted to abolish inadequate one-room schools and insisted that teachers have college degrees which gave black teachers salaries higher than many politicians wanted; and he greatly improved rural education. Perhaps his racial attitudes allowed him to accomplish things the more reserved Owens could not do.[31]

No matter the place or personnel, the process of joining AMA and public schools was often slow and tedious. In 1933, Brownlee first approached the Macon, Georgia, board of education about making Ballard a public senior high with the AMA and board cooperatively supporting it. Serious talks did not begin until 1939, significant cooperation did not occur until 1941, and the merger was not completed until 1949. The most painless transition occurred at Lincoln Academy in North Carolina. Cooperation increased almost from the time of the building of the Rosenwald school, and accelerated when Henry C. McDowell, a 1930 Harmon Award winner and former missionary to Portuguese, West Africa, became principal in 1937. After eighteen years of successful mission work, the American Board wished to make him a "star promoter," but McDowell wanted a challenge rather than spending his years telling people what he had already accomplished. "He is repeating his African success," Brownlee stated in 1939, "getting people to do things they never believed they would do; bringing about inter-racial cooperation in unusual and telling ways; harnessing a number of white indigenous welfare movements to the service of Negroes as well."[32]

During the summer of 1941, McDowell toured thirteen western North Carolina counties where the black population was insufficient to support a black accredited high school. He convinced state agent of Negro Education Nathan C. Newbold to assist him in persuading the counties to unite in providing a dislocation fund to send their students to Lincoln Academy. Twenty-seven such students attended Lincoln in 1941–42. In 1941, McDowell arranged for the state and county to pay eight months' salary for seven

Lincoln Academy teachers with the AMA furnishing the ninth month and providing full salary for eight other teachers. The AMA selected the teachers. Morton strongly approved McDowell's plan because it was "so much in line with our policy of handing over to the state all the traffic will bear but doing everything that will maintain the integrity of the institution." By fall 1941, the state was paying most of the salaries of ten teachers and all of one while the AMA paid all of seven. By 1946, the AMA paid salaries of only the office secretary, house mothers for boys and girls dormitories, and a dietician. Morton remarked that state and county officials constantly insulted teachers at Lincoln School in Marion, Alabama, but Lincoln Academy had "come through the transition with flying colors and our work and the state's is dovetailing with no friction whatever."[33] Lincoln Academy was virtually a public school by 1949, but the AMA continued to bear the expense of providing dormitories for students who lived away from Kings Mountain until the end of the 1954–55 academic year.[34]

Transfer in other states proved more complex, but in Georgia the AMA had a strong ally in Robert L. Cousins, the white state director of Negro Education.[35] Cousins served as liaison in the sometimes rocky relationship between the AMA and education boards responsible for Ballard Normal School and Dorchester Academy. He strongly desired AMA institutions to become public and urged local boards to do more and counseled cooperation and patience to Brownlee and Morton. Although Cousins made significant contributions to black education, his efforts and those of other state agents were aided and partially motivated by blacks' increased willingness—abetted by the NAACP—to go to court to secure better schools. The threat of desegregation caused many whites to look more favorably upon separate and "equal" education. Liberty County, in particular, had been exceedingly backward in educating black youth, but with Cousins's urging, the county board in 1940 agreed to join the AMA in providing a new central high school, bus service, teachers' home, and elementary school. The county promised to support one teacher for every fifteen high school students and one for every twenty elementary pupils, and it would provide supervision and at least half the cost of new buildings and a bus. The AMA furnished the rest.[36] Brownlee and Morton met with Dorchester Academy parents to discuss this agreement. They told them the county wished to take responsibility for educating their children, and asked them to decide whether to accept. They admitted that the new school might not at first meet Dorchester standards but would grow into it, and they warned parents that if they voted to keep Dorchester they would, as previously, be required to pay tuition and buy books, and would retard the county's progress in furnishing public schools. While parents were pleased that the county was ready to cooperate in financing a free school, they worried about its quality and the loss of their nearly one-hundred-year-old community treasure. Morton and Brownlee assured them that the buildings would remain and the AMA would continue to assist them through the Dorchester Community Center. When the vote was taken, not a single negative one was cast, though many citizens later regretted that they had not opposed the move. Classes continued to be held at Dorchester until fall 1942, when the new state-accredited Liberty County Training School opened at Riceboro.[37]

Building a new high school in Macon took longer and cost the AMA far more.[38] Although the Bibb County board of education had summarily rejected his 1933 overture for cooperation, Brownlee again approached the county superintendent in 1936 about the possibility of creating a free accredited black public high school for Macon and with a similar result. Cousins, as at Dorchester, played a positive role. In 1939, he encouraged the board to cooperate and urged Brownlee to try again. The following year, Cousins advised Brownlee to inform Bibb County superintendent Walter P. Jones that Ballard would discontinue grades eight and nine as of June 1940 in order to concentrate upon the upper three grades. This would prove to Jones that the AMA was serious, and "prepare the way for the next steps in the years to come." Dropping two grades would save only about $1,000, "but the primary purpose in all this is to move forward educationally in Macon rather than save money." Outside factors also altered the city board's attitude toward Ballard. The Macon board had profited from Ballard for years because the state had paid a per capita allowance for the three hundred Ballard students, money which never assisted blacks but helped provide good schools for whites. When in 1940 the department of education began assigning money based on the number of children actually taught, the Macon superintendent became more amenable. In 1941, the AMA voted to deed Ballard School and equipment to the board of education for one dollar and share expenses for five years provided the board maintained an A-rated school, retained its black teachers and principal James A. Colston, kept the AMA salary schedule, and hired as future teachers only graduates of accredited colleges.[39] The board rejected the proposal because it could not promise to maintain the AMA's salary schedule and it was reluctant to keep present teachers. Apparently it feared that white teacher Louis Mounts would remain.[40] As Morton wrote, "all our plotting and planning . . . has borne no fruit." Finally in June 1942, Brownlee and Jones, prodded by Cousins, agreed that the county would exercise full control over Ballard and pay most teachers, while the AMA would pay Principal Colston and two teachers and transfer Ballard equipment to the board;

in addition, annually the AMA and the county each would place $5,000 in a fund to be used eventually to build a new accredited high school. Ballard property remained in AMA hands but continued as the high school until the new building was constructed. After numerous delays caused by war short-ages and AMA-board disagreements, Ballard-Hudson High opened in 1949 with 1,200 students and a staff of fifty-five. Fittingly, Brownlee spoke at the November dedication.[41]

After much wrangling and multiple conferences, Morton and Brownlee persuaded local boards to bear a small share of teachers' salaries at Lincoln School and Trinity, thereby allowing students to attend tuition free. The ar-rangement began at Lincoln in 1937–38 and at Trinity in 1943–44. Within three years, high school enrollment at Lincoln jumped from 52 to 260; it in-creased to 430 in six years and to 700 by 1948. Despite the often consider-able loss of quality, public schools clearly reached far more pupils than AMA tuition schools. Though many were distressed at the loss of interracial fac-ulties, other school patrons agreed with the AMA that the gain in students warranted the loss of principle. Brownlee called the agreement at Lincoln "a stride forward interracially" since it was the first time the AMA had been able to cooperate effectively with local officials at Marion, but the Lincoln staff severely suffered from the change. Morton wrote in 1944 that "the teachers have to take so many insults from state and county officials, that I am con-stantly embarrassed and ashamed."[42] The AMA continued to contribute a majority of the budget, but by 1943 the county paid five of twelve teachers. As Brownlee said, "This is one form of what we call a creeping-up, coopera-tive transition from a private, tuition-charging school to a free school."[43] In 1947, Morton declared Lincoln "practically" a state and county institution. The AMA continued to pay the principal, an art and a music teacher, and it operated its community center which included a dropout prevention pro-gram; but Morton was reluctant to deed property to the county board since she feared it would not maintain a quality program. As late as 1954, the AMA still gave the county free use of Lincoln property and equipment and paid a portion of the principal's salary, but it was technically a public facility.[44]

Morton was also slow to press the issue of complete transfer of Trinity School. When state agent E. G. McGehee suggested in 1942 that the city and county would like to take over Trinity, she replied that the city al-ready controlled the grade school and that school and the teaching staff were "in a deplorable condition." Nevertheless, in 1943 Brownlee negotiated an agreement with Limestone County superintendent Walter A. Owens for the county to contribute $3,000 and allow Morton to select the teachers, and Trinity became a free public school. The county initially was often late making payments, but by 1948 the county and state furnished $15,615 of Trinity's $30,465 budget. Although black principal W. Judson King managed to maintain an accredited school, county officials constantly interfered. In 1947, the county temporarily stopped bus service so the children could work. King reported that some of the parents "were prompted—that is a mild word for it—to request that the buses be stopped for two or three weeks. These were the most timid of our country people on whom our community groups are working to get the buses back." The following year King warned that there was trouble on the horizon with the board. "The fact that so many Negroes are going to school some each year has frightened them stiff."[45] Despite tension with the county board, Morton and Brownlee were now eager to reach some agreement before Brownlee retired in October 1950. In June 1950, the AMA promised to deed the Trinity School property to the Limestone County board of education with the stipulations that Trinity be continued at the present site for at least five years, the AMA pay the board $10,000 a year for two years to be matched by $40,000 from the board to build new classrooms and purchase equipment, the board take full responsibility for salaries, and the present inventory remain at Trinity. In addition, the AMA appropriated $12,000 to the school for 1950–51 plus $5,000 toward the building program. In September a state official informed Principal King that the board expected blacks to raise part of its $40,000 share, and King wrote, "clearly brought to my attention that as an employee of local authorities I am not to talk out of school." The board did not fully meet its obligations until 1957, at which time the AMA transmitted a deed and $20,000 to the board. The county board closed Trinity in 1970 rather than integrate it.[46] By 1950, all AMA elementary and secondary schools except Fessenden Academy had closed, had merged with, or were cooperating with the public system. All efforts to make Fessenden a public school failed, and it closed in 1951.

Even though the AMA was funded in part by church donations, the Congregationalists had a tradition of supporting public education and, despite occasional internal tension over the relative value of parochial or secular education, the association continued that trend. Secretaries Beard, Douglass, and Brownlee all favored religious training but were even more devoted to public education, and through persuasion, pressure, diplomacy, encouraging the black community to demand their rights, and financial inducement, they significantly contributed to the development of public schools in the South.

6
AMA Colleges, 1890–1950

AMA colleges were "committed by history and character 'to education for liberation,'" Dr. Wesley A. Hotchkiss declared in 1966. The AMA concept of equality led it from the beginning to demand that African Americans have access to all levels of education. As the *American Missionary* stated in 1893, "The only true ground to take—the only one sanctioned by the Constitution and Christianity—is that the Negroes are men and are entitled to equal rights in church and state, and that they must be prepared for the exercise of these rights." In 1865, recently emancipated blacks were an "undeveloped race," AMA officers believed, but their condition resulted from slavery, not racial characteristics, and education could free them from the baneful effects of servitude. Elementary and secondary education were state responsibilities, they argued, and such association schools should be retained only until states assumed their rightful duties,[1] but black colleges should be permanent.[2] Between 1866 and 1881, the AMA chartered eight "colleges" and assisted in the founding of Howard University. Building and maintaining these colleges was no easy task. For decades higher education for blacks was fiercely contested by whites in both North and South. In 2002, Allen and Jewell stated that "one inescapable lesson is that African Americans have found the road to higher education stony, fraught with obstacles and resistance. In many respects," they add, the pursuit of college training was "an apt metaphor for the larger Black struggles for citizenship, self-determination, and personhood."[3]

Though established primarily for black Americans, the AMA colleges welcomed all races. The founders recognized that few whites would attend, but as Edward P. Smith said when proposing Atlanta University, "I would, by all means open the school to all without distinction of color. Practically, the whites will exclude themselves for awhile—not long—for I am confident we can make it such a school as will attract them over the high wall of prejudice, and in the course of years, will grow to the character and power of a school like Oberlin." Smith was overly optimistic. The only white students in most AMA colleges—except Berea, which had almost equal numbers of black and white students until Kentucky state law mandated segregation in 1904, and Straight, which for a few years taught whites in its law schools—were faculty children.[4]

The establishment of black colleges was, of course, a long-range plan. Capital, facilities, faculty, and qualified students were scarce immediately after the Civil War, but AMA officers dreamed of a day when black youth would have equal opportunity for higher education. When a critic chided the association for calling its chartered institutions universities and colleges when initially they were primary and secondary schools, Secretary Beard replied, "I was at church yesterday. It was Children's Day. The minister baptized twenty babies. I noticed that every one of them got an adult name. The colleges and universities were named all right. Now you bring them up." Horace Mann Bond said the names indicated that "the founders took emancipation seriously, believing that the Civil War had settled . . . the issue of human equality" in the country and that they were "applying, to the newly freed population, the ancient faith in the efficacy of higher education to elevate a people."[5]

Contrary to white southern charges, the colleges did not offer higher education before students were ready. Fisk, clearly the most advanced AMA college, quickly assembled a strong faculty and graduated its first four students in 1875. There were no graduates the following year, and only two in 1877. By 1883, the school enrolled thirty-three college students and enjoyed a growing reputation. A white Nashville reporter in 1885 described Fisk as "the most important and influential institution of its kind in the United States." Among visitors between 1885 and 1900 were Theodore Roosevelt, Frederick Douglass, Adm. George Dewey, Ohio senator John Sherman, and former President Rutherford B. Hayes. Fisk's increasing fame attracted students from the North including W. E. B. Du Bois from Great Barrington, Massachusetts, who graduated in 1888. Du Bois viewed the Fisk faculty as "inspiring and beneficial" and his years on campus as a time of "splendid inspiration." He enrolled at Harvard in 1889, where he found not better teachers, only teachers better known. Nevertheless, the college remained Fisk's smallest department for many years.[6]

Talladega, next in quality to Fisk in the early years, developed more slowly. Organized in 1867 and chartered as a college in 1869, it did not accept its first freshman class of two, Zachariah Jones and John R. Savage, until 1891. They graduated in 1895. Three diplomas were awarded in 1897 and one in 1898. The AMA colleges accepted only those students they believed qualified, and with the exception of a few students such as Du Bois they had to "raise" their own. Zachariah Jones was trained in the Talladega theology department, and John Savage was an 1890 normal school graduate.[7] As late as 1900, Tougaloo College, Tillotson College, and Straight University still concentrated primarily on elementary, secondary, and teacher training. There were only 103 college students enrolled in all AMA institutions in 1890, but that number represented almost one-fifth of all students in southern black colleges.[8]

In the meantime, the colleges emphasized teacher training and college preparatory classes. In 1891, field superintendent W. E. C. Wright encountered AMA-trained black public school teachers throughout the South. In town after town in Texas, he said, he found public schools staffed by graduates of Straight University, Tillotson College, and even the more remote Talladega and Tougaloo. Wright attended the State Teachers' Association meeting in Huntsville, Alabama, where the organization's president informed him that "the great majority of the four hundred present owed their education, directly or indirectly," to the AMA. By 1899, Straight had graduated approximately 120 normal students, and an even larger number were teaching without completing the course. A majority of the one hundred who had graduated from Tougaloo's normal and academy courses were teachers. Of Fisk graduates still living in 1900 and known to Fisk officials, 12 were principals and 45 were teachers in high or normal schools, and 34 were principals and 120 instructors in grammar schools. At least seven hundred Fiskites who never graduated became teachers, and scores of others directed schools during summers, including Du Bois who taught in Lebanon, Tennessee, in a small log hut minus doors and windows in 1886. After three months in which he learned much about the condition of rural blacks, was seduced by his landlady, and was threatened by local whites, Du Bois wrote that he would not take $200 for his experience, but would not go through it again for $300. As early as 1873, Talladega had forty-six normal and seventeen higher normal students, and its 1890–91 catalog boasted with some truth that Talladega afforded "facilities for the training of teachers second to none in the South."[9]

The number of college-preparatory students at AMA schools steadily increased from 151 in 1894 to 198 in 1895 and 330 in 1896, but the effect on college enrollment was negligible. AMA colleges had fewer than 150 students in 1900.[10] Indeed at the turn of the century, the outlook for black colleges was bleak and the mission societies were courting bankruptcy. No black college had sufficient staff, physical plant, scientific equipment, or operating expenses, and none had endowments of any consequence. The AMA's approximately $210,000 appropriation comprised almost twenty-five percent of all northern philanthropic funds for southern black education in 1910. Collections for black education were declining in the North, and southern states furnished almost no aid. The only growth in funds came from blacks themselves. In 1911, H. Paul Douglass reminded the AMA executive committee that in the last few years, despite poverty and discrimination, tuition payments made by black students had risen fifty percent while AMA appropriations had remained static.[11] The impoverishment of both the colleges and their constituents made increase in enrollment difficult.

Despite their defects, the colleges had made significant positive contributions by 1900. W. E. B. Du Bois, who thought the training of teachers was black colleges' most important function to date, wrote in 1903, "Few persons realize how vast a work, how mighty a revolution has been thus accomplished." These colleges "born of the faith and sacrifice of the abolitionists" trained thousands of black teachers. Putting "teachers of their own race and blood" in black schools "placed before the eyes of almost every Negro child an attainable ideal." In the same essay, "The Talented Tenth," Du Bois proclaimed the missionary colleges "trained in Greek and Latin and mathematics, 2000 men; and these men trained a full 50,000 others in morals and manners, and they in turn taught thrift and the alphabet to nine millions of men . . . It was a miracle—the most wonderful peace-battle of the 19th century." In addition, the colleges had produced ministers, physicians, dentists, pharmacists, attorneys, businessmen, and other professionals. These colleges were imperfect, Du Bois admitted, but a "crushing rejoinder" to sneering critics was that "in a single generation they had put thirty thousand teachers in the South" who had "wiped out the illiteracy of the majority of the black people of the land." Those teachers included the many normal and secondary as well as college students.[12]

The colleges grew slowly in the first decade of the twentieth century. Tougaloo, Straight, and Tillotson seldom enrolled more than a few students in college classes.[13] Tillotson had three in 1906 and Tougaloo six in 1908. All faculty, except at Fisk, taught secondary and college-preparatory as well as college classes. The Carnegie Foundation for Advancement of Teaching's definition of a college required that six faculty teach college classes only. Talladega employed its first full-time college teacher in 1909, and did not fully meet the Carnegie requirement until 1921. Even so, it was clearly the best opportunity for black Alabama youth to secure a college education. In 1903, Booker T. Washington wrote Talladega treasurer Edwin C. Silsby about Rhodes Scholarships. "Talladega College is the only institution in Alabama from which we can hope to have a colored student go," Washington stated, "and I believe that if the matter is taken in hand in time enough and all conditions understood that there will be a chance for a Talladega man to go to

Oxford which of course will be a great thing not only for the college but for the race." While Talladega was flattered by Washington's suggestion, the first black Rhodes Scholar, Alain Leroy Locke, graduated from Harvard, not a lowly Alabama black college.[14] In 1908, the AMA taught 10,592 elementary students, 1,166 secondary, 1,696 special students, 147 theological students, and only 159 college students. This small number, Secretary Douglass assured constituents, proved that colleges had "served conditions rather than theories" and took only qualified students. President Isaac M. Agard announced in 1910 that Tillotson now offered "a full collegiate education," though most effort still went into normal and preparatory courses. Straight and Tougaloo were in much the same situation. There remained a great need for all types of schools, but the AMA gradually shifted funds and effort upward. In 1918, the number of elementary students had declined to 4,624 and the secondary students had increased to 3,039 and college to 351, a natural progression of students since 1908. In the same year black colleges awarded 319 bachelor degrees. Fisk gave twenty-eight, Talladega sixteen, Atlanta eleven, and Straight and Tillotson one each.[15]

In the face of southern white hostility and dwindling missionary funds, H. Paul Douglass, who became AMA superintendent of education in 1906, encouraged the appointment of southern white and black men to AMA college boards of trustees. He hoped that southern white trustees would become sufficiently interested in the schools to gather financial support and also act as buffers against those most actively opposed to black higher education. The results were mixed. Blacks were rightly suspicious of white appointees. With few exceptions, such as Vermont-born, Union Army veteran Ira Hobart Evans at Tillotson, most early southern white trustees were strict segregationists and only tepidly supported liberal arts training for blacks. Evans served as president of the Tillotson board from 1909 to 1920 and donated at least $20,000 of his own funds to the school. On the other hand, another white Tillotson trustee and banker, under strong white pressure, resigned from the board and joined the Ku Klux Klan "because the risk did not justify his service."[16] The only white citizen in Mississippi that Douglass could initially persuade to join the Tougaloo board of trustees was Bishop Charles B. Galloway, Methodist Episcopal Church, South, who had publicly declared blacks as men and brothers, eligible for any privileges and agencies that fitted them "for service in the Kingdom of God." Despite Galloway's refusal to share meals with black trustees, Douglass defended his appointment by saying, "because they are so sound on the main issue, it is possible for men of such views to accede to the popular practices of their section in non-essentials like formal racial recognition." When Galloway died, he was succeeded by another bishop, Theodore D. Bratton.[17] Douglass, an out-spoken defender of black rights, temporarily abandoned principle in pursuit of the long-term goal of greater support for black colleges. While some blacks agreed with Douglass, many others protested and demanded more black trustees to counter southern whites. A few blacks had served on AMA college boards of trustees since the early 1890s. Former student Yancey B. Sims was elected to the Talladega board of trustees in 1893 and was succeeded by Nathan B. Young in 1896. George W. Crawford, Talladega class of 1900, joined the board in 1904, and was one of the college's most influential trustees for four decades. George W. Moore, an 1881 Fisk graduate, became a Fisk University trustee in 1885. Still, though blacks remained a minority for many years, they demanded and eventually received greater representation on college boards. The AMA was slower to add women to college boards of trustees, however. Mrs. Arch Trawick was appointed to the Fisk board in 1918, while Juliette Derricotte was the first woman so honored by Talladega in 1926. In 1933, Mrs. Lucius R. Eastman joined the boards of trustees at Straight and Tougaloo, and in the same year Fannie C. Williams, an alumna, was appointed to the Straight College board.[18]

Adding southern trustees failed to alleviate the colleges' dire financial circumstances. Most blacks remained in poverty, southern whites were generally indifferent, and appeals to philanthropic foundations commonly fell upon deaf ears unless requests were for industrial training. AMA schools were reduced to annual begging campaigns to avoid ending the year with a deficit. Faculty constantly solicited northern friends and churches, and presidents were occupied primarily with collections. In 1905, Talladega president Benjamin M. Nyce complained that financial crises prevented any efforts to promote and strengthen the college. In 1908 Fisk president James G. Merrill, plagued by the enemy of all presidents of black colleges, lack of money, resigned in frustration. His valiant efforts to secure foundation support resulted mainly in a $5,000 Slater Fund grant to add a department of applied sciences for secondary students.[19] "The only real difficulty is the money side," Merrill informed trustees, "and this difficulty is so great that I have come to the conclusion that I no longer have a right to continue in my present position."[20]

The only significant foundation support to Fisk in the first decade of the twentieth century came through the efforts of Booker T. Washington and his wife, Margaret Murray Washington, an 1889 Fisk graduate. Though Washington saw the *American Missionary* as a northern journal that had not fallen under his spell, and had written in 1898 that AMA officers "do everything in a sly way to hinder work at Tuskegee," he often hired association college graduates for his faculty, occasionally publicly commended the AMA's work, and later sent sons Booker Jr. to Fisk and Ernest Davidson to Talladega. Fisk had unsuccessfully solicited Andrew Carnegie for years, but in 1908, in part as a favor to Mrs. Washington, Carnegie gave $20,000 for a Fisk library. In 1909, Fisk elected Washington, the most prominent black man in America in the view of philanthropic foundations, to its board of trustees. Fisk president George A. Gates deemed it essential to announce that Washington's selection to the board did not mean, as some Fisk alumni feared, that Fisk would move toward industrial education. Washington had joined the Fisk board, Gates added, "to indicate and emphasize his conviction concerning the value of Fisk's work." Washington rarely attended trustee meetings, but he continued to assist Fisk in fund collecting. In 1910, he wrote Carnegie a personal letter saying, "Fisk University I consider is doing the best work of any institution in the South in purely college directions for the education of our people." Despite Washington's assistance to Fisk, he sometimes found it necessary to rebuke President Gates for the latter's public criticisms of industrial education.[21]

Talladega officials also appealed to Washington for assistance and so coveted his influence with philanthropists that they may have fired William Pickens, black professor of Greek, Latin, and German. Pickens publicly criticized industrial education and Washington in numerous speeches, and Washington complained to the AMA that Pickens repeatedly said that "Tuskegee teaches girls to wash clothes; Talladega teaches them to think." Pickens muted his public criticism of Tuskegee, yet strengthened his ties to Washington's critics. President John M. Metcalf wrote Washington several times requesting fund-raising support, but received no reply. When he informed Washington in 1914 that Pickens had been dismissed, Washington immediately responded with an offer of assistance. Though Pickens had been accused of being uncooperative and missing too many classes while recruiting and soliciting for the NAACP, Washington's views may have influenced the decision to release him.[22]

In 1912, in honor of the fiftieth anniversary of the Emancipation Proclamation, the AMA launched a million-dollar campaign to endow its colleges. Booker T. Washington endorsed the drive, commending the colleges for providing black leadership and the AMA for its unselfish devotion "to the welfare of the South." But slow collections led the association to abandon the effort in 1916 after Fisk's portion had been collected.[23] By 1915, the only black colleges with appreciable endowments were two industrial schools: Hampton with $2,709,344 and Tuskegee with $1,942,112.[24] Lack of adequate funds stunted the growth and seriously affected the quality of AMA colleges. Douglass described the college standards in 1908 as "high rather than broad." Most had "narrow and traditional curriculums," and probably none met the requirements of either northern or southern education associations. Three years later Douglass told the executive committee that the AMA was at the head of all societies supporting black education, but at present "we are not maintaining our higher institutions in an adequate way and in comparison with the best similar schools of other denominations."[25]

Despite foundation indifference to the liberal arts and the AMA's friendship with Washington, it never wavered in its determination to offer a liberal arts education to its students. At the first and second Monhonk Conferences in the Catskills in 1890 and 1891 to discuss black education, Samuel Chapman Armstrong of Hampton Institute and others argued for the Hampton model of industrial education. AMA field secretary Joseph E. Roy, "after making a brilliant defense of blacks' right to higher education, declared that it was 'too late in the history of civilization to impose any repression upon any class of people.'" In 1898, William Hayes Ward, editor of the *Independent* and longtime chairman of the AMA executive committee, chastised President William McKinley for praising Tuskegee for giving blacks practical training rather than "attempting the unattainable" by offering higher literary education. "What there is 'unattainable' to the Negro, or what school offers the unattainable, we do not know," Ward stated.[26] The AMA was not an enemy of industrial education. It approved this type of schooling for both blacks and whites, but not to the exclusion of liberal and higher education. It gladly accepted a $7,500 Slater Fund appropriation to Talladega, Tougaloo, and Straight in 1892, but this was for elementary grades only and did not alter the regular curriculum. In 1903, the *American Missionary* pleaded for liberal arts. "Once let caste be separated by race, color, education and a separate industrial training, and there is no hope for future equality in the republic." "Industrial training and toil has its place and value," the *American Missionary* editorialized in another issue, "but the last chapter will not be written until the door of every honorable employment and profession swings open to the blackest face God's sunshine ever made"—and for that colleges were essential. W. T. B. Williams, field agent for the John F. Slater Fund, praised Talladega in 1906 as "one of the few schools that make a reasonable bid for the development along the lines of higher education," but, he added, "it has yet to prove that it can give industrial work its proper place." Industrial education never took root even in AMA primary and secondary schools and was not a factor in colleges. In his 1916 government report on black education, to be discussed later, Thomas Jesse Jones, director of research for the Phelps-Stokes Fund, complained that only those who worked on the farm to earn tuition obtained farm experience at Talladega. He found no industrial training in colleges at Straight, Tougaloo, Tillotson, and Fisk. Tougaloo owned a large farm and produced much of the cafeteria food, but Jones regretted that agriculture was taught only to eighth graders and first-year normal students. Farmwork, as at Talladega, was performed solely by those earning school expenses. Tillotson offered cooking, sewing, and manual arts only through the ninth grade.[27]

Poverty did not prevent a steady, if uneven and slow, improvement of college quality and faculty, especially at Talladega and Fisk. While many of the first teachers were ministers or teachers better suited to secondary education work, Fisk had some well-trained instructors almost from the beginning. Adam K. Spence, educated at Olivet College, Oberlin, and the University of Michigan, gave up a professorship of foreign languages at Michigan to go to Fisk in 1870. After Du Bois studied at Harvard and in Germany, he pronounced Spence "a great Greek scholar by any comparison." Spence's brother-in-law, Frederick A. Chase, left the presidency of Lyons Collegiate Institute in Lyons (now Clinton), Iowa, in 1872 to establish a science department at Fisk. Henry Swift DeForest, a Yale graduate who became Talladega president in 1879, was also an able classics teacher. The number of women appointed to the college faculty was especially unusual. Women dominated primary education in the United States, but were rare at coeducational colleges. Helen C. Morgan, an 1866 Oberlin graduate who went to Fisk in 1869 as a Latin professor and remained for thirty-eight years, was one of the first women in the country to attain full professor rank at a coeducational college. She declined to leave Fisk for a higher salary at Vassar. In 1910, Talladega employed Clara M. Standish, a 1904 Phi Beta Kappa graduate of Tufts College, to teach chemistry. Standish, who described Talladega as a "centre of enlightenment," remained for twenty years, sent many science students for graduate degrees, and took her place as department head. Standish was, black colleague Marion Cuthbert wrote, "one of those teachers who gave Talladega character in personality, in human relations, and in intellectual achievement." Standish and Morgan seemed to have had no less influence in faculty committees than male teachers.[28]

All colleges had interracial faculties, though at first most blacks were in primary and secondary classes; but as more blacks earned degrees, they joined the college ranks. William Pickens, who left Talladega as a junior and graduated Phi Beta Kappa from Yale in 1903, was hired at Talladega in 1904; and Fisk employed James Dallas Burrus, one of its first four graduates, as an instructor in mathematics in 1875. In 1915, Thomas Jesse Jones listed AMA college faculty by race as follows: Talladega, twenty-nine white, twelve black; Straight, seventeen white, thirteen black; Tillotson, fourteen white, six black;

Tougaloo, twenty-nine white, two black; and Fisk, thirty-one white and fourteen black. At this time, a majority of the black faculty were still teaching below the college rank, but the number increased rapidly after 1920. Many of the first black college faculty were young men fresh from northern graduate study. They secretly thought "that those over thirty were finished," Lura Beam recounted, and "found the dedication of elderly whites quite a bore." Older faculty who were department chairs, lived in scarce campus housing, and occupied most positions of importance, the young men believed, blocked their own dreams of promotions and the convenience of campus homes. It was often single, older white women who stood in their way. Beam once saw a letter from one young black male teacher to another which read, "If that old bitch from Massachusetts would ever die or get through here, I could begin to live."[29] No doubt there was tension between black and white faculty, but the degree to which they lived and worked in harmony in a racially conscious, hostile South was remarkable. Indeed, the above slur may have been based as much on gender and age as race.

College students were so few in number and so mixed with other pupils that no clear picture of them emerges in early college records. Though occasional students such as Du Bois hailed from the North, most came from AMA schools, either the better secondary institutions or the college-preparatory departments. Most were from poor, uneducated families and worked to remain in school. Nearly all took summer jobs, many as teachers, and enrollment was often small in the fall because students were picking cotton. During the growing season some Tougaloo women still followed the plow, the *American Missionary* reported in 1907, "that they may make school possible for themselves." Yet all were not first-generation students. In 1903, twenty-four children of alumni enrolled at Talladega, and in 1907 the AMA noted that children of former graduates increased each year, and in nearly all cases "their heredity and the effects of better home environment are quite evident." Edwin C. Silsby, who knew both students and alumni at Talladega better than anyone, said the greatest difference between second-generation students and others was that the former were more likely to stay in school. They rarely left before graduation, and they came with a larger fund of general knowledge. Alumni children were also better able to pay full tuition.[30]

Rich or poor, students were governed by rigid school rules, and those who refused to conform were removed. A Talladegan was suspended for having sex with the woman who eventually became his wife, and in 1895 a college woman was removed for "misconduct" with a male student off campus during summer vacation. Douglass said Christian education required effective moral control. "Discipline is therefore a sterner reality in these schools than in the average American college. The goings and comings of students is under strict limitations. The oversight of girls is especially conscientious and watchful." Even Douglass, however, questioned the need for such severity with college students. Chapel was mandatory, and Sabbath church attendance was encouraged. The AMA was nonsectarian, however, and, to the chagrin of Congregational supporters, made little effort to proselytize. To Beard, a Congregational minister, church expansion was secondary to education. Douglass left a pastorate when he was unable to alter race relations in Springfield, Missouri, but he never believed "in literal fire and brimstone." Students were far more likely to be Methodists and Baptists than Congregationalists. In 1907, of 510 Straight pupils, 207 were Catholic, 139 Methodist, 72 Baptist, and only 69 Congregational. The remainder were of other Protestant denominations. Only ten Straight students claimed no denominational choice.[31]

Students generally assumed they were fortunate to be in college and accepted rigid rules with minor grumbling, but, as illustrated by Talladega students, they rebelled when they believed they had been wronged. In 1887, the AMA executive committee imposed, over Treasurer Silsby's objection, a cheaper food plan at Talladega with faculty and students eating separately and different fare. Women students led a revolt that forced discontinuance of the new plan, and faculty and students continued to dine together on the same food. Several Talladega women vowed to boycott classes and work assignments in 1895 in protest of disciplinary measures taken against a fellow student. President DeForest, who met with Georgia Patterson, one of the ringleaders, told the Prudential Committee, "I do not remember ever to have met such defiant insolence either in my experience as a county-school teacher, or in my connection with two college faculties in the north." Patterson claimed that faculty "walked over students" because of their race. When Patterson and Emma Ratcliffe were sent home, six male sympathizers boarded the train and rode part of the way with them. President Benjamin M. Nyce provoked a revolt in 1905 when he appointed a southern white to assist the farm superintendent. The previous assistant had been a black man. A former state legislator and friend of the school recommended the assistant, and Nyce, wishing to accommodate a southern supporter, made the appointment. Five student representatives met with Nyce, charged that his appointment of a white southerner was "a blow to their manhood," and demanded the new assistant's removal. Students sent a forcefully worded petition to the AMA which ended, "Through the years we have believed in and loved your sacrificial labors for us, and the aims and ideals of your great organization have developed in our breast. From . . . these aims and ideals, we cannot and will not retreat." Secretary Beard understood the petitioners' suspicions, but argued that racial prejudice was wrong whether directed against black or white. "This is so clearly a case of prejudice," he wrote Nyce, "that we can not go back upon our history to sustain the appeal of the students." As a result "a large number" of disgruntled protesters left school. Most students eventually returned, but they had stood strong against an unwise administrative decision until convinced of their error.[32] They had accepted the AMA's claim that they were equal and should fight for their rights.

In many ways 1917 was a watershed year for AMA colleges and black higher education. Thomas Jesse Jones investigated black education for the Federal Bureau of Education between 1914 to 1916, and in 1917 published a two-volume survey critical of black colleges including those of the AMA. Scholars have disagreed as to Jones's motives. Du Bois charged that Jones emphasized industrial and agricultural training to the detriment of academic education, and said Jones claimed black colleges "must" cooperate with the white South, and called for unity of purpose among educational boards. Since white southerners were generally hostile to black liberal arts colleges and the General Education Board (GEB), created by John D. Rockefeller in 1902, was the most powerful of the educational foundations and had practically surrendered to the white South, Du Bois proclaimed these might be dangerous suggestions. James D. Anderson believes Jones "espoused the Hampton-Tuskegee philosophy," while Anderson and Moss in *Dangerous Donations,* not necessarily sympathetic with Jones's views, suggest he was basically advocating the "progressive era" curriculum he thought best for both black and white schools.[33] Jones reported that of the dozens of black colleges in the South only thirty-three offered any courses of college grade and they enrolled a mere 1,643 students. Only Fisk, Howard, and Meharry Medical College, Jones declared, had "student bodies, teaching force and equipment, and income sufficient to warrant the characterization of 'college.'" There were too many black colleges and they were handicapped by emphasis on a classical curriculum, he added.[34]

Jones was not particularly impressed with AMA schools other than the independent Fisk. Talladega was described as "a school of secondary and collegiate grade with a large elementary enrollment and a theological department." He did add that it was the only black school in Alabama offering college work. Tougaloo's secondary and teacher-training work were effective, and its college course selection good, but Jones concluded the staff was too "fully occupied with the complex system of secondary courses" to handle college courses, and the present number of college students, twenty, did not warrant the additional expense. He recommended that "the college department be strengthened and developed essentially as a college for teachers." Tillotson's teaching force and equipment were "too limited to attempt college work." Straight was "a well managed secondary school with a large elementary enrollment and a few pupils in college classes." Jones advised that efforts to maintain a college "be not allowed to hamper the development of secondary courses adapted to the needs of the pupils." He suggested that Fisk and Howard be adequately financed and that Talladega, Straight, Tougaloo, and Tillotson, among others, be developed into junior colleges.[35]

There was a chorus of black criticism of the Jones survey. Among blacks, historian and founder in 1915 of the Association for the Study of Negro Life and History Carter G. Woodson stated, Jones's "name was mentioned only to be condemned." But as Anderson and Moss point out in *Dangerous Donations,* "if the Jones Report was part of a master plan to restrict black higher education, it failed miserably." Within a decade the number of black college students increased eightfold.[36] There were many reasons for the growth, but the Jones study stimulated support. It definitely affected the AMA. Between 1916 and 1930, the AMA increased its appropriations for black education by five times, and hastened the closing of secondary schools, in part so more could be spent on colleges. In 1921, the AMA dropped the last two years of study at Tillotson and made it a junior college. It also upgraded Brick School and LeMoyne Institute to junior colleges in 1925 and 1927 respectively, and boosted the latter to a four-year college in 1931.[37]

Faculty were indignant when Jones described Talladega's college program as so weak that it should cease to be a four-year college and be developed as a junior college, but ten years later after significant improvement in faculty and curriculum, Dean James T. Cater admitted Jones was correct. Talladega in 1927 was so much superior it hardly resembled the school Jones evaluated in 1916.[38] Black college enrollment grew for other reasons as well. Foundation pressure and support along with states attempting to head off possible desegregation created new high schools, therefore producing more potential students. Also there were larger numbers of second- and third-generation-educated families who could afford to send their children to college, and finally blacks demanded college education for their youth. Black agency cannot be ignored when dealing with higher education. Blacks insisted upon education, including liberal studies. As James D. Anderson has so ably shown, black administrators and instructors managed to teach academic subjects even in county training high schools designed to be basically industrial.[39] And finally, northern philanthropic foundations which previously had financed primarily Tuskegee, Hampton, and their offshoots began to channel funds into liberal arts colleges.[40]

In 1909, H. Paul Douglass lamented "the preoccupation of philanthropy" with industrial education which "made the financial problems of the colleges well-nigh desperate." Du Bois complained in 1912 that during its first ten years the GEB had given $2,107,500 to southern higher education, practically all of it to whites, and in 1916 he wrote that the GEB's appropriation had shown once again "that it does not believe in higher education" for blacks. Yet in 1930, Du Bois conceded that despite its earlier mistakes, the GEB had been "in later years the salvation of education among Negroes." A year earlier the GEB had confessed that prior to 1919 it "had not felt warranted in contributing to any considerable extent to the endowment of Negro colleges." But between 1924 and 1931 it gave $25 million to black schools, much of it to colleges, and the AMA received a sizeable share.[41]

Although the GEB gave limited funds to black colleges prior to 1919, it made an exception for Fisk. In 1911, the GEB promised $60,000 to Fisk if it could raise an additional $240,000, and three years later, a GEB committee speculated whether it should "take hold" of Fisk, the most promising black college, and develop it as a model. Later, Fisk president Fayette Avery McKenzie seized upon this knowledge and requested aid in securing an endowment. In 1921, the GEB pledged $500,000 toward a $1 million endowment if the university could raise the remainder. Shortly after Fisk collected on the pledge in 1927, the GEB granted an additional $400,000 to construct and endow a new library.[42] Talladega had less immediate success. For years school officials vainly solicited the GEB for assistance until in 1921 the board granted $35,000—later increased to $49,000—toward the construction and equipping of a new science building; and in 1922 it gave $5,000 toward enhancing faculty salaries. Then, in January 1928, GEB and Rosenwald Fund officials visited Talladega and concluded "that for serious college work, this is now the best Negro college in the South."[43] Shortly thereafter, the GEB agreed to give $500,000 toward a $1 million endowment if Talladega could raise a half million from other sources within five years. In order to assist, the Rosenwald Fund granted $15,000 for 1929–30, $10,000 for 1930–31, and $5,000 for 1931–32 for annual expenses. Unfortunately the Depression intervened, and Talladega was unable to raise its share until 1936. The GEB generously extended the time limit, and on April 21, 1936, the board of trustees announced that the million-dollar endowment dream was a reality.[44]

When the foundations finally began supporting black colleges, they concentrated their efforts on the most prominent schools, which meant that Tougaloo, Straight, and Tillotson received little support. In 1904, a Tougaloo teacher directly appealed to former Brown University classmate John D. Rockefeller Jr., who forwarded the teacher's letter to the GEB and replied to him that since his father had founded the GEB all applications for southern education went to the board. The appeal failed, as did requests in 1904, 1908, and 1920. Finally in 1924, the GEB promised $25,000 for an academic building if the school could raise a like amount. GEB field agent Leo M. Favrot visited Tougaloo in 1926 and reported that it had the best facilities and faculty of any Mississippi black college, it had superior plant and equipment, the AMA had "greatly increased" its appropriations, and there was "an atmosphere of culture and refinement about the school." But apparently GEB officials were unimpressed since they made no further grants until 1930, when the GEB gave one-third of the cost of a $100,000 building.[45] The best Straight College could get was a $5,000 grant for scientific equipment in 1926.[46] Despite repeated appeals, Tillotson never received GEB funds. In 1931, the GEB rejected President Mary E. Branch's application for a paltry $2,000 for biology equipment with the comment that its policy was not to assist schools not aided in the past, and that foundations were concentrating on a few centers of strategic importance. It did, however, give Bethune-Cookman $2,000 in 1934. Mary McLeod Bethune apparently had more influence than the less well-known Branch.[47]

Dillard University received by far the greatest foundation support of any AMA college. Anderson and Moss claim in *Dangerous Donations* that by 1930 the GEB and other foundations set the "philanthropic agenda for the South," and though religious givers still made large donations for black education, the missionary societies' influence had declined.[48] The AMA and other mission societies still played a major role in black higher education, but they badly needed foundation help and adapted their policies to appeal to the foundations; and the GEB and Julius Rosenwald Fund led the move to create one of the AMA's best schools, Dillard University.[49] In 1928, James P. O'Brien, president of Straight College, solicited a $500 contribution from Edgar B. Stern, a well-known New Orleans businessman and son-in-law of Julius Rosenwald.[50] Stern replied that if $500 was all O'Brien needed he should be able to secure that from the AMA, but if he was "ever interested in bigger things, you will find me ready to help." A few days later Edwin R. Embree, president of the Julius Rosenwald Fund, visited Stern to consider the health, housing, and educational needs of black New Orleanians. They also discussed a possible merger of Straight College and New Orleans University, chartered by the Freedmen's Aid Society of the Methodist Episcopal Church. Both schools were seriously underfunded and competed for the same students. New Orleans University also operated the Flint-Goodridge Hospital for blacks. Stern and Embree speculated that a merger might produce an outstanding black university, which fit the Rosenwald Fund plan of developing major black educational centers at Washington, D.C.; Nashville; Atlanta; and, perhaps, New Orleans—rather than dissipating funds on many small and inefficient colleges.[51]

The idea of a merger was not new. Secretary Douglass had advised it in 1913 and the 1917 Jones report had suggested that New Orleans University be relocated to avoid duplication. In 1928, after seeking and receiving approval from GEB officers, Embree proposed the idea to the AMA and the Department of Education for Negroes of the Methodist Episcopal Church. Secretary Brownlee—who since 1923 had advocated the merger of Tillotson and Samuel Huston, a Methodist Episcopal Church college in Austin, Texas—was enthusiastic if "we could get together on an honest-to-goodness university basis."[52] After considerable infighting, consultation, and temporary stalemates, a plan for unity was completed in 1929 which called for a complete consolidation of Straight College, New Orleans University, and the Flint-Goodridge Hospital. The new institution was named after James H. Dillard, former Tulane president, general agent for the James F. Slater Fund, and proponent of black schooling, though he was associated more with industrial than liberal education.[53] A $2 million fund was created for land purchase and construction. The AMA, GEB, and Methodist Board of Education promised $500,000 each, and the Rosenwald Fund pledged $250,000. The remaining $250,000 was to be collected locally. Edgar B. Stern undertook this chore, became president of the board of trustees, and spent much of his energy and a considerable amount of his money supporting Dillard until his death in 1959. Both the GEB and the Rosenwald Fund consistently supported the school. Between 1930 and 1948, the latter gave $1,056,763.75 to Dillard—more than to any other college. No doubt, Stern's position as a Rosenwald relative and sometimes member of the Fund board were factors in the Rosenwald Fund's contributions, but Embree, then president of the Rosenwald Fund, wrote in 1932 that "there is no single thing in which the Fund has taken part in the past four years that interests me as much as this whole Dillard business." The new eighty-bed Flint-Goodridge Hospital opened in 1932 under the superintendence of a brilliant twenty-seven-year-old black man, Albert W. Dent; and in September 1935 Dillard University began classes with an outstanding faculty led by Dean Horace Mann Bond.[54]

Foundation support and increased AMA appropriations contributed to college growth during the 1920s and 1930s, but outstanding leadership was also significant. Though most major decisions were made in AMA headquarters in New York until the early 1930s, when Brownlee and the executive committee gave school presidents greater power, presidents set the tone on campus and led in money-raising ventures. Mary E. Branch, a dynamic, charismatic black woman who became Tillotson's president, was an example of how to accomplish much with little.[55] Branch, born in Farmville, Virginia, and educated at Hampton Institute, University of Pennsylvania, and the University of Chicago where she received a B.A. in philosophy in 1922 and an M.A. in English in 1925, became president of Tillotson in 1930. The AMA had reduced Tillotson to a junior college in 1925, and when it still failed to compete successfully with the many other black Texas colleges, the association made it a women's college in 1926 and "grandiosely declared that it was to do for the southwest what Wellesley and Mt. Holyoke did for New England." After two prior unsuccessful efforts Brownlee persuaded Branch to leave a higher paying position at Vashon High in St. Louis to face what many thought certain failure in Austin, Texas. Between 1930 and her death in 1944, Branch almost single-handedly transformed Tillotson from a shabby, rundown, poorly led college with a minimal reputation and an enrollment of sixty-five to a modest but well-kept campus with more than seven hundred students and a class–A rating by the SACSS. She immediately energized students, improved the faculty, began refurbishing the campus, and increased college numbers to 139 by fall of 1930. Enhanced enrollment was remarkable given that in 1930 Texas high schools graduated fewer than two thousand students and the state had fourteen black junior and senior colleges. Since Tillotson recruited only women, the pool of available students was further reduced.[56] In 1931–32, Branch offered scholarships to the top two women graduates of every Texas high school and, in 1935, began enrolling males. She introduced football and baseball to attract more men, and by 1937–38 Tillotson boasted 399 students, 152 of whom were males. That year she added a summer school for teachers, which brought total enrollment to 668, an impressive number considering the Depression and that only 2,990 blacks were attending all Texas colleges in 1935. Jessie Daniel Ames, general field secretary of the Commission on Interracial Cooperation, toured the campus in 1938 and wrote to Brownlee, "What Dr. Branch has done at Tillotson is almost a miracle." Branch succeeded with no foundation aid and limited AMA assistance. During her fourteen years at Tillotson the AMA increased its annual appropriation by only approximately $10,000. Despite his admiration of Branch's superb leadership, Brownlee did not see Tillotson as a permanent AMA college and avidly pursued a state takeover or merger with Samuel Huston.[57] In 1942, he described Tillotson as the AMA's strongest college in enrollment, but weakest in "buildings and assurances of enlarged or even continued financial support."[58]

Frederick A. Sumner's presidency at Talladega, 1916–33, was less dramatic than Branch's at Tillotson, but he was a major reason why GEB and Rosenwald Fund agents concluded that Talladega was "the best Negro college in the South." Unlike Branch, Sumner was not a professional educator. Trained at Oberlin College, Hartford Seminary, and Yale University, Sumner left the pastorate of a Milford, Connecticut, Congregational church to go to Talladega. His personality, energy, tact, and readiness to delegate responsibilities to other administrators, especially Dean James T. Cater, compensated for his lack of educational training. His sunny disposition, willingness to abandon outdated regulations, and increased campus democracy created a more collegial atmosphere and endeared him to students, which may explain why the outbreak of student protest so prevalent on black campuses in the post-WWI years was muted at Talladega. With AMA assistance he improved the faculty and increased the number of black teachers from sixteen percent in 1910 to sixty-six percent in 1925. Thirteen of the seventeen new instructors hired in 1931 were African American. Under his leadership, Talladega became a genuine college and earned the coveted A rating by the SACSS. He vastly improved and expanded the campus, and in 1928 initiated a million-dollar endowment campaign. Sumner inspired alumni, faculty, and student loyalty and "gave Talladega the continuity of leadership and harmony that it needed to move into the modern age of education."[59]

Other college presidents performed invaluable service. Buell G. Gallagher, described by a Talladega alumnus as "sincere, dynamic, courageous and progressive," succeeded Sumner and led Talladega through the Depression and the early war years. When he resigned in 1943, he had completed the endowment, further strengthened the faculty, stimulated community service, more aggressively attacked discrimination, built a new library and teachers' home, enhanced Talladega's national prestige, democratized the campus, and imbued the school—at least for a time—with an energy and excitement it had never before experienced. George A. Owens, black business manager at Talladega and Tougaloo, and later president of Tougaloo College, said "Gallagher's system of student voice and academic freedom was really mind-boggling." Such an environment, he added, was an invaluable educational experience "for black kids who have never been able to speak their minds."[60]

Rev. William T. Holmes, "a fearless advocate for equal rights and opportunities for Negroes," went to Tougaloo in 1913 when it was basically a high school. Dean Henry W. Cobb recalled in 1944 that in 1919 the college department "was pretty much a thing of shreds and patches" with most instructors teaching high school classes; but when Holmes left in 1933 it was a liberal arts college. Few colleges made more progress during the Depression than LeMoyne under President Frank Sweeney's leadership. Sweeney, a World War I veteran and Harvard B.A. and M.A. graduate, became president in 1929 and directed LeMoyne from a two-year teacher-training school to a four-year institution. LeMoyne had 84 college students, 170 secondary students, and 165 elementary pupils in 1928. Only one instructor taught college courses exclusively. Ten years later there were four hundred college students and twenty-eight faculty devoted to college work.[61] All of the above presidents had weaknesses and took missteps, but they made progress in spite of worldwide depression, criminally inadequate financial support, an often hostile white South, and a generally indifferent white North.

The AMA colleges remained small, but enrollment steadily increased. In 1925, there were 305 students in college classes, fewer than the 429 LeMoyne alone had in 1939. The number grew to 903 in 1932–33 to 1,359 in 1935–36 and to 2,206 in 1940–41. An additional 512 college students attended summer sessions that year.[62] Statistics indicated increased numbers, and accreditation illustrated enhanced quality. In the late nineteenth century, accrediting associations were formed, but none even considered black colleges—an indication of contempt at worst and indifference at best—until 1928, when the SACSS decided to rate them. Thereafter, accreditation became essential for reputation and fund collecting, and became a major goal of black colleges in the 1930s. As James Anderson says, segregated black colleges "could not exist apart from the power and control of white standardizing agencies." Fisk received an A rating in 1930. Talladega was judged deficient in library equipment and professors' salaries, but was rated A in 1931. Tougaloo and LeMoyne were rated B in 1932, and Tillotson in 1933. LeMoyne was awarded the desired A rating in 1939, Tillotson in 1943, and Tougaloo finally in 1947. The need for accreditation compelled the AMA, despite its poverty, to find ways to improve its colleges.[63]

Despite variation in quality and location, all the colleges faced common issues during the 1920s and 1930s: leadership, faculty, boards of trustees, students, finances, and relationship with the community. Leadership questions often related to race as well as ability. Many of those who advocated black faculty also preferred black leaders. African Americans became principals in AMA schools relatively early, but the association was slow to appoint black college presidents. In a 1920 article, the NAACP periodical *Crisis* claimed that a "glaring weakness" of black colleges was choosing white executives, thereby placing men of inferior intelligence and experience over scholarly blacks. Only two types of white men were accepting such jobs, the author said: those whose careers were ending and who wanted a retirement position, and those whose pay at black schools was greater than their talents could earn from whites.[64] This view was not widespread in AMA colleges in 1920, but as more blacks attained advanced degrees and experience, requests for black leadership increased. The first clamor for a black president came not from African Americans, but from whites in Austin, Texas. When John R. Shilladay, white NAACP secretary, visited Austin in August 1919, several whites including a judge and a constable publicly attacked and severely beat him. The judge denounced northerners who preached social equality, and a deputy sheriff declared that Texas did not want "Negro-loving white men." White hostility quickly focused on Tillotson's interracial faculty, and Austin whites demanded that Tillotson employ only black teachers. The AMA demurred, saying the time was not right for a change. In 1921, local white trustees requested an all-black faculty, warning of serious consequences if President R. W. Fletcher and white teachers came back. The AMA concluded that the principles that sent teachers south in the 1860s were at stake and asked Fletcher and the faculty to return.[65] Soon thereafter, four white trustees resigned, and the Klan sent a threatening letter. Although there were no attacks on students and faculty, the AMA employed a detective agency to investigate Klan activity on campus. A teacher wrote from the Tillotson campus in December 1921: "Tillotson has been having troublesome times this year, but . . . the Ku Klux difficulties seem to have subsided." In 1924, the AMA appointed James T. Hodges as Tillotson's first black president, but it retained some white faculty, which led to more Klan threats. "This fired our old time zeal and led us to support the school on principle if for no other reason," Brownlee said.[66]

Hodges's appointment at Tillotson did not foreshadow a rush to appoint black executives. When Joseph K. Brick School became a junior college in 1925, principal Thomas S. Inborden, an African American, became president; and at Tillotson College, Branch succeeded Hodges in 1930. But the AMA chose no more black managers until 1936. When Dillard was created, the question of the president's race was seriously debated. Edgar Stern and Brownlee were the strongest personalities on the board of trustees. The latter insisted upon an interracial faculty which, he believed, necessitated a black leader or a white man who could comfortably socialize with black students and faculty. Stern denied any preference as to color, but he was a southerner and believed "that if we have a colored president we cannot have a mixed faculty." He respected white Fisk president Thomas E. Jones, but feared social relations problems with a white man at Dillard's helm. He had heard that Mrs. Jones had danced with black faculty at a party and warned "that the day the wife of a white president of Dillard does this, you will find me among the missing trustees of this institution." If a white man were selected, Stern said, he must either be a southerner with sufficient tact to avoid alienating local whites, or a northerner who "must not be a radical on interracial relations."[67] Stern settled on Will W. Alexander, southern white director of the Commission on Interracial Cooperation (CIC), as the proper choice. Embree and GEB representatives told Stern that Alexander's experience with the CIC would enable him to "bring all these diverse interests together in one common purpose and effort." Brownlee fretted about Alexander's refusal to promise to live on campus and socialize with blacks, while Stern favored him in part because he, at that time, accepted segregation.[68] After some harsh letters exchanged between Stern and Brownlee, the board of trustees in a tense March 1931 meeting elected Alexander acting president over Brownlee's protest.[69] When Alexander, who divided time between Dillard and the CIC, resigned in 1936, both Brownlee and Stern enthusiastically endorsed the appointment of black William Stuart Nelson as his successor.[70]

Though Branch and Albert W. Dent, who succeeded Nelson in 1941, were extraordinary administrators, and black William H. Jones followed Branch at Tillotson, the AMA did not select black leaders for LeMoyne until 1943, Talladega in 1952, and Tougaloo in 1964, which created considerable anguish among its black constituents. Some African Americans in Memphis had long advocated black management of LeMoyne, and when Frank Sweeney resigned in 1940 "Negro leadership for Negroes" became their slogan. The local NAACP endorsed Dean Henry Hamilton, and even national NAACP secretary Walter White became involved. Ugly charges and rumors led to the eventual removal of Dean Hamilton, and Brownlee himself directed LeMoyne until 1943 when Dean Hollis F. Price became its first black president.[71] During the period he oversaw LeMoyne, Brownlee divided his time between Memphis and the New York headquarters and was often an absentee president. His successor as AMA executive secretary acidly remarked in 1954 that Brownlee's "experience at LeMoyne was good for Brownlee, but not for LeMoyne."[72]

Even more prolonged bitterness raged at Talladega. When Gallagher resigned in 1943, the board of trustees appointed Dean James T. Cater acting president while it searched for a successor. Black Talladega business manager George A. Owens called Cater "one of those white Negroes from Atlanta." When asked if he meant "white" in complexion or thought, Owens replied, "[c]omplexion. In Atlanta there was a group of them like George and Walter White." Owens thought Cater was unusually talented but exceedingly jealous of his prerogatives as dean. Cater's selection as acting president was appropriate since the school owed much of its educational prominence to him. Both Presidents Sumner and Gallagher concentrated on material needs while Cater successfully directed academic affairs. Cater and many faculty and alumni assumed his contributions warranted promotion to president.

George W. Crawford, a Talladega and Yale University graduate, a founder of the Niagara Movement and the NAACP, and senior member of Talladega's board of trustees, strongly believed Talladega should have a black president, though he did not necessarily sponsor Cater. At a 1942 AMA seminar on race, he had made an eloquent plea for black leadership. Placing paternalistic whites at the head of black schools was perhaps unavoidable earlier, he had stated, but blacks now insisted on positions of responsibility. Those working in black education must learn, Crawford added, "that they are working *with* Negroes," not for them, and beneficent paternalism was no longer acceptable. Unfortunately, a majority of the board thought a white president was needed.[73]

Talladega's board of trustees minutes failed to reveal why trustees—including Brownlee, who as AMA director and a board member had enormous influence—thought a white president necessary, or why Cater was not considered. By 1944, according to Brownlee, Cater was "recognized as the foremost dean" of southern black colleges, and he had done an excellent job at Talladega. His lack of a Ph.D. was considered a detriment, but Brownlee, who had earlier reservations about Albert Dent at Dillard not having an advanced degree, eventually supported his appointment as president at Dillard in 1941, and was pleased with his performance. Interestingly, Gallagher did not consider his dean a suitable replacement. And why a white president? Since the AMA had already appointed several successful black leaders, why should race be a factor at Talladega? Indirect evidence indicates that Brownlee's passion for maintaining an interracial faculty came into play. He had advocated a black president at Dillard in 1931 for the same reason, but Tillotson and Dillard had increasing difficulty in employing whites. Though black faculty were now in a majority, Talladega was still clearly interracial and Brownlee wanted to keep it that way. He apparently believed that in rural Talladega a white president could more easily attract white faculty and keep open communication and peace with wary white neighbors. Talladega and Tougaloo, the two most rural schools, were the last to enjoy black leadership. Brownlee clearly pressured Crawford to support a white candidate. Looking back later in 1949, Crawford wrote Brownlee, "It will be remembered that I have been among those who have felt that our bi-racial set-up should continue as long as possible. I still feel that way but must frankly confess that I am beginning to have misgivings about the validity of my position." In 1944, both Crawford and Brownlee, probably incorrectly, assumed that selecting a black president would endanger retention of an interracial faculty. And yet, as will be shown, in less than a decade, a black president would preside over Talladega's mixed faculty during an even more turbulent period and would be viewed as less threatening than his white predecessor.[74]

After delaying for almost two years, the board selected Adam D. Beittel in 1944. Though Beittel survived until 1952, his position was untenable almost from the beginning. Cater never accepted him and became increasingly uncooperative. He successfully turned most of the black faculty, students, alumni, and older white teachers against him. Some observers believed that Cater was simply angry at not being elected president. Whatever the merits of that claim, it was clear that the dean was unwilling to relinquish control of the school. He had directed academic affairs with limited interference under Presidents Sumner and Gallagher. Beittel, an educator and former dean, became involved in every aspect of the college. Crawford also was invariably critical, blaming Beittel for almost all of the school's ills, including low enrollment. An "institution with a white president has two strikes against it," he told the board of trustees. Though Beittel was a consistent and aggressive opponent of segregation, and his son enrolled at Talladega and pledged a black fraternity, students and alumni charged Beittel with being evasive and compromising on the question of segregation. Certainly Beittel had shortcomings. He was sometimes brusque and irascible, but most who knew him, including black president Hollis F. Price at LeMoyne, considered the above slurs "particularly dastardly." Indeed, local whites saw Beittel as a radical agitator who mingled socially with blacks even at dances. Yet the initial reason for discord was less race than Cater's frustration at being passed over for the presidency.[75] The faculty divided on the issue, but not exclusively along racial lines. As bitterness and hostility accelerated, Cater supporters grasped at any available issue and began to use race as an excuse to attack. The AMA board's closing of Sessions and Drewry in 1948, already discussed, simply provided additional ammunition. Indeed, surface relations between Cater and allies and Beittel were correct, if not cordial, up to that time. Many alumni who preferred black leadership eagerly joined the fray. The contentiousness compelled the trustees to act in order to prevent serious damage to the school. In 1952, it investigated and concluded that Beittel had "been wronged both by the charges against him and by the methods resorted to by those who have attacked him." While the board condemned such injustice, it decided the situation was so explosive Beittel could not effectively administer the college. It removed both Beittel and Cater, and appointed Arthur D. Gray, a Talladega alumnus, as the school's first black president.[76] The board of trustees bore much of the responsibility for the Beittel-Cater controversy. Before Beittel arrived, the long delay in choosing a new leader gave Cater and supporters hope that he might be selected, and allowed anger to fester. There is no evidence that the board told Cater that he could not be considered, why he was not a viable candidate, or that the president must be white, and why that was true. The board's ineptness and Cater's frustration sparked a bitter racial controversy in the AMA's most comfortably interracial college. Even under the best of circumstances, interracial cooperation could be fragile and volatile.

Whether the president was black or white, AMA colleges generally managed to maintain interracial faculties. In 1934, Edgar B. Stern wrote that Dillard's acting president, Will W. Alexander, believed Brownlee had "impugned his motives" for having nominated only blacks for the Dillard faculty. The AMA "crowd," Stern added, "purport to hold the matter of bi-racial faculty as a deep-rooted conviction." Stern was absolutely correct. The AMA on principle insisted upon interracial staffs at all of its colleges. It was seldom easy. At first black faculty were scarce, and by 1940 fewer whites seemed willing to go to black schools, in part because salaries were not competitive. Moreover, interracial experience was often new to both races. When historian Alrutheus A. Taylor went to Fisk in 1926, he found a "most friendly feeling" between blacks and whites, but never having been in that situation and acutely aware of the southern racial codes regarding black men and white females, he had to overcome a reluctance to talk to white women.[77]

Other personnel were simply unfitted for interracial work. A white nurse at Tougaloo was released in 1911 because she "grew to take the southern attitude" toward blacks. Years later Brownlee wrote of a white Tougaloo professor who had charged that the black dean was sometimes impatient with her. Brownlee explained that she was a northern woman with southern sentiments—"by far the most difficult people to deal with"—and for a black person to be impatient with any white was to her almost a crime. "Tougaloo itself has not been devoid of white supremacy to a degree," Brownlee added. On the other hand, Tougaloo terminated a white female teacher in 1923 because she was "too friendly" with black men. During this period AMA officials preferred that interracial contact not include extramarital romance because southern whites charged that mixed faculties encouraged rampant, illicit interracial sex. It was difficult enough, they thought, to protect biracial staffs without giving credence to southern whites' malicious rumors.[78] The AMA became increasingly tolerant on this issue, and interracial liaisons occasionally occurred. For a white woman at Talladega in the early 1940s, a "love affair across race lines" ended abruptly and resulted in a rift with her family and a near "nervous break down." Neither party was reprimanded for the relationship. An interracial marriage at Tougaloo in 1950 may have created a stir in the white community, but it was no problem on campus.[79]

Whites were too often patronizing and many blacks mistrusted whites, whatever their origin, so some misunderstanding was unavoidable. In 1919 at Straight University, "there commenced to be something like trouble between colored and white factions on the faculty. This has been somewhat dissipated by the withdrawal of the causes." Since the divisions were mainly between young black men and older white women, the factors of age, gender, education, and personality may have been as important as race. The young men were frequently better educated than older missionary teachers, and strong-willed, dominant white women with proprietary interest in their institution seemed to thrive in the AMA ranks. The leader of one faction at Straight was Emily Nichols, "the oldest teacher in point of service, and one very influential locally."[80] Alma Hanson worked for the AMA for forty-nine years, eight at Talladega and forty-one at LeMoyne. She was officially treasurer at LeMoyne, but assumed greater responsibilities and was twice acting president. Once during summer vacation a man came to campus and asked to see the president. Hanson climbed down from the top of a building where she was repairing the roof and said, "I am the president." She was devoted to LeMoyne, sometimes paying out of her own pocket when students could not meet obligations, and leaving her estate to fund student scholarships. A black male colleague said she was "courageous, militantly independent . . . and never condescended to any man regardless of his status." Neither was she submissive to any man whatever his race. In a sense she was an equal opportunity offender. At different times a white dean and a black president complained that she was overstepping her authority. There were other such women in the AMA, and it was not surprising that young faculty—black or white, male or female—might resent their authority and attitude. But the divisions were not always between old and young, or missionary teachers and young professionals. In 1940, Frank Sweeney, recently retired LeMoyne president, spoke of "how deep and complete, the lines run in the LeMoyne-Negro-white-world." August Meier, an assistant professor of history at Tougaloo from 1945 to 1949, wrote that some white faculty "are essentially paternalistic and condescendingly sentimental toward Negroes, rather than realistic and genuinely equalitarian," and some black faculty did not wish to associate with whites and indeed wished they were not there.[81]

Given the state of race relations in the country, some racial friction on campus was inevitable, but hostile blacks and condescending whites were not in a majority. Four years after Sweeney spoke of the divisions at LeMoyne, Mary Louise Wright, wife of white dean Jay Wright, branded as false the claim that black suspicion of whites was too great to be overcome. She and her husband had, she announced, "stepped over the color line so to speak."

Though she did not say so, Dean Wright found Alma Hanson much more difficult than most black colleagues, and after noting racial problems at Tougaloo, August Meier added that "many Negroes and whites on the faculty were of course unprejudiced, and enjoyed splendid social relationships with each other and with their students." In any event, the divide at LeMoyne was not as great as Sweeney suggested and was partially due to Sweeney and black dean Henry Hamilton's intense mutual personal dislike.[82] Black–white relations improved when black Hollis F. Price became LeMoyne president in 1943. Price truly believed in an interracial faculty and inspired great loyalty and affection among both black and white colleagues. A white faculty member wrote years later that the "spirit" Price created at LeMoyne, the "mutual respect and affection," the "freedom to be honest, the possibility of disagreeing with the boss," convinced him to remain in college teaching and administration. Price was familiar with white condescension and black racial exclusiveness spawned by generations of mistreatment, and he allowed neither to be openly practiced on campus.[83]

When Du Bois lectured at Talladega in 1928, he was impressed with the "rather unusual collection of white and colored teachers and officers." In 1939 Talladega president Buell G. Gallagher declared that Talladegans believed the races should work and live together "despite all the opposition of the Lily Whites and Mr. Jim Crow on one hand and the narrowness of Black chauvinism on the other." In 1943, *Chicago Defender* reporter Enoc P. Waters described Talladega College as "an oasis of racial democracy in a desert of racial segregation and prejudice. Despite dark surroundings, the torch of enlightenment burns brightly here." Waters found no racial restrictions and saw whites and blacks "mingling freely and with equality." After *Ebony* published a similar article in 1951, Talladega received a letter from a young man in Accra, Gold Coast, West Africa, addressed simply "Talladega College, Oasis in Alabama, U.S.A." Lillian Voorhees, speech teacher and Little Theater director at Talladega, reflected the view of many white faculty when she informed a relative, "I would not choose to work elsewhere than in a Negro college or in Negro education." White faculty seemed no less concerned for students than were their black counterparts. Voorhees and many whites at Talladega and other colleges made teaching and nurturing black youth their life work. White Fisk history professor Theodore S. Currier encouraged young John Hope Franklin to attend his alma mater, Harvard, for graduate training in history. When it appeared Franklin might not be able to finance the venture, Currier went to his Nashville bank and borrowed five hundred dollars. "He placed the entire sum in my hand," noted historian Franklin remembered decades later, "and in a voice I can still recall, he declared, 'Money will not keep you out of Harvard.' "[84]

Of course, there were often significant social and cultural differences between the races, and even though they worked well together, and joined to teach and uplift students, blacks and whites were sometimes less compatible socially. African American faculty, according to one white faculty wife who was at Talladega during WWII years, tended to be more interested in fraternities and sororities and a more formal social life than many antiestablishment whites. Nevertheless, on most campuses black and white staff associated as easily and comfortably after hours as at work.[85]

As the number of black faculty increased, so did the quality of these teachers, but improvement was slow. A 1932 U.S. Office of Education study deplored the lack of research and publications in black colleges, and in 1937 Professor V. V. Oak of North Carolina College repeated the criticism and added that the teachers lacked a professional attitude toward their work. Both charges were relevant to most AMA colleges in the early 1930s. Low salaries, supplementary responsibilities, library deficiencies, heavy teaching loads, absence of encouragement, lack of research funds, and segregated educational associations contributed to these shortcomings. Nevertheless, all the colleges made gains during the 1930s and 1940s. The AMA, boards of trustees, and the GEB made loans to help faculty earn advanced degrees. At least eight Talladegans borrowed money for advanced study between 1935 and 1937. Still others attended summer school, and more of the faculty engaged in research. Charles S. Johnson made Fisk a genuine center of scholarship in the 1930s and 1940s, and sixteen Talladega faculty published books or articles in the mid-1930s. Dillard opened in 1935 with a research-oriented faculty, after president Will W. Alexander and Dean Horace Mann Bond had scoured the country for established black scholars. If Alexander continued to hire at the present rate, Edwin R. Embree had said in 1934, he would assemble at Dillard "the most brilliant faculty of any university in the South. It would be an odd commentary on the times if it were left to a Negro university to show what a real faculty should be in the South."[86] Dillard differed from other AMA staffs in that it was almost exclusively black male. When the school opened in 1935, the faculty had already published more than one hundred articles, theses, musical compositions, monographs, and books, and within six months it had published twenty-four additional articles.[87] Dillard continued to add important scholars, such as historian Benjamin Quarles. Unfortunately, Tougaloo, Tillotson, and LeMoyne lagged behind; Dillard lost some of its best faculty to other schools; and the above stated reasons for limited research continued to plague all AMA colleges. But even those that lacked a strong research faculty had many able devoted teachers.[88]

Who were the students benefiting from the improving faculty? Certainly the profile had changed dramatically since the early years when an illiterate teenager might wander onto campus seeking elementary education. There were still penniless youth with limited educational backgrounds, but there were also more second- and third-generation AMA students and others from certified high schools nationwide. John McCray had been valedictorian at Avery Institute and editor of the *Avery News* when he arrived on the Talladega campus in the early 1930s. There were 30 high school valedictorians in the 129-member Talladega freshman class of 1934, and 16 sons and daughters of Talladegans enrolled in 1936. Success after graduation illustrated these students' ability. Between 1930 and 1938, 103 Talladega graduates enrolled in professional or graduate school, 11 at Columbia University, 12 at the University of Chicago, and 22 at the University of Michigan. Twenty-eight graduates between 1931 and 1941 earned Ph.D.'s, and others became physicians, attorneys, dentists, newspaper editors, and teachers. Dr. Theodore Sherrod, class of 1938, knew of twenty-six M.D.'s or Ph.D.'s from his class alone.[89]

Of course, many college students still suffered serious educational deficiencies. The Talladega graduation rate averaged about sixty percent, but in 1930 it fell to thirty-seven percent. It jumped back up to sixty-seven percent the following year. Lillian Voorhees said in 1921 that Tougaloo students were "starved" for beauty and culture. And as late as 1949 Tougaloo president Harold C. Warren said the college had some outstanding students but Mississippi's inferior system left many unprepared. As a result of uneven and inadequate schooling, he added, "it takes some time to bring the average freshman up to doing work which is honestly on the college level." Warren was seeking funds to offer eight-week remedial sessions each summer. Brownlee bluntly warned Vernon L. Wharton, a visiting white historian-teacher from Millsaps College, that Tougaloo students had "native capacity and potential ability" but "due to handicapped homes and very poor" elementary and high schools, some freshmen were "not beyond bona fide seventh graders." When Margaret McCulloch went to LeMoyne in 1934, she abandoned her "carefully prepared history lecture notes because there was just nothing in [the students'] experience to tie the history to." Although more students were middle class by now, the country's racial system—exacerbated by the Depression—meant family incomes were relatively low. At Talladega, in the three classes of 1937–38, 1938–39, and 1939–40, fifty percent of the students were from families with total annual incomes of nine hundred dollars or less. A 1943–44 profile showed that Tillotson students ranged from comfortable to impoverished. Among parents were sixty-five farmers, twenty-two teachers, seventeen defense workers, seventeen ministers, and two college deans. Other occupations included thirty-nine common laborers, seventy-nine domestics, and thirty-one unemployed. In 1942 Margaret McCulloch told of the daughter of a "derelict artist janitor" who failed at LeMoyne largely because she worked almost full time trying to support herself and younger siblings while taking a full load of classes.[90]

The National Youth Administration (NYA) kept hundreds of AMA students in college during the Depression, but financial exigencies compelled scores of others to withdraw. In 1937 an impecunious Talladega female student resorted to stealing needed underwear from dormitory mates, and the following year a student withdrew because she was embarrassed by "lack of certain essentials." Tougaloo and Tillotson students especially needed help, and some thought the latter received preferential treatment because President Mary E. Branch was on the Texas NYA Negro Advisory Board. Lyndon B. Johnson, then Texas NYA director, had appointed all white advisors to the NYA board. When Washington officials suggested he add some African American members, he resisted saying that if he appointed a black member all present board members would resign, he would be forced to retire, and he would "in all probability be run out of Texas." He did, however, select a black advisory board that included Branch. Though she obviously never had the clout of Mary McLeod Bethune, director of the Negro Division of the NYA, Branch took her duties seriously and secured NYA aid for Tillotson, as well as for other schools, and helped establish several Freshmen College Centers which offered one year of college to black youth whose families were eligible for relief. Johnson reported that Branch had been "extremely helpful" in initiating fifteen different Freshmen College Centers, and had also assisted in selecting schools to be allocated additional funds from unused balances. Tillotson always got its share. NYA deputy director Beatrice Denmark was so pleased with the Negro Advisory Board's work and Texas projects for blacks that she invited Mrs. Eleanor Roosevelt to examine them.[91]

Rich or poor, college students were closely supervised in the early twentieth century. Langston Hughes, in a 1934 *Crisis* article titled "Cowards from the Colleges," attacked the absurd regulations of black institutions which he likened to "monasteries and nunneries in their strictness." In the early years of the twentieth century, fraternization between sexes, alcohol, card playing, and dancing were strictly prohibited. Hughes's description applied primarily to this pre-1920s environment at AMA colleges. Bolder and more confident than previous generations, students in the 1920s protested the "ancient customs and practices" shaped by "benevolent despots" and won concessions.

In 1927, Talladega students convinced the board of trustees to allow mixed social dancing "under strict and adequate supervision" and mixed-company card playing. At Tillotson the deeply religious President Branch viewed old regulations as quaint and abolished compulsory chapel, approved card playing, condoned dances both on and off campus, and allowed women students to receive male callers. Students also won the right to organize fraternities and sororities. Talladega students first unsuccessfully requested Greek organizations in 1919. Finally in 1924 the board of trustees reluctantly permitted fraternities, and added sororities the following year. Branch, herself an Alpha Kappa Alpha sorority member, welcomed sororities and fraternities to Tillotson's campus in 1935, and they were accepted at Dillard in 1936. A few critics contended that the Greek organizations, while increasing social activity, had a deleterious impact. Talladega student John McCray claimed in 1934 that they had "done more to retard a united student progress on this campus than any other single agency. They have polluted student elections, formed social 'clicks,' and nurtured a clannish and individual conceit." President Gallagher denounced them as "little nests of sham aristocracy," and charged that some of them chose members "on the basis of color, money, and campus prestige." If he were a race-hating demagogue, he stated, he would send anonymous checks to "my allies in the Greek organizations" on black campuses. Even sorority member and student Catherine Cater admitted in 1937 that many members had "lost sight of the finer ideals and purposes of the early organizations."[92]

Raymond Wolters's *The New Negro on Campus: Black College Rebellions of the 1920s* effectively describes the new ferment on campuses during this period, including the Fisk revolt that ousted a white president in 1925.[93] Students on other AMA campuses frequently criticized the leadership but focused more on greater student freedom and democracy. Most association colleges established student governments, Tougaloo women struck in 1930 to prevent the employment of a matron thought to be anti-black, and Talladega women demanded equal rights with men. In 1937, the latter banded together to elect Catherine A. Cater student body president, the first female to be so honored, and campaigned for equal financial aid. Men were only thirty-seven percent of the student population, they charged, yet comprised sixty-three percent of those on the NYA and college payroll. Male students also were given the higher salaried positions receiving seventy-five percent of all student aid. The next year Talladega coeds announced that "[t]he fight for women's freedom takes on a new vigor on campus." They had won "the rights to smoking, unlimited use of radios and lights, free entrance into extracurricular activities" and were now demanding the choice to leave campus without permission. They were almost certainly influenced by the presence of strong female role models such as dean of women Hilda Davis; Margaret Montgomery and Martha Jane Gibson, teachers of English; and Lillian Voorhees, teacher of speech and theater.[94]

Students also intensified their attacks on off-campus discrimination. In April 1933, Talladega students invited Mary White Ovington, who was observing the Scottsboro Boys' trial for the NAACP, to campus to discuss the case. The next year students and faculty collected funds to help finance an appeal, but the *Talladega Student* feared that "inane prejudices" would prevent justice being done. Tillotson, LeMoyne, Dillard, and Talladega formed student chapters of the NAACP in the 1930s, and Dillard and Talladega students demonstrated against lynching in February 1937. Talladega students initiated a voter-registration drive in 1938, and solicited new NAACP members. "The combination will afford a stronger basis for appealing to the court officials for the right to vote," they stated. The next year Talladega students, "greatly incensed" at the "police brutality" shown by an officer attempting to control a waiting line of theatergoers, boycotted a downtown theater.[95] Perhaps more threatening to their white neighbors, AMA college students hosted at least ten interracial conferences between 1929 and 1936. The Fellowship of Reconciliation held an interracial retreat at LeMoyne from December 27, 1929 to January 1, 1930. Nearly forty people almost equally divided between black and white met to probe racial problems. "The fellowship was wonderful to behold," the *American Missionary* reported, and southern white and black youth eating together "augurs well for the future."[96]

Just as there were occasional tensions among the faculty and students, so were there on the boards of trustees. Members were black and white, and from North and South. With the exception of Dillard, where the AMA and Methodist board each selected six trustees who then chose five more, the boards were dominated by AMA appointees and the executive secretary who was always on the board had unusual influence. Brownlee, a persuasive leader, was secretary from 1920 to 1950 and often got his way, except at Dillard where Edgar Stern was president of the board. If Stern and Brownlee agreed on an issue, it generally became board policy. White southern trustees were most often prominent businessmen with an occasional church bishop thrown in at Tougaloo. No matter how supportive of their respective colleges, southern white trustees during the early years tended to be segregationists, and in the case of Hugh L. McElderry at Talladega more inclined toward industrial education. A longtime trustee, McElderry became increasingly disillusioned as Talladega grew in stature as a college and flaunted its interracial character. In 1929 he wrote Julius Rosenwald complaining that

Talladega no longer trained black nurses and was neglecting its farm. He urged Rosenwald to talk with GEB officers, an indication of foundation power, and "shape things down here along Tuskegee lines and in line with the thought of Booker T. Washington." Unless Talladega moved in this direction "instead of teaching Latin, Greek and higher math and with it the inculcation of social equality," it might not only lose him as a trustee, but reverse the recent southern trend "of doing all possible for Negro improvement." After an unsatisfactory meeting with President Sumner, McElderry resigned in July 1929.[97]

White trustees who made significant contributions included C. Arthur Bruce at LeMoyne and Stern at Dillard. Bruce, co-owner of a Memphis lumber company, became chairman of the board of trustees when LeMoyne became a four-year college in 1934 and so remained until 1960. During the 1940 quarrel over the presidency, national NAACP secretary Walter White charged that Bruce was a "notorious" lily-white Tennessee Republican. Brownlee responded that he had not appeared to be lily-white when dining with White's brother George, or when fraternizing with black members of the National Committee on Interracial Activities of the Boy Scouts. Bruce was cautious about alienating Memphis whites, but worked closely with black president Hollis F. Price who said Bruce was "instrumental in the growth and accreditation of LeMoyne," and that no one was more responsible for LeMoyne's great progress from 1934 to 1960.[98] A dilemma for all AMA presidents was whether or to what degree to accommodate themselves to whites who did not fully share their interracial ideals in order to benefit their institution. With the exception of Brownlee, Stern was the most powerful trustee of any AMA college. For thirty years he devoted much of his energy, influence, and money—including one check of $100,000—to Dillard. Along the way he personally financed summer courses for scores of black physicians; invited black contralto Marian Anderson, long before she became famous, into his home to expose her talent to New Orleans white society; became fast friends with his African American protégé Albert W. Dent, whom he regularly welcomed into his home for social events; and gradually, if reluctantly, softened his earlier stance on segregation. Stern learned, grew, and changed, and as biographer Gerda Klein explains, when the desegregation struggle began in New Orleans in the 1950s the Sterns "threw their prestige, their means, and their efforts" into the cause. Critics flooded their mailbox with "the most virulent kind" of hate mail.[99]

Black trustees were often alumni or noted northerners such as Judge Hubert T. Delany, a leading Harlem citizen appointed to the Talladega board in 1942. The most distinguished and one of the most powerful black trustees was 1914 Talladega graduate Dr. Theodore K. Lawless, a dermatologist, millionaire philanthropist, and 1954 Spingarn Award winner for notable achievement. The son of AMA district superintendent of churches Dr. Alfred Lawless, he graduated from Northwestern University Medical School in 1919 and did additional study at Columbia and Harvard Universities, and in Paris; Freiburg, Germany; and Vienna. A Jewish professor helped him secure recommendations for study abroad. Lawless later recalled that "it was a noteworthy fact in my own life experience that of the twelve letters I obtained, eleven were from Jewish physicians." Perhaps in recognition of their assistance, he later established a dermatology clinic in a Jerusalem hospital. He served on the board of trustees of almost all AMA colleges at one time or another and contributed thousands of dollars, including arranging the purchase of a $700,000 apartment complex for faculty housing at Dillard. He believed that blacks had been on the receiving end too long and should give more. Lawless was not just a figurehead trustee. He took an active role and frequently irritated presidents and other board members. The *Chicago Defender* said of him, "Sometimes gruff in inter-personal relations, Dr. Lawless was never a candidate for any popularity contest. Nevertheless, his basic humanitarianism and his countless acts of philanthropy endeared him to thousands."[100]

No matter how calm the campus and congenial the faculty, students, and trustees, relationships with surrounding white communities, with few exceptions, ranged from grudging acceptance to indifference to active hostility. Whites who left campus likely met with cold civility at best, and blacks encountered segregation, discrimination, suspicion, and occasional violence. Gallagher thought he was fortunate when he boasted that during his ten years at Talladega only one shot was fired at his house. The Tougaloo entrance sign was constantly riddled with bullets. When President Harold C. Warren went there in 1947 he had the sign rebuilt, but bullets soon defaced it beyond recognition. Violence was never far away at Tougaloo. In 1925 four hooded white men attacked Tougaloo student Myrtle Wilson and her physician fiancé as they were riding in his new car. The men shot and brutally beat the doctor, who urged Wilson to flee. In her attempt to escape, she got entangled in a barbed wire fence and damaged one eye so badly it had to be removed. New Orleans whites were unhappy when in 1933 Straight president Charles B. Austin exhorted a First African Baptist Church congregation to consolidate their votes in order to have a voice in government and to educate their youth so they "might take part in this great democracy." There were a few tense days at LeMoyne in 1943 when President Hollis Price invited A. Philip Randolph to speak on campus after city officials prevented his speaking at a black church. Later Price wrote thankfully, "He came, he spoke very well and the buildings remain standing." Price added that it took all his ingenuity to live peaceably with Memphis whites "while still holding to any principles."[101]

Staff and students were frequently reminded of their "place" in society. Dillard president Albert W. Dent was denied three times before being allowed to register to vote in New Orleans. Travel to AMA annual meetings or on vacation was often an ordeal. In 1942, Tillotson president Mary E. Branch and dean William H. Jones, in Nashville for an AMA meeting, could not get Pullman reservations back to Austin, Texas, and had a "most disagreeable" return trip. Jones stood up the entire five hundred miles from Little Rock to Austin. Trainmen in 1942 assaulted several Talladega students riding the L&N Railroad from Birmingham to Nashville. Town-gown relationships were often volatile. Talladega permitted females to go to town on Saturday only in an emergency, dean of women Hilda Davis wrote in 1948, because the town on that day tended to be crowded with rural whites hostile "to Negroes of the type which the college students represent." A few whites showed a friendly interest and sometimes attended campus entertainments, but an early 1950s study of the city of Talladega indicated that a majority of whites dealt with the college in much the same way they handled "most unpleasant subjects, by avoiding contact with the offending institution." Avoidance was preferable to violence and the Klan visits to campus in 1948 and 1949. As late as 1950, Talladega students reminded the WHTB radio station that "its announcers need not refer to Negroes as 'niggers' in its newscasts."[102]

World War II interrupted the natural progression of AMA colleges and affected almost every facet of their existence. Black faculty and students were keenly aware of conditions in Europe and were divided over whether the United States should join the Allies. They saw the irony of fighting to preserve democracy abroad while being denied it at home. Talladega student Lofton Mitchell questioned what the country was defending and against whom. He had heard of fighting to save democracy and of President Franklin D. Roosevelt's wish to spread democracy. "How, I should like to know," he wrote, "can an insect spread a disease he does not have? We have no democracy in this country. The South is as Fascistic as Germany and Italy. The North is as treacherous and imperialistic as England." Why should blacks support such a system? President Gallagher thought the "Jim Crow processes" of the entire military and government effort were a "stinging slap in the face" of patriotic blacks, and students and faculty were not immune to it. After Pearl Harbor, blacks generally supported the war, but they continued to demand changes at home. In 1942, the LeMoyne faculty administered a questionnaire in an attempt to judge students' attitude toward the war. Questions and responses included: "Do you think that Negroes should be compelled to fight?" Eighty-two answered yes, 105 answered no. "Does your heart quicken when you hear the National Anthem of America?" Seventy-six answered yes, 108 responded no. "Do the words of the song 'My Country 'Tis of Thee' express your opinion of America?" Fifty-four answered yes, 128 answered no. "Do you experience a thrill when listening to 'Lift Every Voice and Sing?' One hundred and fifty-five answered yes, thirty-nine said no. One hundred and sixty-four thought blacks should use the war as an opportunity to demand greater recognition. Clearly they were not unquestioning patriots. Despite their skepticism, once the war began AMA students and alumni supported the war just as they had the Spanish American War and World War I. Sixty-five Talladega alumni were in the military by November 1942, and many more either joined the military or were drafted before the war ended. Tougaloo's flag had 125 stars in April 1944, one gold for a graduate recently killed in the Pacific.[103]

The war catapulted the country out of the Depression which brought slightly increased enrollment. Higher salaries and expanding summer employment enabled more students to pay their tuition. In 1941, Tillotson and Tougaloo saw their largest college enrollments ever—690 and 162 respectively. Tillotson's college population jumped to 814 in 1943–44. Unfortunately, male enrollment plummeted during the war. In 1943 LeMoyne boasted only twenty-one males, and in 1945 Talladega reached a low of thirty-seven men.[104] The war also depleted the male faculty. "We lost our instructor in speech this week," Dean James T. Cater wryly wrote in 1945. "He has gone to a CO camp at the government's invitation." Far more faculty enlisted or were drafted. Hollis Price complained in 1942 that not only had LeMoyne lost many faculty to the draft, but the War Production's Board also insisted that the school sell one-fourth of its typewriters for Army use. Price lost two more faculty to the military the next year, and Brownlee feared that lack of instructors might prevent some of the schools from opening in the fall of 1944. The faculty shortage was complicated by low salaries. Dillard and Talladega were "practically in accord" with the SACSS salary minimum, but LeMoyne was below and Tillotson and Tougaloo were lower still.[105] Defense jobs often paid better, and some faculty left to join black state colleges which were now being better funded. In 1943, Dillard also lost two men to white colleges. Allison Davis went to the University of Chicago and Charles W. Buggs became professor of bacteriology at the Medical College of Wayne State University.[106]

Although the war ended the national depression, it failed to improve the

AMA's financial health. When Tougaloo president Judson Cross asked for $1,500 for salary increases in 1941, Brownlee could only suggest that he take the money from other campus sources or raise tuition. The 1942 decision to discontinue secondary schools and feature colleges and race relations brought no new funds. The board of directors of the Board of Home Missions actually reduced the AMA appropriation by $32,000 for 1942–43, and refused to raise it for 1944–45. This combined with the steep increase in prices brought a considerable reduction in cash flow. Only more students paying tuition prevented the schools from losing ground. Rising costs made even keeping adequate food in school cafeterias difficult, and scarce materials and limited money prohibited new building or even major repairs. When the war began Tillotson had "miserable equipment" and buildings in need of renovation, and both deteriorated further. Tougaloo women abandoned a crumbling dormitory and moved into one vacated by men now in the military.[107] The only positive financial news came from Dillard. In 1940, Dent and Stern initiated a drive for a $3 million endowment. The AMA pledged $1 million; the Methodist Board of Education, GEB, and Rosenwald Fund added $500,000 each; and in June 1944 Dent announced the completion of a successful campaign.[108]

In view of the AMA's tenuous financial situation, it was not surprising that the association looked favorably upon any new attempts to support black education. All AMA colleges, except Talladega, were founding members of the United Negro College Fund (UNCF) created in 1943. Fearing the fund would interfere with Talladega's own solicitations, President Gallagher declined to cooperate, but Talladega joined immediately after his resignation, and in 1948 President Adam Beittel remarked that the UNCF income was an essential part of Talladega's budget. Brownlee enthusiastically supported the UNCF. Even if the schools had larger endowments (Fisk and Dillard, $3 million; Talladega, $1 million; and the others virtually none), Brownlee said in 1946 that they needed more than the AMA could possibly provide, and the UNCF had been their "life-saver" during the war years. The influx of returning veterans also helped balance the budget.[109]

"The college no longer resembles a female school," the Talladega Freshman News Sheet announced in April 1947. "Since the vets are returning it looks once again like a co-educational school." In fall 1947, Talladega had 362 students: 192 women and 170 men, the best balance of men and women in school history. Seventy-six males were veterans. Other colleges enjoyed a similar temporary climb in male students. In 1948, Dillard had 162 veterans, and the next year Tillotson enrolled 268 former military men counting 114 in summer classes. Chrystine Shackles, who was a history professor at Tillotson during that time, has said veterans brought new life to campus. Classroom discussions were more stimulating, and students seemed more militant. Margaret McCulloch saw similar differences at LeMoyne. Our males have returned, she wrote in 1946, "veterans—young men who have lived from end to end of the earth, gained a new world outlook and bear themselves with a new manliness and vigor as *men*, not as Negro men."[110]

By 1949 veterans were declining in number, and maintaining enrollment became a permanent problem at most private black schools. The Talladega faculty noted "a relatively new element" in the quest for students in 1947. It was "the *improved character*" of state institutions with their lower tuition costs "and other inducements made possible by increased support from state legislatures." In an attempt to maintain the fraud of separate but equal, all southern legislatures had increased funding for their black colleges. Black public colleges had been negligible competition prior to 1920, but they grew rapidly from that date onward. There had been forty students in private black colleges to one in public colleges in 1914. The ratio declined to 3 to 1 in 1926, 1.5 to 1 in 1935, and in 1953 black public four-year colleges enrolled fifty-seven percent of all African American college students.[111] The Tougaloo faculty noted in 1951 that state colleges not only were cheaper, but also offered attractive scholarships to the best high school students. Tougaloo, according to another report, had somehow to cope with the "free-flowing scholarships" of state institutions. Those sixty-five football players "Alcorn College hurled against us in our final game, get all-expenses for four years in college," said faculty member William Bender. The athletic programs resulting from full scholarships in football and other sports, and the school spirit it stimulated, also attracted students. After Mississippi began putting more state money in Jackson College (now Jackson State University) in the late 1940s, AMA officials debated closing Tougaloo. The campus had deteriorated during the war, and it had little endowment, had a small enrollment, and was unpopular with white Mississippians. AMA secretary Philip M. Widenhouse in 1951 doubted it could successfully compete with state schools, but based on the "quality of students . . . and ability of some few devoted faculty" he thought it should continue. Samuel C. Kincheloe, chairman of the AMA executive committee, made a personal survey of the state. He soon concluded that of all the areas in which the association worked, it was most needed in Mississippi. The greatest white opposition to Tougaloo, he wrote, was to the interracial faculty which in itself was an indication of why the AMA should be there. Rather than abandoning it, the AMA increased its support of Tougaloo. Black public colleges competed as fiercely for faculty as for students. In 1944, Hollis Price said he saw no way LeMoyne could compete with Tennessee A&I's "lavish expenditures" for both students and instructors. Florida A&M in 1947 offered one of Price's faculty $1,500 more annually. It was going to be increasingly difficult, Price feared, to keep LeMoyne from becoming a refuge for "mediocre and frustrated" teachers. The AMA colleges could only continue to struggle for money, students, faculty, and against segregation and discrimination.[112]

Anderson and Moss state in *Dangerous Donations* that "[a] keen observer might well have predicted in 1930 that the expansion of southern black education almost guaranteed a future challenge to white supremacy and Jim Crow." The AMA's interracial colleges by their very presence defied the South's racial code, and faculty and students had consistently, cautiously, and sometimes successfully spoken out against the many injustices perpetrated against blacks. For example, in 1894, Straight University professor George W. Henderson persuaded Louisiana's Roman Catholic hierarchy, Tulane University president William P. Johnson, and Rev. Benjamin M. Palmer, pastor of New Orleans' First Presbyterian Church, to petition the Louisiana legislature against lynching. Edwin C. Silsby, who served Talladega College from 1885 to 1916, helped organize the black Alabama State Teachers Association, denounced the state poll tax and other laws which limited black political participation, and demanded greater local and state support for black public schools. Booker T. Washington declared that Silsby was "more than willing to be identified with us anywhere under any circumstances."[113]

More aggressive action began in the 1930s with interracial conferences, and the war accelerated AMA defiance of injustice and segregation. Brownlee stated in 1943 that the war, which had increased racial tension on campus, might be wholesome as it meant an awakening awareness of the evils of segregation. In 1941 the Talladega NAACP youth council conducted a fund drive to aid in the fight to equalize black and white teachers' salaries, and encouraged patronizing black businesses. Faculty member David Rasmussen was arrested, jailed, and fined for eating with blacks in a Birmingham restaurant. In 1942, Talladega's President Gallagher, with threat of federal intervention, pressured local companies to hire blacks, and the school purchased a projector and showed movies on campus "to avoid the fetid Jim Crow balcony of downtown theaters."[114] At Tillotson, President Branch insisted upon mixed seating for all college programs, sponsored interracial student meetings, served on the Texas State Interracial Committee, and organized and became president of the Austin chapter and then the Texas branch of the NAACP. Every single Tillotson faculty member was an NAACP member in 1942–43. In New Orleans, Albert W. Dent was vice chairman of the Citizens Committee on Race Relations and helped organize the Louisiana Institute on Race Relations in 1945.[115]

In 1946 Tougaloo staff members W. A. Bender and Richard A. Daniels and two students attempted to vote. Bender, state president of the NAACP, and the students were driven from the polls; and Daniels, who tried to vote at Gulfport, was beaten, arrested, and thrown in jail, where he was almost killed. Bender publicly testified that he had heard Senator Theodore Bilbo in two separate speeches say "Keep the n-r away from the polls by seeing him the night before the election . . . I'll forgive you for all that you do to him." Brownlee wrote Bender, "My heart swelled with a deep-down pride when I read your testimony at the Bilbo hearing. Thank God for your integrity and courage. Whatever the outcome of the hearing, the fact that it took place is a significant milestone along Freedom Road." Ruth Barefield-Pendleton, who attended Tougaloo in the late 1940s and was later secretary of the Central Committee for Birmingham, Alabama's civil rights campaign, said Tougaloo was "the only island of light in a sea of darkness" in Mississippi.[116]

President Adam D. Beittel of Talladega began attacking discrimination and segregation almost from the day he arrived on campus. In 1946, he demanded that the city commission provide black children with the same supervised summer recreation white children enjoyed; he fumed about the segregated hospital; he lectured the white ministerial alliance on brotherhood; he joined the Negro Conference of Alabama, a black ministerial association; and he urged the mayor to employ black policemen.[117] Soon local whites viewed him as a "needler," "agitator," "radical," and "dangerous" man. Beittel achieved statewide notoriety when he protested to Gov. James E. Folsom about unequal salaries for black and white teachers, asked Gov. E. Persons to investigate alleged police brutality in Birmingham, and complained to Birmingham commissioner of public safety Eugene "Bull" Connor about discrimination against Talladega students.[118] Beittel brought unwanted national publicity to Alabama in 1949. The University of Alabama invited Talladega students to enter artwork in a judged exhibition as a part of ceremonies inaugurating a new art museum. Dr. Francis Taylor, director of the New York Metropolitan Museum of Art, and Dr. Thomas Munro of the Cleveland Art Museum were on the program. Talladega forwarded students' projects and asked if those exhibiting could attend some of the functions. When the head of the university art department said no, Beittel withdrew students' contributions, publicly condemned the segregated proceedings, wrote influential men throughout the country, and received public support from John Dewey, Rockwell Kent, Max Weber, and others. The *New York Times* covered the controversy, and both Munro and Taylor withdrew.[119] More white Alabamians began to agree with those in Talladega that Beittel was a menace.

Local white hostility deepened when Talladega hosted a biracial student conference on civil rights on April 9–11, 1948. Several white students from Alabama schools attended. It was "vitally important for the future of the South and our nation," Beittel said in an opening address, "to have American youth cross the barriers of segregation and mingle together in discussion and debate." The nearly one hundred participants resolved that "the evil of all forms of segregation and discrimination based on race, creed, color or national origin" be eliminated and recommended passage of a federal anti-lynching law, jury service for all races, right of all qualified voters to vote in primaries, employment of black policemen, an end to segregation in all public and private institutions, and abolition of poll tax and restrictive covenants. Whites were outraged. Local white trustee Samuel B. Wilson angrily insisted that Beittel allow no more such conferences, and the Talladega Chamber of Commerce withdrew its sponsorship of the United Negro College Fund. With his usual candor, Beittel charged Wilson and the Chamber of Commerce with attempting to deny students the right to take "an educational and constructive approach" to problems of discrimination. Communists in Russia and Nazis in Germany had agreed on one thing, he added: "Only the approved point of view may be proclaimed." Wilson resigned a few months later. The local newspaper editor blamed President Harry S. Truman as well as Beittel. He doubted that Talladega would have sponsored the conference "held in an atmosphere of complete social equality" except for Truman's call for civil rights legislation. "Racial agitators," emboldened by Truman, the editor wrote indignantly, had "dropped all pretense of not desiring social mingling of the races." Perhaps he was unaware that a year earlier Beittel had invited white students to socialize with Talladega students in his home. The editor promised that the students' call for desegregation would never occur. The federal government and all of the United Nations lacked the power to destroy segregation. "Not all the hosts that ever marched could do it."[120] Beittel, undeterred by white criticism, instituted an exchange program with northern colleges, which brought a white student to Talladega in 1948. In 1951, claiming that Talladega should not wait idly until the Supreme Court desegregated southern white colleges, Beittel opened the school's scholarship examination to all races. He managed to recruit one native white Alabamian, Frank Laraway, who enrolled in 1952.[121]

While white southerners considered college activists radical, their actions were in reality generally cautious and measured. Though their position was not as untenable as state black institutions, which were totally dependent upon state legislatures, AMA colleges still looked to whites for donations, were under white supervision, and were surrounded by whites hostile to desegregation; and leaders knew that moving too quickly could result in loss of life and property. When the Klan burned a cross on the Talladega campus in 1948 and paraded through again in 1949, it was not just showing off its new sheets and hoods. They were delivering a warning. Beittel was clearly the AMA president most active in battling segregation from 1944 to 1952. His color probably allowed him to do things that black presidents could not do in Memphis and New Orleans. Moreover, Talladega was a small town, and the college had a greater impact there than institutions in larger cities. White teacher Margaret Scott stated that Talladega "belonged to the segregated South," but she believed the extended presence of the college kept the town from being as volatile as Selma or other towns.[122]

Although most AMA colleges shared in postwar prosperity—Talladega's budget rose from $233,000 in 1943–44 to $410,717 in 1951–52—they were still seriously underfunded. When Brownlee retired in 1950, he warned his successor, Philip Widenhouse, that the colleges were at a crossroads. None had adequate financial support to face the future securely. How, he asked, "are they to survive from an economic standpoint in competition with state institutions?" That same year President Warren stated that the task of maintaining a faculty at Tougaloo was "a constant scramble" since restricted funds prohibited his competing with state salaries; and, he added, the handicap was becoming greater. The competition for students was equally intense. Other presidents had similar laments, and within a few years white colleges were offering scholarships to exceptional black students who traditionally attended AMA and other private schools. Desegregation, so long fought for by faculty and students, seriously damaged the very colleges that produced many of the civil rights leaders. Sociologists Walter R. Allen and Joseph O. Jewell claim that during the twenty years after the historic 1954 Brown decision declaring segregated schools unconstitutional, blacks "participated in a second 'Great Migration.'" This time it was not from south to north, but from historically black colleges and universities (HBCUs) to predominantly white colleges. By 1967–68, there were more than 130,000 African American students enrolled in formerly white institutions who might have been attending HBCUs. The succeeding decades were fraught with peril for private black schools.[123] Despite inadequate endowments, competition with state black colleges and traditionally white schools, and the Board of Home Missions' absorption of the AMA, the original institutions survived.[124] They continued to struggle to balance budgets, nurture students, retain adequate faculty, and steadily chisel away at segregation and discrimination. Between

1890 and 1950, AMA colleges graduated only several thousand students, but their impact was incalculable. AMA and other historically black colleges and universities "functioned as multifaceted institutions," providing a majority of black teachers; educated ministers; doctors; dentists; attorneys; and social, political, business, professional, and civil rights leaders for the black community.[125]

7

Race Relations Department

Shortly after the Interstate Commerce Commission abolished segregation in interstate travel in November 1955, Robert L. Carter, NAACP counsel, declared he could never have won the case without the assistance of Herman H. Long and the AMA's Race Relations Department. This was only one of many instances in which the department had attacked segregation since Fred L. Brownlee had created it in 1942.[1] From the time he became corresponding secretary in 1920, Brownlee had grown increasingly sensitive to and concerned about racism. In 1924, he urged AMA members to free themselves "from the dangers of paternalism and face the future courageously on the principles of democracy." The AMA must give African Americans greater leadership roles in its schools, he added, while continuing to maintain interracial faculties and resist "the danger of falling into the present, natural tendency toward racial segregation." Speaking to a large missions audience in 1929, Brownlee held up a rusty chain which, he said, had ringed the necks of African men and women during slavery. It had been easier to sunder those shackles, he declared, than to convince many whites that blacks "should have a real opportunity for the finest things in life." The next year, he warned that "soul-crushing and spirit-enslaving" segregation must be eliminated voluntarily through love or an explosion might result. Suppression of "the voice of intelligent interracial unrest" was as futile as plugging "the spout of a steaming tea-kettle" and expecting "the lid to stay on." Much had been done for blacks, he exclaimed, but little "on the basis of true interracialism with them." Institutional "Christianity and interracial fellowship" were at a crossroad, he cautioned. "If love is to have its way then Christians will have to become more like their Master."[2]

Brownlee, an admirer of the NAACP's "numerous achievements" and "virile stand for righteousness," addressed its twenty-second annual meeting at Pittsburgh in 1931, and attacked "missionary associations and ... interracial movements for advocating interracialism" and then adopting or allowing segregated programs. Brownlee now considered racism the most difficult problem in the United States, ranking in importance with world peace. White America must experience "a fundamental change of heart, mind, and soul" before it could atone for the inhumanity it had shown and continued to show black Americans, he proclaimed. In 1936, Brownlee lamented that ninety years after the AMA's creation, the black man remained "not only America's 'forgotten man,' but its most sinned-against, neglected, shunted aside, suppressed and repressed man." A virulent racial virus undermined the health of United States democracy, rendered Christianity anemic, and made "callow the soul of him who does the discriminating." Abraham Lincoln had declared that the country could not survive half slave and half free. Brownlee questioned whether it could continue "nine-tenths caste and one-tenth outcaste."[3] He made "Erasing the Color Line" the focus of his 1937 annual report, led the AMA in financially supporting the NAACP and other organizations seeking to improve race relations, and attacked segregation personally when he could. Although he freely mingled with blacks in churches, in schools, and in their homes in Mississippi and Alabama, he did not aggressively try to desegregate public accommodations in the South at this time. He did, however, protest segregated hotels and restaurants elsewhere, including in New York City.[4] In 1940 Brownlee toured the West with black friends Dr. Charles S. and Marie Johnson, and Josie Sellars. They were well received everywhere except at the Totem Pole Café at the edge of Yellowstone Park where the waitress refused to serve them. They immediately left and dined at a nearby establishment without incident. Brownlee complained to Montana governor Roy E. Ayers about the affront to his friends, and suggested Ayers inform the proprietor of the Totem Pole that he disagreed with his policy. Such action would mean much, Brownlee wrote, to "our American democracy toward the solution of a very vexing problem which eats, like a worm, at the heart of our commonwealth."[5]

Brownlee grew increasingly frustrated with northern indifference to racial discrimination, and with his own inability to effect change. Soon after joining the AMA, he learned the futility of pointing out to whites that their conduct was inconsistent with their professed beliefs. When he turned to black friends and told them the AMA should more actively attack discrimination, they responded with a smile and apparent indifference. He was puzzled by their seeming disinterest until he invited several leading black men to his office to discuss the issue. They examined race relations and possible approaches to improvement, but frankly told Brownlee that they had limited faith in the AMA's, and more important, the church's, willingness to act.

Church members were more likely to talk brotherhood than practice it, they charged. Brownlee could hardly disagree. The AMA consistently advocated black education as a means of liberation, and gave far more than mere lip service to equal rights, but its divisional committee showed only minor interest in doing more directly in race relations.[6] It was not until 1940, according to Brownlee, that "we began to take in earnest" what the black men had discussed in his office. At an AMA divisional committee meeting, Brownlee confessed that he was "haunted by a sense of frustration" about race relations. Charles S. Johnson, race relations expert and noted black sociologist at Fisk University, present as a consultant, began "talking in his quiet way" about methods of dealing with racial strife. Ruth Morton, whom Johnson later said was "one of the minds and spirits that gave birth" to the race relations department, told of some racial work being done in Chicago. Brownlee and Morton decided to investigate possible ways in which the AMA could take a more active role in fighting segregation and racism.[7]

By 1940, Brownlee was clearly determined to place greater emphasis on improving race relations. Equality had always been the association's aim, but, wrote Brownlee, "we had not kept as close to the firing line as we should have." Offering education, publicizing discrimination, lobbying politicians, and appealing to conscience and goodwill had failed to bring necessary change, and new methods must be tried. "Are we to solve the problem of integrating Negroes in American life on the basis of our democratic principles," he asked, "or are we to head toward racial war because of continued injustices and discrimination?" In his opinion, the possibility of World War II further heightened the glaring contrast between U.S. preachment and practice. He believed that the AMA could render service in quiet, often behind-the-scenes, effective ways. Such work could best be done by "an intelligent, level-headed Negro in whom men of brains, leadership and authority have confidence." He clearly was thinking of Charles S. Johnson of Fisk, whom he considered "the best qualified man in the United States in the realm of race and race relations."[8]

In October 1941, Brownlee invited numerous experts to attend a two-day seminar on "racialism" at Broadway Tabernacle in New York City, to be held on January 16–17, 1942. Little did he know that by then the Japanese would have bombed Pearl Harbor, forcing the country into war. Attendees included the presidents of AMA and other black colleges, representatives of philanthropic boards, and government officials.[9] Though males were in a majority, there was more than a sprinkling of women, including Ruth Morton; Tillotson College president Mary Elizabeth Branch; and Jessie Daniel Ames, founder of the Association of Southern Women for the Prevention of Lynching. Brownlee opened the seminar by branding racialism the "major issue, the fundamental problem, the disease at the heart of white and Negro relations." "We are questioning," he added, "the integrity of the United States in fighting for democracy while still so deficient in practicing it." Underlying the undemocratic treatment of blacks, Brownlee stated, was the generally accepted doctrine of racial inferiority. The purpose of the seminar was to face racism squarely, and to seek ways to eliminate it.[10]

After lengthy discussions, Edwin R. Embree, president of the Rosenwald Fund, moved that seminar participants ask the AMA to establish a commission with a budget sufficient to circulate materials and rally forces against discrimination. This motion planted the seed that grew into the Race Relations Department. Embree's motion was seconded, but then, according to Talladega College president Buell Gallagher, representatives of the various Board of Home Missions agencies "began a frantic job of mending their own fences and putting up 'No Trespassing' signs." The normally optimistic Gallagher doubted that the AMA could act. His pessimism was unwarranted. In April, Brownlee informed Embree that the seminar provided "the shock I wanted . . . so far as the AMA is concerned. It awakened some people who needed to be shaken up, persons who hold the destiny of the A.M.A. in their hands." On January 26, the AMA executive committee resolved to concentrate its attention on race, and to employ a director to develop a "noninstitutional type of pioneering work" in race relations.[11] Of course, the AMA decision had to be approved by the Board of Home Missions (BHM) and the General Council of Congregational Christian Churches. Both did so in June 1942, and Brownlee's dream of a special department of race relations could now become a reality. He planned to initiate a new era in AMA history "of more direct, cooperative service" looking toward securing full citizenship rights and privileges for black Americans. The AMA had long ago chosen "the conciliatory and educational way," Brownlee stated, and it had been a reasonable and good way. The association had "never compromised on principle" and had "always maintained genuine fellowship" in its schools, but the NAACP, born as a direct action agency, had "succeeded in getting many things done which the A.M.A. would have taken much longer to accomplish." The Race Relations Department would be more action oriented than the schools. Brownlee also hoped to use AMA colleges and cooperative centers more effectively "as agencies in their own communities to better race relations." He saw the Race Relations Department, schools, and community centers as partners in the struggle for equal rights, and he fervently believed that race relations work was "the core of everything the A.M.A. has done, is now doing and hopes to do for years to come." The AMA's new thrust, he reminded BHM members, did not absolve them of personal responsibility. "Our convictions needed to be sharpened," he added, "our consciences made more sensitive, our imaginations more creative, and our souls inspired with a new sense of mission." He urged northern Christians to tackle "fearlessly, courageously, and intelligently" such questions as restrictive real estate covenants, fair employment practices, the poll tax, white primary elections, and hospital and sanitation facilities.[12]

Brownlee often doubted that ordinary white BHM members shared his passion for black equality, and no doubt he was in advance of many. Numerous northern churchmen denied his claim that segregation was "a vicious system, a sin against God, a disgrace to man," and others were uncomfortable with Brownlee's liberal attitude toward interracial marriage. Blacks, he often proclaimed, had the right to marry, fraternize, and worship with whomever they pleased. In 1940 he suggested that amalgamation was the ultimate solution to racial prejudice. Ferdinand Q. Blanchard, a devoted AMA supporter and officer, and a Brownlee confidant, reflected the views of many liberal northern whites when he wrote in 1945 that Brownlee, having worked with privileged blacks and having argued "inflexibly from premise to conclusion" so long and relentlessly, failed to take the other side into account. There were reasons for discrimination besides racial prejudice, he said. "The race issue is not the simple thing you suggest, between being mean and kind," Blanchard added. All blacks were not of the quality of the AMA's college professors. Blanchard vehemently protested racial prejudice but apparently found class discrimination less reprehensible.[13]

A race relations department had been authorized but remained to be created. What should be its responsibilities, and who should direct it? There was no need to duplicate the NAACP, the National Urban League, and other such organizations, but Brownlee believed the AMA could provide a mediating influence by functioning in "an advisory capacity with and through" existing public and private institutions and agencies. The department would operate on "an educational, moral suasion, conciliation basis, and seek in practical ways" to deal with problems lying behind racial dissatisfaction, including housing, employment, recreation, and health. Brownlee told Claude A. Barnett, head of the Associated Negro Press, that the AMA's aim was to alter "color caste legalized by Jim Crow laws," to be "a sharp spear, goading into action all who" were inclined to improve race relations, and to make "miserable the Bilbos and Talmadges everywhere."[14] Since Brownlee supervised the schools, colleges, and community centers, thereby leaving limited time for the new department, the direction it took and its success would depend largely upon its director; and Brownlee was determined that Charles S. Johnson fill that role.

Edwin R. Embree, Johnson's friend and fellow worker, seconded Brownlee's effort to make Johnson director of the newly created Race Relations Department. Johnson, a Rosenwald Fund trustee since 1934, was its part-time director of research, as well as chairman of the social science department at Fisk University. Embree's and Brownlee's mutual admiration of Johnson led them to cooperate temporarily in employing him.[15] Brownlee invited Embree to a November meeting at Fisk where all AMA college presidents, deans, and school principals discussed the AMA's future work as it moved "toward concentration in the field of racism." Embree wrote to Brownlee afterward, "The plans that you and I are making for union of effort through a great personality [Johnson] are exciting indeed." In December the BHM executive committee approved the AMA's recommendation that Johnson become director of the Race Relations Department effective January 1, 1943. At the same time he became director of the Rosenwald Fund's race relations program.[16]

Born in Bristol, Virginia, on July 24, 1893, Johnson was educated at Wayland Academy and Virginia Union University where he graduated in 1916. After graduation he moved to Chicago, secured work as a night watchman and stevedore, and enrolled at the University of Chicago, where as a graduate student in sociology he came under the direction of Albion Small and Robert E. Park. Richard Robbins in *Sidelines Activist: Charles S. Johnson and the Struggle for Civil Rights,* says Park, impressed by his young student's "brilliance in ordering facts and in conducting scrupulously scholarly research," became a friend, mentor, sponsor, and "a signal influence on his life and work." Upon Park's recommendation, Johnson became director of research and investigation for the Chicago Urban League. A Carnegie grant allowed him to study the Great Migration and make a survey of blacks in Milwaukee, similar to studies later done for Fisk and the Race Relations Department.[17] Johnson interrupted his research career in 1918 to enlist in the Army, where, as a regimental sergeant major in the 803rd Pioneer Infantry Regiment, he took part in the Meuse-Argonne offensive. Although he and other blacks came under direct enemy fire for their country, Johnson witnessed whites beat and harass black soldiers both at the point of embarkation in France and after unloading in Norfolk, Virginia.[18]

Johnson returned to Chicago just a week prior to the terrifying race riot which began July 27, 1919. During thirteen days of horror, 38 people were killed and 537 were injured. Johnson was shot at while dragging others to safety. He later presented a plan to study the riot's causes, which led to his appointment as associate executive secretary of Chicago's Commission on Race Relations, a post-riot creation of Illinois governor Frank O. Lowden. Johnson devised the research strategy and wrote at least seven chapters of the resulting *The Negro in Chicago*. Robbins claims this initiated Johnson's "basic approach to race relations research" and "made him a major player for the next three decades." It also acquainted him with philanthropist Julius Rosenwald, a commission member who developed great respect for the black investigator.[19] Before the report on the riot appeared, Johnson moved to New York to become director of the National Urban League's new department of Research and Investigation. In addition to conducting a number of social surveys, Johnson in 1923 founded and became the editor of *Opportunity*, the league's magazine. Its purpose was to stimulate pride in past racial achievements, and Johnson used it to attack racism and to encourage black creativity in the arts. He and *Opportunity*, along with *Crisis*, published black authors, offered prizes, and held receptions, thereby becoming midwife to the Harlem Renaissance.[20] Robert E. Hemenway, Zora Neale Hurston's biographer, declares that Johnson "single-handedly turned *Opportunity* into an expression of 'New Negro' thought," which meant that blacks would not passively accept a subordinate role.[21]

In the meantime, Johnson continued significant research for the Urban League. According to Robbins, these studies were of two kinds: community surveys of black life and sociological essays on race relations. His reputation for research eventually resulted in his leaving the excitement and lively social life of Harlem in 1928 for the confined campus of the small but dynamic Fisk University. When, a year earlier, the Laura Spelman Rockefeller Memorial Foundation funded a department of social science research at Fisk to make original studies of black life and to train black researchers for education and social service positions, Johnson was a logical choice to be its head. Although research was limited at most small, underfunded black colleges, Johnson developed Fisk into a genuine center of scholarship with an excellent social science faculty, and with a direct pipeline to the major philanthropic foundations. Between 1928 and 1940, the Fisk social science faculty published twenty-three books and scores of articles, and trained many young black scholars in race relations. Johnson, says historian August Meier, created the "Fisk Machine" through which most of the foundation research money was channeled.[22] Johnson sat on the boards of many philanthropic agencies, and money for black sociologists went primarily to Fisk. His Fisk associates called him "the most powerful Negro" in America.[23] Most of the Fisk studies were meant to explain blacks to whites and to suggest ways to improve black life, but Johnson intended his studies to do more than enlighten a few scholars. One aspect of his work was a "distinctive deployment of the research-advocacy role as a strategy of change, as a means of persuasion to induce the makers of public policy to act more decisively to end racial segregation." Johnson's goal was always integration, but integration "tempered by cultural pluralism." Desegregation did not mean rejecting black culture. He assumed that blacks were making, and would continue to make, "significant contributions to the larger American culture."[24]

Johnson's scholarship and his personal contacts undoubtedly influenced some New Deal measures during the Great Depression. John Egerton, in *Speak Now against the Day: The Generation before the Civil Rights Movement in the South,* praises Johnson, Edwin R. Embree, and Will W. Alexander for "the role they played in the desegregation of the New Deal." In addition, Johnson, a prominent leader of the Commission on Interracial Cooperation, helped form its successor, the Southern Regional Council; he served on national panels of religion, race relations, labor, and education; and he was active in several professional social science societies. Little wonder that Brownlee thought Johnson was the best choice to head the AMA's initiative against discrimination. *Advance* magazine described him in 1943 as "the world's leading authority on the Negro" and one of the country's most competent sociologists.[25]

Johnson officially became director of the Race Relations Department on January 1, 1943, and had a staff of nine in place by June.[26] Ira DeA. Reid, professor of sociology at Atlanta University, was one-third time and associate director. Reid, who had succeeded Johnson as director of research for the National Urban League, went to Atlanta in 1930 to work with W. E. B. Du Bois, former *Crisis* editor, historian, sociologist, and propagandist, and was a talented scholar. Horace Mann Bond, educator, historian, and president of Fort Valley State College, collaborated on special projects. The most significant appointment after Johnson was Herman H. Long, who became associate director when Johnson became president of Fisk in 1946, and director of the department upon Johnson's death in October 1957. Long, a star basketball and football player, graduated from Talladega College cum laude in 1935, and the following year earned a master's degree in psychology from the School of Religious Education, Hartford Seminary Foundation in Hartford, Connecticut. Long became an instructor of psychology at Miles College in Birmingham in 1936. In the fall of 1939, he enrolled in the University of Michigan to work on a Ph.D. in psychology, and in 1944 joined the Race Relations Department.[27]

The need for racial amelioration was so urgent Johnson feared that some might expect sudden miracles. He knew progress would be reluctant and erratic since he was dealing with "the same slow-moving elements of custom and tradition and problems of human behavior that have resisted the high principles of Christian democracy since the founding of the nation." But he was eager to get started. He perceived the department's task as understanding racial problems and bringing the best experience of the social sciences to bear upon them.[28] Johnson's academic approach to race relations caused some, especially northern blacks, to brand him as too cautious. In historian Rayford Logan's view, he was "right of center," and another black critic called him "an establishment nigger." In reality Johnson was angry about racial discrimination and spent his adult life working tirelessly to eradicate it. One acquaintance referred to his "capacity for great but controlled indignation," which he channeled into his scholarship. Egerton has accurately described Johnson's situation: "To be black and southern in those perilous times, and to stake out a position at variance with the canons of segregation and white supremacy, required a mixture of conservatism and a tactful independence that few non-Southerners could understand or appreciate." Aggressiveness, an iron will, and a clear sense of purpose were not enough, Egerton adds; "Br'er Rabbit smarts-craftiness, sagacity, a smooth line, and an instinct for survival" were necessary. Johnson and other black pragmatists, "using whatever tools they could get their hands on[,] . . . chipped away at the mighty rock of segregation."[29] Southern whites certainly did not consider Johnson too cautious. They saw him as a disruptive troublemaker. Much of the black criticism of Johnson came later, and it was unfair to hold Johnson, as Richard Robbins suggests, "to some litmus test of militancy, constructed twenty years after his death, and applied *after* the ensuing civil rights revolution and the collapse of racial segregation in the South."[30]

Johnson sincerely believed, as did Du Bois, that "thorough, disciplined research" revealing the degree and depth of racial discrimination was one of many methods of effecting social change. He did not naively think that impeccable research would alter southern white opinion, but his experience with New Deal agencies caused him to hope that it might "induce the makers of public policy to act more decisively to combat racial discrimination, and to end racial segregation." During his early career Johnson was careful to avoid alienating southern white liberals. Blacks needed any friends they could find, he believed, even if these friends did not favor complete equality. Black northern journalists such as Roi Otley sometimes accused him of being a pawn of white leaders, but Lewis W. Jones, who lived in the South and knew Johnson well, saw him "as a shrewd man building Trojan horses in the center of Jim Crow." For years Johnson fumed silently because whites in the

Commission on Interracial Cooperation, and later on the Southern Regional Council, refused to declare publicly against segregation. In a 1945 speech at an interracial institute in Richmond, Virginia, Johnson said he sought to find a bridge that could lead to understanding "in a situation in which collective action" was vital. Perhaps an accord might be reached, he continued, between blacks and sympathetic whites by ceasing to demand of each other what was for the present impossible, and by cooperating in those areas where there was agreement: programs seeking better facilities, more equal opportunities, and fuller participation in the obligations and privileges of citizenship. Yet he was chairman of the drafting committee that wrote the "Durham Statement" in October 1942 which proclaimed a "fundamental opposition to the principle and practice of compulsory segregation." Sixty black leaders met in Durham, North Carolina, and called for the abolition of racial discrimination in every form even though they knew such a statement would alienate many of their white allies. Richard Robbins suggests that Johnson, preparing the Durham draft "which would for the first time come out directly against segregation, was *for that time* evoking a spirit of nonviolent combat akin to that of the four black students" who in 1960 "prepared their sit-in at Woolworth's lunch counter to protest denial of service" in Greensboro, North Carolina.[31] Johnson's ultimate aim was always total destruction of segregation and discrimination.

Even before the staff was complete, in 1943 Johnson and the Race Relations Department began a flurry of activity, and there was much to do. Black soldiers were discriminated against and frequently abused. Race relations were poor in the South and were worsening in the North. The large African American migration to the North and West in search of employment created new tension areas. The black population in Los Angeles doubled between 1940 and 1945. It grew by seventy-seven percent in Chicago in the 1940s, and the growth was also great in the industrial cities such as Seattle, Portland, and San Francisco. Johnson and his group were facing the kinds of problems described by a concerned Portland, Oregon, citizen who wrote to Brownlee in January 1944 seeking help. There had been a sixfold increase in blacks there since the war began, and proper housing was unavailable. Realtors refused to sell to African Americans, and "white only" signs began appearing prominently at restaurants. The situation was seriously aggravated by a large influx of white southern workers. Portland blacks were accustomed to a subordinate social position but were not used to some of the more flagrant discriminatory practices associated with the South. Many of the new black residents, he continued, were from New York, Chicago, and other eastern cities, and their aggressiveness alarmed local whites and blacks alike. Others thought the southern blacks there, while less confrontational, responded to "crude and emotional religious patterns." There was tension on crowded transit facilities which both blacks and whites used, and white fear was accentuated by a report that two thousand black soldiers were to be housed nearby.[32]

The lack of adequate housing, receptive schools, and friendly local governments, combined with strong racial prejudice stirred by local demagogues, created a volatile atmosphere in many northern cities. On June 20, 1943, a race riot exploded in Detroit which killed thirty-four people. Additional outbreaks occurred in Mobile, Alabama; Beaumont, Texas; and other areas. The department identified 242 racial clashes in 47 cities and towns in 1943. The riots in Detroit and Mobile were caused largely by the employment of or upgrading of black workers. The Race Relations Department sent black minister Harold M. Kingsley, a veteran AMA worker, to Detroit, and Henry C. McDowell, former missionary to Africa and principal of Lincoln Academy, to Mobile as common ground workers. Their stated objective was to help forestall a recurrence of violence, to rebuild community trust and tolerance, and "most important to chart the inciting source of the difficulty" so that methods could be devised to assist future threatened areas—a tall order for two men with no formal training as mediators and with no authority. Brownlee informed McDowell that he was to be "a combination of detective, investigator, social engineer" and a representative of the government, the Race Relations Department, and the AMA. Although the expectations for Kingsley and McDowell were unrealistic, this established the tradition of sending common ground workers to tension areas.[33]

In the meantime, Johnson and associates made a survey of racial tension in industry, housing, transportation, rural America, the military, and other problem areas, published in 1943 as *To Stem This Tide: A Survey of Racial Tension Areas in the United States.* Johnson pinpointed areas in which problems were likely to occur and tried to devise methods of avoiding conflict. Johnson and Horace Mann Bond also wrote *Into the Main Stream,* a manual of sound racial practices for interracial communities, while the staff, including Margaret C. McCulloch, prepared twelve lessons for the Methodist Church on "The Golden Rule and Race Relations," and *Manners and Minorities,* dealing with personal etiquette in direct interracial relations. In order to inform people of what was being done in the field, the department in cooperation with the Rosenwald Fund printed "The Monthly Summary of Events and Trends in Race Relations." (By 1945 the "Monthly Summary" was being sent to approximately seven thousand people and organizations.) Investigation and publication were only a small part of what the department was doing in 1943. Ira DeA. Reid was training additional common ground workers in Atlanta, while Johnson helped create and became first chairman of the executive committee of the interracial Southern Regional Council. The department also informed government agencies of the spread of racial hostility and worked with church and youth groups interested in improving racial relations. Johnson made scores of speeches and consulted with officials in San Francisco, Los Angeles, Boston, Utica, and St. Louis, thus beginning an important Race Relations Department innovation—the self-survey.[34]

By the end of 1943 Johnson and Brownlee had, with few exceptions, basically determined the paths that the department would follow in its efforts to deal with racial problems. These included education of individuals, groups, and organizations; use of common ground workers, community self-surveys, school programs, and race relations institutes; and investigations designed to alter behavior and influence public policy. At first Johnson thought that common ground workers would play a major role in the department's activities. The plan was not to subsidize permanent persons in hot spots, but to send help when invited. Kingsley and McDowell apparently had no appreciable impact in Detroit and Mobile, but some workers had at least limited influence. Kingsley helped develop an interracial and intercultural program in Los Angeles in 1944, and Grace C. Jones spent six months in Detroit in 1944–45 educating leaders.[35]

Jones had earned a B.A. in 1929 from New Orleans University (now Dillard) and a master's in psychology from the University of Michigan in 1941. She resigned as psychologist of the Girl's Industrial School in Delaware, Ohio, in 1943 to join the Race Relations Department. In April 1944 Johnson sent her to Detroit to advise public school officials. The superintendent of Detroit Public Schools, Warren E. Bow, viewing her as "a very helpful person," requested that she return the next year to assist in developing a program of intercultural education and democratic human relations. She returned in January 1945 and consulted in at least 58 of the city's 250 schools. Certainly advice was needed. Guest School, a local white high school, formed a cooperative program with a fellow black school and, until Jones scrapped the idea, planned to entertain black guests with a blackface comedy act. A joint venture in which the black chorus director of the fellow school directed a mixed chorus of both schools in singing the Negro national anthem, "Lift Every Voice and Sing," went well. With a little advice from her, the intercultural program at Guest, Jones wrote, was "progressing remarkably." Jones encountered insensitivity and ignorance more often than outright hostility. While at Detroit she went to Ypsilanti to confer with the school superintendent and businessmen. Her working notes indicate some of their comments: "Negro rowdies coming down on our establishment and wrecking it"; "If you serve acceptable Negroes the others will come, too, and drive trade away"; "You'll have to give the Negro what he wants—or you may have something happening like in Detroit." Jones's final comment was "fear, fear, fear!!" There was more than enough racial bias outside the South, but at least some areas recognized that and requested help. In return Jones and others exerted a positive, though limited, influence. Common ground workers dispatched to southern cities went primarily as investigators rather than as mediators and educators.[36] These employees went to several other cities, but more and more they were assigned to other duties, especially the community self-surveys conducted by the department.[37]

Both Charles S. Johnson and Herman H. Long, who cooperated in originating the self-survey, thought it was the most important technique the Race Relations Department devised, and other experts agreed.[38] The Catholic journal *Interracial Review* called it a "true pioneering" effort. The National Council for Civil Rights sponsored a planning conference on the use of the self-survey in 1949 and invited Long to present two papers.[39] According to Johnson, the self-survey was "a planned and deliberate effort in social engineering, combining the values of scientific fact finding with those of effective community organization, with social action directed toward the concrete goal of changing local policies and practices" of community agencies and institutions. Local leaders had to be concerned and willing to learn in order for the system to work, but that was also its great advantage. The department entered a city only upon request. Staff experts then made contact with and formed a board of top business, educational, political, professional, and community leaders. With the power and prestige of the community behind them, working committees of local people, trained and directed by the department, went into the community to find the facts. They studied housing, neighborhood covenants, banking, employment, churches, social welfare agencies, schools—any area where discrimination might create tension. The survey became an effort of united community groups, and thus more acceptable than a blueprint imposed by outsiders. Long believed that the survey became "in essence, a social process grafted onto the community structure . . . drawing its dynamics from the sustaining life of the community." Some of the scholarly dispassionate observation was thereby lost, he admitted, but community participation maximized the potential of the research program to create social change. In addition to directing the survey, the staff attempted to sensitize school administrators and inform employers and labor groups of the possible consequences of refusing jobs to blacks.[40] Since it was a local effort, and those involved occasionally learned much about themselves as well as the recent black immigrants they feared, the results and changes were sometimes substantial.

The idea of self-surveys began to germinate in Johnson's and Long's minds after San Francisco officials asked for help in 1943. Wartime migration had tripled the city's population in three years. Whites, fearing that trouble lay ahead and unsure of what to do, sought Johnson's advice. The race relations staff, led by Herman Long, conferred with city leaders and guided a survey of housing, labor, industry, schools, churches, hospitals, public accommodations, and community relations generally. The survey revealed widespread segregation and discrimination, but whites also learned that blacks' needs and wants resembled theirs, and that "they were in no way special—except as discrimination had created special problems." As a result of the investigation and recommendations, the city established a Mayor's Committee on Unity to continue the work, and established an Urban League to help immigrants find employment. The city hired black teachers in the public schools for the first time; appointed a black principal; added blacks to the police force; solicited black doctors, nurses, social, and recreation workers; and began plans for housing developments. In addition, the San Francisco Telephone Company employed black operators. The survey was "a major factor in preventing the spread of racial hysteria into open conflict," Long believed.[41]

In 1945, several Pittsburgh, Pennsylvania, agencies and interracial organizations requested assistance in making "a self appraisal" of problems and resources with a view to determining "constructive programs of action." Johnson sent Herman Long and four common ground workers to help.[42] As a result of the survey, the city council established a Mayor's Council on Civic Unity, department stores hired black saleswomen, the Retail Merchants Association adopted a fair promotion policy, and the public schools added a program of intercultural education, especially for administrators. More important than these immediate results, perhaps, the survey committee formulated an extensive master plan of action relating to labor and industry, education, housing, churches, government, and social and health agencies. It established goals to be met on a time schedule. The department always hoped that the survey would energize progressives in the community and was merely the beginning of long-range efforts to improve race relations.[43]

One of the department's greatest successes occurred in Minneapolis, which was experiencing postwar racial unrest similar to that of many other northern cities. In late 1946, the city requested Race Relations Department assistance. Several months of fieldwork and analysis began in the spring of 1947. The young, dynamic mayor and future United States senator and vice

president, Hubert H. Humphrey, proclaimed that the "well planned and exe-
cuted" self-survey was "the most important and significant project" the city
undertook during his administration. Long and Humphrey formed a close
bond which led Humphrey to accept an appointment to the Race Relations Department advisory committee and to cooperate with Long in the
interest of racial progress after he was elected to the United States Senate.[44] According to the *Minneapolis Star,* the investigation revealed discrimination in industry, labor, housing, hospitals, public schools—indeed in almost every facet of Minneapolis life. Blacks, Jews, and Japanese-Americans
were generally excluded from civic organizations. The results of the survey
were "more successful than the most sanguine had expected." As often happened, some changes occurred before the survey was completed. One aim
of the Race Relations Department was to involve and sensitize large numbers of people who then, it hoped, would make individual efforts to improve
race relations; and it worked in Minneapolis. Even before Long and his colleagues completed their survey and made recommendations, the city commission passed fair-employment and anti-hate ordinances. While the Race
Relations Department could not claim much credit for these advances, the
self-survey "brought the heavy impact of community-wide citizen attention
and participation," which added to the needed effort. Additional changes included the adoption of a policy of making all emergency housing available
without color distinction, the formal advocation by the Minneapolis Board
of Realtors of state enabling legislation for public housing, the hiring of the
first black public school teachers, and employment of the first black nurses in
two city hospitals. The Minneapolis survey attracted considerable national
publicity and led many other communities to ask for Race Relations Department aid.[45]

Most of the cities seeking assistance were outside the South, but in August 1953, the Maryland Commission on Interracial Problems and Relations
invited Herman Long to aid in conducting a self-survey of Baltimore. The
commission, established by the Maryland General Assembly in 1951, concluded that enlightening the public about conditions under which minorities lived in Baltimore might contribute toward improving those conditions.
Commission members had read about the Race Relations Department self-
surveys in national magazines and newspapers and asked Long to direct the
project and to train 350 volunteer workers to do the interviews.[46] He agreed
to do so without charge. Long encouraged using local volunteer interviewers
for two reasons. It was cheaper, but more important, Long believed that when
people took the time to study racial discrimination they "usually become
anxious to do something about it." Sixty-eight organizations and five hun-

dred volunteer workers eventually participated in the survey of education, employment, housing, public accommodations, hospitals, interfaith relations, and social welfare agencies. In April 1954, the AMA Divisional Committee reported that the survey had "already been a potent force toward better race relations." Some theaters and lunch counters in department and five-and-dime stores had desegregated, and city officials were advocating integrated public housing. No one claimed that the self-surveys solved all or even most of the racial problems in the communities concerned, but greater sensitivity to minorities and at least some progress usually occurred. The CBS television network was sufficiently impressed with the results of the Baltimore survey to include it in its thirty-minute program *The Search* on March 20, 1955, dealing with contributions made to improving American life. Long was interviewed and performed admirably.[47]

In the meantime, the AMA's annual Race Relations Institute was attracting national attention. In July 1944, Johnson held a three-week seminar at Fisk University "to provide an intensive and practical" course in race relations for those "who were concerned in their own communities with programs of amelioration." Johnson's reputation enabled him over the years to bring almost every leading race relations specialist, black and white, together with an impressive number of prominent community, government, union, and educational leaders to study race relations. The 1944 institute had 137 participants—81 white, 55 black, 1 Japanese, 90 from the South, and 47 from the North. Johnson, Brownlee, and Ruth Morton, the resident faculty, were aided by numerous consultants. Morton enthusiastically wrote that it "was the most thrilling experience of its kind" she had ever had and many other participants agreed. The institute, which Johnson referred to as a "Laboratory for Scientific Social Engineering in Human Relations," became an annual affair (sessions were shortened from three to two weeks in 1948) and consistently drew distinguished faculty and participants.[48]

Patrick J. Gilpin, a Johnson biographer, believes the institutes might be Johnson's greatest contribution to race relations. Yet there was nothing particularly new about a race relations institute. Johnson himself had hosted such events at Swarthmore College since 1933, but the Fisk institutes were held in the South where discussion of race was discouraged and segregation was held sacred. In a region where violation of racial customs often provoked violence, men and women of different races met unsegregated on the Fisk campus, studied, lived, ate, and roomed together, condemned segregation and sought ways to undermine it. The *Pittsburgh Courier* reported that the consensus at the 1947 institute was that segregation, a relic of "barbaric ages," must be replaced by unity, friendship, understanding, and cooperation. The

Fig. 10. Race Relations Department Institute participants, 1947 (Courtesy of Amistad Research Center, Tulane University, New Orleans, Louisiana)

institute was of national consequence, Johnson declared in 1947, because, as the only meeting of its kind held in the South, it symbolized "a constructive approach to the problem in the area where the heart of the problem lies." This, Johnson added, gave the institute significance "extending far beyond the immediate sessions themselves." Egerton has proclaimed that when Johnson initiated the Race Relations Institute he "took a bold but calculated step beyond his time or place. He had the stature to get nationally prominent blacks and whites to participate . . . and the courage to withstand local white criticism," even when white Fisk president Thomas Elsa Jones "nearly caved in to pressure." Local newspapers frequently condemned the institutes, and the Nashville police often arrived on campus prior to evening sessions and engaged in day-to-day harassment. Before the third annual institute, James G. Stahlman, publisher and owner of the *Nashville Banner,* and other community leaders visited President Jones and demanded that the institutes be stopped. Some observers thought Jones was ready to concede, but Johnson stood firm.[49] Johnson had remained in interracial organizations that failed to oppose segregation because he thought blacks needed the support of white liberals, but he insisted on integration at the institutes.

Not surprisingly, some Tennessee whites suspected the presence of outside agitators in the institutes. In 1945, the *Nashville Banner* charged that two attendees, James Dombrowski and Margaret Gelders Frantz of the Southern Conference for Human Welfare, had "communist associations of various sorts." Many Tennessee whites assumed that Communists must be involved, and constantly attacked Johnson and the institute. Interestingly, while whites believed that "Reds" had infiltrated the institute, Benjamin J. Davis Jr., a top black Communist leader, charged Johnson with letting Willard S. Townsend, president of United Transport Service Employees of America, and George L. P. Weaver of the Congress of Industrial Organizations (CIO) use the institute as a platform to attack the Communist Party. At the 1947 institute, Townsend condemned the "plague of intrigue that Communists have injected into democratic and free labor unions of the world." Townsend, an African American who was elected a vice president of the AFL-CIO in 1955, attended several institutes.[50]

A general pattern soon developed for the institutes. Johnson opened each session with a state of race relations message, and then consultants—sixty in 1946—gave a series of addresses and workshops to participants. Names of faculty and consultants often read like a Who's Who in race relations. Topics discussed in 1947 included Group Tensions, Constitutional Steps toward Equal Rights, An Affirmative Radicalism, Christian Church and Race Relations, and Education for Democratic Human Relations. President Harry S. Truman's 1946 creation of the President's Committee on Civil Rights was widely discussed.[51] A *Chicago Daily News* reporter remarked that the 1947 institute lectures were "pretty much on the academic side, and not calculated to jar a strange visitor out of his nap." Most attendees, however, found the sessions exciting, and they also learned in bull sessions and individual discussions, or as Mrs. Opal G. Gruner, a white volunteer from Minneapolis, said, "the experience of living in a dormitory with a mixed group is in itself an education." And all lectures were not academic treatises. In 1950, NAACP counsel Thurgood Marshall eloquently urged all qualified blacks to apply for admission to public universities. "We now have the tools to destroy all governmentally imposed racial segregation," he boasted, but added that it would require time, courage, and determination. While the Chicago reporter thought the talks esoteric and too academic for the average person, Johnson found them exhilarating. The simple act of bringing together the consultants and lecturers, all of whom were active throughout the country in various types of race relations programs, had been beneficial, he said. "The resulting cross-fertilization and mutual stimulation would have been valuable to us," he declared, "even if there had been no members to listen to the exchange of ideas." Of course the sessions were held for those attending, not for the consultants, and it was hoped that they would have a leavening effect when they carried the message back to their agencies and communities, and in many instances it worked. When Minnesota governor Luther V. Yougdahl issued an order on November 22, 1949, desegregating the state national guard, he quoted from a summer institute lecture to explain his decision. More than 1,300 community leaders attended the institute during its first ten years, which Johnson believed was "significant."[52]

Participants in 1948 included representatives of several denominations, YWCA officers, labor leaders, members of several race relations commissions, staffs of mayors of Chicago and Minneapolis, numerous schoolteachers, presidents of black colleges, black specialists from federal and state governments, and officials from the National Urban League and the NAACP. Charles H. Houston, NAACP counsel, returned to the institute every year until his death "as a means of broadening his own thinking in the legal struggle for constitutional rights." Houston's successor, Thurgood Marshall, who played a leading role in the destruction of legal segregation and was a future United States Supreme Court justice, continued the tradition.[53] Institute members most often represented churches, agencies, school districts, commissions, or government, but numerous individuals chose to attend and used the experience to good advantage. Mrs. Genevieve Steefel of Minneapolis attended at her own expense in 1945, and returned home to initiate a citywide race relations program backed by Mayor Hubert Humphrey. Her efforts may have led to the later city self-survey discussed previously. A St. Louis schoolteacher participant assisted in establishing a desegregated art center and a school in her city, and the 1946 institute inspired a Baltimore woman to help organize that city's first race relations institute. Others were less successful in bringing change to their communities. Paul M. Clanton, a white Pine Bluff, Arkansas, businessman, attended the institute in 1946. Although he, "an average businessman," felt out of his element surrounded by educators, he was impressed with the hospitality and genuine interest manifested by all. He attended hoping to learn how to persuade business associates and friends to think on race relations "honestly, straight, fairly and sincerely." "I've learned to smile and understand when I'm called a 'Nigger Lover,'" he wrote Long three years later. Black acquaintances were confident of his sincerity, but, he added, "I really haven't made much headway with my own friends and associates." Clanton learned what most well-meaning southerners, black and white, already knew: segregation and discrimination entrenched by decades of custom and laws were not easily eradicated.[54]

Although the institute was primarily for adults, especially program or agency leaders, youth were not ignored. Hollis F. Price, LeMoyne College president, suggested in 1945 sending some outstanding AMA college students to the institute. Other AMA college presidents and Brownlee, who wanted the schools to play a larger role in race relations, agreed. Beginning in 1946 two students from each AMA college were annually given scholarships to attend. Each college supported one student while the institute funded the other. In 1947, Rev. James A. Glaiser, pastor of the Westfield, New York, Methodist church, proposed the idea of a junior institute to Johnson. As a result, twenty-nine excited white high school students spent thirteen days at Fisk. They attended the regular lectures and discussions, stayed in the same dorms, and went swimming and dancing with black youth. The students learned a great deal, including that not all blacks necessarily welcomed their presence. Two of the group walking near Fisk were shocked when an elderly black woman screamed at them: "White trash, why don't you go back where you belong?"[55]

From the beginning, the national media gave the institute wide and relatively favorable notice. Black-owned newspapers usually announced the institute program (at least ten did in 1947), and occasionally sent reporters to cover some of the sessions. Nashville's *Tennessean* and *Banner* closely followed daily proceedings, as did a few other newspapers. A *Time* reporter went to the first institute in 1944 on the mistaken theory that it might be "an extreme leftist affair." The next day he registered and remained for the entire session. John N. Popham, a Virginia native and the *New York Times'* first southern correspondent, attended periodically. Correspondents for northern papers were generally positive. Edwin A. Lahey, *Chicago Daily News* wrote in 1947 that "quietly with no tub thumping and no demagoguery, the ripples of influence from this annual meeting lap steadily against the rocks of prejudice and discrimination in America." Saville R. Davis of the *Christian Science Monitor* was so impressed he found it difficult "not to seize a typewriter and report that democracy is safe—safe at the core." The institute was not filled with raging radicals intent on the overthrow of the government, Davis reminded fearful whites. "Social change in the face of the towering complexities of this problem here in the South, is not being pressed to the point of explosion." The leaders were not willful incendiaries, simply men and women who deeply felt the shame of discrimination and second-class citizenship forced upon them, but who were also intensely loyal to the country which had "left them for so long an aggrieved minority." Johnson was pleased with Davis's interpretation. He was angry about racial injustice in America, but he intended to work for change within the system.[56]

Interest in the summer institutes spawned a number of local programs directed by the Race Relations Department. They were short two- to three-day programs of intensive study designed to provide "concerned persons with concrete suggestions for doing a better job of democratic living." More than 350 people registered for a March 12–16, 1945, session at Richmond, Virginia. Albert W. Dent, Dillard University president, and Edgar B. Stern, chairman of the Dillard board of trustees, organized the November 5–7, 1945, institute led by Herman Long in New Orleans. Seven hundred and fifteen people registered and still more attended the New Orleans institute. Other institutes were held in St. Louis, Missouri; Little Rock, Arkansas; Raleigh, North Carolina; and Birmingham, Alabama. If judged by later problems in some of those cities, the institutes had limited impact, but the January 15–18, 1947, session in Baltimore with Brownlee as the major speaker was definitely positive. Almost three thousand attended one or more sessions. Results were seen in community planning, and by local organizations justifying their progressive stands by quoting institute speakers. The NAACP on two occasions used institute discussions in presenting its case on housing issues and the location of a new black school. Participants petitioned the mayor and city officials for a Mayor's Commission on Human Relations. Just as the woman who had attended the earlier Fisk session helped initiate the Baltimore race relations institute, some of the participants encouraged and cooperated with the later city self-survey.[57]

The early institutes featured academic lectures on race, psychology, and other subjects as well as talks on practical methods of ameliorating racial tension, but by 1949 the sessions had taken on a new, less academic tone and more discussions of how to attack discrimination. Some observers assumed this was because Herman Long, thought to be more of an activist than Johnson, became associate director of the Race Relations Department in 1946 after Johnson became president of Fisk University. More likely it was a natural progression. In October 1944, Margaret McCulloch—former history professor at LeMoyne College, social worker, race relations volunteer with the Fellowship of Reconciliation, and now editorial assistant of the Race Relations Department—wrote, "Amazing changes are taking place within the AMA staff. Johnson himself is changing deeply." McCulloch, who had been impatient with Johnson's deliberate approach, was happy to see him moving away from "his vague amorphous notion of 'letting the facts speak for themselves.'"[58] Johnson continued to deliver the welcoming addresses and helped organize the programs after Long became associate director. The 1949 institute, entitled "Implementing Civil Rights," included sessions on segregated housing, desegregation of the military, developing city nondiscrimination policies, community organizing, political implications of human rights, opening labor and industry to blacks, group tensions, and college admission practices. In his opening statement, Johnson warned that race had "become the scale on which democracy" was "being weighed in a world relentlessly forced to choose between ideologies." If racial problems were not solved, he continued, the United States faced "a national defeat from within through loss of one's faith in their very reason for living." No longer would Johnson say as he had in 1947 that the institute was not "designed as an action group, but . . . as a medium of enlightenment with a view to making social action more intelligent." The institutes remained a medium of enlightenment, but Johnson now admitted there was a desperate need for immediate change and progress.[59]

By 1950, the Fisk program was far from standing alone. There were ninety-one institutes of varying length and quality that year; nevertheless, the institute at Fisk was still unique, in part because it was in Nashville. It would be simple, a participant wrote, to hold the conference in a northern city, but its "importance was augmented by its being held where the work has to be done." Ruth Morton agreed that staging the institute "in the very heart of the spot where race difficulties are at their peak" was one of its genuine values. Certainly others thought the Fisk institute still important, and although there were more students and teachers attending than previously, agency and other significant leaders were still present. In 1950, participants included twenty-two students; forty-two teachers; seven ministers, rabbis, priests, and one bishop; twenty-four members of race relations committees; eighteen community organization personnel; representatives of nineteen church organizations; nine homemakers; three social workers; three government officials; and five labor leaders. In 1953, Bernard Crick, a visiting scholar from England, was impressed with almost everything at the institute, including "the vast amount of quiet preparatory spadework toward integration." It was, he thought, a model in race relations with delegates black and white from North and South living, eating, and working together "in complete equality and ease." The campus was "an island in a segregated town." In 1955, Long, hardly an unbiased observer, argued that the institute was "the most distinctive and important leadership training effort in intergroup relations in the country" because it was the oldest, involved the largest number of participants, drew from the most extensive geographical area, had the largest and most varied lecturers and resource leaders, and most important, was the only national effort located in the South. The novelty had worn off, but the institute was still needed and provided a useful service.[60]

Johnson and Long eagerly anticipated the 1954 session because of school desegregation. Months before the Supreme Court declared segregated schools illegal in *Brown v. The Board of Education of Topeka, Kansas* (May 17, 1954), Johnson and Long had planned the 1954 session around the theme "Meeting the Challenge of Integration." Both men had provided information to the NAACP counsel in the case. Thurgood Marshall "emphasized the value of Johnson's contribution," and they were ecstatic about the decision. In his keynote address, Johnson called *Brown* "the most affirmative and unequivocal national pronouncement in human rights" since the Emancipation Proclamation. It was, he added, a bold "mandate regarding the nation's conception of its commitment to fundamental rights." AMA officials, equally jubilant, called a meeting of presidents and principals of all of its schools to discuss methods of implementing the decision.[61]

Johnson and Long had no delusions that desegregation would be easy, but both probably initially underestimated how difficult it would be. In his keynote address at the 1954 institute, Johnson reminded his listeners that the court decision merely cleared the way for integration by removing legal barriers. "Integration must be achieved in the local setting, and by means best suited to the area." Long advised distinguishing between "pure ideal" and reality. There was not now and probably never would be perfect integration in the country. "What we are trying to achieve," he added, "is the establishment of conditions under which people, regardless of race, can make mutually helpful adjustments to one another." Long predicted that the governors of Georgia, South Carolina, and Mississippi would erect the greatest obstacles. The immediate need, he stated, was to develop an enlightened public to counteract the scare tactics the governors would undoubtedly use. Long thought the 1954 institute was one of the best ever because of the interest generated by the *Brown* case. He was pleased that thirty-one southern school superintendents and administrators attended at least some of the sessions. Perhaps suggestive of the institute's reputation, Alvin M. Rucker, a consultant to the President's Committee on Government, brought a special message from Vice President Richard M. Nixon to the 1954 session. Nixon regretted that his busy schedule prevented him from speaking at the institute; however, Rucker announced, "Mr. Nixon has instructed me to convey to you his admiration for the splendid work being done here and to assure you that both he and the president subscribe to the high objectives of your program." Nixon recognized the expediency of acknowledging the Race Relations Department. The next year James P. Mitchell, United States Secretary of Labor, spoke at the institute.[62]

Desegregation became the major focus of the institutes for the next several years. The 1955 session, "New Horizons in Human Relations: Closing the Gap between the Court and the Community," attracted the staff of the Southern Regional Council and several other interracial agencies. Johnson and Long assisted the Southern Regional Council in program planning and directing the recently formed eleven state councils through which the council launched its programs for school desegregation. These sessions were not popular with much of the white South. A Tennessee resident wrote Long that his support of desegregation was "right down the commie road." The *Brown* decision, he added, was a Russian-sponsored trick to destroy the United States. He warned Long that "all the pink pimps . . . Egg Heads . . . Starry-Eyed do-gooders and desegregation buzzards" would learn that they could not "push Negroes down we white Americans throats and we won't have any integration regardless of what Russia, Asia or Africa thinks." Such threats were ineffective. In 1956, an indication that the department was becoming more activist, Long and Johnson invited Dr. Martin Luther King Jr. to speak on "The Montgomery Story," thus providing what historians Patrick J. Gilpin and Marybeth Gasman call "the first truly interracial forum in the South," allowing King to proclaim "the message of the Montgomery Improvement Association to the nation." Johnson approved King's approach and told institute members that racism was a "malignancy" which endangered "the entire national fabric" and could not "be cured by temporizing compromise."[63]

Long and Johnson did not limit their attack on segregation to their Race Relations Department work. From the beginning Long, an active NAACP member, went beyond his department responsibilities and attacked discrimination wherever he saw it. He took public issue with Tennessee governor Gordon Browning who in 1949 was quoted as seeing no harm in the Klan burning crosses. "I don't reckon there is any harm in burning a cross if they don't whip nobody," he stated. In the same year Long was credited with "stimulating" the Nashville city council to enact anti-mask and cross-burning ordinances. In 1952, he and other black golfers brought suit against the Nashville Board of Park Commissioners to desegregate city golf courses. Judge Robert N. Wilkin, District Court of the United States for the Middle District of Tennessee, not only decided against them but gratuitously lectured Long and his friends. Those who "intentionally or unwittingly" overburdened "democratic and legal processes" were destroying the "delicate balance and apportionment of powers upon which our way of life depends" and thereby, the judge said, played "into the hands of revolutionaries." While they might think they were champions of freedom and liberalism, Wilkin added, they were "bringing about a totalitarianism which will destroy the very object that they seek to serve." Long appealed, and in February 1954 federal judge Elmer D. Davis ordered that blacks be allowed to play one of the three public courses on certain days of the week until a new nine-hole course could be opened for African Americans. The black golfers continued to fight to open all courses to them at all times. Long also served on the Nashville NAACP radio and on other committees from 1952 forward; worked locally and nationally for black voting rights; and personally attempted to desegregate Nashville public schools when, in September 1955, he, as a representative of parents and the NAACP, took five children to enroll in the Glen Elementary School. Principal Mary Brent politely told Long that she had no authority to accept black children.[64]

In most of the South, the reception of those attempting to integrate schools was less polite. By 1956, Johnson and Long were both more pessimistic about desegregating schools. Although by October 1956, 797 school districts had desegregated since the decision of May 1954, there were only 319,184 black students in these recently desegregated schools and 2,400,000 southern black children still in all-black schools; and attempts to desegregate were becoming increasingly violent. Alabama, Florida, Georgia, Louisiana, Mississippi, North Carolina, South Carolina, and Virginia had no desegregated districts. In 1956, a white mob kept blacks from enrolling in Mansfield, Texas, and the national guard was called out in Sturgis, Kentucky, to disperse a white mob determined to prevent school integration. In that same year Senator Harry Byrd of Virginia called for "massive resistance" to school desegregation, 101 southern congressmen signed the Southern Manifesto calling the *Brown* decision a "clear abuse of judicial power," and Autherine Lucy was expelled from the University of Alabama. And worse was yet to come. There were later eruptions of violence in Little Rock, Arkansas; Oxford, Mississippi; and scores of other southern cities. Television viewers throughout the land witnessed the humiliating spectacle of adult white racists abusing and screaming at small black children. Long lamented that segregationists fomented violence—or threatened to—as a strategy to prevent integration. Such efforts were so well organized and supported, he said, that the possibility of violence was "a reality which any community beginning desegregation—even those with the most positive orientation—now confronts." In September 1957, shortly before his death, Johnson noted "the thinning ranks of white liberal advocates of civil rights in the tense post-

Brown atmosphere." He had seen whites drift out of the Southern Regional Council when finally in 1951 it announced that "segregation must go," and even more white liberals became invisible after the *Brown* case. The South, "provincial and isolationist to the core," he wrote sadly, would never voluntarily integrate. Johnson died on October 27, 1957, at a Louisville, Kentucky, railroad station while en route to New York City for a meeting with the Fisk University board of trustees. The AMA named Long director of the Race Relations Department soon afterward.[65]

Charles S. Johnson made significant contributions to the AMA and race relations. Richard Robbins says he was by no means a Booker T. Washington, but neither was he as outspoken a militant as Du Bois. He was a "conciliatory realist" who was "also a liberal advocate for change, one whose realism necessitated interracial cooperation . . . but whose strategy of conciliation never required abandoning the core principle of total opposition to all forms of racial injustice." Gilpin and Gasman claim that "[h]e was not a radical, but a diplomat who, through his collaborations, realized many of the ideas of thinkers more radical than himself." Moreover, they said the Race Relations Department under Johnson's leadership "became the intellectual basis for much of the race relations and civil rights struggle prior to the era of Martin Luther King Jr." Indeed, without Johnson and the Race Relations Department, "the dramatic events that began to crystallize in the mid-1950s" around King might "have been delayed several more years."[66]

Long was an excellent choice to succeed Johnson. He had learned from both Johnson and experience, and he had become an outstanding race relations expert. In 1954, the *New York Times* could accurately call him "one of the South's foremost authorities on racial tensions." Long was remarkably energetic and, unlike Johnson who always had other major responsibilities, could devote full time to the cause. He was the department's best ambassador to the Congregational Christian Churches which helped support it, and he had an extensive network of friends in government and in race relations.[67] Long was a member of many organizations—for example, the Christian and Jews Commission on School Integration, and the National Conference of Christians and Jews—was a close friend and advisor to Thurgood Marshall, was on the board of the Southern Regional Council and president (1955) of the National Conference of Intergroup Relations Officials, and made scores of speeches annually. He cooperated with the Highlander Folk School in Monteagle, Tennessee, under attack as being Communist inspired for its devotion to desegregation, and in 1955 he was elected to the Highlander executive council. Long seldom shied away from unpopular causes and organizations. He served on the board of the Southern Conference Education Fund, probably the most radical southern organization fighting segregation. When one of its members, Carl Braden, was red-baited and railroaded into prison (after he refused to answer several questions before the House Un-American Activities Committee), Long supported him with money and letters, and even visited the White House on Braden's behalf. Despite his constant activity, Long's major focus was always the Race Relations Department, including the institute which he had directed since 1946.[68]

The institute met annually until 1969, and continued to advocate integration and justice for all minorities. While the major focus had been on African Americans, the Race Relations Department had never been concerned solely with them. The 1957 session included eight American Indian delegates, as well as Spanish-speaking members from the Southwest and from Puerto Rico. Long found the "cross-fertilization" of experience and ideas from diverse minority groups helpful. Still, desegregation was the institute's major goal. The 1958 delegates—though approving President Dwight D. Eisenhower's sending troops to protect black students in Little Rock—petitioned him, after Long criticized the administration for its silence and ambivalence, to provide greater moral leadership and to call a national conference on the issue of desegregation of public schools. It was obvious, they wrote, that the massive resistance to the *Brown* decision made "imperative the calling of such a conference at the earliest possible date." Institute delegates had become, as Long said in his 1965 keynote address, "actionists" and social engineers seeking the best methods of implementing federal law and integrating American society. Interestingly, in 1965 Long emphasized the urgency of finding ways to prevent the civil rights movement from being "engulfed by extremes of black nationalism," which, he warned, might divert attention from remaining needed reforms and threaten the goals of the revolution. Long understood the black power cry—"a generalized, highly emotional slogan—wonderfully expressive of elements of self-pride which has so long been denied"; but he feared that practically it would be divisive, and potentially could divide blacks by class. Black nationalists were, however, welcomed to the institute. In 1968, Clifton H. Johnson, now director of the Race Relations Department, reported that the summer institute was the largest ever and included young radicals, black nationalists, and "many others who were having their first interracial experience."[69]

The impact of the Race Relations Institute is difficult to assess.[70] It obviously did not influence many staunch racists, but the institutes gave Johnson, Charles H. Houston and Thurgood Marshall of the NAACP, Martin Luther King Jr., and others a public forum from which to attack discrimination and functioned as a training center for thousands of union, race commission, government, church, and school leaders, thus, in Johnson's words, "planting a ferment" throughout the community. Nearly all national race relations organizations sent personnel to the institute at one time or another, as did major religious denominations. During its first ten years, union representatives were prominent at the institute. Surely these leaders had some influence on their constituents. And individuals sometimes effected change, as mentioned earlier. Even small contributions were appreciated. In 1960, Long wrote of Mrs. Mary Porter Evarts of Columbia, Tennessee, who attended an early institute and who had "continued a deep and abiding interest" ever since. Her children were on "the right side of the issue," and she had recently sent two hundred dollars to support the sit-in movement. Evarts had moved to Maryland but remained involved in interracial activity. One institute participant withheld family funds from a hospital until it agreed to accept and treat black patients, and hundreds of others attacked segregation and discrimination in their communities. In the fight against racism, every soldier counted.[71]

The Race Relations Department's investigations probably had a more readily measurable impact than the institute. One of Johnson's main goals was to influence public policy, and he early concluded that areas in which the department might succeed were racially restrictive covenants and segregation in interstate railroad transportation. Long, under Johnson's supervision, investigated Chicago, St. Louis, and other cities and brought the "whole sordid story of race restrictive covenants" before the American public a strategic two months before arguments were presented to the U.S. Supreme Court. The study, published as *People v. Property: Race Restrictive Covenants in Housing* (1947), revealed the part played by real estate agents, bankers, and "the basically subversive nature" of many neighborhood associations. Restrictive covenants in Chicago, the authors contended, segregated blacks more rigidly than they were segregated in Nashville. Johnson and Long denied the common charge that integration lowered property values and provoked racial tension and riots. The trouble, they argued, was really caused by segregation and the patterns it created. As soon as the study was off the press, the department sent ten copies of *People v. Property* to NAACP counsel Charles H. Houston, who was arguing two cases, *Hurd v. Hodge* and *Urcido v. Hodge,* before the U.S. Supreme Court. Long also sent ten copies to the clerk of the Supreme Court. Houston acknowledged receipt of the books and added, "I . . . can't tell you how important it is." Houston prepared a special brief based on Long's findings and sent each judge a copy of the book. Finally in May 1948, the court in *Shelley v. Kraemer* declared restrictive covenants not enforceable in law. Houston telegraphed congratulations to Long and Johnson. Johnson was modest about the department's role, saying that the book was but one of many factors considered by the court. Still, the report was a part of the record and, Johnson added, "has been used again and again since the decision in making clear to the public the principles and facts on which the decision was based."[72]

The department got quick results from its study of real estate covenants. A positive response to the investigation of segregation of interstate railroad transportation took much longer. Johnson took up this issue because the court and the Interstate Commerce Commission seemed to be moving in the direction of desegregation. In 1946 the Supreme Court in *Morgan v. The Commonwealth of Virginia* agreed with the NAACP that laws requiring segregation on interstate buses were an unreasonable burden on interstate commerce and were therefore invalid. At its October 1949 session, the Court heard *Henderson v. The U.S.,* which challenged segregation in dining cars on railroads. The case began in 1942 when Elmer W. Henderson, field representative of the President's Committee on Fair Employment Practices, was denied seating in the curtained-off "conditionally reserved" section for blacks because whites were sitting there. The Race Relations Department filed an *amicus curia* brief in the case, and Johnson's 1943 publication, *Patterns of Negro Segregation,* was used. In 1950, the Court outlawed dining car segregation and ordered railroads to permit African Americans to occupy any empty dining room seat. Even before the decision, Johnson and Long had decided that desegregation of railroads was an issue that might soon be subject to legislative or administrative action, and they began a study of discrimination on railroads.[73] Between November 1949 and June 1950, two teams of investigators—J. Leon Holly, black, and Edward Chesky, white; and Grace C. Jones, black, and Jeanette Harris, white—made forty-six trips on twenty-seven different trains on nineteen interstate railroads documenting discrimination and how and when it was imposed. The trips covered approximately 28,000 miles, and the teams interviewed 290 black passengers. Long also recorded his experience on several trips, and eventually published the findings in 1952 as *Segregation in Interstate Railway Coach Travel,* but he began aggressively using preliminary information in 1949 in an attempt to influence legislation.[74]

In May 1949, he sent a memorandum, "Segregated Interstate Public Travel," to Senator Hubert H. Humphrey, whom he had known since the Minneapolis self-survey, saying he hoped it would be useful to the senator "in considering legislation in this vital area." "In a very real sense," Long told Humphrey, "segregation as a public practice and an expression of national and local policy is the core of the civil rights issue. It is an important symbol of racism, and it is the new frontier of the advance toward the establishment of full and democratic human rights." He warned Humphrey that legislative attack upon segregation was "beset with hazards and difficulties," and probably should not be attempted without reasonable certainty of winning or willingness to lose in the interest of gains made in public education made by the attempt. Nevertheless, the recent advances against segregation made through the Supreme Court, outlawing restrictive covenants and ruling against segregated buses, "should be the basis in the national public policy upon which tactical moves can be made, legislatively and otherwise." Long suggested three strategic areas for activity: abolition of segregation in the District of Columbia, the armed forces, and interstate travel. Interstate travel was especially important, he claimed, because it involved a large number of people and was a "vast network of communication and movement essential to our national life." Long had clearly gone beyond the role of a scholar presenting raw data. For the next five years he frequently contacted Humphrey and many other congressmen. When *Segregation in Interstate Railway Coach Travel* was published, he sent copies to congressmen, including Tennessee senator Estes Kefauver, Supreme Court justices, newspapers, and legislative aides. He corresponded with Dr. Max M. Kapelman, legislative counsel to Humphrey, and members of the Committee on Interstate and Foreign Commerce who would be most likely to deal with any bill outlawing segregation on interstate travel. He also made several trips to Washington to discuss tactics.[75]

Long was encouraged in 1953 when Rep. Adam Clayton Powell of New York and Senator Humphrey introduced a bill to make segregation on interstate railways unlawful. These bills were unsuccessful, but a later one at least received committee approval. Phineas Indritz, Office of the Solicitor, U.S. Department of Interior, wrote Long in December 1953 that he had used *Segregation in Interstate Railway Coach Travel* "with considerable effectiveness" in his efforts to obtain administration support for bills pending in Congress to outlaw segregation. Indritz asked for more copies of the book to distribute to other government agencies concerned with the problem. Rep. John W. Heselton, Massachusetts, discussed Long's report before introducing a bill to ban segregation on interstate transportation on January 18, 1954. In May 1954, Long appeared before the Committee on Interstate and Foreign Commerce as an expert witness, and *Segregation in Interstate Railway Coach Travel* was filed as part of the hearing. Unfortunately, the bill H.R. 7304 was approved by the commerce committee but was never brought to the floor. Heselton reported that House Speaker Joe Martin had no objection to the bill, but Sam Rayburn, the Democratic minority leader, did. Heselton promised to refile in January 1955.[76]

While Long was lobbying Congress for legislation to end discrimination in railway travel, he was also working with the NAACP which was attacking the same issue through the Interstate Commerce Commission. In September 1952, Thurgood Marshall asked for a copy of Long's report on interstate travel to use "in an overall case to be filed this fall." Long, who was still writing the final draft, sent three sections a few days later. As soon as the report was published, he forwarded copies to the NAACP. Assistant counsel Robert L. Carter read the book and informed Long that it was "a wonderful job" and "just the type of thing we need for our omnibus complaint about which we talked when you saw us in New York." On December 21, 1953, Carter and Marshall filed complaint Number 31423 with the Interstate Commerce Commission. They cited Long's survey in their brief. A trial hearing was scheduled for July 27, 1954. Carter, who had already conferred with Long in Washington, asked him to appear as an expert witness, and to arrive in D.C. on July 25 "so that we can go over the material and decide on the form of presentation." Long appeared directly before the trial examiner, who recommended that segregation be ended. In November 1955, the full commission declared that segregation on interstate transportation was unlawful and ordered the cessation of such in rail, bus, water, and air transportation by January 10, 1956. Actual compliance was inconsistent, but several railroads, including the Southern Railroad and the Louisville and Nashville, removed "white" and "colored" signs from their waiting rooms and desegregated coaches. As late as 1959, however, Long informed the Tennessee Advisory Committee on Civil Rights and the President's Commission on Civil Rights that while Nashville, Knoxville, and Chattanooga had desegregated local bus transportation facilities, some areas had not.[77] It remained for the 1961 Freedom Riders finally to force the end of segregated transportation and facilities in the Deep South.

Long was justifiably proud that he and the Race Relations Department "had a direct hand" in ending segregation in interstate travel. It showed the value of long-range strategy and planning, he told the AMA executive committee, "as well as how research can be used as an aid to enlighten policy decisions in race relations." Carter, Marshall, and others gave him much credit. Walter Washington, principal of black Summer Hill High School in Clinton, Mississippi, wrote Long that desegregation of transportation was a major contribution "toward bringing into existence true democracy," and Long's generous and longtime interest, he continued, had significantly contributed to the decision. He paid "great tribute" to Long and his staff for presenting scientific evidence which, coupled with other activities, brought about "a new day in transportation for the Negro, particularly in the South."[78]

Other Race Relations Department staff fought discrimination in different ways. One of the most unusual methods was the circulation throughout the country of the "Races of Mankind" exhibit. Based on *Races of Mankind* by Ruth Benedict and Gene Weltfish, anthropologists at the Cranbrook Institute of Science at Bloomfield Hills, Michigan, had built it to correct "false concepts dealing with race and nationality." The AMA purchased the exhibit, and in 1944 staff member Edmonia Grant began taking it around the country. In the fall of 1944, she displayed it at Atlanta University and Emory University in Atlanta as well as at a number of churches. It opened on February 1, 1945, in the main New York City public library with excellent radio and newspaper publicity. Mayor Fiorello LaGuardia and Fannie Hurst, writer and patron of black artists, were among the dignitaries present for the opening. The exhibit proved so bulky and expensive to ship that in 1945 the AMA prepared a series of eighteen posters depicting its most important scenes. During the next five years the department distributed more than fifteen thousand sets of posters, mostly to classrooms, accompanied by discussion materials developed to aid teachers.[79]

More useful was a series of short books and pamphlets, including two by Margaret C. McCulloch, an occasional staff member. McCulloch, a Phi Beta Kappa, earned a B.A. in history at Wellesley College in Wellesley, Massachusetts, in 1923, and left her New Jersey home to go south to teach in black schools in South Carolina and Alabama. She also took an M.A. in history at the University of North Carolina in 1934. After teaching social sciences at LeMoyne College in Memphis, Tennessee, from 1934 to 1940, she resigned to spend much of the next two decades establishing and working, often without salary, in community centers in Nashville and Memphis. In each city she deliberately selected residences that bordered on both black and white communities. She identified herself with the organizations and activities of each and thereby became a liaison between blacks and whites. In order to assist Johnson, and to earn money for her private interracial activities, McCulloch accepted a position with the Race Relations Department in 1943. "I'm really very deeply happy over this," McCulloch wrote her mother about her new job. "It means that I shall be a part in shaping what is, I believe, the most pioneering, extensive, and significant endeavor in this field for the next few decades." McCulloch often lectured or directed workshops for the institute. In 1959, she led a clinic on "Techniques of Interracial Work in the South." Many participants praised the clinic, which was unsurprising since LeMoyne students had considered her a remarkable teacher. In addition to performing editorial responsibilities, doing research whenever needed, and providing assistance in the institutes, McCulloch wrote *Segrega-*

tion: A Challenge to Democracy (1950) and *Integration-Promise-Process-Problems* (1952), both widely distributed, especially among interracial organizations and churches. The former discusses the evils of segregation, while the latter is a primer on how to achieve integration and why it should be done. Many interested people found it helpful. In February 1955, the Detroit Commission on Community Relations ordered two hundred copies, and the National Education Association asked for one hundred. The department produced many other educational pamphlets and books designed to reduce discrimination and ameliorate racial tension, and sent them free or at cost to any organization desiring them.[80]

While Long, Johnson, and other staff members' responsibilities were many and diverse, John Hope II, appointed director of industrial relations in 1945, focused on industrial relations counseling with the ultimate goal of moving toward economic democracy. Born in Atlanta, Georgia, in 1909, Hope was the son of John Hope, educator, activist, and president of Atlanta University. John Hope II, an economist, was educated at Morehouse in Atlanta and at Brown University. During World War II, he served in the Atlanta office of the Fair Employment Practices Committee. His interest in economics, fair employment, and research made him a natural choice to head the industrial relations section of the Race Relations Department. His charge was to work with labor unions, industry, and local, state, and federal governments for the full acceptance of black workers. Some of his earliest activity was with the self-surveys. He persuaded businessmen and trade unions in Minneapolis and Pittsburgh "to face the facts" on fair employment. Both top management and labor leaders often accepted his findings even though he revealed their shortcomings. He further met with ranking executives of the automobile industry and leaders of the United Auto Workers.[81]

Hope worked tirelessly to integrate blacks into labor unions, which had traditionally excluded them. At least thirty American Federation of Labor unions, including airline pilots, railroad telegraphers, glass workers, and plumbers, denied blacks membership in 1943. The Detroit riot was triggered, in part, when 26,000 white workers struck the Packard Motor Plant in protest against black workers, and the Mobile disturbance began when black workers were upgraded. But in 1944, Sidney Hillman, leader of the Congress of Industrial Organization, declared that the interests of blacks and organized workers were the same. He placed some African Americans on the CIO's Political Action Committee, but persuading white unionists to accept blacks was not easy, even in the North. In April 1948, the chairman of the Civil Rights Committee, New Jersey State Council, CIO, wrote Johnson asking for advice and materials. As already seen, union representatives were usually present at the summer institutes, but Hope went to the unions also. He ordinarily, with union assistance, investigated conditions—conducting a type of self-survey—and then made recommendations. One of his most successful efforts was with the United Packing Workers of America (UPWA), CIO. It was a cooperative venture initiated in 1949 between the union and the Race Relations Department, with Hope and assistants providing technical assistance and consultation. Hope examined the treatment of minorities, and how closely practice measured up to the union's stated antidiscrimination and civil rights policies. After discovering a great distance between practice and profession nationally, Hope made "rank-and-file" studies in Kansas City; Omaha, Nebraska; Atlanta; and Fort Worth, Texas.[82]

The Kansas City study (1950) revealed that black workers, skilled and unskilled, had less take-home pay than whites, that they filed a higher percentage of complaints, and that many workers were unaware of the union's antidiscrimination policy. The union instituted an "action program," and Hope and Louis Krainock, union educational director, held leadership training classes involving twelve Kansas City locals. A follow-up study in 1951 showed positive results. The UPWA was using labor-management machinery to eliminate discrimination, its antidiscrimination committee was elevated to department level, a full-time educational director was added to the staff, discriminatory hiring had been broken down in several plants, and segregated facilities had been eliminated in many cities. The Kansas City plan, under the union and Hope's leadership, fostered the desegregation of some community facilities, including theaters. Hotels in several places opened to African Americans when the UPWA refused to hold conventions in cities with segregated public accommodations. Most of these positive changes occurred in the North and West. Even a strong union antidiscrimination stance failed to bring immediate implementation in the South.[83]

By the time he resigned in 1961, Hope had made hundreds of talks, and counseled even larger numbers of people. He learned that effective counseling was not limited to employers, unions, or government officials. Sometimes talks to church groups, personnel managers, or committee members brought results, but more often he investigated employment discrimination or other factors affecting black workers, such as inadequate housing. He wrote two books, *Equality of Opportunity: A Union Approach to Fair Employment* (1956) and *Three Southern Plants of International Harvester Company* (1953), and several reports. In 1959, he prepared a ninety-eight-page report on black workers for the U.S. Senate, Special Committee on Unemployment Problems. Herman Long in 1962 testified before the U.S. House, Special Committee on Employment and Education based on Hope's study of race practices in

Tennessee, Kentucky, South Carolina, and West Virginia industries. There was still severe discrimination against black workers who were kept in marginal positions, Long declared, "by a vicious cycle of departures and preferences of which industrial procedures" were "a prominent and determining aspect." Although much progress had been made since World War II, neither studies, counseling, union support, nor government fair employment decrees brought equality in the workplace. Black-union relations remained strained. The International Brotherhood of Electrical Workers in Cleveland, and the Bricklayers, Masons and Marble Masons Protective Association in Milwaukee did not admit blacks until 1958, and they did so then only because AFL-CIO president George Meany threatened to revoke their charters. Many other unions did not accept African Americans, and blacks still tended to be "last hired, first fired." In March 1958, the African American unemployment rate was 14.4 percent, the highest in eleven years. It was 6.9 percent for whites. Hope resigned in 1961 to become assistant executive director of the President's Committee on Equal Employment Opportunity, but the Race Relations Department continued to fight to end discrimination against black workers. In 1962, Long and Vivian W. Henderson published *Jobs and Color: Negro Employment in Tennessee State Government* for the Tennessee Commission on Human Relations.[84]

Brownlee as chief executive officer of the AMA vigorously defended the Race Relations Department until his mandatory retirement in 1950. Many department friends feared it would suffer in Brownlee's absence because his reputation and influence had enabled him to fend off attacks from within the BHM, which now largely determined the AMA's budget. Fortunately, his successors, Philip M. Widenhouse and Wesley A. Hotchkiss, continued to support the department, but there were problems. Brownlee had secured approval for the department, but from the beginning church support ranged from strong to indifferent to outright hostile. In November 1944, Long and Edmonia Grant attended a national board meeting of the Congregational Christian Church to familiarize members with their work. Long was astounded at "the distance between our program and the Ecclesiastical Division and their lack of information." When Long was appointed associate director of the Race Relations Institute, Ruth Morton congratulated him and added, "It will be good to have you more closely associated with us in our many struggles with our executive committee."[85]

The problem was not that the church was unsympathetic to the department's goals. The Council for Social Action, a church agency that Brownlee advised, had long been troubled about racism, and in 1946 the General Council of the Congregational Christian Church repented of the sin of racial segregation and stated that society could not be ridded of discrimination until the Christian church rose above the color line and became truly inclusive. The BHM, with the AMA's somewhat reluctant financial support, created the Committee on Church and Race with Rev. Galen R. Weaver as its director. The committee, scheduled to last two years and concerned about racism generally, was to deal specifically with the church.[86] The major issue between the AMA and the church was that the Race Relations Department had no religious emphasis, paid too little attention to the church, and gave it too little credit. Many ministers complained that the department's literature failed to mention the church or BHM and that it was commonly called the Fisk Race Relations Department. If it was Fisk's department, one board member said, let Fisk pay for it. Others argued that the Race Relations Department received too large a portion of the budget, around $40,000 annually. In 1948, William F. Frazier, treasurer of the Board of Home Missions of the Congregational Christian Church, argued that a $20,000 bequest to the AMA which Brownlee wanted to use for the department should be used as current BHM income to be fair to sister agencies that had yielded to the department. Brownlee resisted, and Frazier warned him that "at the first breath of trouble drastic cuts" would be made in the AMA's current budget. When the two-year limit on the Committee on Church and Race expired, some board members wished to continue it or set up a separate race relations department. In a victory for the department, Brownlee persuaded the BHM to add Weaver to the Race Relations Department staff. Weaver became the "Specialist in Religion and Race" and race relations secretary for the Council for Social Action.[87]

Weaver, a sincere, able man, was a useful addition to the staff, but unfortunately under the "merger" the department advisory committee, previously composed primarily of AMA-appointed members, changed. Under the new plan there was a committee of twenty, six selected by the AMA divisional committee (subject to approval by the Board of Home Missions), six chosen by the Council for Social Action (clearly a church agency), and the remaining eight elected by the above. This committee was often less sympathetic to the department than earlier ones, and many members continued to think it had a too limited connection to religion and the church.[88] On the other hand, too few church members knew of the department's work. Brownlee complained that getting an adequate budget was a constant struggle, and that the Board of Home Missions was "very weakly committed to this phase of the work." He thought treasurer William F. Frazier wished to dissolve the department completely. Church representatives continued to complain about the department, and in 1956 insisted that it be evaluated by outside consultants. Positive reports did not end the grumbling. In response to church complaints that the department ignored it, Long investigated segregation in the Congregational Christian Church and published a report entitled *Fellowship for Whom: A Study of Racial Inclusiveness in the Congregational Churches* (1958). Long concluded that the church was moving toward desegregation with "glacial slowness." The relationship between the department and church continued to be fretful. In 1960, the Board of Home Missions' Committee on Internal Structure considered removing the Race Relations Department from the AMA division altogether.[89]

The Race Relations Department remained with the AMA—now the Division of Higher Education and the AMA—and although budget struggles continued, it was relatively secure after 1960; but its best years were probably over, even though its research and the annual institutes remained useful and Long continued his frenetic pace in 1959–60. He was in constant demand throughout the country. In 1959, he was the keynote speaker for the Detroit Commission on Human Relations leadership clinic. Soon afterward he had a luncheon meeting with Helen Fuller, managing editor of the *New Republic,* who sought information for an article on southerners and schools. He participated in a civil rights legislation seminar organized by Republican senator Jacob K. Javits of New York, and was on the program of the National Civil Liberties Clearing House in Washington, D.C. An active member and vice president of the Southern Conference Educational Fund, Inc., Long arranged for selected members to meet with Roy Wilkins of the NAACP, forced the desegregation of the school on Stewart Air Force Base in Tennessee, worked for school desegregation and a law curbing Ku Klux Klan activity in Nashville, and acted as liaison between benefactors and those in need. When supporter Fowler McCormick sent five hundred dollars to the department for "improving racial understanding," Long used it to help send twenty-two black children, who had been shut out of their schools in Warren County, Virginia, to Washington, D.C., to enroll in public schools. He was similarly busy in other years. In 1960–61, he directed the department, conducted research, made scores of speeches, consulted with dozens of organizations, and supported the Nashville sit-ins. He made two talks and advised twenty of the most influential leaders of the current sit-in movement at a Special Southern Student Leadership Seminar held at Fisk in July 1961. He was an expert witness in a Tennessee desegregation case, testified before a U.S. House Special subcommittee chaired by James Roosevelt, and was on the program of the Michigan NAACP convention. He was so busy that he rejected an invitation to be a delegate from the National Urban League to the White House Conference on Aging held January 9–12, 1961. The above is only a sample of Long's activities, and these were in addition to his normal responsibilities. He belonged to almost every organization devoted to improving conditions of African Americans.[90]

Probably no person in the United States was more active than Long in fighting discrimination, and he had an able staff to assist him. Nevertheless, the department was not as significant as it had been. Maintaining its budget required an annual struggle. Numerous organizations and government agencies were doing similar work. Though it was less active than it would become, the federal government had passed the civil rights bills of 1957 and 1960, the first since Reconstruction, and more legislation was forthcoming. Then the department received a serious blow in 1964 when Long resigned to become president of Talladega College. He had declined several previous offers of academic positions. In 1958, he had rejected an opportunity to become head of the sociology department and editor of *Phylon* at Atlanta University. When asked in 1959 if he would consider the presidency of Lincoln University in Pennsylvania, he replied, "I suppose that I have never viewed myself in the image of a college president, and I cannot now imagine that the clothing would fit very well." Yet in 1964, he was willing to take on the task. Heading his alma mater was attractive. Alumni wanted him, it was an AMA college, and AMA administrators knew and respected him; but he may also have been influenced by the knowledge that the Race Relations Department had outlived its years of greatest usefulness.[91]

Long remained active in race relations work and continued to assist in the summer institutes, but the department faltered for two years without a full-time director. In 1966, the AMA finally appointed a young white historian, Clifton H. Johnson, director. Johnson had taken a leave of absence from AMA's LeMoyne College in 1961 to catalog the AMA archives, which had been housed at Fisk since the 1940s.[92] After two years of cataloging and arranging documents, Johnson opened the collection for use in late 1963. Scholars, especially historians, eagerly descended upon Fisk which, Johnson concluded, indicated the need for more sources for the study of black America. No single academic center systematically collected source material on African Americans, which led Johnson to propose to Wesley A. Hotchkiss, now AMA leader, that the AMA archives be used as a nucleus for collecting materials on black Americans. Johnson and Hotchkiss presented the idea to the presidents of the six AMA colleges who agreed in principle. Funding was another matter. Finally in spring of 1966, Hotchkiss suggested that the proposed center, now being called the Amistad Research Center, and the Race Relations Department be placed under one director. On September 1, 1966, the Race Relations Department became a division of the Amistad Research

Center (ARC) under Johnson's leadership. The department continued to support research and the summer institutes for a time, but Johnson's greatest contribution was almost singlehandedly to build over the next thirty years the Amistad Research Center into one of the finest collections of African American source materials available. As Johnson said in proposing the research center, the Race Relations Department had "been extraordinarily influential in dismantling the massive structures of segregation," but the end of that stage of the struggle was in sight. The next step was the more difficult process of integration, and research was essential in understanding and guiding the process. The Amistad Research Center, as successor to the Race Relations Department, Johnson hoped, "would carry that great tradition on into the next phase of the integration of our society."[93]

8

Afterword

As already seen, the American Missionary Association in 1937, over Brownlee's strenuous objections, legally gave up its independence to the Board of Home Missions of the Congregational Christian Church.[1] The association, however, remained a separate division, retained control of its legacies, and under Brownlee managed to carry on its normal work even though the Board of Home Missions (BHM) had final say over the budget. William F. Frazier, architect of the 1937 union and the most powerful BHM official, was the first board executive vice president, and clashed often with Brownlee who resented his oversight and interference with the AMA. Frazier resigned to become BHM treasurer and was replaced by executive vice president Truman B. Douglass, a nephew of former AMA secretary H. Paul Douglass, who mollified Brownlee somewhat. Though they occasionally disagreed, especially over the importance of church work, Douglass and Brownlee generally cooperated in maintaining association schools and community centers, but the latter's independence sometimes irritated even Douglass.[2] The tension between Brownlee and BHM treasurer Frazier continued. Both were honest, efficient, dedicated men who simply disagreed on many issues. Personality, finance, social and political views, and especially direction of the BHM contributed to their differences. The treasurer was conservative on most political and social issues, while Brownlee was an ardent New Dealer and supported almost any reform movement. Fortunately, Frazier approved the black colleges, but sometimes he attempted to reward his favorites contrary to Brownlee's recommendations and he was unenthusiastic about community centers and functional education. He preferred a less independent AMA and more control of its funds. Frazier could not subordinate the association and gain complete mastery of its finances without firing Brownlee, which, according to Frazier's successor, Howard E. Spragg, "would have meant a first class fight." Moreover, Spragg added, Brownlee knew a great deal about finance. He "did a lot of fancy bookkeeping and hid funds" which Frazier unsuccessfully tried "to grab."[3] The AMA legacies and endowment, more than $17 million in 1954, continued to go to the AMA though their use had to be approved by the BHM; but, as Brownlee had warned, church funds for the association declined significantly after the various mission agencies were unified.[4]

Both Frazier and Douglass were pleased when Brownlee retired in 1950, and they sought a new secretary who was not associated with the AMA, a person whose first loyalty, unlike Brownlee's, was to the BHM rather than to a single division. They selected Philip Widenhouse, the AMA's first southern-born leader. Born in Concord, North Carolina, on February 21, 1911, Widenhouse graduated from Wofford College in 1932 and the Chicago Theological Seminary in 1936. During his last two years in seminary, he worked in the BHM Department of Research and Survey. As an ordained Congregational minister, he led churches in Chicago and Atlanta before becoming Director of Research in Church Planning for the Council of Churches in Washington, D.C., in 1943. He joined the Board of Home Missions in 1945, first as assistant in city work, and later as Director of Interdivisional Coordination with responsibility for relating the work of the divisions, including the AMA, to the general BHM administration. Who better to become a BHM rather than an AMA loyalist?[5] Much to his superiors' dismay, as Widenhouse became more acquainted with and devoted to AMA work, he attempted to—and to a degree did—assert some of the same independence Brownlee had exercised; but real power belonged to the Board of Home Missions since it made policy and appropriations. Once the BHM made appropriations to the AMA, however, Widenhouse and successors, with advice of their administrative committees, were relatively free to allocate funds in accordance with AMA principles.[6]

The Board of Home Missions further absorbed the AMA in 1956 when it created the Division of Higher Education and the American Missionary Association, which combined AMA activities and colleges with white denominational schools. The ideal of desegregation was a stated motive for the new division. Both the AMA and the BHM advocated integration, and separate organizations for black and white colleges seemed to give lie to their claims. Widenhouse, a sincere integrationist who supported the 1956 change, now supervised both black and white institutions. Desegregation was only one reason for the change. The reorganization was also another method of compelling greater AMA subordination. Some BHM members apparently wished to delete American Missionary Association from the title altogether, but most black members, including black college presidents, considered the

AMA "their" organization and objected. The name was retained not to give the AMA or black colleges more prominence than white schools, but to please the black constituency. The AMA name may have been kept for still another reason. Spragg claimed that churches gave less and less to the AMA, a mere pittance in the later years, but they used the American Missionary Association "as a promotional gimmick to raise money for the church," money which then went "to a thousand different things."[7]

In 1958, Wesley A. Hotchkiss succeeded Widenhouse, who resigned to become president of Rocky Mountain College in Billings, Montana. And although Hotchkiss was a vigorous advocate for AMA issues until his 1982 retirement, he was aware from the beginning that he was a BHM employee assigned to the AMA.[8] Unlike Brownlee and, to a lesser extent, Widenhouse, Hotchkiss was under no illusions that the AMA was or could ever again be even semi-independent. Two reorganizations occurred early in Hotchkiss's administration. In 1961, the Board of Home Missions became the United Church Board for Homeland Ministries (UCBHM), in part to accommodate the agencies of the former Evangelical and German Reformed Churches which had joined the Congregational Christian Church in 1957 to form the United Church of Christ (UCC). Then in 1963, the AMA colleges were transferred to the Council for Higher Education of the UCC. Neither change seriously affected AMA efforts.[9] More important was Howard E. Spragg's election as BHM treasurer. Spragg became director of the BHM Puerto Rican mission in January 1949. Puerto Rico was still under AMA supervision, and he worked for a short time with Brownlee. In 1952, he became AMA secretary, assisting Widenhouse with the colleges and community centers. Two years later executive vice president Truman Douglass appointed him general secretary of administration for the BHM, in which position he lobbied for the merger that created the United Church of Christ. In 1959, he succeeded Frazier as BHM treasurer, the most powerful BHM position under both him and his predecessor. Spragg knew and appreciated the AMA tradition and worked well with Hotchkiss. At the same time he was determined to further unify the various BHM divisions, and when he succeeded Douglass as executive vice president in 1968 he insisted that other United Church Board for Homeland Ministries divisions take on more minority issues. During Douglass's tenure, the AMA had been responsible for most of the work with African Americans. Some association supporters saw Spragg's actions as further diluting AMA influence. He viewed it as responsible statesmanship and a reasonable effort to deal with serious American problems.[10]

Despite loss of independence, the AMA through the Board of Home

Missions and the United Church Board for Homeland Ministries continued to support, though far from lavishly, the colleges, the Race Relations Department, and later the Amistad Research Center. In 1960–61, it allocated $476,000 to the colleges, and requested and received BHM approval for an additional $50,000 for construction of a library at LeMoyne from the AMA Unexpended Property and Plant Account and another $50,000 from its Capital Fund Equipment Account for other college services. Additionally, it financially assisted six faculty in pursuing advanced degrees. In 1964, Hotchkiss and the AMA helped secure Ford Foundations grants for Fisk, LeMoyne, Dillard, and Tougaloo, and in 1967 it gave $504,667 to the colleges and $68,800 to the Race Relations Department.[11]

The AMA and its officers actively encouraged the colleges' civil rights activities, for example, Talladega College sit-ins in downtown drugstores in 1962, and Tougaloo students' sit-ins at the Jackson, Mississippi, public library in 1961 and drugstores in 1963. All the AMA colleges became more or less headquarters for civil rights agitation. Fisk University, with assistance from Herman Long and the Race Relations Department, trained many students for sit-ins, nonviolent marches, and demonstrations. Tougaloo was especially considered a significant center in the struggle for black freedom. In 1955, white trustee Barron C. Rickettes warned Philip Widenhouse that "many influential politicians and businessmen already hold the opinion that Tougaloo College is one of the principal centers of de-segregation in the state." In the early 1960s, the Mississippi White Citizens Council, claiming that material secured from FBI director J. Edgar Hoover proved that Tougaloo was "a hot bed of communism," tried to force the retirement of Adam D. Beittel, the fiery activist president.[12] A legislator unsuccessfully introduced a bill to revoke Tougaloo's charter.[13] The AMA supported the colleges' efforts to secure civil rights, sponsored citizenship schools at Dorchester Center, and made grants to various civil rights organizations, including $11,000 to the Southern Christian Leadership Conference (SCLC) in 1966 "for a general education and voter registration program."[14]

Obviously AMA funding was only a small portion of the colleges' budgets. The United Negro College Fund exceeded the AMA's contribution to Talladega in 1964–65, and beginning in 1960 both Hotchkiss and Spragg encouraged the schools to become ever more independent. College boards of trustees began to play a greater role, and Hotchkiss and Spragg, though they were trustees too, made fewer decisions. Spragg remembered that he and Hotchkiss urged the colleges "to be self-financing to a large degree, self-directing, self-controlled." Some of the presidents feared that the push toward greater independence foreshadowed a loss of even partial AMA and

UCBHM funding. In reality, the colleges had long been responsible for supplementing their budgets, and Spragg's policy of independence was not as unique as he suspected. The presidents did not lose their traditional funding, but U.S. government agencies soon far outstripped the UCBHM in support of AMA colleges. In 1962–63, the government contributed less than $30,000 to Talladega, but federal money began to flow to historically black colleges and universities (HBCUs) from the College Work Study program under authorization of 1964 poverty legislation and Title III of the Higher Education Act of 1965, Strengthening Developing Institutions. In 1967, the government gave Talladega $210,950 in Equal Opportunity Grants alone. By 1969–70, the federal government sent $857,545 to Talladega, more than its total 1964 budget. The same was true at other AMA colleges. Indeed, it is likely that some private black colleges would have folded during the 1970s without federal government assistance. Still, AMA or UCBHM funding to association institutions was important, consistent, and badly needed.[15] Moreover, the AMA frequently supplemented its modest annual appropriations with special grants for construction or equipment, and it also encouraged the churches, which were giving less directly to the AMA, to assist its colleges. In 1971, the United Church of Christ General Synod voted to launch a $10 million fund-raising campaign in 1973 for the colleges. In the meantime, it made a $1.5 million emergency grant to the colleges and gave an additional $1.5 million in 1973. In 2006, the United Church of Christ gave $1 million to Dillard to assist in recovery from Hurricane Katrina and an additional $500,000 each to Talladega and LeMoyne-Owen college.[16]

The AMA also continued to fund the Race Relations Department and later the Amistad Research Center. Clifton H. Johnson—a combination scholar, archivist, collector, diplomat, lobbyist, and extraordinary fundraiser—transformed the Amistad Research Center (ARC), which began primarily with AMA documents, into a major repository of African American materials. In 1969, he convinced the AMA and UCBHM to allow the ARC to incorporate so it could solicit funds as an independent institution. Additionally, at Johnson's urging, the AMA gradually increased its annual appropriation, gave frequent small donations, and in 1981 made a $900,000 endowment grant to the center. Both Spragg and Hotchkiss claimed credit for the grant. Of course, that was only a small amount of the money that Johnson collected over the years.[17]

In 1985, the Division of Higher Education was eliminated, and a new division, Education and Publications, was created. The AMA still existed within Education and Publications, and according to general secretary Nanette M.

Roberts, would "deal with the kind of issues of social justice for which the AMA is famous."[18] The change scarcely altered the AMA's role. In fact, Roberts managed to secure a slight increase in funding for the colleges. More significant, in 1987 the AMA's financial endowment, maintained intact since its founding, was completely absorbed by the United Church Board for Homeland Ministries. The UCBHM continued to support the AMA colleges, civil rights, and black equality, and the AMA name was retained. But a vibrant, independent American Missionary Association, which for more than a century had held aloft the torch of equality, was no more.[19]

Note on Sources

As noted in endnote 3 of the preface, the American Missionary Association has been thoroughly researched from its founding through the Reconstruction years, but there is no complete treatment of it after 1890. There is, however, a relatively rich literature on this extraordinary organization. Especially useful for an insider view are books by three corresponding secretaries: Augustus Field Beard, *A Crusade of Brotherhood: A History of the American Missionary Association* (Boston, 1909); Harlan Paul Douglass, *Christian Reconstruction in the South* (Boston, 1909); and Fred L. Brownlee, *New Day Ascending* (Boston, 1946). While these books were in-house efforts to publicize the AMA, they reveal much about the association's leadership, teachers, schools, aims, financial problems, and efforts to integrate blacks into American life. Joyce Hollyday's *On the Heels of Freedom: The American Missionary Association's Bold Campaign to Educate Minds, Open Hearts, and Heal the Soul of a Divided Nation* (New York, 2005), sponsored by the United Church of Christ, may indicate a renewed church interest in African American colleges and issues. Although not specifically on the AMA, James D. Anderson's impressive *The Education of Blacks in the South, 1860–1935* (Chapel Hill, 1988) helps place the AMA educational work in context with other education societies and the limited public schools.

Historically black colleges and universities have been and remain vitally important to the black community. They have trained much of the country's African American leadership and continue to assist thousands of black youth to improve their opportunities in life. There are dozens of books on the role of and the need for black colleges, but too few histories have been written about individual institutions. Fortunately, there are several studies of AMA colleges. Clarice T. Campbell and Oscar A. Rogers Jr., *Mississippi: The View from Tougaloo* (Jackson, MS, 1979) is especially good on the college's struggle against segregation and for equal rights. Maxine D. Jones and Joe M. Richardson, *Talladega College: The First Century* (Tuscaloosa, AL, 1990), and Richardson, *A History of Fisk University, 1865–1946* (Tuscaloosa, 1980) trace two of the AMA's best-known institutions, but the latter ends before the tenure of Fisk's most famous and first black president, Charles S. Johnson.

Patrick J. Gilpin and Marybeth Gasman, *Charles S. Johnson: Leadership beyond the Veil in the Age of Jim Crow* (Albany, NY, 2003), and Richard Robbins, *Sidelines Activist: Charles S. Johnson and the Struggle for Civil Rights* (Jackson, MS, 1996) deal adequately with Johnson as a college president. Shawn C. Comminey, "A History of Straight College, 1869–1935," (PhD diss., Florida State University, 2003) traces Straight until it merged with New Orleans University to become Dillard University. Atlanta University became independent soon after its founding, but Joseph O. Jewell's discussion of northern teachers' influence on students and community in *Race, Social Reform, and the Making of a Middle Class: The American Missionary Association and Black Atlanta, 1870–1900* (Lanham, MD, 2007) is pertinent to all AMA colleges. Two earlier books on Atlanta University are Myron Adams, *A History of Atlanta University* (Atlanta, 1930), and Clarence A. Bacote, *The Story of Atlanta University: A Century of Service, 1865–1965* (Atlanta, 1969).

In *Stand and Prosper: Private Black Colleges and Their Students* (Princeton, NJ, 2001), Henry N. Drewry and Humphrey Doermann praise the accomplishments of private black colleges in the face of economic scarcity and discrimination, and make a strong case for their continuance. They often use AMA schools as examples, and Drewry, who attended Talladega College, adds a special chapter on his alma mater. Addie Louise Butler focuses on three very different types of schools in *The Distinctive Black College: Talladega, Tuskegee, and Morehouse* (Metuchen, NJ, 1977); and Michael R. Heintze, *Private Black Colleges in Texas, 1865–1954* (College Station, TX, 1985) illustrates the financial weaknesses and instability of many private black colleges and provides a pattern against which to measure AMA institutions. Tillotson College history professor Chrystine I. Shackles presents a favorable picture of her institution during World War II and the postwar years in *Reminiscences of Huston-Tillotson College* (Austin, TX, 1973). August Meier's *A White Scholar and the Black Community, 1945–1965* (Amherst, MA, 1992), though occasionally overly critical of colleagues and select administrators, is a generally objective and perceptive recounting of the experiences of an activist white teacher at both Tougaloo College and Fisk University. While Eric Anderson and Alfred A. Moss Jr.'s *Dangerous Donations: Northern Philanthropy and Southern Black Education, 1902–1930* (Columbia, MO, 1999) is not about the AMA, it is useful for tracing philanthropic societies' early reluctance to support black liberal arts colleges. When philanthropists did finally decide to fund liberal arts colleges, AMA schools received a large share.

The AMA's colleges taught hundreds in the early years. Its secondary and elementary schools trained thousands. An indication of the importance of the AMA's educational efforts is that its secondary-elementary schools have attracted three book-length studies and several articles. Titus Brown, *Faithful, Firm, and True: African American Education in the South* (Macon, GA, 2002), and Edmund L. Drago, *Initiative, Paternalism, and Race Relations: Charleston's Avery Normal Institute* (Athens, GA, 1990) deal not only with Ballard Normal School and Avery Institute, but also with the surrounding black community. Drago's thoughtful discussion of intraracial prejudice is applicable to other black schools in major southern cities. Dawn J. Herd-Clark, "Dorchester Academy: The American Missionary Association in Liberty County, Georgia, 1867–1950," (PhD diss., Florida State University, 1999) traces Dorchester Academy from a one-room, one-teacher school to a twelve-grade institution with dormitories, and the only place in Liberty County where black youth could attend high school before 1942. As a teacher in an AMA school beginning in 1908 in Wilmington, North Carolina, and as AMA assistant superintendent of education from 1911 to 1919, Lura Beam was thoroughly familiar with AMA activities. In *He Called Them by the Lightning: A Teacher's Odyssey in the Negro South, 1908–1919* (Indianapolis, 1967), Beam draws an intimate portrait of teachers and curriculum during her tenure. Surprisingly, she probably overestimated the black-white and old-young division in the schools and gave too little credit to female principals. Raymond J. Pitts, *Reflections on a Cherished Past* (Sacramento, CA, 1980) is based on questionnaires he sent to 147 women and 56 men who attended Ballard Normal School between 1868 and 1942. Most respondents remembered their Ballard experience favorably. Less has been written on the AMA's purely elementary schools, which in scores of areas provided the only educational opportunity for black children.

There is no general study of the American Missionary Association's civil rights activities, but Ralph E. Luker, in *The Social Gospel in Black and White: American Racial Reform, 1885–1912* (Chapel Hill, 1991), clearly illustrates that the AMA was in the forefront of the northern fight against lynching, segregation, and disfranchisement. Gilpin and Gasman and Robbins, mentioned above, discuss the Race Relations Department during its early years when Charles S. Johnson was director. Keith Berry, "Charles S. Johnson, Fisk University, and the Struggle for Civil Rights, 1945–1970" (PhD diss., Florida State University, 2005) includes two chapters on the Race Relations Department. Katrina Marie Sanders, *"Intelligent and Effective Direction": The Fisk University Race Relations Institute and the Struggle for Civil Rights, 1944–1969"* (New York, 2005) is a detailed treatment of the Race Relations Institutes.

The most essential materials for this portrayal of the American Missionary Association's efforts to bring blacks into the mainstream of American life were the primary sources found in the Amistad Research Center, and in the archives of AMA colleges and schools. The American Missionary Association Archives, and the American Missionary Association Archives, Addendum, located at the Amistad Research Center, contain thousands of letters and documents written by faculty, students, staff, administrators, friends, and opponents. Included in this collection are files of the corresponding secretaries, the AMA Executive Committee, colleges, community centers, Race Relations Department, and most secondary schools. The Amistad Research Center also houses the United Church Board for Homeland Ministries Race Relations Department records, microfilm of the Charles S. Johnson Papers, and dozens of other helpful collections, plus selected correspondence with the General Education Board and the Julius Rosenwald Fund. The *American Missionary* not only kept AMA supporters up to date on southern schools, but also informed readers of southern white racism, violence, and discrimination along with the association's response. There is a vast literature on African American education in the nineteenth and twentieth centuries, all of which cannot be acknowledged in a brief bibliographical essay. The many sources that contributed most directly to this study are noted in the endnotes.

Notes

In citing works in the notes, short titles have occasionally been used. Works frequently cited are identified by the following abbreviations:

AM *American Missionary*
AMA American Missionary·
  Association

AMAA American Missionary
  Association Archives
UCBHMA United Church Board
  for Homeland Ministries Archives

PREFACE

1. For a detailed study of the organization and prewar activities of the American Missionary Association, see Clifton H. Johnson, "The American Missionary Association, 1841–1861: A Study of Christian Abolitionism" (PhD diss., University of North Carolina, 1958).

2. Mrs. S. F. Venatta was on a steamer near Helena, Arkansas, when the boat was attacked by Confederates. She was struck in the shoulder by a six-pound minnie ball which literally shattered her body. Her husband received a minnie ball in the thigh. J. R. Locky statement, 5 January 1864, AMAA, Amistad Research Center, Tulane University, New Orleans, Louisiana.

3. Studies specifically dealing with the AMA during the Civil War and Reconstruction include: Patricia C. Click, *Time Full of Trial: The Roanoke Island Freedmen's Colony, 1862–1867* (Chapel Hill, 2001); Clara DeBoer, *Be Jubilant My Feet: African American Abolitionists in the American Missionary Association, 1839–1861* (New York, 1994); Richard B. Drake, "The American Missionary Association and the Southern Negro, 1861–1888" (PhD diss., Emory University, 1957); Jacqueline Jones, *Soldiers of Light and Love: Northern Teachers and Georgia Blacks, 1865–1873* (Chapel Hill, 1980); Maxine D. Jones, "A Glorious Work: The American Missionary Association and Black North Carolinians, 1863–1880" (PhD diss., Florida State University, 1982); Joe M. Richardson, *Christian Reconstruction: The American Missionary Association and Southern Blacks, 1861–1890* (Athens, GA, 1986). Although not specifically on

the AMA, Heather Andrea Williams, *Self-Taught:African American Education in Slavery and Freedom* (Chapel Hill, 2005) frequently uses AMA sources. Other books on black education during the period are Ronald E. Butchart, *Northern Schools, Southern Blacks, and Reconstruction: Freedmen's Education, 1862–1875* (Westport, CT, 1980); and Robert C. Morris, *Reading, 'Riting, and Reconstruction: The Education of Freedmen in the South, 1861–1870* (Chicago, 1981).

4. Joyce Hollyday, *On the Heels of Freedom: The American Missionary Association's Bold Campaign to Educate Minds, Open Hearts, and Heal the Soul of a Divided Nation* (New York, 2005), ix.

5. *AM* 55 (July 1901): 139; *AM* 57 (December 1903): 324; *AM* 58 (October 1904): 253; *AM* 61 (September 1907): 201–2; *AM* 64 (May 1910): 123; *AM* 65 (March 1911): 793; *AM* 65 (September 1911): 317; *AM* 70 (December 1916): 488; *AM* 65 (March 1911): 791; Ralph E. Luker, *The Social Gospel in Black and White:American Racial Reform, 1885–1912* (Chapel Hill, 1991), 200, 2003.

6. Luker, *The Social Gospel in Black and White*, 5, 114; *Forty-Ninth Annual Report of the AMA* (New York, 1895), 7–8; *AM* 51 (March 1897): 81; *AM* 67 (April 1913): 34; *AM* 67 (August 1913): 287; Lucien C. Warner to Gov. Frank O. Lowden, 17 December 1917, in AM 71 (September 1917): 259; *AM* 73 (May 1919): 101; *AM* 73 (February 1919): 613–14; *Eighty-Seventh Annual Report of the AMA* (New York, 1933), 16–17; AMA administrative committee minutes, 24 January 1934, February 1937, 17–18 October 1938, AMAA, Addendum, Amistad Research Center, Tulane University, New Orleans, Louisiana.

7. As will be seen later, the AMA legally opposed the Florida segregation law aimed at Orange Park School and the Kentucky law aimed, in part, at Berea College. *AM* 59 (April 1905): 125; *AM* 55 (April 1901): 91; *AM* 67 (November 1913): 476–77; *AM* 68 (April 1914): 36; *AM* 73 (October 1919): 347; *Sixty-Eighth Annual Report of the AMA* (New York, 1914), 93; *AM* 82 (February 1928): 67; *AM* 32 (February 1936): 52.

8. George E. Mowry, *The Era of Theodore Roosevelt, 1900–1912* (New York, 1958), 212–14; *Fifty-Fifth Annual Report of the AMA* (New York, 1901), 5–6; *AM* 61 (February 1907): 68; *AM* 62 (December 1908): 324.

9. Lura Beam, who was with the AMA from 1908 to 1919, wrote in the 1960s that there was an annual AMA search for hotels that would accept black delegates to the national convention. "Suave proposals that Negroes ride in the freight elevator and have their meals in their rooms got short shrift." The association approved the Niagara Movement and supported the NAACP. It often contributed to NAACP anti-lynching and other campaigns. In 1911 it noted the NAACP's new journal *The Crisis* and reprinted its salutary. Lura Beam, *He Called Them by the Lightning: A Teacher's Odyssey in the Negro South, 1908–1919* (Indianapolis, 1967), 119–20; *AM* 59 (September 1905): 203–4; *AM* 62 (October 1908): 258; *AM* 65 (February 1911): 727; Luker, *The Social Gospel in Black and White*, 254.

10. The association branded *The Birth of a Nation* depiction of Reconstruction as false and recommended black former Mississippi congressman John R. Lynch's *The*

Facts of Reconstruction as more accurate. *AM* 69 (August 1915): 281–82; *AM* 69 (October 1915): 409; *AM* 75 (February 1921): 606–8; John Hope Franklin and Alfred A. Moss Jr., *From Slavery to Freedom: A History of Negro Americans* (6th ed., New York, 1988), 293; John Hope Franklin, *Mirror to America: The Autobiography of John Hope Franklin* (New York, 2005), 140; Luker, *Social Gospel in Black and White,* 289, 296.

11. The *American Missionary* reported in June 1919 that no one who believed in human brotherhood could read Du Bois's report of his visit to black soldiers in France without having his fighting instincts aroused. Some white officers of black troops had disgraced the principles for which the United States was fighting. The southern attitude of these officers was reprehensible, but the general order warning French officers and citizens from associating with black Americans was worse. *AM* 73 (June 1919): 158–59; *AM* 73 (September 1919): 285–86.

12. *Seventy-Third Annual Report of the AMA* (New York, 1919), 31–32; *AM* 73 (December 1919): 483; *AM* 73 (July 1919): 221.

13. AMA executive committee minutes, 11 March 1924, AMAA, Addendum.

14. *AM* 77 (February 1923): 603; *AM* 80 (July 1926): 168; *AM* 80 (October 1926): 273.

15. For more on the Scottsboro case, see: Dan T. Carter, *Scottsboro: A Tragedy of the American South* (Baton Rouge, 1969), and James E. Goodman, *Stories of Scottsboro* (New York, 1994); *Eighty-Fifth Annual Report of the AMA* (New York, 1931), 44; *AM* 87 (May 1933): 584, 594; AMA administrative committee minutes, 10 July 1934, 9 April 1935; AMA executive committee minutes, 11 December 1934, AMAA, Addendum.

16. *AM* 44 (December 1890): 435; *AM* 44 (June 1890): 175. Ryder quoted in Luker, *Social Gospel in Black and White,* 118–19; *AM* 58 (March 1904): 69.

17. Many African American teachers continued to think that teaching equality, self-confidence, and self-respect was revolutionary. Edouard Plummer, a New York junior high teacher since the 1960s, proclaimed in the late 1990s, quoting novelist James Baldwin, that "[t]eaching black children is a revolutionary act." Michele Foster, *Black Teachers on Teaching* (New York, 1997), xxv.

18. Luker, *Social Gospel in Black and White,* 29, 222–23; Adam Fairclough, *Teaching Equality: Black Schools in the Age of Jim Crow* (Athens, GA, 2001), 9.

CHAPTER 1

1. The AMA generally defined common schools as ungraded elementary schools, though occasionally it used the term for its graded elementary schools. Many of the common schools went only through the fourth grade. *AM* 49 (April 1895): 137; *AM* 52 (December 1989): 163; James D. Anderson, *The Education of Blacks in the South, 1860–1935* (Chapel Hill, 1988), 148.

2. *AM* 53 (December 1899): 157; *AM* 47 (November 1893): 346; *AM* 55 (July 1901): 153.

3. *AM* 70 (May 1916): 100; Joanna A. Greenlee, Teacher's Record, AMAA,

Addendum; H. Paul Douglass, *Christian Reconstruction in the South* (Boston, 1909), 213–15; *Allen Normal and Industrial School Catalog, 1905–6* (1906), 19.

4. Fred L. Brownlee, *New Day Ascending* (Boston, 1946), 78; *Cotton Valley School* (Pamphlet, New York, 1948), 2; Alice B. Donaldson, "News from Cotton Valley," mimeograph newsletter, 18 September 1943, box 9, folder 18, Cotton Valley School, AMAA, Addendum; *AM* 50 (May 1986): 156–57.

5. Joe M. Richardson, "Cotton Valley School: 'Bridging the Gap between the School and the Community,'" *Southern Studies* 6 (Fall 1995): 67–70; Douglass, *Christian Reconstruction in the South* 219–20; Brownlee, *New Day Ascending* 128; Samuel C. Adams, interviews with Mrs. Emma C. Boyd and Mr. and Mrs. N. L. Johnson, 7 February 1947, box 9, folder 5, Cotton Valley School.

6. *AM* 50 (May 1986): 157; *AM* 54 (April 1900): 68–69; A. F. Beard to AMA executive committee, 4 April 1893, box 1, folder 33, Beard to My Beloved Cousin, 8 March 1932, box 1, folder 10, A. F. Beard Papers, Amistad Research Center.

7. Douglass, *Christian Reconstruction in the South* 221–23; *AM* 54 (April 1900): 69; *AM* 60 (October 1906): 246–47; *AM* 59 (March 1905): 77–78; *AM* 66 (January 1912): 584; *Alumni Directory of Fisk University* (Nashville, 1930), 105, 137.

8. Janet Sharp Hermann, *The Pursuit of a Dream* (New York, 1981), 224, 229–32, 237; *Fifty-Fourth Annual Report of the AMA* (New York, 1900), 67; *AM* 63 (September 1909): 588; AMA executive committee minutes, 12 March 1918, AMAA, Addendum.

9. *AM* 56 (January 1902): 17–18; *AM* 56 (November 1902): 450; *AM* 59 (October 1905): 246; AMA executive committee minutes, 6 May 1902, AMAA, Addendum.

10. AMA executive committee minutes, 4 May 1892; AMA mission committee minutes, 29 May 1930, AMAA, Addendum; *AM* 56 (May 1902): 239–40; *AM* 63 (July 1909): 514.

11. *AM* 56 (May 1902): 241–43; *AM* 58 (September 1904): 209; AMA executive committee minutes, 11 June, 9 July 1901, AMAA, Addendum; Douglass, *Christian Reconstruction in the South,* 264.

12. *AM* 63 (July 1909): 514–15; U.S. Bureau of Education, *Negro Education: A Study of the Private and Higher Schools for Colored People in the United States* (2 vols., Washington, DC, 1917), 2:369.

13. *AM* 59 (December 1905): 305; *AM* 61 (June 1907): 165–66; *Fifty-Ninth Annual Report of the AMA* (New York, 1905), 15, 42, 47; H. Paul Douglass, "Report on Mount Herman Seminary," March 1907, Douglass Letter book, Beam-Douglass Collection, Amistad Research Center; Douglass, *Christian Reconstruction in the South,* 237–38.

14. Leslie K. Dunlap, "The Reform of Rape Law and the Problem of White Men: Age of Consent Campaign in the South, 1885–1910," in Martha Hodes, ed., *Sex, Love, Race: Crossing Boundaries in North American History* (New York, 1999), 363, 357–61. See also: Helen Griffith, *Dauntless in Mississippi: The Life of Sarah A. Dickey, 1838–1904* (South Hadley, MA, 1965).

15. *AM* 61 (September 1907): 211–14; *AM* 75 (October 1921): 263; *AM* 51 (April

1897): 119–20, 121; *AM* 54 (April 1900): 69; *AM* 69 (February 1915): 669; *AM* 70 (May 1916): 100; Douglass, *Christian Reconstruction in the South,* 221–22.

16. Washington Gladden quoted in Luker, *Social Gospel in Black and White,* 222–23; *AM* 55 (January 1900): 22; *AM* 63 (July 1909): 511–12; *AM* 61 (June 1907): 164; *AM* 61 (November 1907): 284; *AM* 57 (October 1903): 237–39; *AM* 58 (November 1904): 276; *Fifty-Seventh Annual Report of the AMA* (New York, 1903), 40, 104.

17. U.S. Bureau of Education, *Negro Education* 2:351, 369; Leon F. Litwack, *Trouble in Mind: Black Southerners in the Age of Jim Crow* (New York, 1998), 53.

18. AMA executive committee minutes, 12 September 1911, AMAA, Addendum; *AM* 65 (November 1911): 463; Lura Beam, *He Called Them by the Lightning,* 142–45.

19. *AM* 63 (July 1909): 511–12; *AM* 57 (March 1903): 71.

20. Douglass, *Christian Reconstruction in the South,* 222–23; *AM* 54 (April 1900): 69.

21. AMA executive committee minutes, 14 December 1891, AMAA, Addendum; *AM* 47 (November 1893): 346; Grace Carruthers, Teacher's Record, 1916–28, AMAA, Addendum.

22. *AM* 63 (February 1909): 49; Douglass, *Christian Reconstruction in the South,* 219; Julia M. Johnson speech, "The School and Its Community," 26 January 1955, box 11, folder 22, Cotton Valley School; Etta Cottin, Teacher's Record, AMAA, Addendum.

23. Richardson, "Cotton Valley School: 'Bridging the Gap between the School and the Community,'" 70; *AM* 71 (March 1917): 666.

24. AMA executive committee minutes, 9 January, 13 March 1917, AMAA, Addendum.

25. *Seventy-Eighth Annual Report of the AMA* (New York, 1924), 21.

26. Samuel C. Adams interviews with Addie B. Williams and Willola Anderson, 4 February 1947; undated interviews with Mrs. Marjorie L. S. Ball and Mrs. Evelyn M. Black, box 9, folder 7, Cotton Valley School.

27. Undated interview (1946 or 1947) with Mrs. Lorene W. J. Hastings; undated interview with Mary Promise; Samuel Adams interview with Willola Anderson, February 4, 1947, and Willie Mitchell, February 11, 1947, box 9, folder 7, Cotton Valley School; undated interview with Mrs. Evelyn M. Black, box 9, folder 7, Cotton Valley School.

28. Undated interviews (1946 or 1947) with Mrs. Lorene W. J. Hastings and Mrs. Evelyn M. Black. Black quoted music teacher Mrs. Elinor L. H. Foster, box 9, folder 7, Cotton Valley School; *Seventy-Eighth Annual Report of the AMA* (1924), 21; Ruth A. Morton to Vivian R. Belk, 6 June 1941, box 8, folder 10, Ruth A. Morton to Marjorie J. Green, 3 February 1945, box 9, folder 17; Fisk University, "A Community Survey of Cotton Valley, Macon County, Alabama," typescript, 47–49, 74, box 9, folder 10; undated interviews with Mrs. Marjorie L. S. Ball and Mrs. Evelyn Black, box 9, folder 7, Cotton Valley School; *AM* 70 (May 1916): 100; *AM* 69 (February 1915): 669.

29. *AM* 61 (September 1907): 211–14; E. Franklin Frazier, "A Survey of the

Community about Cotton Valley School, Fort Davis, Alabama," December 1925, ii, 3, 4, 9, 10, 11–13, box 10, Cotton Valley School. Frazier submitted an unnumbered thirty-four-page report. The author numbered the copy used for this study.

30. Herman H. Long, "No Hiding Place: The Negro Search," 25 October 11, 1962, box 3, folder 7, Herman H. Long Papers, Amistad Research Center; *AM* 61 (September 1907): 211–14; Fisk University, "A Community Survey of Cotton Valley, Macon County, Alabama," 62, 64, 68–70, box 9, folder 10; undated interviews with Mrs. Lorene W. J. Hastings and Mrs. Evelyn M. Black, box 9, folder 7, Ruth A. Morton to Julia M. Johnson, 20 April 1949, box 8, folder 23, Myrtle W. Knight to Dear Friends, 13 December 1936, Dorothy P. Childs to Dear Friends, 3 February 1936, box 11, folder 20, undated list of former graduates of Cotton Valley, box 11, folder 17, Cotton Valley School; Fred L. Brownlee, *A Continuing Service* (New York, 1938), 20.

31. Brownlee, *New Day Ascending*, 128; *AM* 56 (January 1902): 17–18; U.S. Bureau of Education, *Negro Education*, 2:61, 351, 369.

32. *AM* 49 (April 1895): 137; *AM* 52 (December 1898): 163; Litwack, *Trouble in Mind*, 68; Frazier, "Survey of the Community about Cotton Valley School," 11–13.

33. *AM* 61 (October 1907): 250–51; *AM* 62 (December 1908): 306; *AM* 66 (April 1912): 24; Beam, *He Called Them by the Lightning*, 125.

34. Millie Belle Davis to J. W. Cooper, 4 June 1908, Beam-Douglass Collection, 1906–18, AMAA, Addendum.

35. Beam, *He Called Them by the Lightning*, 134; *AM* 47 (January 1893): 3.

36. *AM* 45 (March 1891): 91; *AM* 52 (December 1898): 164; *AM* 62 (March 1908): 68; *AM* 59 (March 1905): 76; Beam, *He Called Them by the Lightning*, 134.

37. For more on the Jeanes Foundation, see: Lance G. E. Jones, *The Jeanes Teacher in the United States, 1908–1933* (Chapel Hill, 1937); *AM* 59 (December 1905): 303; *AM* 61 (November 1907): 283; *AM* 64 (November 1910): 530; Anderson, *Education of Blacks in the South*, 86.

38. *AM* 59 (February 1905): 55; *AM* 59 (May 1905): 157; Frazier, "Survey of the Community about Cotton Valley School," 13, 15.

39. *AM* 60 (March 1906): 85–86.

40. AMA executive committee minutes, 13 May 1924, AMAA, Addendum; AMA administrative committee minutes, 14 February 1933, AMAA, Addendum; *Seventy-Eighth Annual Report of the AMA* (1924), 21–22.

41. *Seventy-Eighth Annual Report of the AMA* (1924), 21; *Missionary Herald* 135 (June 1939): 238; Brownlee, *Continuing Service*, 20; Ruth A. Morton to Julia M. Johnson, 8 August, 4 September 1946, box 8, folders 18, 7, 19, Cotton Valley School, AMAA, Addendum; Division of Higher Education and AMA minutes, 11 April 1961, box 363, General Secretary Correspondence, AMAA, Addendum.

CHAPTER 2

1. *AM* 50 (September 1896): 277; *AM* 62 (March 1908): 65; *AM* 64 (April 1910): 27–28; A. F. Beard to AMA executive committee, 4 April 1893, box 1, folder 33,

A. F. Beard Papers; *Forty-Ninth Annual Report of the AMA* (1895), 22–23; Richardson, *Christian Reconstruction*, 113–19.

2. Anderson, *Education of Blacks in the South*, 110–14, 197; Douglass, *Christian Reconstruction in the South*, 225–25; *AM* 66 (July 1912): 223; *AM* 68 (May 1914): 99–100; Michael W. Homel, "Two Worlds of Race? Urban Blacks and Public Schools, North and South, 1865–1940," in David N. Plank and Rick Ginsberg, eds., *Southern Cities, Southern Schools: Public Education in the Urban South* (New York, 1990), 251–52; Statistics on Education in Georgia, 1930, box 87, folder 14, Julius Rosenwald Fund Papers, microfilm, Amistad Research Center; Ambrose Caliver, *Education of Negro Teachers* (Westport, CT, reprint, 1970), 4.

3. Richardson, *Christian Reconstruction*, 113–14; *AM* 47 (November 1893): 348; *AM* 61 (November 1907): 283; *AM* 62 (November 1908): 286–87.

4. Other AMA normal and secondary schools included Peabody Academy, Troy, North Carolina; Chandler Normal, Lexington, Kentucky; Burrell Normal, Florence, Alabama; Lincoln School, Meridian, Mississippi; Knox Institute, Athens, Georgia; Brewer Normal, Greenwood, South Carolina; Lincoln Academy, Kings Mountain, North Carolina; and Orange Park Normal School, Orange Park, Florida. Charlotte Hawkins Brown's, Palmer Memorial Institute was associated with the AMA from 1924 to 1933.

5. Titus Brown, *Faithful, Firm, and True: African American Education in the South* (Macon, GA, 2002) and Edmund L. Drago, *Initiative, Paternalism, and Race Relations: Charleston's Avery Normal Institute* (Athens, GA, 1990).

6. Drago, *Initiative, Paternalism, and Race Relations*, 96; Brown, *Faithful, Firm, and True*, 93–94; *AM* 59 (November 1905): 270; H. Paul Douglass, "The Story of Emerson Institute" (AMA Pamphlet, 1910), 13, Small Field Records, box 200, folder 2, Series AMAA, Addendum.

7. Horace Mann Bond, *Black American Scholars: A Study of Their Beginnings* (Detroit, 1972), 41–42; Horace Mann Bond, "The American Missionary Association Colleges and the Great Society," *Inauguration of Herman Hodge Long as Ninth President of Talladega College* (New York, 1965) 14–17; Richardson, *Christian Reconstruction*, 115; Coretta Scott King, *My Life with Martin Luther King, Jr.* (New York, 1969), 25–26, 35–37; W. Judson King to Ruth Morton, 9 September 1950, King to Philip Widenhouse, 7 March 1951, R. F. Johnson to Howard C. Spragg, 13 August 1954, box 3, Trinity School, AMAA, Addendum; Hollyday, *On the Heels of Freedom*, 168.

8. The AMA began development of agricultural high schools in 1907. They were to teach a traditional high school curriculum plus "do such work as is accomplished by the standard schools of this type" in the Midwest. In 1910 the following were listed as agricultural schools: Lincoln Normal in Marion, Alabama; Fessenden Academy in Martin, Florida; Dorchester Academy in Liberty County, Georgia; Lincoln Academy in Kings Mountain, North Carolina; Brewer Normal in Greenwood, South Carolina; Gloucester High School in Cappahosic, Virginia; and J. K. Brick School in Enfield, North Carolina. *AM* 64 (November 1910): 531–32; Douglass, *Christian Reconstruction in the South*, 230–32.

9. For a detailed study of Dorchester see: Dawn J. Herd-Clark, "Dorchester

Academy: The American Missionary Association in Liberty County, Georgia, 1867–1950," (PhD diss., Florida State University, 1999); Douglass, *Christian Reconstruction in the South*, 232–35; *AM* 50 (July 1896): 224; *AM* 57 (March 1903): 80.

10. H. Paul Douglass, "Report on Dorchester Academy," January 1907, Douglass Letter book, January–October 1907, Beam-Douglass Collection, Amistad Research Center.

11. Joe M. Richardson, "Allen Normal School: Training 'Leaders of Righteousness' 1885–1933," *Journal of Southwest Georgia History* 12 (Fall 1997): 1–26; "The Quitman School—The Burning and the Rebuilding," typescript, box 204, folder 10, 1886, Small Field Records, AMAA, Addendum; *AM* 51 (June 1897): 197–98; *Allen Normal and Industrial Catalog, 1905–6*, 6–8.

12. *AM* 58 (March 1904): 77; *AM* 78 (December 1924): 347; *AM* 67 (March 1913): 743; *AM* 62 (December 1908): 314; *AM* 45 (October 1891): 354; *AM* 67 (April 1913): 27; *AM* 80 (January 1926): 409–10; Raymond G. Von Tobel to My Dear Friends, 15 March 1930, Ballard School, box 78, folder 1, AMAA, Addendum; Ann Short Chirhart, *Torches of Light: Georgia Teachers and the Coming of the Modern South* (Athens, GA, 2005), 46–47.

13. *AM* 67 (February 1913): 677; *AM* 73 (March 1919): 674; *AM* 75 (May 1921): 98.

14. Litwack, *Trouble in Mind*, 54; Henry Hugh Proctor, *Between Black and White: Autobiographical Sketches* (Freeport, NY, 1971), 15; Glenda Elizabeth Gilmore, *Gender and Jim Crow: Women and the Politics of White Supremacy in North Carolina, 1896–1920* (Chapel Hill, 1996), 36.

15. *AM* 45 (November 1891): 411; *AM* 50 (September 1896): 285; *AM* 56 (May 1902): 233; *AM* 66 (December 1912): 542.

16. *AM* 71 (July 1917): 219; *AM* 76 (February 1922): 524; M. L. Phillips, *Fifteen Years at Lincoln School* (AMA Pamphlet, New York, 1912), 7.

17. Anderson, *Education of Blacks in the South*, 156; Richardson, *Christian Reconstruction*, 237; *AM* 66 (December 1912): 542; "Lincoln School, Marion, Alabama," undated typescript, Lincoln School, box 15, folder 1, AMAA, Addendum; Mary L. Phillips, *Lincoln Normal School* (Pamphlet 1902?); *AM* 52 (December 1898): 165, 210–11; *AM* 58 (June 1904): 174–78.

18. Robert G. Sherer, "Let Us Make Men: Negro Education in Nineteenth-Century Alabama" (PhD diss.: University of North Carolina, 1970), 308; *AM* 47 (November 1893): 361; *Huntsville Gazette*, 26 November 1881.

19. H. Paul Douglass to J. W. Cooper, 16 March 1907, 16 September 1907, Beam-Douglass Collection, Amistad Research Center; *AM* 61 (June 1907): 164; *AM* 61 (October 1907): 243; *AM* 62 (October 1908): 249–51; Brownlee, *New Day Ascending*, 121–22.

20. Litwack, *Trouble in Mind*, 53, 91, 95. According to Michael Dennis, prominent southern educators advocated disfranchisement and industrial education as a way to bring peace to the South. He mentions specifically Edwin Alderman, president of the University of Virginia; Samuel Chiles Mitchell, president of the University of South

Carolina; Walter Barnard Hill, chancellor of the University of Georgia; and Charles Dabney, president of the University of Tennessee. Michael Dennis, "Schooling along the Color Line: Progressives and the Education of Blacks in the New South," *Journal of Negro Education* 67 (Spring 1998): 142–45.

21. *AM* 51 (April 1897): 124; William N. Sheats to J. M. Slater, 26 October 1903, Superintendent of Public Instruction Letter Book, vol. 24, Florida State Archives, Tallahassee, Florida; *(Charleston) News and Courier* quoted in *AM* 58 (October 1904): 238; *Crisis* 19 (November 1919): 349; Beam, *He Called Them by the Lightning*, 225.

22. Franklin and Moss, *From Slavery to Freedom*, 238; Luker, *Social Gospel in Black and White*, 289, 296; *AM* 60 (October 1906): 270; *AM* 60 (December 1906): 315–16, 325, 328–29; *Crisis* 1 (January 1911): 7; Litwack, *Trouble in Mind*, 188; Douglass, *Christian Reconstruction in the South*, 59; *Crisis* 2 (May 1911): 32.

23. *AM* 70 (April 1916): 30; *AM* 67 (April 1913): 30; Beam, *He Called Them by the Lightning*, 48.

24. For more on Judge Horton and his attempts to treat the Scottsboro defendants fairly, see: Dan T. Carter, *Scottsboro: A Tragedy of the American South* (Baton Rouge, 1969), 184, 193–239, 245–46, 264–69. Jay T. Wright, "Trinity School, Midyear Report," January 1941, box 4, Brownlee to Wright, 10 March 1941, box 1, Trinity School, AMAA, Addendum. *Seventy-Fourth Annual Report of the AMA* (New York, 1920), 10; *AM* 77 (July 1923): 218; Alfred E. Lawless to F. L. Brownlee, 27 April 1921, box 8, folder 1, J. Stanley and Kathryn T. Stanley Papers, Amistad Research Center.

25. *AM* 79 (April 1925): 11; *Seventy-Eighth Annual Report of the AMA* (1924), 14; *AM* 82 (January 1928): 21; *Missionary Herald* 132 (February 1936): 63–64; King, *My Life with Martin Luther King, Jr.*, 36.

26. U.S. Office of Education, *Negro Education: A Survey of Private and Higher Schools for Colored People in the United States,* Bulletin, 1916, no. 39 (Washington 1917), 162–69; *AM* 46 (March 1892): 75; *AM* 53 (July 1899): 65; *AM* 50 (August 1896): 251; *AM* 71 (March 1917): 667; *AM* 73 (January 1919): 545. Missionary barrels were still being sent to the colleges in the 1950s.

27. *AM* 71 (January 1917): 518; *AM* 78 (September 1924): 206; *AM* 49 (August 1895): 263–64; *AM* 49 (September 1895): 287; Douglass, *Christian Reconstruction in the South,* 263–64; *AM* 47 (February 1893): 38, 42; *AM* 68 (October 1914): 410.

28. Richardson, "Allen Normal School," 13; Drago, *Initiative, Paternalism, and Race Relations,* 154–55; *AM* 59 (April 1905): 122; AMA executive committee minutes, 10 March 1914, AMAA, Addendum.

29. *AM* 55 (January 1901): 21; *AM* 66 (July 1912): 223; *AM* 67 (April 1913): 30; *AM* 72 (June 1918): 166; *AM* 57 (March 1903): 81; *Brewer Normal School* (Brochure, 1918), box 213, folder 13, Small Field Records, Series A, AMAA, Addendum.

30. Information from results of Georgia state teachers' examinations from *Atlanta Independent,* 21 March 1889, cited in Joseph Oscar Jewell, "Black Ivy: The American Missionary Association and the Black Upper Class in Atlanta, Georgia, 1875–1915," (PhD diss., UCLA, 1998), 84; *AM* 54 (October 1900): 152–53; *AM* 56 (December 1902): 499–500; *AM* 70 (July 1916): 222; *Crisis* 36 (February 1929): 65.

31. *AM* 66 (April 1912): 25; *AM* 61 (June 1907): 183; Cornelia M. Curtis, undated memoir, Thomasville Historical Society, Thomasville, Georgia; *AM* 70 (July 1916): 222.

32. Franklin, *Mirror to America,* 379–80; Linda Perkins, "Education," in Darlene Clark Hine, Elsa Barkley Brown, and Rosalyn Terborg-Penn, eds., *Black Women in America: An Historical Encyclopedia* (Bloomington, 1994), 384–85; Chirhart, *Torches of Light* 54; Omelia T. Robinson, "Contributions of Black American Academic Women to American Higher Education" (PhD diss., Wayne State University, 1978), 63.

33. Beam told of the white father of one of the families at her school who "came to the school once a month to pay the tuition and sign the report cards. He waited uneasily until the principal came for he wanted to talk . . . about his children's prospects for college." Most of the fair-skinned children had light-skinned parents, however, rather than white ones. AMA executive committee minutes, 12 May 1914, AMAA, Addendum; Beam, *He Called Them by the Lightning,* 29; Margaret H. Scott statement, 23 September 1936, Margaret H. Scott Papers, Amistad Research Center.

34. Beam, *He Called Them by the Lightning,* 89; Drago, *Initiative, Paternalism, and Race Relations,* 132–33.

35. H. Paul Douglass, "Report on Beach Institute," January 1907, Douglass Letter book, January–October 1907, Beam-Douglass Collection; *AM* 73 (July 1919): 228; Beam, *He Called Them by the Lightning,* 29; Drago, *Initiative, Paternalism, and Race Relations,* 132–33, 183–92.

36. Joe M. Richardson, "'The Nest of Vile Fanatics': William N. Sheats and the Orange Park School," *Florida Historical Quarterly* 64 (April 1986): 393–406; Wali R. Kharif, "The Refinement of Racial Segregation in Florida after the Civil War" (PhD diss., Florida State University, 1983), 183–84; (*Jacksonville) Florida Times-Union,* 21 June 1896; *AM* 49 (January 1895): 287.

37. Florida, *Report of the Superintendent of Public Instruction, 1894* (Tallahassee, 1894), 71; W. N. Sheats to J. C. Hartzwell, 14 June 1895, Superintendent of Public Instruction Letter book, 25 February 1895–25 September 1897, Florida State Archives, Tallahassee, Florida; Sheats statement against Orange Park in Jacksonville *Florida Times-Union,* 5 October 1895; Florida, *Acts and Resolutions, 1895* (Tallahassee, 1895), 96–97.

38. Copy of motion to quash indictment against teachers, 21 October 1896, in records of the Fourth Judicial Circuit of Florida, Clay County Courthouse; *New York Times,* 23 October 1896, 24 October 1896; William N. Sheats [compiler], *Digest of the Laws of the State of Florida with the Regulations of the State Board of Education and the Instruction Forms of the Department of Education* (Tallahassee 1915), lxxxvii; Richardson, "'The Nest Of Vile Fanatics': William N. Sheats and the Orange Park School," 403–6.

39. *AM* 57 (January 1903): 16; Beam, *He Called Them by the Lightning,* 8, 9, 11, 14; *AM* 73 (July 1919): 229; *AM* 71 (October 1917): 329; *Eighty-First Annual Report of the AMA* (New York, 1927), 22, 51; Lorena Derby, Teacher's Record, AMAA, Addendum.

40. For more on southern white moderate Cable, see: Arlin Turner, "George W. Cable's Beginnings as a Reformer," *Journal of Southern History* 17 (May 1951): 136–51; Arlin Turner, *George W. Cable: A Biography* (Durham, NC, 1956) and Turner, ed., *The Negro Question: A Selection of Writings on Civil Rights in the South*, by George W. Cable (Garden City, NY, 1958).

41. Beam, *He Called Them by the Lightning*, 18, 19, 26, 175–76; Franklin and Moss, *From Slavery to Freedom*, 288; *AM* 66 (April 1912): 26.

42. Michael Fultz, "Teacher Training and African American Education in the South, 1900–1940," *Journal of Negro Education* 64 (Spring 1995): 197–201.

43. Professor Francis T. Waters claimed that Gregory Normal Institute furnished most of the teachers for eastern North Carolina, including Wilmington city schools. By 1900 hundreds of LeMoyne students and former students were teaching. The Shelby County, Tennessee, county superintendent of education said LeMoyne graduates filled the bulk of county schools. He was pleased that they had moral training as well as book knowledge. Principal O. Faduma of Peabody Academy in Troy, North Carolina, said ninety percent of the teachers in Montgomery County, North Carolina, came from Peabody. In 1914, three-fourths of Perry County, Alabama, teachers were trained at Lincoln Normal. *AM* 49 (July 1895): 226; *AM* 55 (October 1901): 203; *AM* 51 (April 1897): 122; *AM* 54 (October 1900): 150; *AM* 66 (July 1912): 227; *AM* 69 (September 1915): 331.

44. Ballard principal Raymond G. Von Tobel wrote in 1930 that more than eighty percent of teachers in Macon County's black public schools were Ballard graduates. Raymond G. Von Tobel to Dear Friends, 11 January 1930, box 1, folder 1, Raymond G. Von Tobel papers, Amistad Research Center; *AM* 58 (March 1904): 76; *AM* 51 (December 1897): 268; *AM* 56 (January 1902): 19–20; *AM* 84 (February 1930): 172; Brown, *Faithful, Firm, and True*, 145.

45. *AM* 45 (July 1891): 264; *AM* 56 (March 1902): 135; *AM* 47 (April 1893): 117; *AM* 56 (July 1902): 329; *AM* 60 (April 1906): 115–16; *AM* 72 (June 1918): 167; Diane Ravitch, *The Revisionists Revised: A Critique of the Radical Attack on the Schools* (New York, 1978), 67; *Eighty-Ninth Annual Report of the AMA* (New York, 1935), 37.

46. Drago, *Initiative, Paternalism, and Race Relations*, 127.

47. For more on Clark, who became a noted South Carolina civil rights activist, see: Septima Poinsette Clark, *Echo in My Soul* (New York, 1962) and Cynthia Stokes Brown, ed., *Ready from Within: Septima Clark and the Civil Rights Movement* (Trenton, NJ, 1990).

48. Drago, *Initiative, Paternalism, and Race Relations*, 150–54; Bureau of Census, *Negro Population 1790–1915* (Washington, DC, 1918), 404; Franklin and Moss, *From Slavery to Freedom*, 362–63; Michael Fultz, "African American Teachers in the South: Powerlessness and the Ironies of Expectations and Protest," *History of Education Quarterly* 35 (Winter 1995): 114; Michele Foster, *Black Teachers on Teaching*, 23–25. For more on Mamie Fields, see: Mamie Garvin Fields with Karen Fields, *Lemon Swamp and Other Places: A Carolina Memoir* (New York, 1983).

49. Stephanie J. Shaw, *What a Woman Ought to Be and Do: Black Professional Women*

Workers during the Jim Crow Era (Chicago, 1996), 74, 76–77; Ann Short Chirhart, "'Gardens of Education': Beulah Rucker and African American Culture in the Twentieth-Century Georgia Upcountry," *Georgia Historical Quarterly* 82 (Winter 1998): 836–37; Chirhart, *Torches of Light*, 12, 35–36.

50. See Brown, *Faithful, Firm, and True*, chapter 8, and Drago, *Initiative, Paternalism, and Race Relations* for alumni at Ballard and Avery; *Catalogue of Knox Institute and Industrial School, 1924–25* (Athens, GA, 1924), 27–31; *AM* 56 (July 1902): 327; *Mobile Register*, 30 May 1909, 4; *Emerson Normal Institute Catalog, 1900–1901* (Mobile, 1901), 5–9.

51. Rev. Robert Sheaff, a Bowdoin College and Bangor Seminary graduate, was appointed principal of Dorchester in October 1918 and released in 1920. He was honest and showed good judgment in dealing with teachers but, Secretary Brownlee said, he had "no fundamental understanding of Negroes." His wife, the matron and preceptress, lacked deep understanding of black girls. Robert Sheaff, Teacher's Record, AMAA, Addendum.

52. AMA, Teacher's Record, AMAA, Addendum; H. S. Barnwell to Mrs. R. G. Von Tobel, 30 July 1935, box 8, folder 8, J. Stanley and Kathryn T. Stanley Papers, Amistad Research Center; Fred L. Brownlee to Frank Sweeney, 17 July 1935, Frederick L. Brownlee Papers, Amistad Research Center; *AM* 60 (October 1906): 23; AMA executive committee minutes, 12 September 1911, AMAA, Addendum; Beam, *He Called Them by the Lightning*, 120, 140.

53. *Eighty-Seventh Annual Report of the AMA* (1933), 59–60; AMA executive committee minutes, 11 June 1921, AMAA, Addendum; AMA administrative committee minutes, 25 April 1933, AMAA, Addendum; AMA, *Accelerating Social Evolution* (New York, 1939), 21; *AM* 82 (January 1928): 21.

54. *Missionary Herald* 135 (August 1939): 337; *AM* 81 (May 1927): 621–22; H. Paul Douglass, "Report on Lincoln Normal School," 1907, Douglass Letter book, Beam-Douglass Collection; H. Paul Douglass to J. W. Cooper, 27 November 1909, Beam-Douglass Collection; Maxine D. Jones and Joe M. Richardson, *Talladega College: The First Century* (Tuscaloosa, AL, 1990), 87; Mary E. Phillips, Teacher's Record, AMAA, Addendum; Idella J. Childs speech presenting Phillips for induction into Alabama Women's Hall of Fame, 13 October 1988, Lincoln School, box 18, folder 17, AMAA, Addendum; Brownlee, *New Day Ascending*, 126; Hollyday, *On the Heels of Freedom*, 175; Beam, *He Called Them by the Lightning*, 34.

55. H. Paul Douglass to J. W. Cooper, 29 November 1908, Beam-Douglass Collection; Margaret H. Allison, Teacher's Record, AMAA, Addendum; Beam, *He Called Them by the Lightning*, 142.

56. Ida F. Hubbard, principal of Slater Training School in Knoxville, Tennessee, said in 1897 that blacks were "religious and emotional, with an evil inheritance which will take years to overcome; the elements for character building still crude and home life defective; families living in one room." *AM* 51 (December 1894): 294.

57. Katherine M. Rowley to Dear Classmates, 19 December 1901, *The Third Annual Class Letter, Class of 1899* (Oberlin, 1902), 46; *AM* 71 (July 1917): 219–20;

J. Taylor Stanley, *A History of Black Congregational Christian Churches of the South* (New York, 1978), 1; Wayne J. Urban, *Black Scholar: Horace Mann Bond* (Athens, 1992), 14, 16.

58. Vanessa Siddle Walker, *Their Highest Potential: An African American School Community in the Segregated South* (Chapel Hill, 1996), 88–89, 201–2; Raymond J. Pitts, *Reflections on a Cherished Past* (Sacramento, CA, 1980), 2, 14, 15, 36, 47–48, 58, 60, 73. Lillian Roundtree Ford, Bertha Hill, Charles E. Holmes, Judson D. Howard, James C. Johnson, Nellvina Ming LaBeach, Ruth Howard Davis, Alumni Questionnaire, Ballard School, box 80, folders 12–16, AMAA, Addendum.

59. Pitts, *Reflections on a Cherished Past,* 49, 55, 85; Birtill T. Barrow, Teacher's Record, AMAA, Addendum; Charles Killens to Raymond J. Pitts, 24 January 1980, Ballard School, box 79, folder 2; Louis H. Mounts to Fred L. Brownlee, 3 August 1938, Ballard School, box 78, folder 1, AMAA, Addendum.

60. All of the quotes in the above paragraph are found in Hollyday, *On the Heels of Freedom,* 166–71.

61. More than any other AMA corresponding secretary, Brownlee learned from African Americans, and was able to work *with* them. In this particular instance he may have been talking as much or more to church supporters who, Brownlee believed, were not zealous enough in supporting black rights. *Eighty-Third Annual Report of the AMA* (New York, 1929), 8.

62. Richardson, *Christian Reconstruction,* 114, 191, 207; AMA executive committee minutes, 14 April 1890, AMAA, Addendum; A. F. Beard to AMA executive committee, 4 April 1893, box 1, folder 33, Beard to My Dear Cousinly Friend (Fred L. Brownlee), 13 January 1933, box 1, folder 10, A. F. Beard Papers; *AM* 57 (March 1903): 74–75.

63. *AM* 51 (December 1897): 269–70; *Fifty-Fourth Annual Report of the AMA* (New York, 1900), 22; *AM* 55 (January 1901): 22; *AM* 58 (February 1904): 35.

64. *Eighty-First Annual Report of the AMA* (1927), 11, 15; *AM* 77 (January 1923): 537; *Crisis* 22 (August 1921): 177; *Crisis* 34 (October 1927): 267; AMA executive committee minutes, 19 April 1927, AMAA, Addendum.

65. *AM* 61 (February 1907): 41; *AM* 67 (August 1913): 277–78; *AM* 70 (May 1916): 90–93; *AM* 71 (September 1917): 265–66; *AM* 72 (July 1918): 219; Douglass, *Christian Reconstruction in the South,* 135, 143; *AM* 75 (May 1921): 95; H. Paul Douglass to J. W. Cooper, 25 January 1910, Beam-Douglass Collection; George F. Bagby, "William G. Price and the Gloucester Agricultural and Industrial School," *Virginia Magazine of History and Biography* 108 (2000): 45, 59, 67.

66. Joe M. Richardson, "Joseph L. Wiley: A Black Florida Educator," *Florida Historical Quarterly* 71 (April 1993): 458–72; *Who's Who of the Colored Race* (Chicago, 1915), 283; *Crisis* 7 (December 1913): 65; *Ocala Evening Star,* 6 September 1915; Beam, *He Called Them by the Lightning,* 89; M. D. Potter to N. A. A. C. P., 25 June 1937, Papers of the NAACP, Part 7, The Anti-Lynching Campaign, 1912–1953, Series A: Reel 10, Group 1, Series C Box C-353, Microfilm.

67. White later became promotional secretary when the missions boards merged

in 1935. H. Paul Douglass, "Report on Burrell Normal School," March 1907, Douglass Letter book, Beam-Douglass Collection; *Crisis* 7 (March 1914): 221; *Missionary Herald* 133 (November 1937): 508; AMA missions committee minutes, 11 May 1920 and 12 May 1925, AMAA, Addendum; *Crisis* 33 (January 1927): 148–49; *Missionary Herald* 141 (April 1945): 48.

68. Frank B. Stevens, Teacher's Record, AMAA, Addendum; Drago, *Initiative, Paternalism, and Race Relations,* 117–18, 139–95; Herd-Clark, "Dorchester Academy," 137–67; *AM* 65 (March 1911): 784–85; AMA missions committee minutes, 13 April 1920, 18 June 1920, 18 April 1922, AMAA, Addendum.

69. *AM* 76 (June 1922): 134; *Eighty-Sixth Annual Report of the AMA* (New York, 1932), 20; F. L. Brownlee to Marion V. Cuthbert, 19 September 1944, box 238, Race Relations Department, AMAA, Addendum; *Crisis* 50 (February 1943): 45; Jessie Carney Smith, ed., *Notable Black American Women* (Detroit, 1992), 245–46; Marion V. Cuthbert, Teacher's Record, AMAA, Addendum; *AM* 76 (April 1922): 14; *AM* 80 (January 1926): 407; Fred L. Brownlee to Ethel W. Stallings, 8 February 1944, box 107, folder 6, Tougaloo College, AMAA, Addendum.

70. Chirhart, *Torches of Light,* 44; Linda M. Perkins, "The Impact of the 'Cult of True Womanhood' on the Education of Black Women," *Journal of Social Issues* 39.3 (1983): 17; James L. Leloudis, *Schooling the New South: Pedagogy, Self, and Society in North Carolina, 1880–1920* (Chapel Hill, 1996), 186–88.

71. Jacqueline Jones, *Labor of Love, Labor of Sorrow: Black Women, Work, and the Family from Slavery to the Present* (New York, 1985), 144, 200; Henry Allen Bullock, *A History of Negro Education in the South from 1619 to the Present* (Cambridge, MA, 1967), 181; Foster, *Black Teachers on Teaching,* xvii; AMA executive committee minutes, 9 March 1920, AMAA, Addendum.

72. Drago, *Initiative, Paternalism, and Race Relations,* 154; Fred L. Brownlee to My Dear Miss Hansen, 1 May 1922, Anna Maria Hansen Jamison Papers, Amistad Research Center; Ruth D. Anderson, Teacher's Record, AMA executive committee minutes, 12 May 1925, AMAA, Addendum.

73. Ruth A. Morton to Ruth M. Stuart, 13 July 1938, box 1, Trinity School; Morton to Inez Fant, 19 May 1938, box 1, Trinity School, AMAA, Addendum; Morton to Wilfred Gamble, 25 April 1941, Lincoln School, AMAA, Addendum; Board of Home Missions committee minutes, 15–16 April 1941, AMAA, Addendum.

74. In 1908, AMA treasurer Henry W. Hubbard visited Ballard and was extremely impressed with the cultured, refined black faculty. *AM* 56 (June 1892): 299; *AM* 62 (April 1908): 112; Brown, *Faithful, Firm, and True,* 104; *Mobile Register,* 30 May 1909; *AM* 67 (February 1913): 675; *AM* 69 (May 1915): 96; *(Mobile) Inner City News,* 27 May 1995, 3; Margaret H. Scott to Dear Sister, 23 September 1936 and 14 October 1936, Margaret H. Scott Papers.

75. Black leaders in Mobile asked Brownlee to hire a white principal probably because they assumed that it would make retaining a mixed faculty more likely. Brownlee said he appreciated the recommendation, but thought it "much better to have an efficient colored man at the head of the school than to get a white man who is not

up to the task." F. L. Brownlee to Alfred E. Lawless, 11 May 1921, box 8, folder 1, J. Stanley and Kathryn T. Stanley Papers; *AM* 75 (May 1921): 93–94; *AM* 85 (September 1931): 1195; A. F. Beard to My Dear Brownlee, 8 February 1933, box 1, folder 1, A. F. Beard Papers; Ruth A. Morton to Cassius M. Plair, 22 August 1938, box 12, folder 4, Lincoln School; Helen P. Desort to W. R. Ireland, 28 February 1944, box 34, General Secretary Correspondence, AMAA, Addendum; *Missionary Herald* 132 (January 1936): 18.

76. See Brown, *Faithful, Firm, and True,* and Drago, *Initiative, Paternalism, and Race Relations: Charleston's Avery Normal Institute* for detailed accounts of industrial training at Ballard and Avery.

77. Edmund T. Ware, Atlanta University chaplain, denied Dickerman's charge that the AMA taught social equality. That faculty and students shared the same table in the dining room did not make them social equals, Ware said, but the missionaries believed that because "God was no respecter of persons . . . that men had no right to be. They believed in universal brotherhood." Luker, *Social Gospel in Black and White,* 153; *AM* 66 (April 1912): 25; *AM* 51 (September 1897): 226; *AM* 65 (December 1911): 528; Alfred A. Moss Jr., *The American Negro Academy: Voice of the Talented Tenth* (Baton Rouge, 1981), 73–74.

78. Douglass, *Christian Reconstruction in the South,* 280–81; Luker, *Social Gospel in Black and White,* 148–49, 152; *AM* 64 (November 1910): 528.

79. W. M. Holloway to John L. Wiley, 2 January 1907, Superintendent of Public Instruction Letter book, vol. 33, Florida State Archives, Tallahassee, Florida.

80. Beam, *He Called Them by the Lightning,* 123–25; AMA executive committee minutes, 14 December 1909, 5 April 1910, 10 September 1918, AMAA, Addendum; *Eighty-Ninth Annual Report of the AMA* (1935), 90; Ferdinand Q. Blanchard to F. L. Brownlee, 13 June 1950, Frederick L. Brownlee Papers, Amistad Research Center.

81. *AM* 78 (December 1924): 348; Brownlee, *New Day Ascending* 133; *Eighty-Second Annual Report of the AMA* (New York, 1928), 26; *Eighty-Fifth Annual Report of the AMA* (1931), 32.

82. *Eighty-Sixth Annual Report of the AMA* (1932), 9; *Eighty-Eighth Annual Report of the AMA* (New York, 1934), 50; *Southern Association of Colleges and Secondary Schools: Approved List of Colleges and Secondary Schools for Negro Youth* (no publisher, place, or date of publication listed); Raymond G. Von Tobel to Dear Friends, 5 March 1934, box 78, folder 1, Ballard School; Brownlee, *A Continuing Service* 33; Hollyday, *On the Heels of Freedom* 144; Henry N. Drewry and Humphrey Doermann, *Stand and Prosper: Private Black Colleges and Their Students* (Princeton, NJ, 2001), 72.

83. In 1948 Ruth Morton wrote of the unnatural separation of males and females in earlier AMA schools and suggested that students were happier and no more delinquent under more relaxed rules. Ruth A. Morton to John A. Buggs, 11 March 1948, John A. Buggs Papers, Amistad Research Center; Beam, *He Called Them by the Lightning,* 134; *AM* 57 (April 1903): 103; *AM* 69 (May 1915): 98; *AM* 61 (June 1907): 184; *AM* 58 (December 1904): 312; *AM* 64 (May 1910): 116–17.

84. Richardson, "Allen Normal School," 8–9; *AM* 47 (February 1893): 39; *AM*

62 (January 1908): 1; Beam, *He Called Them by the Lightning,* 134; *AM* 78 (October 1924): 254–55; *AM* 77 (November 1923): 417–78.

85. *AM* 78 (December 1924): 348; *AM* 77 (May 1923): 101; Hollyday, *On the Heels of Freedom,* 175.

86. Drago, *Initiative, Paternalism, and Race Relations,* 148; *Eighty-Sixth Annual Report of the AMA* (1932), 35; *Eighty-Ninth Annual Report of the AMA* (1935), 66; Brown, *Faithful, Firm, and True,* 117–21.

87. Cornelia M. Curtis, undated memoir, Thomasville Historical Society, Thomasville, Georgia; William W. Rogers, *Thomas County, 1865–1900* (Tallahassee, 1973), 240; Bagby, "William G. Price and the Gloucester Agricultural and Industrial School," 68, 73; Drago, *Initiative, Paternalism, and Race Relations,* 169–70; *Eighty-sixth Annual Report of the AMA* (1932), 32; *Eighty-Third Annual Report of the AMA* (New York, 1929), 34; *Eighty-Eighth Annual Report of the AMA* (1934), 48.

88. *AM* 47 (November 1893): 348; *AM* 45 (November 1891): 375; *Eightieth Annual Report of the AMA* (New York, 1926), 45; *Eighty-Fifth Annual Report of the AMA* (1931), 52.

89. Richardson, *Christian Reconstruction,* 109–12; AMA executive committee minutes, 9 June 1908, AMAA, Addendum; *AM* 58 (November 1904): 276; *AM* 59 (December 1905): 305.

90. Brownlee lists AMA annual receipts 1846–47 to 1944–45 in *New Day Ascending,* 271–72; *Eighty-Second Annual Report of the AMA,* (New York, 1928), 12–13; AMA administrative committee minutes, 10 April 1928, AMAA, Addendum; *Eighty-Seventh Annual Report of the AMA* (1933), 60.

91. *AM* 70 (April 1916): 24–25; *Eighty-First Annual Report of the AMA* (New York, 1927), 24; *Eighty-Second Annual Report of the AMA* (1928), 26; *AM* 63 (October 1910): 655; *Eighty-Fourth Annual Report of the AMA* (New York, 1930), 39; Drago, *Initiative, Paternalism, and Race Relations,* 154.

92. Income dropped from a high of $1,634,047 in 1927–28 to $798,678 in 1932–33, to $533,315 in 1937–38 to $528,705 in 1942–43. Increased war employment and stimulation of the economy did not appreciably increase AMA revenues. Brownlee, *New Day Ascending,* 272.

93. AMA administrative committee minutes, 13 December 1932 and 15 September 1936, AMAA, Addendum; F. L. Brownlee to Dr. William H. Morgan, 19 November 1943, box 324, General Secretary Correspondence; *Eighty-Fifth Annual Report of the AMA* (1931), 34; *Eighty-Seventh Annual Report of the AMA* (1933), 30; Ruth A. Morton to Earnest A. Smith, 19 April 1944, box 13, folder 8, Lincoln School; Fred L. Brownlee to Jay R. Stocking, 14 November 1933, in *AM* 87 (7 December 1933): 1129.

94. For a general discussion of the NYA and black schools, see: Paula S. Fass, *Outside In: Minorities and the Transformation of American Education* (New York, 1989), 124–34; *Eighty-Ninth Annual Report of the AMA* (1935), 31, 35, 67; Raymond G. Von Tobel to My Dear Friends, 11 January 1930, 15 October 1932, and 6 November 1933,

box 1, folder 1, Raymond G. Von Tobel Papers; *Eighty-Seventh Annual Report of the AMA* (1933), 45, 47; *AM* 87 (6 July 1933): 743; *The Ballardite*, 27 May 1937; *Ninetieth Annual Report of the AMA* (New York, 1936), 39; Hollyday, *On the Heels of Freedom*, 165–66; Brown, *Faithful, Firm, and True*, 130–31. For more on the NYA in Georgia, see: Florence Fleming Corley, "The National Youth Administration in Georgia: A New Deal for Young Blacks and Women," *Georgia Historical Quarterly* 77 (Winter 1993): 728–56.

95. Fred L. Brownlee to H. S. Barnwell, 5 March 1936, box 8, folder 9, J. Stanley and Kathryn T. Stanley Papers; Drago, *Initiative, Paternalism, and Race Relations*, 198–99.

CHAPTER 3

1. Presidents included Merrill Edward Gates (1892–98), president of both Rutgers and Amherst Colleges, and Dr. Cyrus Northrup (1909–13), professor at Yale and president of the University of Minnesota for twenty-seven years. Vice presidents included U.S. Supreme Court justice David J. Brewer and Justice Robert Roberts Bishop, associate justice of the Massachusetts Supreme Court, eminent jurist, and trustee of Phillips Academy and Andover Theological Seminary. *Seventy-Sixth Annual Report of the AMA* (New York, 1922), 38; *AM* 61 (February 1907): 35; *Sixty-Third Annual Report of the AMA* (New York, 1908), 8.

2. Jacob Henry Dorn, *Washington Gladden: Prophet of the Social Gospel* (Columbus, OH, 1967), 126, 128, 296–98, 301; Luker, *Social Gospel in Black and White*, 203, 244–45. See also Gladden's *The Negro's Southern Neighbors and His Southern Friends* (New York, 1903) and *Recollections* (Boston, 1909).

3. Dorn, *Washington Gladden*, 36–37; Luker, *Social Gospel in Black and White*, 244–48; Amory H. Bradford, *My Brother* (Boston, 1909); *AM* 59 (November 1905): 81; *AM* 64 (April 1910): 1–2; *AM* 61 (December 1907): 312–14.

4. The only examples of "discourteous correspondence" found related to letters informing principals that they had exceeded their budgets or that they should consider retirement. Richardson, *Christian Reconstruction*, 87; Brownlee, *New Day Ascending*, 259–61; Augustus F. Beard, *Crusade of Brotherhood* (Boston, 1909), 314; Luker, *Social Gospel in Black and White*, 264.

5. Many members remained on the committee for years which provided continuity. For example, Charles A. Hull was on the executive committee from 1879 to 1884, and then joined again in 1888 as chairman and retained that position until his death in 1912. Dr. Lucien C. Warner was an active member of the executive committee for thirty-three years, ending his service in 1925. The committee nearly always included a sprinkling of businessmen such as Samuel S. Marples, a prominent member of the New York City Produce Exchange, and Thomas E. Stillman, attorney and director of the Southern Pacific Railway Company, and officer and director in "various financial activities." AMA executive committee minutes, 8 April 1913,

11 April 1916, 10 October 1916, and 10 November 1925, AMAA, Addendum; Beam, *He Called Them by the Lightning,* 116–18; *Fifty-Seventh Annual Report of the AMA* (1903), 36; *Sixtieth Annual Report of the AMA* (New York, 1906), 30.

6. *Eighty-Eighth Annual Report of the AMA* (1934), 99; *AM* 87 (February 1933): 135; *AM* 87 (June 1933): 654; *AM* 83 (January 1929): 133; *AM* 57 (December 1903): 311; Fred L. Brownlee, *August Field Beard, 1833–1924* (flyer, 1934), box 1, folder 32, unidentified newspaper obituary 1934, box 1, folder 30, A. F. Beard Papers; F. L. Brownlee, "A Cultural Autobiography," n.d., in Frederick L. Brownlee Papers.

7. AMA executive committee minutes, 14 April 1890, AMAA, Addendum; *AM* 57 (December 1903): 311; *AM* 82 (December 1928): 438; Beam, *He Called Them by the Lightning,* 123.

8. Unidentified newspaper clipping, box 1, folder 13, Frederick L. Brownlee Papers; AMA executive committee minutes, 10 February 1903, AMAA, Addendum; *AM* 57 (April 1903): 101; *AM* 70 (May 1916): 89–90; H. Paul Douglass to My Dear Father and Mother, 21 July 1906, H. Paul Douglass Papers, Amistad Research Center.

9. Rena Douglass to Dear Mother, 19 April 1906; H. Paul Douglass to My Dear Father and Mother, 21 July 1906, H. Paul Douglass Papers.

10. After three years of teaching in AMA schools, Lura Beam became assistant superintendent of education in 1911. Douglass was quite comfortable in delegating important responsibilities to Beam. AMA executive committee minutes, 12 September 1911, AMAA, Addendum.

11. *AM* 60 (October 1906): 232; Beam, *He Called Them by the Lightning,* 122–25; Luker, *Social Gospel in Black and White,* 268, 302, 304–5, 310–11; Douglass, *Christian Reconstruction in the South,* 20–26, 30–34, 378–79; AMA executive committee minutes, 11 September 1906, 14 December 1909, 5 April 1910, 10 September 1918, and 23 July 1918, AMAA, Addendum; Ferdinand Q. Blanchard to F. L. Brownlee, 13 June 1950, Frederick L. Brownlee Papers; A. F. Beard to F. L. Brownlee, 18 July 1933, box 1, folder 11, A. F. Beard Papers. Cady quoted in *Eighty-Ninth Annual Report of the AMA* (1935), 90; *Advance* 137 (October 1945): 9–11.

12. AMA executive committee minutes, 31 October 1918, 9 September, 14 October 1919, and 14 September 1920, AMAA, Addendum; *AM* 72 (December 1918): 474.

13. AMA executive committee minutes, 12 October 1920, AMAA, Addendum; *AM* 74 (December 1920): 460; *AM* 86 (3 November 1932): 429; Dorn, *Washington Gladden,* 122; Typed statement of education and career to 1920, Frederick L. Brownlee Papers; List of Brownlee's characteristics by Lillian Voorhees at time of Brownlee's death, n.d., box 15, folder 8, Lillian W. Voorhees Papers, Amistad Research Center; Statement on Brownlee's visit to New Orleans church, Mrs. Geneva Smith interview with Joe M. Richardson, 12 May 1993, New Orleans, Louisiana; Hollis Price quoted in Harold W. Lundy, "A Study of the Transition from White to Black Presidents at Three Selected Schools Founded by the American Missionary Association" (PhD diss., University of Wisconsin, 1978), 590.

14. Alfred E. Lawless to Fred L. Brownlee, 5 May 1921, box 8, folder 1, J. Stanley and Kathryn T. Stanley Papers; Alfred E. Lawless, "Report at the AMA Annual Meeting," Detroit, Michigan, 8 November 1922, box 12, folder 12, J. Stanley and Kathryn T. Stanley Papers; A. F. Beard to Ruth Brownlee, 8 March 1932, box 1, folder 10, A. F. Beard Papers; Fred L. Brownlee to Warren W. Pickett, 26 March 1941, General Secretary Correspondence, AMAA, Addendum.

15. *Southern News,* November 1924, pages unnumbered; H. H. Proctor to F. L. Brownlee, 26 September 1925, 8 October 1925, box 1, folder 20, Henry Hugh Proctor and Adeline Proctor Papers, Amistad Research Center; Frederick L. Brownlee, "Experience in Work with Negroes," *Missionary Review of the World* 59 (June 1936): 311–12; *Eighty-Fourth Annual Report of the AMA* (1930), 4.

16. *AM* 81 (December 1927): 880–81; AMA administrative committee minutes, 23 May 1932, AMAA, Addendum; F. L. Brownlee to Frank Sweeney, 9 January 1930, Frederick L. Brownlee Papers; *Crisis* 30 (August 1925): 192.

17. Ryder was a Congregational minister who became AMA field superintendent in 1884, district secretary in Boston in 1889, and assistant corresponding secretary in 1892 and secretary in 1895. Cady was also a Congregational minister, long concerned with social application of Christianity. An eloquent speaker, Cady fought racial injustice while urging support for AMA work. In 1936, a longtime AMA supporter said Cady was the most persuasive AMA champion in the last twenty-five years. His two passions were black rights and temperance. *AM* 71 (November 1917): 405, 407; *Crisis* 15 (April 1918): 279; *Crisis* 22 (June 1921): 78; *Missionary Herald* 136 (January 1940): 1–4; *Missionary Herald* 132 (July 1936): 309.

18. A potential wealthy donor was persuaded to visit one of the colleges to see if he might wish to support it. On the edge of campus he met a young couple in a hack. He instructed his driver to return him to the hotel. "I have seen all I need to see. When they can ride in hacks, they can pay for their own education." Richardson, *Christian Reconstruction* 92–95; *AM* 71 (May 1917): 90; *Fifty-Third Annual Report of the AMA* (New York, 1899), 97; *Eighty-Second Annual Report of the AMA* (1928), 57; Beam, *He Called Them by the Lightning,* 118; *Seventy-Third Annual Report of the AMA* (1919), 29; *AM* 58 (November 1904): 279; *Seventy-Ninth Annual Report of the AMA* (New York, 1925), 47; For annual receipts from 1846 to 1946, see Brownlee, *New Day Ascending,* 271–72.

19. Naturally, legacy income varied. Between 1916 and 1930 legacies ranged from $63,783.99 in 1916 to $325,416.15 in 1925–26. *AM* 70 (May 1916): 96–97; *Eighty-Fourth Annual Report of the AMA* (1930), 59.

20. Hand, born in New England, went south in 1818 to join an uncle in business at Augusta, Georgia. He took over his uncle's cotton brokerage business and expanded it. When the Civil War began he was arrested as a spy. He was later released, but felt compelled to remain in the South. At war's end he moved to Connecticut. His sympathy for blacks led him to establish the Hand Fund. *AM* 86 (4 February 1932): 137, 162; Howard T. Oedel, *Daniel Hand of Madison, Connecticut, 1801–1891* (Madison, CT,

1973); George A. Wilcox, *A Christian Philanthropist: A Sketch of the Life of Mr. Daniel Hand, and of His Benefaction to the American Missionary Association for the Education of the Colored People in the Southern States of America* (New York, 1889).

21. Richardson, *Christian Reconstruction,* 92–95; *Forty-Sixth Annual Report of the AMA* (New York, 1892), 81; *AM* 70 (May 1916): 96–97; *Eighty-Fourth Annual Report of the AMA* (1930), 59.

22. Hall also left money to Berea College, and stipulated that none of his gift to Berea "be used for the education of the colored race, inasmuch as my gift to the American Missionary Association may be largely applied to education of such race." Quote from Brownlee, *New Day Ascending,* 279.

23. By 1948 the Charles M. Hall Fund had grown to $8,348,071.05 and the Hand Fund to $1,507,959.17. The association badly needed money, and for years it adopted a policy that the Hand Fund grant's conditions required only that the capital remain at $1,500,000 and used growth as well as income. When Richard H. Dubie became treasurer of the United Church Board for Homeland Ministries in 1968, he changed that policy and began to reserve growth as well as income which enabled the United Church of Christ to give Dillard University one million dollars to help repair damage caused by Hurricane Katrina. Clifton H. Johnson, e-mail to Joe M. Richardson, 12 June 2006; *United Church News* (June/July 2006): A7; F. L. Brownlee to Dr. Frazier and members of the Unity Committee, 23 December 1936, General Secretary Correspondence; Brownlee, *New Day Ascending,* 272–73, 278–79; *Eighty-Second Annual Report of the AMA* (1928), 58; *AM* 80 (July 1926): 178. A. Sharp to F. L. Brownlee, 28 January 1949, General Secretary Correspondence; *Eighty-Sixth Annual Report of the AMA* (1932), 64. *Ninetieth Annual Report of the AMA* (New York, 1936), 11.

24. Sixty-eight percent of expenditures was for work with southern blacks, 6.1 percent for Puerto Rico, 4.4 percent for American Indians, 2.6 percent for southern highlanders, 1.5 percent for cooperatives, 6 percent for annuities, 5.4 percent for administration, 4.7 percent for promotions, 1.9 percent for the Southwest and Utah. Decade receipts found in Brownlee, *New Day Ascending,* 271–72; *AM* 49 (October 1895): 314; *Seventy-Fifth Annual Report of the AMA* (New York, 1921), 25; *Eighty-Sixth Annual Report of the AMA* (1932), 64.

25. In 1890 corresponding secretary Michael E. Strieby, a Congregational minister, warned the AMA executive committee that Congregationalists posed a danger to the association as many thought it should be disbanded. AMA executive committee minutes, 14 April 1890, AMAA, Addendum.

26. Annual meetings continued to be held separately, but biennial meetings were held jointly with the National Council.

27. Brownlee, *New Day Ascending,* 262; *Missionary Herald* 133 (February 1937): 49; *Missionary Herald* 134 (November 1938): 515–16; *Sixty-Eighth Annual Report of the AMA* (1914), 6–8.

28. *Seventieth Annual Report of the AMA* (New York, 1916), 8–10; *Seventy-Second Annual Report of the AMA* (New York, 1919), 8–9.

29. *AM* 79 (January 1925): 393; *AM* 79 (June 1925): 105; *AM* 79 (July 1925): 156;

AM 79 (October 1925): 250, 253; George L. Cady to William H. Day, 4 June 1925, Ferdinand Q. Blanchard to Irving C. Gaylord, 5 June 1925, Gaylord to Cady, 30 July 1925, Gaylord to Thomas H. Hood, 25 November 1925, General Secretary Correspondence.

30. Apportionment was as follows: foreign work (American Board) 37 percent, AMA 9 percent, extension boards 15.5 percent, ministerial boards 6 percent, education society 7 percent, and state missionary work 25.5 percent. By 1933–34 the AMA was receiving only seven percent of mission funds. *Eightieth Annual Report of the AMA* (New York, 1925), 4; *Eighty-First Annual Report of the AMA* (1927), 7; *AM* 80 (July 1926): 178; *AM* 81 (March 1927): 511; *Eighty-Eighth Annual Report of the AMA* (1934), 73–74; F. L. Brownlee to Ferdinand Q. Blanchard, 9 April 1936, Frederick L. Brownlee Papers.

31. Brownlee was responding to Ferdinand Q. Blanchard, who had served on the executive committee from 1909 to 1936. Blanchard said he could not have stayed after 1936, but the AMA was fortunate that Brownlee had remained. Ferdinand Q. Blanchard to F. L. Brownlee, 27 June 1946, Brownlee to Blanchard, 2 July 1946, Blanchard to Brownlee, 8 August 1950, Frederick L. Brownlee Papers.

32. The Congregational and Christian churches had merged in 1929.

33. Frederick L. Brownlee, *Perplexing Realities* (New York, 1937), 3, 69–70. After 1936, the AMA no longer made its usual annual report. The BHM reported for all societies. Brownlee then began publishing short statements of AMA affairs such as *Perplexing Realities*; F. L. Brownlee to Dr. Frazier and members of the unity committee, 23 December 1936, General Secretary Correspondence.

34. Ferdinand Q. Blanchard to Philip Widenhouse, 2 May 1950, box 329, General Secretary Correspondence; J. E. McAfee to F. L. Brownlee, 25 March 1939, Frederick L. Brownlee Papers; Fred McCuistion interview with Ruth A. Morton, 1 October 1941, box 295, General Education Board Files, Series I, Subseries II, Rockefeller Archives Center, microfilm, Amistad Research Center; AMA division committee minutes, 4 December 1950, box 362, General Secretary Correspondence; Fred L. Brownlee, "Yesterday and Tomorrow," typescript, 28 July 1950, Frederick L. Brownlee Papers; Ruth A. Morton to Charles T. Akre, 12 April 1950, box 329, General Secretary Correspondence; F. L. Brownlee to Charles S. Johnson, 1950, box 29, folder 10, Charles S. Johnson Papers, Amistad Research Center.

CHAPTER 4

1. *Eighty-Ninth Annual Report of the AMA* (1935), 27–28.

2. Brownlee did not say the schools were isolated from blacks, but he said, using Ballard as an example, that the school's "work of tomorrow depends upon the awakening of the Negroes themselves to what remains to be done and can be done provided they put their shoulders to the wheel and plan collectively." Brownlee, *New Day Ascending,* 140.

3. Luker says that, while a pastor in Ames, Iowa, Douglass used the term *social*

gospel a decade before writing *Christian Reconstruction in the South* in 1909; Luker, *Social Gospel in Black and White*, 1, 13–14. *AM* 58 (September 1904): 209; *AM* 54 (April 1900): 67–68; Douglass, *Christian Reconstruction in the South*, 253, 257; Drago, *Initiative, Paternalism, and Race Relations*, 172–73, 175.

4. *AM* 57 (May 1903): 150; *AM* 60 (June 1906): 169; *AM* 62 (January 1908): 13–14; *AM* 71 (July 1917): 217–18; Douglass, *Christian Reconstruction in the South*, 116.

5. *AM* 64 (May 1910): 115–16; *AM* 68 (April 1914): 32–33; *AM* 67 (February 1913): 675; *Ocala (Florida) Banner*, 24 March 1916; Jones and Richardson, *Talladega College*, 118–19.

6. There were many donations to the hospital. Lincoln Hospital in New York City provided one of the most useful by sending its superintendent of nurses training, a Miss Ford, to spend several weeks helping to open the hospital and organize a nurses training school—all of this at no cost to the AMA. *AM* 78 (May 1924): 57.

7. *Eightieth Annual Report of the AMA* (1926), 24, 48; *Eighty-Seventh Annual Report of the AMA* (1933), 65.

8. AMA executive committee minutes, 14 April 1914, 10 June 1919, 13 February 1923, and 14 May 1925, AMAA, Addendum; AMA, *Doors to Health: A Medical Ministry for America* (Brochure, n.d.) in General Education Board Files, Series 3, Subseries I, box 90; *Seventy-Eighth Annual Report of the AMA* (1924), 11; *Seventy-Ninth Annual Report of the AMA* (1925), 9; Dr. Pauline Dinkins, Teacher's Record, AMAA, Addendum; AMA missions committee minutes, 8 December 1925, AMAA, Addendum; *Eightieth Annual Report of the AMA* (1926), 24, 78; *Eighty-Ninth Annual Report of the AMA* (1935), 73–74, 80; *Ninetieth Annual Report of the AMA* (1936), 46; Richardson, "Cotton Valley School," 74–75.

9. Drago, *Initiative, Paternalism, and Race Relations*, 198; *AM* 79 (April 1925): 11; *Missionary Herald* 134 (February 1938): 55–56; Fred L. Brownlee, Proposed Field Budget for 1945–46, box 326, General Secretary Correspondence; Fred L. Brownlee and Ruth Morton, *Bread and Molasses* (New York, 1940), 3, 4, 6.

10. Fred L. Brownlee, Suggestions for Kings Mountain Conference, 8–15 June 1932 and 29 January 1932, box 8, folder 5, J. Stanley and Kathryn T. Stanley Papers; *Eighty-Ninth Annual Report of the AMA* (1935), 37; *Missionary Herald* 137 (May 1941): 26; Brownlee, *Perplexing Realities*, 8; Brownlee and Morton, *Bread and Molasses*, 11–12; Fred L. Brownlee to Edgar B. Stern, 12 December 1938, box 88, folder 4, Dillard University, AMAA, Addendum; Brownlee to Frank Sweeney, 5 March 1936, Frederick L. Brownlee Papers.

11. Progressive education was a late-nineteenth and early-twentieth-century reform movement which advocated a more flexible classroom approach, including personal attention to students, problem-solving methods, and more democratic participation. Jay M. Shafritz, Richard P. Koeppe, and Elizabeth W. Soper, eds., *The Facts on File Dictionary of Education* (New York, 1988), 369–70.

12. Brownlee told Tougaloo teacher Ethna B. Winston that he favored experimental education which was, he said, admirably described in Dewey's *Experience and Education;* Fred L. Brownlee to Ethna B. Winston, 13 December 1938, box 106,

folder 9, Tougaloo College, AMAA, Addendum. See also Brownlee to Margaret C. McCulloch, 21 February 1941, box 14, folder 16, LeMoyne-Owen College, AMAA, Addendum.

13. For treatment of Dewey's educational philosophy and the progressive education movement, see: Harry G. Good and James D. Teller, *A History of Western Education* (3rd ed., London, 1969), 552–53; David B. Tyack, ed., *Turning Points in American Educational History* (Waltham, MA, 1967), 319–20; Walter Feinberg, *Reason and Rhetoric: The Intellectual Foundations of Twentieth Century Liberal Educational Policy* (New York, 1975), 139; Lita Linzer Schwartz, *American Education: A Problem Centered Approach* (Boston, 1969), 70–71.

14. Brownlee and Morton, *Bread and Molasses,* 7; Carter V. Good, *Dictionary of Education* (New York, 1945), 174; Olive Dame Campbell, *The Danish Folk School: Its Influence in the Life of Denmark and the North* (New York, 1928), v, vii–viii; Rolland G. Paulston, *Other Dreams, Other Schools: Folk Colleges in Social and Ethnic Movements* (Pittsburgh, 1980), 187–89.

15. Pat McNelly, ed., *The First Forty Years: John C. Campbell Folk School* (Brasstown, NC, 1966); Fred L. Brownlee to H. S. Barnwell, 5 March 1936, box 8, folder 9, J. Stanley and Kathryn T. Stanley Papers; F. L. Brownlee, Proposed Field Budget for 1945–46, box 326, General Secretary Correspondence; Brownlee to Philip M. Widenhouse, 19 June 1954, box 331, General Secretary Correspondence.

16. In April 1934, the AMA administrative committee voted that the necessity for reorganization meant discontinuance of the position of associate executive secretary. In September it placed Daniel on leave of absence with pay from October to December of that year. The committee recorded "its respect for Dr. Daniel's unusual intellectual gifts, his skillful approach to social problems, and his keen scientific and constructive judgment." AMA administrative committee minutes, 10 April 1934 and 11 September 1934, AMAA, Addendum.

17. Brownlee, "Yesterday and Tomorrow"; T. Matsumoto to F. L. Brownlee, 8 January 1942, box 2, Trinity School, AMAA, Addendum; *Missionary Herald* 131 (August 1935): 364–65; *Eighty-Ninth Annual Report of the AMA* (1935), 42; Fred L. Brownlee to Quincy W. Wales, 19 October 1944, box 325, General Secretary Correspondence.

18. Ruth Morton years later recalled that once in stage fright while waiting to give a speech, she asked Brownlee about the AMA's philosophy of community living. He scribbled an answer. "The developing of an adequate philosophy of community living accepts the fact of the solidarity of the human race and is based on respect for people as persons. It includes provisions for economic security, physical health, social welfare, intellectual growth, aesthetic satisfaction, and spiritual well being for all individuals. It places full responsibility on individuals to discover for themselves the necessary political safeguards for democratic freedom." Ruth Morton, "Philosophy and Principles of the American Missionary Association Community Centers," speech given at Tuskegee Institute, 6 July 1948, undated AMA pamphlet in Ruth Morton Scrapbook, Amistad Research Center.

19. Brownlee, "Yesterday and Tomorrow"; *Eighty-Ninth Annual Report of the AMA* (1935), 42; *Ninetieth Annual Report of the AMA* (1936), 38.

20. Morton told Brownlee that she had always despised "old maids who run around telling how much they had been admired in their youth." She had been in love and engaged to marry, Morton added, but both had fumbled and she would not now marry the man if she could. Ruth A. Morton to F. L. Brownlee, 18 February 1936, Frederick L. Brownlee Papers.

21. Ruth A. Morton to F. L. Brownlee, 18 February 1936, Frederick L. Brownlee Papers; AMA administrative committee minutes, 11 February 1936 and 9 April 1936, AMAA, Addendum.

22. Brownlee, *Perplexing Realities*, 31–32; Margaret H. Scott to Dear Sister, 14 October 1936; Scott to Dear Book Club, 27 November 1936, Margaret H. Scott Papers.

23. Brownlee, *Continuing Service*, 22; Brownlee and Morton, *Bread and Molasses*, 10.

24. Harold F. Clark to Godwin Watson, 3 June 1940, box 4; Jay T. Wright vita, 10 July 1940, box 1; Jay T. Wright to F. L. Brownlee, 21 September 1940, box 1; Ruth A. Morton to Wright, 28 November 1940, box 1; Mary Davis to Morton, 11 December 1940, box 1; Wright to Brownlee, 17 December 1940 and 23 February 1941, box 1, Trinity School; Ruth A. Morton to Mr. Reynolds, 27 November 1940, box 78, folder 3, Ballard School.

25. Morton said that Wright "is a genius in the field of education. He knows more about functional education, the training of teachers, and can actually put his theories into practice better than any person I have ever known." She added that he was "erratic in personality" and a poor financial administrator. Ruth A. Morton evaluation, 29 April 1942, box 4, Memorandum Covering Conference with Mr. Jay Wright in Athens, Alabama, on May 14, 1942, and Comments Thereon, box 4; Fred L. Brownlee to Louise H. Allyn, 15 January and 27 March 1941, box 1, Trinity School, John A. Buggs, "Resume of Six Years of an Educational Experiment," 1948, 1, TC/Adm. 4/13/2/59, Talladega College Archives, Talladega, Alabama.

26. Josie Belle Sellers, Teacher's Record, Amistad Research Center; Brownlee, *A Continuing Service* 24; *Missionary Herald* 134 (August 1938): 363; Fred L. Brownlee, *Accelerating Evolution* (New York, 1939), 15; Fessenden *Sparks,* 20 September 1940, 20 October 1940, 27 November 1940, 6 March 1941, 17 May 1941; Ruth A. Morton to Frank Sweeney, 18 January 1939, box 147, folder 17, LeMoyne-Owen College, AMAA, Addendum.

27. Ruth A. Morton to L. M. Hickman, 10 April 1942, box 323, General Secretary Correspondence; *Missionary Herald* 135 (June 1939): 238–39; Brownlee, *Continuing Service,* 20.

28. Helen Desort to Enoch Bell, 16 September 1941, box 323, General Secretary Correspondence; *Tampa Bulletin,* 16 June 1951; Ruth A. Morton to Jay T. Wright, 1 August 1942, box 2, Trinity School; Ruth A. Morton to John A. Buggs, 19 October 1942, box 1, folder 3, John A. Buggs Papers, Amistad Research Center; Fred L.

Brownlee unaddressed form letter, 26 October 1949, box 50, Fessenden Academy AMAA [New] Addendum.

29. In 1948 Buggs wrote a fifty-page summary of the thought leading to this program of studies, a discussion of how it was implemented, and the successes and failures. Buggs, "Resume of Six Years of an Educational Experiment."

30. Buggs, "Resume of Six Years of an Educational Experiment," 4–5, 11, 13–14.

31. At the end of six years, Buggs claimed that of the thirty-eight instructors he had hired, only four were completely satisfactory. Five others adjusted sufficiently to make them useful to the program. In 1948 Buggs claimed that the social science teacher was the most important one for implementing the program, and the present one was "absolutely worthless." The math teacher was questionable. Only five of the present teachers would be seriously missed if they left, he claimed. Buggs, "Resume of Six Years of an Educational Experiment," 33.

32. Buggs, "Resume of Six Years of an Educational Experiment," 14–26; Report of the Board of Home Missions of the Congregational and Christian Churches for the year ended 31 May 1944, 22–23, in Associations, Conferences and Organizations, TC/Ass. 2/4/2/1; *(Fessenden) Student Voice,* 2 March 1943, 22 April 1949.

33. Buggs, "Resume of Six Years of an Educational Experiment," 24–26.

34. F. L. Brownlee, *Seeking a Way* (New York, 1944), 5; Buggs, "Resume of Six Years of an Educational Experiment," 34–39.

35. Fred L. Brownlee to W. T. Pelham, 22 December 1947, box 202, folder 5, Small Field Records, AMAA, Addendum; Buggs, "Resume of Six Years of an Educational Experiment," 27–31.

36. Brownlee, normally a "realistic idealist," sounded more like a dreamer when talking about functional education. In 1938, speaking of Fessenden, he said he was concerned about youth, their health, how they would make a decent living, their homes, what kind of citizens they would become, how they might fill their leisure hours with wholesome recreation, and "how life may become for them an integrated scale of values culminating in religious reverence for all that is highest and best and most beautiful." *Missionary Herald* 134 (August 1938): 358; Brownlee, *Perplexing Realities,* 8.

37. Brownlee, *Perplexing Realities,* 8; Fred Gamble to Helen Desort, 3 November 1940, General Secretary Correspondence; Ruth A. Morton to Wilfred Gamble, 20 September 1940, box 12, folder 11, Lincoln School.

38. Unfortunately, there is some evidence that Williams was pleased because he thought the school might become more like the Brick Rural Life Center and a demonstration farm. D. E. Williams to F. L. Brownlee, 31 October 1938 and 26 January 1939, Frederick L. Brownlee Papers.

39. Benson Y. Landis to F. L. Brownlee, 18 September 1940; Thomas Jesse Jones to Brownlee, 18 September 1940; Jones to Anson Phelps Stokes, 31 October 1940, Frederick L. Brownlee Papers; Ruth A. Morton to Jay T. Wright, 17 July 1941, box 1, Trinity School.

40. Drago, *Initiative, Paternalism, and Race Relations,* 200, 206–8, 227; Brown, *Faithful, Firm, and True,* 127; Brownlee, *Perplexing Realities,* 33–35.

41. The three counties were Halifax, Nash, and Edgecomb. Brownlee said in 1946 that the AMA provided "partial salaries of several teachers for three years," but administrative minutes offered the Brick high school faculty "free of charge" for 1933–34 if counties would operate a free school. Brownlee, *New Day Ascending,* 150; Board of Home Missions administrative committee minutes, 25 April 1933, AMAA, Addendum.

42. Jackson Davis to Leo M. Favrot, 19 May 1932, box 403, GEB Files, Series I, Subseries III, Rockefeller Archive Center; Jackson Davis interview with Brownlee, 11 January 1933, box 403, GEB Files, Series I, Subseries III, Rockefeller Archive Center, Microfilm, Amistad Research Center; Brownlee, *New Day Ascending,* 149–50; Fred L. Brownlee, "Changing Conditions in a Dynamic Society," typescript, 1 June 1954, 16, Frederick L. Brownlee Papers.

43. Fred L. Brownlee notation, 5 April 1950, on his January 1934 outline of plan for Brick in Ruth Morton Scrapbook, Amistad Research Center. A later statement said the Brick property was "saved from sale by a margin of only one vote" in the AMA divisional committee. Statement in unidentified typescript of Brick Rural Life School, Ruth Morton Scrapbook, Amistad Research Center.

44. *Missionary Herald* 132 (February 1936): 79; Brownlee, "Changing Conditions in a Dynamic Society," 17–18.

45. Brownlee, *New Day Ascending,* 151–52; Brownlee, "Changing Conditions in a Dynamic Society," 17–18; *Missionary Herald* 132 (February 1936): 79; *Eighty-Ninth Annual Report of the AMA* (1935), 71–72.

46. Although Brick Rural Life School was Brownlee's idea, he gave Ruth A. Morton and Neill A. McLean much of the credit for its creative development. Fred L. Brownlee notation, 5 April 1950, on his January 1934 outline of plan for Brick Rural Life School, Ruth Morton Scrapbook.

47. *Missionary Herald* 136 (May 1940): 26; *Missionary Herald* 135 (February 1939): 56; *Missionary Herald* 136 (September 1940): 20–21; *Missionary Herald* 137 (December 1941): 39; Fred L. Brownlee and Ruth Morton, *Shackled Still* (New York, 1942), 11–12; Ruth A. Morton to Mrs. Mildred E. Eakin, 20 September 1940, General Secretary Correspondence.

48. Morton and Brownlee gave different numbers including seven members with seventeen dollars and thirty-four members with sixty-eight dollars. No doubt it started with the former, but quickly grew to the latter. Ruth A. Morton to Samuel C. Adams, 23 April 1948, box 14, folder 9, Lincoln School; Brownlee, *New Day Ascending,* 152.

49. In 1934, Congress passed the Federal Credit Union Act, which authorized state credit unions to organize under federal charter. Nathan A. Pitts, *The Cooperative Movement in Negro Communities of North Carolina* (Washington, DC, 1950), 24.

50. Brownlee and Morton, *Bread and Molasses,* 6; Brownlee, *Perplexing Realities,* 38; Fred L. Brownlee, *Freedom Stepping Ahead* (New York, 1947), 3; Brownlee, *New*

Day Ascending, 152–53; Pitts, *The Cooperative Movement in Negro Communities of North Carolina*, 25; AMA divisional committee minutes, 21 September 1942, AMAA, Addendum.

51. Pitts, *The Cooperative Movement in Negro Communities of North Carolina*, 21, 24–25, 57, 81, 84–85; *New York Times*, 29 December 1946.

52. Undated Ruth Morton notation on undated picture of a black man showing two white men how to use the cannery, Ruth Morton Scrapbook; The same picture and a brief article appeared in *Ebony* (September 1947): 21.

53. *Missionary Herald* 135 (February 1939): 57; Brownlee, *New Day Ascending* 157; Ruth Morton notation on undated picture of Brick men building a bedstead and bookcase. Ruth Morton Scrapbook; Brownlee, "Yesterday and Tomorrow."

54. Brownlee, *New Day Ascending*, 159; Neill A. McLean to Ruth A. Morton, January 1943, Ruth Morton Scrapbook. The September 1947 issue of *Ebony* (page 23) had a picture of Reid; he was still robust and healthy looking.

55. McLean's report to the Fisk University Race Relations Institute, in *Nashville Banner*, 13 July 1947; Neill A. McLean to Ruth A, Morton, January 1943, Ruth Morton Scrapbook.

56. Unfortunately, Nathan Pitts claims that the county discontinued the service in 1945. It is not clear whether the assistance came from the state or from the county with federal assistance. Community groups continued to study and stress health care, pure water, sanitation, and good nutrition. Pitts, *The Cooperative Movement in Negro Communities of North Carolina*, 68–70; Activities of the Brick Rural Health Center during 1944, unsigned statement in Ruth Morton Scrapbook; Brownlee, *New Day Ascending*, 156; Brownlee and Morton, *Shackled Still*, 10.

57. Apparently Brownlee wanted the North Carolina Council of Credit Unions and Cooperatives to join Brick or perhaps even take over the Brick program. The AMA was ready to contribute $237,000, including part of the Brick plantation, to a five-year program if the GEB and Rosenwald Fund would support it. F. L. Brownlee to Neill McLean, 3 January 1946, box 327, General Secretary Correspondence; Lee Brooks to Jackson Davis, 28 February 1946, box 327, General Secretary Correspondence.

58. AMA division committee minutes, 27 July 1945, 19 February 1946, AMAA, Addendum; F. L. Brownlee to Jackson Davis, 15 March 1946, box 403, GEB Files, Series I, Subseries III, Rockefeller Archives Center, Microfilm; Flora M. Rhind memorandum, 21–22 January 1947, box 403, GEB Files, Series I, Subseries III, Rockefeller Archives Center; F. L. Brownlee to Lee Brooks, 13 March 1947, box 327, General Secretary Correspondence.

59. McLean claimed in 1947 that black North Carolinians had eighty-two credit unions, twenty community canneries, one marketing association, one burial association, six coop stores, two community health and hospitalization plans, twenty-two heavy machinery coops, two poultry developments, seven curb markets, and a saw- and gristmill. McLean's statement to the Fisk University Race Relations Institute, cited in *Nashville Banner*, 14 July 1947; F. L. Brownlee to Flora M. Rhind, 22 April

236 / Notes to Pages 91–93

1947, box 403, GEB Files, Series I, Subseries III, Rockefeller Archives Center; Pitts, *The Cooperative Movement in Negro Communities of North Carolina*, 24; *New York Times*, 29 December 1946; Ruth Morton in AMA division committee minutes, 20 January 1947, AMAA, Addendum.

60. W. Judson King to Ruth Morton, 21 July 1947, 19 January 1948, 6 November 1948, 2 February 1949, 22 July 1949, 26 July 1949, and 14 May 1950, box 3, Trinity School; King to F. L. Brownlee, 4 August 1947, 5 September 1947, 27 September 1947, 12 February 1948, and 22 May 1950, box 3, Trinity School; *Trinity School* (Pamphlet, New York, 1948), 7.

61. Ruth A. Morton to Olive J. Williams, 5 August 1938, box 12, folder 4; L. A. Locklair to Morton, 3 December 1941, box 12, folder 19; Wilfred Gamble to F. L. Brownlee, 13 January 1942, box 13, folder 1; Brownlee to Gamble, 23 January 1942, box 13, folder 1; Morton to Gamble, 22 February 1942, box 13, folder 2, Lincoln School.

62. Fred Gamble to F. L. Brownlee, 29 September 1943, box 13, folder 6; Ruth A. Morton to Earnest A. Smith, 17 November 1943, box 13, folder 7, Lincoln School; F. L. Brownlee to E. E. Day, 9 November 1943, box 324, General Secretary Correspondence.

63. Earnest A. Smith to Ruth A. Morton, 14 February 1944, box 13, folder 9; Ulysses Fowler to Morton, 16 June 1944, box 13, folder 9; Smith to Morton, 12 July 1944, box 13, folder 9; Morton to Smith, 25 July 1944, box 13, folder 10; Morton to Ralph Martin, 5 January 1945, box 13, folder 12, Lincoln School.

64. Samuel C. Adams Jr., Teacher's Record; Ruth A. Morton to Samuel C. Adams, 7 June 1949, box 14, folder 16; Adams to Morton, 19 April 1948, box 14, folder 9; Adams to Morton, 15 May 1948, box 14, folder 9; Morton to Adams 19 May 1948, box 14, folder 10; Ruth Morton, undated [1950] memorandum on Marion Center, box 14, folder 20, Lincoln School.

65. For a detailed view of the Dorchester Cooperative Center, see: Herd-Clark, "Dorchester Academy," chapters 9 and 10.

66. According to Brownlee, Liberty County blacks owned four hundred farms. Blacks resented whites buying land in the region and criticized blacks who sold to them. Fred L. Brownlee to Ruth Morton and Claudius Turner, 6 May 1944, box 72, folder 8; Turner to Brownlee, 30 January 1945, box 72, folder 10, Dorchester Academy; AMA division committee minutes, 27 September 1948, box 362, General Secretary Correspondence.

67. Herd-Clark, "Dorchester Academy," 208–10; *Savannah Tribune*, 14 September 1938, 1, 4; *Savannah Tribune*, 9 February 1939, 7; *Savannah Tribune*, 13 April 1939, 7; Brownlee and Morton, *Bread and Molasses*, 11.

68. Board of Home Missions executive committee minutes, 16–17 April 1940, AMAA, Addendum; Brownlee and Morton, *Bread and Molasses*, 26; Ruth A. Morton to H. C. McDowell, 29 July 1941, box 137, folder 7, Lincoln Academy; Herd-Clark, "Dorchester Academy," 212; AMA division committee minutes, 26 April 1943, box 362, General Secretary Correspondence.

69. Brownlee, *New Day Ascending,* 162; Herd-Clark, "Dorchester Academy," 214–15.

70. Herd-Clark, "Dorchester Academy," 228, 232–33; Brownlee, *New Day Ascending,* 163.

71. Ruth A. Morton to Herman H. Long, 2 February 1948, box 1, folder 10, Race Relations Department, United Church for Homeland Ministries Archives, Amistad Research Center; Loren Miller, *The Petitioners: The Story of the Supreme Court of the United States and the Negro* (New York, 1967), 294–95; Turner's appeal, To Whom It Might Concern, 9 February 1946, box 72, folder 10, Dorchester Academy; Herd-Clark, "Dorchester Academy," 265.

72. Claudius Turner to Ruth A. Morton, 19 April 1946, box 72, folder 10, Dorchester Academy; Herd-Clark, "Dorchester Academy," 237–38.

73. In 1992, former AMA leader Wesley Hotchkiss recalled that long before he joined the AMA (he did not remember the exact date) he was working with rural churches in the South and attended a political action committee meeting and was impressed. Though the committee thought the time was not right to put up black candidates, Hotchkiss believed the Dorchester Center was having a major impact on county politics. Clifton H. Johnson interview with Wesley Hotchkiss, 11 November 1992, box 39, folder 8, Clifton H. Johnson Papers, Amistad Research Center; Claudius Turner to Ruth A. Morton, 19 April 1946, box 72, folder 10; Turner to Morton, 1 July 1946, folder 11; Turner to Brownlee, 8 July 1946 and 10 December 1946, folder 11, Dorchester Academy; Ruth A. Morton speech to Fisk University Race Relations Institute, 1949, Race Relations Department, UCBHMA, Amistad Research Center; Herd-Clark, "Dorchester Academy," 264–83.

74. Fred L. Brownlee to John A. Buggs, 23 February 1945, box 1, folder 12; Buggs to Ruth A. Morton, box 1, folder 13; Brownlee to Buggs, 6 August 1946, box 1, folder 22; Buggs to Morton, 21 September 1947 and 2 October 1947, box 1, folder 28; List of Courses in the Technical Arts Division, Fessenden Academy, box 7, folder 6, John A. Buggs Papers, Amistad Research Center; AMA divisional committee minutes, 19 February 1946, AMAA, Addendum.

75. Buggs had to overcome many difficulties in finally securing a technical arts building. Morton blamed opposition of white politicians for the problem. Many Marion County whites were alarmed at Buggs's activism. AMA division committee minutes, 23 April 1945, box 362, General Secretary Correspondence.

76. Fred L. Brownlee to John A. Buggs, 20 February 1948, box 1, folder 29; Buggs to Brownlee, 26 February 1948, box 1, folder 29; Buggs to Brownlee, 11 March 1948 and 13 April 1948, box 1, folder 30, John A. Buggs Papers.

77. Ruth A. Morton to John A. Buggs, 4 June 1951, box 2, folder 12; Buggs to Fred L. Brownlee, 15 September 1943, box 1, folder 8; Buggs to Brownlee, 9 August 1945, box 1, folder 14, John A. Buggs Papers.

78. Brownlee, *New Day Ascending,* 143; John A. Buggs, Personal Data Sheet, 25 May 1951, box 7, folder 22, John A. Buggs Papers; *Tampa Bulletin,* 16 June 1951.

79. *Tampa Bulletin,* 9 June 1951, 16 June 1951; Ruth A. Morton statement in Min-

utes of the Committee on Future of Fessenden, New York City, 28–29 November 1949, box 50, Fessenden Academy; *The Student's Voice (Fessenden)*, 11 March 1947, 26 November 1948, and undated copy 1949; John A. Buggs to Ruth A. Morton, 24 August 1949, box 2, folder 3; Buggs to Fred L. Brownlee, 2 December 1949, box 2, folder 4, John A. Buggs Papers.

80. Fred L. Brownlee to John A. Buggs, 2 March 1949, Adam D. Beittel Papers, TC/Adm. 4/13/2/59, Talladega College Archives; Buggs to Adam D. Beittel, 28 April 1949, Adam D. Beittel Papers, TC/Adm. 4/13/2/59, Talladega College Archives; Buggs to Philip M. Widenhouse, 20 March 1951, box 3, folder 1, Samuel C. Kincheloe Papers, Amistad Research Center.

81. On three different occasions, Buggs had arranged for Florida A&M College to offer extension courses at Fessenden. Each time A&M agreed and then withdrew, which had increased Morton's suspicions about Bethune and Williams. Ruth A. Morton to Philip M. Widenhouse, 1 November 1950, box 2, folder 9, John A. Buggs Papers.

82. In January 1953, the Marion County Board of Public Instruction purchased Fessenden Academy and thirty acres of land to be used as a black high school for north Marion County. Broward Lovell, *Gone with the Hickory Stick: School Days in Marion County 1865–1960* (Ocala, FL, 1975), 214; AMA division committee minutes, 17 April 1951, box 362, AMAA, Addendum; John A. Buggs to Ruth A. Morton, 1 May 1951, box 2, folder 10, John A. Buggs Papers.

83. Brownlee asked Johnson to destroy this letter after reading it. Fortunately for historians he did not. Fred L. Brownlee to Charles S. Johnson, 1950, box 29, folder 10, Charles S. Johnson Papers, Microfilm, Amistad Research Center.

84. Fred L. Brownlee to Charles S. Johnson, 1950, box 29, folder 10, Charles S. Johnson Papers, Microfilm, Amistad Research Center; John A. Buggs to Ruth A. Morton, 10 March 1951, box 2, folder 9, John A. Buggs Papers; Ruth A. Morton to Samuel C. Adams Jr., 23 April 1949, box 14, folder 15, Lincoln School. Truman Douglass wrote that so many AMA schools had been turned over to public authorities that a director of schools was no longer needed. However, experience proved that was untrue, and Howard Spragg was later appointed to assist AMA executive secretary Philip Widenhouse. Truman B. Douglass to General Secretaries, 26 February 1951, box 12, folder 19, Race Relations Department, UCBHMA; Herman H. Long to Philip M. Widenhouse, 14 March 1951, box 240, Race Relations Department, AMAA, Addendum.

85. Truman B. Douglass to P. M. Widenhouse, 16 April 1953, box 331; Widenhouse to Gertrude Richards, 25 May 1955, box 332, AMA division committee minutes, 30 January 1956, 3 April 1956, and 19 June 1956, box 363, General Secretary Correspondence; Howard E. Spragg to Samuel C. Kincheloe, 18 March 1953, box 3, folder 9, Samuel C. Kincheloe Papers.

86. The Highlander Folk School in Monteagle, Tennessee, had successfully held citizenship schools to train grassroots leaders to lead the fight against segregation and for black voter registration. Herman Long of the AMA Race Relations Department had worked with the program for years. Highlander had been under state at-

tack, and in 1961 the AMA agreed to let Highlander use Dorchester Academy for citizenship schools. The AMA agreed to "participate fully in the citizenship school program, including administering the grant, provided the AMA relationship could be with the citizenship committee." Highlander turned the citizenship schools over to the citizenship committee and out from under the school. It was a committee of four, with Herman Long as one of the members. At his request he was replaced by Wesley Hotchkiss, AMA general secretary. The Field Grant was actually to the Southern Christian Leadership Conference, but was administered by the AMA and the schools directed by Andrew Young. Myles Horton to Citizenship School Program Committee and staff, 21 June 1961, box 21, folder 4; Myles Horton report to Citizenship School Committee, 30 June 1961, box 21, folder 5; Minutes of Citizenship School Committee meeting, 30 June 1961, box 21, folder 5; Wesley A. Hotchkiss to Rev. Andrew J. Young, 11 October 1961, box 4, folder 15, Race Relations Department, UCBHMA; Clifton H. Johnson interview with Wesley Hotchkiss, 12 November 1992, box 39, folder 8, Clifton H. Johnson Papers.

87. Howard E. Spragg to Wesley Hotchkiss, 14 September 1953, box 331, Gladys Williams to Mrs. Mitchell, 7 October 1954, box 332, Division of Higher Education and AMA committee minutes, 25 September 1956, 30 October 1961, and 1 May 1962, box 363, General Secretary Correspondence; 28 January 1963, 9 July 1965, box 364, General Secretary Correspondence; Andrew Young, *An Easy Burden: The Civil Rights Movement and the Transformation of America* (New York, 1996), 135, 153, 154. For more information on the Dorchester citizenship schools, see: Hollyday, *On the Heels of Freedom,* 188, and Brown, *Ready from Within,* 62–66.

88. In 1970, DCC property was conveyed to the Dorchester Improvement Association. Division of Higher Education and AMA committee minutes, 2 February 1970, box 364, General Secretary Correspondence; *Eighty-Ninth Annual Report of the AMA* (1935), 27–28.

CHAPTER 5

1. *AM* 9 (August 1865): 180–81; Richardson, *Christian Reconstruction,* 109.

2. The AMA, more than some other mission societies, worked with states in building up primary schools, and was less likely to graft elementary parochial schools onto its churches. The Freedmen's Bureau strongly supported public schools and commended the AMA on its stance on public education. Though by the 1870s the AMA was supported primarily by Congregationalists, the Congregationalists had a strong tradition of supporting public education. Brownlee, *New Day Ascending,* 114; Richardson, *Christian Reconstruction,* 109–11; Fred L. Brownlee to Philip Widenhouse, 7 March 1954, box 331, General Secretary Correspondence.

3. Richardson, *Christian Reconstruction,* 109–11; *AM* 12 (April 1868): 84; *AM* 13 (November 1869): 241; Brownlee, *New Day Ascending,* 114.

4. H. M. Turner quoted in R. F. Markham to M. E. Strieby, 12 November 1875, AMAA.

5. In fact, the AMA resumed control of a few schools transferred earlier, in-

cluding Washburn Seminary in Beaufort, North Carolina, turned over to the county during Reconstruction. When the county abandoned Washburn in 1888, the AMA took it over and operated it until 1923, when it became a public school again. Washburn Seminary, undated typescript, box 211, Small Field Records, Series A, AMAA, Addendum.

6. AMA executive committee minutes, 9 June 1908, AMAA, Addendum; *AM* 58 (November 1904): 276; *AM* 59 (December 1905): 305; *AM* 59 (January 1905): 10.

7. AMA executive committee minutes, 11 September 1906, 5 April 1910, and 10 March 1919, AMAA, Addendum; *AM* 72 (April 1918): 36; Beam, *He Called Them by the Lightning,* 124, 136–37.

8. AMA Schools Closed or Subsidy Discontinued since 1906, undated list in Beam-Douglass Collection; AMA executive committee minutes, 14 April 1914 and 10 March 1919, AMAA, Addendum; *Seventy-Second Annual Report of the AMA* (1919), 7; *Seventy-Third Annual Report of the AMA* (1919), 12–13; Brownlee, "Changing Conditions in a Dynamic Society"; *AM* 74 (May 1920): 72; Anderson, *Education of Blacks in the South,* 197, 202.

9. The response to the proposed closing of the three schools persuaded the AMA executive committee that it could better utilize alumni and friends, and it organized chapters of the AMA League to develop alumni loyalty and giving. Within two years, the chapters had contributed $15,000 for schools. *Seventy-Fourth Annual Report of the AMA* (1920), 12, 13, 30; *Seventy-Sixth Annual Report of the AMA* (1922), 7–17; AMA executive committee minutes, 10 June 1919, 18 June 1920, 14 February 1922, and 19 October 1926, AMAA, Addendum.

10. *Seventy-Fifth Annual Report of the AMA* (New York, 1921), 12–13; *AM* 77 (October 1923): 347.

11. Emerson remained a public high school until 1929, when it became a junior high until it closed in 1970. The school building was razed in 1972 as part of Mobile's city renewal. *Mobile Press Register,* 3 June 1955, 4a.

12. *Eightieth Annual Report of the AMA* (1926), 18; Brownlee, "Changing Conditions in a Dynamic Society."

13. Fred L. Brownlee to Alfred E. Lawless, 4 May 1921, box 8, folder 1, J. Stanley and Kathryn T. Stanley Papers; *AM* 75 (June 1921): 93; Beam, *He Called Them by the Lightning,* 228.

14. Brownlee, "Changing Conditions in a Dynamic Society"; *Eightieth Annual Report of the AMA* (1926), 22–23; *Eighty-Fourth Annual Report of the AMA* (1930), 24; *Eighty-Sixth Annual Report of the AMA* (1932), 51; AMA administrative committee minutes, 14 February 1933 and 10 September 1935, AMAA, Addendum; *Missionary Herald* 132 (February 1936): 53–55.

15. In 1928, Brownlee said some secondary schools should continue as prep schools to do for blacks what "New England academies and private schools all over the land have done and are doing for white youth." *Eighty-Second Annual Report of the AMA* (1928), 9; F. L. Brownlee to H. S. Barnwell, 26 May 1936, box 8, folder 9, J. Stanley and Kathryn T. Stanley Papers.

16. AMA administrative committee minutes, 13 March 1928, 12 June 1928, 1 April 1934, and 11 February 1936, AMAA, Addendum; Brownlee, "Changing Conditions in a Dynamic Society"; *Eighty-Third Annual Report of the AMA* (1929), 13; *Eighty-Fourth Annual Report of the AMA* (1930), 10.

17. Richardson, "Allen Normal School," 24–25; AMA administrative committee minutes, 25 April 1933, AMAA, Addendum; Bagby, "William G. Price and the Gloucester Agricultural and Industrial School," 80–81.

18. AMA administrative committee minutes, 14 February 1933 and 10 April 1934, AMAA, Addendum; *Missionary Herald* 130 (April 1934): 114–15.

19. AMA administrative committee minutes, 9 April 1935, 10 September 1935, and 14 April 1936, AMAA, Addendum; AMA divisional committee minutes, 15 June 1937, AMAA, Addendum; *Missionary Herald* 133 (November 1937): 509; Ruth A. Morton to W. Judson King, 18 May 1949, box 3, Trinity School; Edwin R. Embree to F. L. Brownlee, 29 November 1937, box 163, folder 7, Julius Rosenwald Fund Papers; Horace Mann Bond to Embree, 14 July 1937, box 175, folder 2, Julius Rosenwald Fund Papers.

20. Brownlee, "Yesterday and Tomorrow"; Eric Anderson and Alfred A. Moss Jr., *Dangerous Donations: Northern Philanthropy and Southern Black Education, 1902–1930* (Columbia, MO, 1999), 217.

21. Ruth Morton statement about Avery in AMA division committee minutes, 24 January 1943, box 362, General Secretary Correspondence; Ruth Morton to F. L. Brownlee, 9 March 1944, box 324, General Secretary Correspondence.

22. Brownlee and Morton, *Shackled Still,* 7; Lewis H. Mounts to F. L. Brownlee, 30 March 1941; Brownlee to Walter P. Jones, 17 April 1941; Brownlee to Mounts, 21 April 1941, box 78, folder 6, Ballard School.

23. Jones and Richardson, *Talladega College,* 155–56; Talladega College board of trustees minutes, 25 November 1946, TC/Adm. 3/3/2/2; A. D. Beittel to F. L. Brownlee, 8 May 1947; Brownlee to Beittel, 20 May 1947, TC/Adm. 4/13/2/27.

24. In an attempt to console faculty, the trustees promised that money saved by closing Sessions and Drewry would be used to enhance salaries and to furnish tutors for faculty children so they would not have to attend segregated schools. Jones and Richardson, *Talladega College,* 156–57; H. A. David to A. D. Beittel, 11 November 1947, TC/Adm. 4/13/2/96.

25. Rosenwald and supporters launched a rural school building program in 1914, which by 1932 had resulted in building almost five thousand rural schools. Though the Rosenwald Fund contributed less than rural blacks, 15.36 percent to 16.64 percent, these schools were called Rosenwald schools. Whites contributed about 4.27 percent, while 63.73 percent came from taxes collected primarily from blacks. This was another indication of blacks' willingness to sacrifice for their children's education. Anderson, *Education of Blacks in the South,* 153–55; S. L. Smith, *Builders of Goodwill: The Story of the State Agents of Negro Education in the South, 1910 to 1950* (Nashville, 1950), 65–67; Thomas W. Hanchett, "The Rosenwald Schools and Black Education in North Carolina," *North Carolina Historical Review* 65 (October 1988): 387.

26. *Eighty-Ninth Annual Report of the AMA* (1936), 40; *AM* 77 (May 1923): 97; Brownlee, *New Day Ascending,* 131–33; *Seventy-Eighth Annual Report of the AMA* (1924), 17–18; *Eightieth Annual Report of the AMA* (1926), 21.

27. AMA administrative committee minutes, 10 April 1938, AMAA, Addendum; AMA missions committee minutes, 9 September 1930, AMAA, Addendum; *Eighty-Seventh Annual Report of the AMA* (1933), 46; *Eighty-Eighth Annual Report of the AMA* (1934), 49; *AM* 87 (4 May 1933): 574.

28. AMA administrative committee minutes, 14 February 1933, 25 April 1933, and 14 April 1936, AMAA, Addendum; Brownlee, *New Day Ascending,* 127.

29. The Charleston city board leased Avery for $1,500 per year for twenty years, retained principal John F. Potts, and promised to operate Avery as a "college-preparatory high school." Drago, *Initiative, Paternalism, and Race Relations,* 246–47. See Drago, chapter 7 for Avery as a public school.

30. In 1949, Walker claimed that within the last seven years Perry County had built forty modern classrooms for blacks, consolidated seventeen schools, and was now running nineteen schoolbuses for black children. L. G. Walker to Ruth A. Morton, 18 February 1949, box 14, folder 14, Lincoln School.

31. Fred L. Brownlee to Quincy W. Wales, 19 October 1944, box 325, General Secretary Correspondence; W. Judson King to Brownlee, 12 February 1948; Brownlee to King, 18 February 1948; King to Ruth A. Morton, 26 September 1949; Morton to W. A. Owens, 1 November 1948, box 3, Trinity School.

32. AMA divisional committee minutes, 15 June 1937, AMAA, Addendum; *Amistad* 7 (January 1930): 11; Henry C. McDowell, Teacher's Record, AMAA, Addendum, Amistad Research Center; F. L. Brownlee to Paul R. Reynolds, 22 November 1939, General Secretary Correspondence.

33. Ruth A. Morton to H. C. McDowell, 24 March 1941, box 137, folder 5; McDowell to Morton, 24 July 1941 and 25 July 1941, box 137, folder 7; McDowell to Helen P. Desort, 1 September 1941, box 137, folder 8; McDowell to N. C. Newbold, 8 June 1941, box 137, folder 7, Lincoln Academy; AMA division committee minutes, 24 February 1943 and 19 February 1946, box 362, General Secretary Correspondence; Morton to Evalee Evans, 12 December 1944, box 13, folder 12, Lincoln School.

34. AMA division committee minutes, 18 April 1949 and 23 June 1954, AMAA, Addendum; Howard Spragg to Hunter Huss, 6 July 1954, box 138, folder 18, Lincoln Academy.

35. S. L. Smith credits Cousins with "almost unbelievable developments in various phases of Negro education," especially in raising the standards of teaching and promoting an extensive school library program. In 1940 Ruth Morton also stated that Cousins had done a remarkable job in providing adequate public school for Georgia black children. Smith, *Builders of Goodwill,* 22. Ruth A. Morton to Mrs. Robert P. Trask, 2 November 1940, box 72, folder 4, Dorchester Academy.

36. See Herd-Clark, "Dorchester Academy," 198–207, for a fuller account of the AMA relinquishing Dorchester Academy.

37. *Missionary Herald* 136 (November 1940): 20–21; Fred L. Brownlee to Robert L. Cousins, 14 March 1940; Brownlee to H. Bacon, 9 May 1940, box 72, folder 2, Dorchester Academy; Brownlee to Nellie E. Chaffee, 31 August 1944, box 325, General Secretary Correspondence; Brownlee and Morton, *Bread and Molasses,* 12.

38. See Brown, *Faithful, Firm, and True,* chapter 7, for a more detailed treatment of the discontinuance of Ballard.

39. The AMA offered 6/14 of a $14,000 budget for 1941–42, 5/14 for 1942–43, 4/14 for 1943–44, 3/14 for 1944–45, and 2/14 for 1945–46. Afterward the county would pay full costs. Fred L. Brownlee to Walter P. Jones, 17 April 1941, box 78, folder 6, Ballard School.

40. AMA division committee minutes, 23 February 1939, AMAA, Addendum; A Report with Recommendation to the Director of the Board of Home Missions by the American Missionary Association Division Committee Meeting of March 9–10, 1940, Common Ground and Race Relations Work, AMAA, Addendum; Fred L. Brownlee to Walter P. Jones, 17 April 1941, box 78, folder 6; Jones to Brownlee, box 78, folder 7; Ruth A. Morton to James A. Colston, 14 May 1941, box 78, folder 7; Colston to Morton, 17 May 1941, box 78, folder 7, Ballard School.

41. The *(Macon) Telegraph,* 6 August 1949, claimed the new school enrolled approximately 1,400 students; Fred L. Brownlee to Mark Smith, 21 April 1942; Smith to Brownlee, 8 June 1942, box 78, folder 10, Ballard School; Brown, *Faithful, Firm, and True,* 135–36.

42. AMA division committee and Board of Home Missions executive committee vote, 15 June 1937, AMAA, Addendum; Brownlee, *Perplexing Realities,* 32; Brownlee, *Continuing Service,* 22; Ruth A. Morton to E. G. McGehee Jr., 20 October 1940, General Secretary Correspondence; Morton to Evalee Evans, 12 December 1944, box 13, folder 12, Lincoln School.

43. Morton wanted to retain Lincoln as long as possible because she did not trust the county to maintain an accredited school, but in 1942, the board of directors of the Board of Home Missions voted to discontinue secondary schools as quickly as they could be turned over to public officials. Ruth A. Morton to Fred A. Gamble, 16 February 1942 and 1 May 1942, box 13, folder 3 and 4, Lincoln School.

44. Fred L. Brownlee to Earnest E. Day, 9 November 1943, box 324, General Secretary Correspondence; AMA division committee minutes, 24 January 1943, AMAA, Addendum; Ruth A. Morton to E. G. McGehee, 9 May 1947, box 14, folder 3, Lincoln School; Fred L. Brownlee, "Changing Conditions in a Dynamic Society."

45. Ruth A. Morton to E. G. McGehee, 10 April 1942, box 323, General Secretary Correspondence; F. L. Brownlee to W. A. Owens, 29 April 1943; Owens to Brownlee, 6 May 1943; W. Judson King to Helen Wernert, 22 October 1943, box 2; King to Morton, 30 September 1947, box 3; King to Morton, 8 May 1948, box 3, Trinity School.

46. The AMA formally deeded the land to the board in December 1956 but refused to release the $20,000 until the building was completed. The check was

sent December 20, 1957. AMA division committee minutes, 13 February 1950 and 21 June 1950, AMAA, Addendum; W. Judson King to Ruth A. Morton, 9 September 1950; Morton to King, 14 December 1950; King to Philip M. Widenhouse, 7 March 1951; Widenhouse to R. F. Johnson, 13 September 1954 and 16 April 1956; Philip M. Widenhouse to William Nelson, 31 December 1956; Helen Wernert to G. H. Roberts, 20 December 1957; Athens-Limestone Community Association to Wesley A. Hotchkiss, 28 September 1981, box 3, Trinity School.

CHAPTER 6

1. Richardson, *Christian Reconstruction,* 123; *AM* 47 (October 1893): 309; Anderson, *Education of Blacks in the South,* 242–43.

2. The American Missionary Association was only one of several mission societies establishing colleges. Other significant societies include the Freedmen's Aid Society of the Methodist Episcopal Church, the American Baptist Home Mission Society, the Presbyterian Board of Missions for Freedmen, the African Methodist Episcopal Church, and the African Methodist Episcopal Zion Church.

3. The eight chartered institutions the AMA founded or helped found were Atlanta University, Atlanta, Georgia; Berea College, Berea, Kentucky; Hampton Institute, Hampton, Virginia; Fisk University, Nashville, Tennessee; Talladega College, Talladega, Alabama; Tougaloo College, Tougaloo, Mississippi; Straight College, New Orleans, Louisiana; and Tillotson College, Austin, Texas. Hampton Institute quickly became independent of the AMA. The AMA deeded Fisk property to the Fisk board of trustees in 1875. The AMA retained the right to approve appointments to the board of trustees and continued to give support and guidance. In Fisk's early efforts to secure an endowment, the AMA assisted it more than the association's other colleges. Atlanta University became completely independent in 1892 when the AMA gave its usual $3,000 annual grant, cancelled a $3,000 mortgage, deeded valuable land to the school, and relinquished AMA representation on the board of trustees. The AMA urged the founding of Howard University and paid the first teacher's salary. It was the chief supporter of the Howard theological department since the government could not support theological studies. Richardson, *Christian Reconstruction,* 293: Joe M. Richardson, *A History of Fisk University, 1865–1946* (Tuscaloosa, AL, 1980), 42; *Forty-Sixth Annual Report of the AMA* (1892), 34; Dwight O. W. Holmes, "Fifty Years of Howard University," *Journal of Negro History* 3 (October 1918): 369, 373; Walter R. Allen and Joseph D. Jewell, "A Backward Glance Forward: Past, Present, and Future Perspectives on Historically Black Colleges and Universities," *Review of Higher Education* 25 (Spring 2002): 257.

4. Berea remained biracial until 1904, when the Kentucky legislature mandated segregation in all schools. Berea, true to its principles, defied the law. It was indicted, convicted, and fined $1,000. It appealed first to the state supreme court and lost. It then appealed to the United States Supreme Court, which in 1906 in *Berea College v. Kentucky* decided in favor of Kentucky. Miller, *The Petitioners,* 197; Richardson,

Christian Reconstruction, 124, 297; E. P. Smith to M. E. Strieby, 28 April 1866, AMAA; Brownlee, *New Day Ascending,* 94.

5. Beard quoted in Brownlee, *New Day Ascending,* 178; Bond quoted in Anderson, *Education of Blacks in the South,* 242–43.

6. Richardson, *History of Fisk University,* 46–47, 50; W. E. B. Du Bois, *Dusk of Dawn: An Essay toward an Autobiography of a Race Concept* (New York, 1940), 30–31; W. E. B. Du Bois, "My Evolving Program for Negro Freedom," in Rayford W. Logan, ed., *What the Negro Wants* (Chapel Hill, 1944), 36–39; Francis L. Broderick, *W.E.B. Du Bois: Negro Leader in a Time of Crisis* (Stanford, CA, 1959), 7–9; *Fisk Herald,* July 1886, 6; *Fisk Herald,* October 1886, 6–7.

7. Jones and Richardson, *Talladega College,* 49–50; *Talladega College Catalog, 1894–95,* 15; *Talladega College Catalog, 1899–1900,* 8. .

8. According to the U.S. Commissioner of Education, the total number of black college students in the United States in 1889–90 was 811, 238 of whom were in northern schools. There were 573 pupils enrolled in 22 southern colleges, 103 of them in AMA institutions. U.S. Commissioner of Education, *Report for the Year 1889–90* (2 vols., Washington, DC, 1893), 2:1088; *AM* 45 (November 1891): 385. For more on Straight University and Tougaloo College, see: Shawn C. Comminey, "A History of Straight College, 1869–1935," (PhD diss., Florida State University, 2003), and Clarice T. Campbell, "History of Tougaloo College," (PhD diss., University of Mississippi, 1970).

9. *AM* 45 (July 1891): 252; *AM* 53 (July 1899): 54; *AM* 55 (April 1901): 67; Richardson, *History of Fisk University,* 49–50, 53; David Levering Lewis, *W. E. B. Du Bois: Biography of a Race, 1868–1919* (New York, 1993), 71; Jones and Richardson, *Talladega College,* 19, 51.

10. The actual number of college students is difficult to discern since AMA records sometimes include Fisk and sometimes not. Then in 1901, AMA statistics sometimes included J. S. Green College in Demorest, Georgia, which was for whites. In 1898, Fisk had fifty-four college students, and in 1900 the other AMA schools had eighty-five. There were also in 1900 ninety-five theological students, some of whom also took college courses. U.S. Commissioner of Education, *Report of the Year 1897–98,* II, 2494–95; *AM* 55 (January 1901): 23.

11. *AM* 48 (November 1894): 388–89; *AM* 49 (November 1895): 354; *AM* 51 (December 1897): 267; Anderson, *Education of Blacks in the South,* 248; Anderson and Moss, *Dangerous Donations,* 219; AMA executive committee minutes, 11 April 1911, AMAA, Addendum.

12. W. E. B. Du Bois, "The Talented Tenth," in Julius Lester, *The Seventh Son: The Thought and Writings of W. E. B. Du Bois* (2 vols., New York, 1971), 1:391, 394–95, 397; Du Bois quoted in Anderson, *Education of Blacks in the South,* 244–45.

13. College budgets tended to indicate the quality of the schools. In 1905 school expenses were as follows: Fisk, $28,490.98; Talladega, $27,464.64; Tougaloo, $20,259.93; Straight, $14,781.47; and Tillotson, $5,571.40. Tougaloo's budget was larger than expected because of its large farm and large number of poverty-stricken

students. Tillotson was always a kind of AMA stepchild. Other colleges were older, closer, and more often visited. *Forty-Ninth Annual Report of the AMA* (1895), 67–71.

14. Locke was at Oxford 1907–10. B. T. Washington to My Dear Prof. Silsby, 11 February 1903, Louis R. Harlan and Raymond W. Smock, eds., *Booker T. Washington Papers* (11 vols., Urbana, 1977), 7:69.

15. *AM* 62 (November 1908): 199, 286; *AM* 64 (February 1910): 978; *Sixtieth Annual Report of the AMA* (1906), 38; Douglass, *Christian Reconstruction in the South*, 241; *Seventy-Third Annual Report of the AMA* (New York, 1919), 12; *Crisis* 18 (July 1919): 135–37.

16. Major Evans, who won a medal of honor for bravery at Hatcher's Run, Virginia, on April 2, 1865, went south after the war with Union occupation forces. He moved to Texas and became a businessman and banker. *Tillotson College Catalog, 1922–23*, 4; *The New Handbook of Texas* (6 vols., Austin, 1996), 1:701; Mabel Clayton Williams, "The History of Tillotson College" (M.A. thesis, Texas Southern University, 1967), 78; Beam, *He Called Them by the Lightning*, 124.

17. Douglass, *Christian Reconstruction in the South*, 115; *Sixty-First Annual Report of the AMA* (New York, 1907), 5, 36; *AM* 63 (July 1909): 519; *Tougaloo News*, May 1938, 1.

18. Du Bois was one of those critical of southern white trustees. Douglass responded, "Dr. Du Bois certainly does not doubt that Bishop Galloway accorded him full rights of spiritual manhood, freely and without condescension . . . whatever his habits as to eating with negroes." Douglass, *Christian Reconstruction in the South* 115; Jones and Richardson, *Talladega College*, 70, 115, 138, 151; *Alumni Directory of Fisk University* (Nashville, 1930), 17, 47; *Straight College Bulletin*, August 1933, 6; Biographical sketch of Fannie C. Williams, typescript, box 1, folder 2, Fannie C. Williams Papers, Amistad Research Center; *Tougaloo News, Catalog Number, 1935–1936*, 2.

19. Benjamin M. Nyce to H. W. Hubbard, 19 May 1905, TC/Adm. 2/1/5; Benjamin M. Nyce to Wallace Buttrick, 7 April 1905, TC/Adm. 2/1/5; Minutes of the Fisk Board of Trustees, 25 June 1908 and 6 October 1909, Fisk University Archives; Jones and Richardson, *Talladega College*, 74; Richardson, *History of Fisk University*, 61–63.

20. The small Slater Fund grant was enough to alarm many Fisk graduates who saw it as a surrender to industrial education. Du Bois addressed the 1908 graduating class and spoke to the issue. Later he admitted, "Perhaps we were over fearful, but I thought then that I was stemming a tide." Du Bois believed Merrill's resignation was in part a result of the speech. "I was sorry for that. I did not mean this as a personal attack." The Department of Applied Sciences was dropped in 1909. W. E. B. Du Bois, "Galileo Galilei," in *The Education of Black People: Ten Critiques, 1906–1960* (Amherst, MA, 1973), 17–30.

21. Richardson, *History of Fisk University*, 67–68; Luker, *Social Gospel in Black and White*, 139; B. T. Washington to J. G. Merrill, 10 January 1908, 25 February 1908, 7 March 1908, and 2 July 1908; E. L. Parks to B. T. Washington, 22 January 1908 and 4 February 1908; P. D. Cravath to B. T. Washington, 28 October 1909 and 13 No-

vember 1909; B. T. Washington to Cravath, 16 November 1909; B. T. Washington to George A. Gates, 12 April 1910 and 21 May 1910; B. T. Washington to Andrew Carnegie, 18 October 1910; B. T. Washington to W. G. Waterman, 18 November 1910; Waterman to B. T. Washington, 27 October 1910; J. E. Bertram to B. T. Washington, 1910, Booker T. Washington Papers, Library of Congress; *Fisk University News,* February 1910, 2.

22. B. T. Washington to J. G. Merrill, 10 January 1908, 7 March 1908, and 28 July 1908; Merrill to B. T. Washington, 2 July 1908; P. D. Cravath to B. T. Washington, 28 October 1909 and 13 November 1909; B. T. Washington to Cravath, 17 November 1909, Booker T. Washington Papers, Library of Congress; Richardson, *History of Fisk University,* 67; Talladega board of trustees minutes, 27 March 1914, TC/Adm. 3/3/1; Sheldon Avery, "Up from Washington: William Pickens and the Negro Struggle for Equality, 1900–1954," (PhD diss., University of Oregon, 1970), 24–27, 33, 34; Jones and Richardson, *Talladega College,* 86.

23. The endowment was to be divided as follows: Fisk, $250,000; Talladega, Tougaloo, Straight, Tillotson, and the white school Piedmont College, $150,000 each. AMA executive committee minutes, 12 November 1912 and 10 December 1912, AMAA, Addendum; *AM* 66 (December 1912): 545; *AM* 67 (March 1913): 740; *AM* 68 (April 1914): 22–23; *AM* 70 (December 1916): 487.

24. In 1919 the AMA reported endowments as follows: Talladega, $102,229.67; Straight, $19,012.84; and Tougaloo, $6,760. Fisk handled its endowment separately from the AMA. *Seventy-Third Annual Report of the AMA* (1919), 75.

25. Endowments for Hampton and Tuskegee found in *Crisis* 10 (July 1915): 111; Douglass, *Christian Reconstruction in the South,* 151; AMA executive committee minutes, 14 February 1911, AMAA, Addendum; Jones and Richardson, *Talladega College,* 79.

26. For more on Roy's AMA activities, see: Joseph E. Roy, *Pilgrim's Letters, Bits of Current History Picked up in the West and the South, during the Last Thirty Years, for the Independent, the Congregationalist, and the Advance* (Boston, 1888); qtd. in Anderson, *Education of Blacks in the South,* 71–72.

27. AMA executive committee minutes, 14 November 1892, AMAA, Addendum; *AM* 47 (October 1893): 308–9; *AM* 57 (March 1903): 78; *AM* 57 (February 1903): 53; W. T. B. Williams to B. M. Nyce, 13 January 1906, box 11, GEB Files, Series I, Subseries I, Rockefeller Archives Center; Thomas Jesse Jones, *Negro Education: A Study of the Private and Higher Schools for Colored People in the United States* (2 vols., Washington, DC, 1917), 2:85, 303, 358, 537, 596.

28. Richardson, *History of Fisk University,* 20–21; Jones and Richardson, *Talladega College,* 82–83, 134; Clara M. Standish to Dear Friends, November 1910, TC/Assn. 2/2/3; Rowland Cross, "A Tribute to Clara Standish," n.d., TC/Adm. 7/5/1/1.

29. Jones and Richardson, *Talladega College,* 70–71, 83–87, 105; Joe M. Richardson, "A Negro Success Story: James Dallas Burrus," *Journal of Negro History* 50 (October 1965): 274–82; Thomas Jesse Jones, *Negro Education,* 2:83, 302, 357, 536, 596; Beam, *He Called Them by the Lightning,* 153–54.

30. *AM* 55 (January 1901): 68; *AM* 60 (September 1906): 205; *AM* 61 (February 1907): 44, 46; *AM* 57 (June 1903): 173; Maxine D. Jones, "Edwin Chalmers Silsby and Talladega College," *Alabama Review* 41 (October 1988): 271–88.

31. *AM* 62 (October 1908): 248; Comminey, "History of Straight College," 132; Beam, *He Called Them by the Lightning,* 124; Minutes of Talladega College Prudential Committee, 5 April 1892 and 19 November 1895, TC/Adm. 7/4/6/2/3/3; Jones and Richardson, *Talladega College,* 58; Douglass, *Christian Reconstruction in the South,* 244.

32. "The Affair at Talladega College," n.d., leaflet, TC/Adm. 4/8/4/1/1; *Mobile Weekly Press,* 3 February 1906; A. F. Beard to Charles Alexander, 8 February 1906, in *Alexander's Magazine,* February 1906, 23; Jones and Richardson, *Talladega College,* 58–63, 73, 75–77.

33. For divergent interpretations of the Jones study, see: W. E. B. Du Bois, "Negro Education," *Crisis* 15 (February 1918): 173–78; Du Bois, "Thomas Jesse Jones," *Crisis* 20 (October 1921): 252–56; Louis Harlan, *Separate and Unequal: Public School Campaigns and Racism in the Southern Seaboard States, 1901–1915* (New York, 1968); Anderson, *Education of Blacks in the South,* 250–51, 256–57; Anderson and Moss, *Dangerous Donations,* 203–9.

34. Thomas Jesse Jones, *Negro Education,* 1:55–60.

35. Thomas Jesse Jones, *Negro Education,* 1:55–60, 32, 83, 304, 357–58, 537–38, 596–97.

36. Qtd. in Anderson and Moss, *Dangerous Donations,* 203–4, 210–11.

37. *Seventy-Eighth Annual Report of the AMA* (1924), 17; *Seventy-Ninth Annual Report of the AMA* (1925), 9; *AM* 78 (October 1924): 248; *Eighty-First Annual Report of the AMA* (1927), 19; *Eighty-Fourth Annual Report of the AMA* (1930), 36; Chrystine I. Shackles, *Reminiscences of Huston-Tillotson College* (Austin, TX, 1973), 4.

38. In 1927, U.S. Bureau of Education representatives visited Talladega and declared it "the best college" they had surveyed. Anderson and Moss, *Dangerous Donations,* 193–94; AMA executive committee minutes, 10 May 1921, AMAA, Addendum; James T. Cater, "Report of the Dean to President Sumner, 1927," TC/Adm. 6/7/4/2; Jones and Richardson, *Talladega College,* 107.

39. For example, a visitor to the Haywood County Training School in Tennessee found black instructors teaching Latin and ignoring industrial work. Anderson, *Education of Blacks in the South,* 142.

40. See Anderson, *Education of Blacks in the South,* for the founding and activities of the various philanthropic boards. The most significant was the General Education Board created by John D. Rockefeller in 1902.

41. In 1915 the *Crisis* reported that the GEB had donated only $144,000 for black higher education and half of that went to Fisk. Douglass, *Christian Reconstruction in the South,* 243; *Crisis* 4 (October 1912): 270; *Crisis* 9 (February 1915): 165; *Crisis* 12 (May 1916): 29; *Crisis* 13 (December 1916): 90; *Crisis* 13 (March 1917): 242; Du Bois, "The General Education Board," *Crisis* 37 (July 1930): 230; Richardson, *History of Fisk University,* 68; Anderson and Moss, *Dangerous Donations,* 95.

42. James D. Anderson suggests that the "industrial philanthropists" attempted to change Fisk's liberal arts bent and turn the school in a direction more sympathetic to them. They wished for, he says, an industrially trained black workforce. James D. Anderson, "Northern Philanthropy and the Training of Black Leadership: Fisk University, A Case Study, 1915–1930," in Vincent P. Franklin and James D. Anderson, eds., *New Perspectives on Black Educational History* (Boston, 1978), 97–111; Raymond B. Fosdick, *Adventure in Giving: The Story of the General Education Board* (New York, 1962), 190; *Crisis* 3 (April 1911): 245; Richardson, *History of Fisk University,* 68, 81, 112, 124; L. S. Shores to C. H. Milam, 20 August 1930, Fisk University Library; *Eighty-Fourth Annual Report of the AMA* (1930), 34.

43. Talladega had dramatically improved since the Jones report. S. L. Smith, director of Southern schools for the Julius Rosenwald Fund, reported in 1930 that "we feel that it is one of the good colleges of the South." S. L. Smith to Edwin R. Embree, 7 October 1930, box 55, folder 1, Julius Rosenwald Fund Papers, microfilm, Amistad Research Center.

44. In 1913 the GEB had denied Talladega's request for funds with the excuse that new demands were being made for expansion of its farm demonstration and allied "forms of rural work." Talladega was rejected again in 1914 and 1915. E. C. Sage to J. M. P. Metcalf, 26 May 1913; Sage to Lucien C. Warner, 4 June 1914; Sage to F. L. Brownlee, 21 November 1921; Sage to F. A. Sumner, 25 February 1922; W. W. Brierley to Brownlee, 27 November 1923; H. J. Thorkelson, Memorandum re visit of Talladega College, Talladega, Alabama, 17 January 1928; F. A. Sumner to W. W. Brierley, 11 June 1928, GEB Files, Series I, Subseries I, box 11, Rockefeller Archives Center, microfilm, Amistad Research Center; Edwin R. Embree to Sumner, 14 May 1929, Rosenwald Fund Papers, box 255, folder 1, microfilm, Amistad Research Center.

45. Though the 1926 report on Tougaloo is unsigned, other letters indicate that Favrot visited and wrote the report. [Leo M. Favrot], Report on Tougaloo College, 18 October 1926; W. J. Ballou to My Dear Rockefeller, 4 May 1904; J. D. Rockefeller Jr. to Dear Ballou, 13 May 1904; Rockefeller to Wallace Buttrick, 13 May 1904; Tougaloo undated application, December 1908; W. T. Holmes to GEB, 28 June 1913; Jackson Davis statement, 7 April 1920; E. C. Sage memorandum, 16 February 1921; W. W. Brierley to W. T. Holmes, 27 November 1923; H. J. Thorkelson memo, 3 March 1926, Thorkelson to Holmes, 16 December 1926; Holmes and James B. Scott to Brierley, 13 January 1930, box 91, GEB Files, Series I, Subseries I, Rockefeller Archives Center; W. T. Holmes to S. F. Smith, 25 March 1930, box 356, folder 12, Julius Rosenwald Fund Papers.

46. In 1915, the AMA executive committee—perhaps as an indication of its limited expectations—renamed Straight University "Straight College." Comminey, "A History of Straight College," 201.

47. H. Paul Douglass first applied to the GEB for aid for Tillotson in 1913. H. Paul Douglass to GEB, 13 May 1913; Leo M. Favrot interview with Mary E. Branch, 30 August 1932; W. W. Brierley, 15 October 1932, box 168, GEB Files, Series I, Subseries I, Rockefeller Archives Center; Mary M. Bethune to W. W. Brierley, 28 March

1934, Mary McLeod Bethune Papers, The Bethune-Cookman College Collection, 1922–55, microfilm, Robert M. Strozier, Florida State University.

48. Anderson and Moss, *Dangerous Donations,* 194–95.

49. For a detailed discussion of the founding of Dillard University, see: Clifton H. Johnson, "White Philanthropy Builds a Black School," Clifton H. Johnson Papers, Amistad Research Center; Joe M. Richardson, "Edgar B. Stern: A White New Orleans Philanthropist Helps Build a Black University," *Journal of Negro History* 82 (Summer 1997): 328–42.

50. The best treatment of Stern is found in a biography of his wife. Gerda W. Klein, *A Passion for Sharing: The Life of Edith Rosenwald Stern* (Chappaqua, NY, 1984). Numerous Stern letters can be found in the Rosenwald Fund Papers, and in the Dillard Papers, AMAA, Addendum.

51. Fred L. Brownlee, "Beginnings of Dillard University," 28 April 1961, Frederick L. Brownlee Papers; Edwin R. Embree to Julius Rosenwald, 31 January 1928, box 90, folder 8, Julius Rosenwald Fund Papers; Clifton H. Johnson, "White Philanthropy Builds a Black School," 20, 24–25.

52. In 1923, at Brownlee's suggestion, the AMA executive committee authorized an informal conference with the M. E. Church Board of Education about the possibility of combining Tillotson and Samuel Huston. AMA executive committee minutes, 11 September 1923, AMAA, Addendum; Fred L. Brownlee to Edwin R. Embree, 18 December 1928, box 191, folder 7, Julius Rosenwald Fund Papers; Brownlee to Leo M. Favrot, 18 December 1928, box 89, GEB Files, Series I, Subseries I, Rockefeller Archive Center.

53. Dillard sometimes seemed to advocate industrial education for African Americans because it was the only type of education acceptable to many southern whites. Michael Fultz said Dillard "consciously utilized diplomacy and tact in labeling the schools 'county training schools' rather than the high schools he hoped they would— and did, by the late 1920s and early 1930s—eventually become." Fultz, "Teacher Training and African American Education in the South," 203.

54. AMA executive committee minutes, 8 July 1913, AMAA, Addendum; Thomas Jesse Jones, *Negro Education,* 1:67; Clifton H. Johnson, "White Philanthropy Builds a Black School," 29; Richardson, "Edgar B. Stern," 329–40; Edwin R. Embree to Edith R. Stern, 5 March 1928, box 140, folder 5; Edgar B. Stern to Embree, 22 March 1928, box 352, folder 4; Embree to Stern, 26 February 1932, box 140, folder 7, Julius Rosenwald Fund Papers; AMA administrative committee minutes, 12 March 1929 and 11 June 1929, AMAA, Addendum; Minutes of the Merger Conference, Board of Education and the American Missionary Association, 21–22 February 1929, GEB files, Series I, Subseries I, box 89, Rockefeller Archives Center.

55. For more on Tillotson and Branch, see: Shackles, *Reminiscences of Huston-Tillotson College;* Olive D. Brown and Michael R. Heintze, "Mary Branch: Private College Educator," in Alwyn Barr and Robert A. Calvert, eds., *Black Leaders: Texans for Their Times* (Austin, TX, 1981); Joe M. Richardson, "Mary E. Branch: African

American Educator and College President," *Southern Studies,* New Series, 7 (Winter 1996): 53–78.

56. Texas, Department of Education, *Negro Education in Texas,* Bulletin No. 24 (Austin, 1931), 25; Michael R. Heintze, *Private Black Colleges in Texas, 1865–1954* (College Station, TX, 1985), 102; Richardson, "Mary E. Branch," 58; Elizabeth L. Ihle, ed., *Black Women in Higher Education* (New York, 1992), 175–78.

57. Brownlee was in constant contact with University of Texas president Homer Rainey, and seriously hoped that the state could be persuaded to assume control of Tillotson. In 1943 he suggested to Rainey that the AMA might deed the Tillotson property to the University of Texas and promise an annual subsidy for a number of years. He asked Rainey to suggest ways to proceed to preserve Tillotson College and its traditions, values, and property "for the racial and interracial good of Texas and our country at large." Fred L. Brownlee to Homer Rainey, 9 January 1942, Huston-Tillotson Records; AMA administrative committee minutes, 16 April 1929; Brownlee to Rainey, 9 November 1943, box 214, folder 18, Small Field Records, Series A, AMAA, Addendum; Jessie Daniel Ames to Fred L. Brownlee, 31 October 1938, Frederick L. Brownlee Papers; For more on Ames, see: Jacquelyn Dowd Hall, *Revolt against Chivalry: Jessie Daniel Ames and the Women's Campaign against Lynching* (New York, 1979).

58. Richardson, "Mary E. Branch," 58, 61; Mary E. Branch to Fred McCuistion, 3 February 1941, box 168, GEB Files Series I, Subseries I, Rockefeller Archive Center.

59. Jones and Richardson, *Talladega College,* 89–110; Clara Standish to Dear Friends, October 1916; Standish to Dear Friends, October 1925; Standish to Dear Friends, April 1923, TC/Assn. 2/2/3; Oscar Lawless to E. C. Silsby, 19 November 1917, Edwin C. Silsby Correspondence 1/1; *Talladegan* 50 (November 1931): 5; *AM* 87 (August 1933): 808.

60. *Talladegan* 61 (January 1944): 5; Jones and Richardson, *Talladega College,* 111–42; Clifton H. Johnson interview with George A. Owens, 24 November 2000, box 11, folder 11, Clifton H. Johnson Papers.

61. *Missionary Herald* 136 (November 1940): 48; *Missionary Herald* 134 (February 1938): 61; *Eighty-Eighth Annual Report of the AMA* (1934), 45; *Tougaloo News* 54 (January 1944): 10; Frank Sweeney, Teacher's Record, AMAA, Addendum.

62. Tougaloo jumped from ten students in 1920 to almost two hundred in 1940. *Seventy-Sixth Annual Report of the AMA* (1922), 10; *Seventy-Ninth Annual Report of the AMA* (1925), 40; *Eighty-Seventh Annual Report of the AMA* (1933), 64; *Crisis* 47 (August 1940): 237; Brownlee and Morton, *Shackled Still,* 20; Brownlee, *New Day Ascending,* 192.

63. Anderson, *Education of Blacks in the South,* 250–51; *Eighty-Sixth Annual Report of the AMA* (1932), 9; Fred L. Brownlee to Edwin R. Embree, 22 September 1932, box 355, folder 1, Julius Rosenwald Fund Papers; *AM* 86 (February 1932): 139; *Eighty-Seventh Annual Report of the AMA* (1933), 41–42; Frank Sweeney to Fred L. Brown-

lee, 1 April 1939, Frederick L. Brownlee Papers; AMA division committee minutes, 8 December 1947, box 362, General Secretary Correspondence; Heintze, *Private Black Colleges in Texas,* 65.

64. G. David Houston, "Weaknesses of the Negro College," *Crisis* 20 (July 1920): 123.

65. All except two black teachers volunteered to return. *Crisis* 18 (October 1919): 300–301; *Crisis* 20 (June 1920): 72; AMA executive committee minutes, 10 February 1920, 13 April 1920, 12 October 1920, 13 September 1921, 11 October 1921, 9 November 1921, and 13 December 1921, AMAA, Addendum.

66. C. S. Wilcox to Anna Maria Hansen, 23 December 1921, Anna Maria Hansen Papers, Amistad Research Center; Fred L. Brownlee, "Tillotson College," undated typescript, Huston-Tillotson, AMAA, Addendum; Heintze, *Private Black Colleges in Texas,* 118–19.

67. Edgar B. Stern to Edwin R. Embree, 8 July 1931, box 191, folder 8; Stern to Thomas F. Holgate, 26 June 1930, box 191, folder 7; Stern to George Arthur, 12 December 1930, box 140, folder 6; Stern to Holgate, 8 January 1931, box 191, folder 8, Julius Rosenwald Fund Papers.

68. In 1947 black scholar J. Max Bond reminded Alexander of the time he greeted him at a meeting and Alexander turned his back and refused to shake hands. Robert C. Weaver, first black racial advisor to the U.S. Department of the Interior, remembered in 1961 that when he initially met him Alexander advocated separate and equal, but had shifted his position by the early 1940s. Stern also altered his stance on segregation. J. Max Bond to Will W. Alexander, 18 August 1947, box 94, folder 6, Julius Rosenwald Fund Papers; Robert C. Weaver, "Dedicatory Address at the dedication of the Will W. Alexander Library at Dillard University," 22 October 1961, box 2, folder 10, Albert W. and Ernestine Jessie C. Dent Family Papers, Amistad Research Center; Wilma Dykeman and James R. Stokely, *Seeds of Southern Change: The Life of Will Alexander* (Chicago, 1962), 172.

69. Alexander apparently preferred the title "administrator" or "acting president" to that of president, perhaps because he was often off campus and because he considered it as a temporary appointment. Edgar B. Stern to George Arthur, 7 March 1931, 1 April 1931; Robert E. Jones to Edwin R. Embree, 7 March 1931; F. L. Brownlee to Stern, 3 March 1931, 13 March 1931; Stern to Brownlee, 16 March 1931; Stern to Embree, 6 April 1931, box 191, folder 8; Embree to Will W. Alexander, 10 July 1931; Stern to Alexander, 6 July 1931, box 191, folder 9, Julius Rosenwald Fund Papers; Richardson, "Edgar B. Stern," 328–35.

70. Nelson had been assistant to Howard University president Mordecai Johnson, and president of Shaw University, where, wrote Stern, he did "wonders with it." Edgar B. Stern to Edwin R. Embree, 19 March 1936, box 192, folder 1, Julius Rosenwald Fund Papers.

71. It was clear that Hamilton badly wanted to be president and had the support of many friends and probably the local NAACP. It was equally clear that he and Sweeney disliked each other, and that Sweeney was not completely sympathetic to

the desire for black leadership. He wrote Brownlee, "For years I have been stung by the expressions of a little group that has constantly deprecated and criticized white leadership" and which had become an "enervating factor in my life and in the life of the institution." Frank Sweeney to F. L. Brownlee, 20 January 1940; Brownlee to Sweeney, 23 January 1940; Walter White to Dear Fred [Brownlee] and George [N. White], 1 April 1940; Brownlee to Walter White, 22 April 1940; T. R. McLemore to Brownlee, 6 June 1940, box 148, folders 4–8, LeMoyne-Owen College, Amistad Research Center.

72. Philip M. Widenhouse to Samuel C. Kincheloe, 26 November 1954, box 110, folder 8, Tougaloo College.

73. Clifton H. Johnson interview with George A. Owens, 24 November 2000, box 11, folder 11, Clifton H. Johnson Papers; Jones and Richardson, *Talladega College*, 143–67.

74. F.L Brownlee to T. Douglass, 15 June 1944, George W. Crawford to F.L. Brownlee, 10 October 1949, General Secretary Correspondence.

75. Business manager George Owens thought the problem began in part because Sumner and Gallagher had basically permitted Cater to run academic affairs on campus. Owens claimed that Cater was a master diplomat who, with the support of a few faculty, had been able to control the college under the democratic system installed by Gallagher. Beittel was more a hands-on president who insisted on playing a greater role in decision making, which Cater believed rightfully belonged to himself. Clifton H. Johnson interview with George A. Owens, 24 November 2000; Jones and Richardson, *Talladega College*, 155.

76. Arthur D. Gray, who succeeded Beittel, suggested years later that much of the discord was the result of Cater's frustration at being passed over for the presidency. In 1954 Truman Douglass wrote of the Talladega situation, "We now know that there has been an individual who had incited a campaign of real subversion and that Dr. Beittel was a victim of his malice." The conviction that Beittel had been seriously wronged no doubt played a role in the AMA later appointing him president of Tougaloo. Arthur D. Gray to D. P. Cottrell, 27 April 1963, TC/Adm. 2/2/2; Jones and Richardson, *Talladega College*, 143–67, 296n.85; Adam D. Beittel to George W. Crawford, 29 April 1952, George W. Crawford Papers, in Board of Trustees Papers, TC/Adm. 3/5/10; Solon T. Kimball and Marion Pearsall, *The Talladega Story: A Study in Community Process* (University, AL, 1954), 123–24; George W. Crawford presentation, Seminar on American Racialism Held by The American Missionary Association Division at the Broadway Tabernacle Church, New York City on January 16, 1942, Buell G. Gallagher Papers, TC/Adm. 4/11/2/13; Crawford statement, Trustee of Talladega College minutes, 19 November 1951, TC/Adm. 3/3/2/2; Drewry and Doermann, *Stand and Prosper*, 148–51; Philip M. Widenhouse to Samuel C. Kincheloe, 20 May 1952; Kincheloe to Widenhouse, 22 May 1952, box 3, folder 7, Samuel C. Kincheloe Papers.

77. Edgar B. Stern to Edwin R. Embree, 22 December 1934, box 141, folder 1, Julius Rosenwald Fund Papers; James P. Woods III, "Alrutheus Ambush Taylor, 1893–

1954: Segregated Historian of Reconstruction," (M.A. thesis, Louisiana State University, 1969), 70.

78. In 1942 Talladega president Buell Gallagher said "a whispering campaign, stemming from persons in high position" had sought to stir up racial animosity in Alabama. "As one small facet of this general campaign throughout the state, completely false and unfounded stories about Talladega College are passing from clacking tongues to ready ears." Rumors about black and white faculty were of a sexual nature. Buell G. Gallagher, *Sinews in Your Wings, America! The Report of the Ninth Year in the Administration of the Sixth President of Talladega College Covering the Year 1941–42* (Talladega, 1942), 7. Horacetina W. Crawley, Teacher's Record, Amistad Research Center; F. L. Brownlee to Harold C. Warren, 24 June 1947, box 108, folder 14, Tougaloo College, AMAA, Addendum; Henrietta Alma Quarles application, 3 June 1947, Adam D. Beittel Papers, TC/Adm. 4/13/2/148.

79. Alma Spar, Teacher's Record, AMAA, Addendum; Hilda Davis to Eleanor French, 26 October 1944, TC/Adm. 8/4/6/2/33/2; August Meier, *A White Scholar and the Black Community* (Amherst, 1992), 10.

80. [Lura Beam], Straight College, January 1919, box 90, folder 2, Dillard University.

81. Hanson was acting president in 1928 and again in 1940. Though older missionary women were often paid less than men, Brownlee revised her salary upward when she became acting president in 1928 to make it slightly more than the dean's. Hollis Price was the black LeMoyne College president who complained that Hanson overstepped her authority. He probably said it with a tolerant smile since he had great admiration and affection for her. F. L. Brownlee telegram to Alma C. Hanson, 27 September 1928; Brownlee to Hanson, 29 May 1940, Frederick L. Brownlee Papers; *LeMoynite* 36 (February 1963), 1–2; Division of Higher Education and AMA committee minutes, 28 January 1963, General Secretary Correspondence; Dr. Walter W. Gibson, *Tribute to a Great Lady* (Pamphlet, Memphis, 1967); Hollis F. Price to F. L. Brownlee, 10 August 1943; Brownlee to Price, 12 August 1943; Price to Brownlee, 16 August 1943, box 150, folder 10, LeMoyne-Owen; story of Hanson coming down off roof to announce that she was president, Clifton H. Johnson statement to Joe M. Richardson, 25 September 1990; Frank Sweeney to F. L. Brownlee, 12 December 1940, Frederick L. Brownlee Papers; August Meier and Chester Slocum, "Tougaloo College Revisited," *Unitarian Christian Register* 130 (November 1951): 29–30.

82. Margaret McCulloch, a white teacher who went to LeMoyne in 1934, tended to agree with President Sweeney about the black-white division. In the spring of 1940 the faculty decided that too many LeMoyne students were deficient in background and voted to adopt a new curriculum for freshmen and sophomores. For the first two years students were placed in an interdisciplinary program studying such areas as health, economics, and job skills in their regular academic classes. When the fall semester began, the faculty voted to abandon the program accepted in the spring. "Amid great confusion it gradually transpired," McCulloch wrote, "that some members of the faculty and staff spent the summer attacking the plan as a plot of the white

members to destroy the institution because they considered Negroes inferior and incapable of 'white education.'" Both Sweeney and McCulloch resigned. The plan closely resembled Brownlee's wish for more functional education. McCulloch moved to Nashville and later joined the AMA's Race Relations Department. Margaret C. McCulloch, "Excerpts on the Nashville Years," handwritten statement by McCulloch, box 1, folder 5, Margaret C. McCulloch Papers, Amistad Research Center.

83. Ernest Hooper to Hollis F. Price, 24 June 1979, Hollis Price Family Papers, Amistad Research Center; Mary Louise Wright to F. L. Brownlee, 11 May 1944, box 150, folder 19, LeMoyne-Owen College; Meier and Slocum, "Tougaloo College Revisited," 30; Hollis F. Price to Galen R. Weaver, 6 October 1946, box 151, folder 10, LeMoyne-Owen College; Crisis 36 (February 1929): 68.

84. Jones and Richardson, Talladega College, 121; Talladegan 57 (November 1939): 1; Chicago Defender, 20 February 1943; Adam D. Beittel to John H. Johnson of Ebony, 14 July 1951, Adam D. Beittel Papers, TC/Adm. 4/13/2/53; Lillian Voorhees to Helen Voorhees, 24 May 1943, Lillian Voorhees Papers; Franklin, Mirror to America, 59–60.

85. For a perceptive view of race relations on black campuses by a white scholar who taught at Tougaloo, Fisk, and Morgan State University, and visited many black campuses see, Meier, White Scholar and the Black Community, 52–72. Meier identified the following article as being from Talladega. A Former Faculty Wife, "A Note on Intergroup Conditioning and Conflict among an Interracial Faculty at a Negro College," Social Forces 27 (October 1948): 430–33.

86. In addition to Bond, already a recognized scholar, the faculty included Charles W. Buggs, biology; Allison Davis, sociology; S. Randolph Edmonds, dramatics; Frederick Hall, music; Norman A. Holmes, religion and philosophy; Clarence T. Mason, chemistry; and Randolph Moses, English. List of faculty, May 1936, part III, reel 3, Horace Mann Bond Papers; U.S. Department of Interior, Office of Education, Education of Negro Teachers, Bulletin no. 10 (Washington, DC, 1933), 113; V. V. Oak, "Some Outstanding Defects in Institutions of Higher Education for Negroes," School and Society 46 (18 September 1937): 357–59; Edwin R. Embree to Edgar B. Stern, 14 June 1934, box 141, folder 1, Julius Rosenwald Fund Papers; Bond to Walter L. Wright, 13 April 1936, part III, reel e, Horace Mann Bond Papers.

87. A list of the 1936 faculty in the Horace Mann Bond Papers named only one woman, Wilhelmina E. Carothers, the librarian. Horace Mann Bond to Walter L. Wright, 13 April 1936, Bond to W. S. Nelson, 13 April 1936, List of Faculty, May 1936, part III, reel 2, Horace Mann Bond Papers; Horace Mann Bond to Will W. Alexander, 13 June 1934, part III, reel 2, Horace Mann Bond Papers.

88. Brownlee gave Bond most of the credit for recruiting faculty and teachers and outlining the academic program since Alexander was rarely on campus. He was not even there for opening day. Fred L. Brownlee, "Dillard University up to 1945," Dillard Bulletin 10 (October 1945): 6; Lundy, "Study of the Transition from White to Black Presidents," 214.

89. AM 79 (July 1925): 157; list of graduates attending graduate or professional

school, Buell G. Gallagher Papers, TC/Adm. 4/11/4/3; Jones and Richardson, *Talladega College,* 124.

90. "First Annual Report of the Sixth President of Talladega College Covering the Academic Year 1933–34," mimeograph copy, Buell G. Gallagher Papers, TC/Adm. 4/11/4/2/1; Buell G. Gallagher, *Straight ahead in Heavy Seas: The Second Annual Report of the Sixth President of Talladega College Covering the Academic Year 1934–1935* (Talladega, 1935), 11–15; Lillian Voorhees to Friends All, 30 January 1921, box 17, folder 6, Lillian W. Voorhees Papers; Harold C. Warren to F. L. Brownlee, 5 December 1949, box 109, folder 7; Brownlee to Vernon L. Wharton, 12 August 1946, box 108, folder 3, Tougaloo College; Margaret C. McCulloch to Dear Family, 12 September 1958, box 1, folder 6; McCulloch to Dear Mother, 1942, box 1, folder 5, Margaret C. McCulloch Papers; *Talladegan* 55 (January 1938): 3; *Talladegan* 56 (November 1938): 6–7; *Talladegan* 57 (November 1939): 9; Richardson, "Mary E. Branch," 58.

91. Hilda A. Davis to Mildred Martin, 11 March 1937; Davis to E. H. Gibbs, 23 March 1938, Dean of Women, TC/Adm. 8/4/6/2/1/1/1; Lyndon B. Johnson to Richard R. Brown, 7 December 1935, box 8; Mary E. Branch to Johnson, 11 March 1936; Lyndon B. Johnson, "Special Report of Negro Activity of the National Youth Administration in Texas," 5 March 1936, box 9; Juanita J. Sadler to Johnson, 9 April 1936, box 8; Beatrice Denmark to Richard R. Brown, 9 February 1937, box 6, NYA Papers, Lyndon B. Johnson Papers, LBJ Library, Austin, Texas.

92. D'alelia Ransom, a Talladega student, charged that Greek organizations on campus had "much the same thoughts as the Ku Klux Klaners: " 'I will not admit you because of looks, color, or dress.'" *Talladega Student* 15 (November 1937): 3; Langston Hughes, "Cowards from the Colleges," *Crisis* 41 (August 1934): 226; *(Talladega) Mule's Ear* 2 (February 1926): 3; *(Talladega) Mule's Ear* 2 (March 1926): 4; Jones and Richardson, *Talladega College,* 91–93; Shackles, *Reminiscences of Huston-Tillotson College,* 27–29, 39–40; Mabel Clayton Williams, "History of Tillotson College," 105–6; Heintze, *Private Black Colleges in Texas,* 104, 169; Richardson, "Mary E. Branch," 61; Horace Mann Bond to W. S. Nelson, 6 May 1936, part III, reel 2, Horace Mann Bond Papers; *(Talladega) Mule's Ear* 11 (February 1935): 4–5; Buell G. Gallagher, "Negro Youth and the Struggle for Democracy," address to youth chapter of NAACP, Atlanta, 3 October 1942, Buell G. Gallagher Papers, TC/Adm. 1/11/5; *Talladega Student* 15 (November 1937): 4.

93. For more on the Fisk revolt, see Raymond Wolters, *The New Negro on Campus: Black College Rebellions of the 1920s* (Princeton, NJ, 1975), 29–69, and Richardson, *History of Fisk University,* 84–100. It should be noted that white Fayette A. McKenzie who was ousted was replaced by another white man, Thomas E. Jones, who was generally popular with both students and alumni.

94. Wolters, *New Negro on Campus;* Laura H. Bates, Teacher's Record, Amistad Research Center; *Talladega Student* 15 (November 1937): 10; *Talladega Student* 16 (November 1938): 12.

95. *(Talladega) Mule's Ear* 9 (April 1933): 9; *Talladegan* 52 (January 1935): 15; *Talladega Student* 12 (February 1936): 20; *Talladegan* 55 (May 1938): 16; *Crisis* 44 (March

1937): 91; *Crisis* 45 (November 1938): 368; *Crisis* 48 (February 1941): 55; *Crisis* 49 (May 1942): 170; Heintze, *Private Black Colleges in Texas,* 105; *Talladega Student* 16 (December 1938): 7; *Talladega Student* 16 (June 1939): 18; *Crisis,* 43 (December 1936): 378.

96. *AM* 84 (13 March 1930): 344; *Crisis* 37 (February 1930): 60; Mary E. Branch to Father O'Donnell, 3 February 1933, Mary E. Branch Papers, Downs-Jones Library, Huston-Tillotson College, Austin, Texas; *(Talladega) Mule's Ear* 9 (April–May 1933): 10; *Talladegan* 52 (May 1935): 3; *Talladegan* 54 (May 1937): 11; *(Pittsburgh) Courier,* 14 December 1935.

97. Lundy, "Study of the Transition from White to Black Presidents," 653; Hugh L. McElderry to Julius Rosenwald, 24 June 1929, 17 July 1929, and 26 July 1929, box 355, folder 1, Julius Rosenwald Fund Papers.

98. Walter White to Dear Fred and George, 1 April 1940, box 148, folder 6; Fred L. Brownlee to White, 22 April 1940, box 148, folder 6; Charter of Incorporation of board of trustees of LeMoyne College, 8 May 1934, box 154, folder 11; C. Arthur Bruce to Brownlee, 29 December 1943, box 150, folder 14, LeMoyne-Owen College; *LeMoynite* 48 (May 1967): 3.

99. Richardson, "Edgar B. Stern," 328–42; Klein, *Passion for Sharing,* 203–5, 210; Dykeman and Stokely, *Seeds of Southern Change,* 169–70.

100. *Crisis* 27 (April 1924): 263; Theodore K. Lawless statement, 6 December 1970, box 92, folder 11, Dillard University; Washington *Evening Star,* 5 September 1970; *Talladega Student* 33 (November 1954): 4; "Skin Wizard of the World," *Ebony* 1 (February 1946): 7–13; *Chicago Defender,* 8 May 1971.

101. Buell G. Gallagher to Charles Sternberg, 22 June 1962, Herman H. Long Papers, TC/Adm. 4/15/12/285; Ruth A. Morton to Ralph R. Shrader, 29 August 1959, box 329, General Secretary Correspondence; Lillian Voorhees to Dear Friends, 1925, box 17, folder 6, Lillian Voorhees Papers; undated clipping, probably around 1950, *(Jackson) Clarion Ledger; (Straight College) Crimson Courier,* January 1933, 3; Hollis F. Price to F. L. Brownlee, 20 November 1943, box 150, folder 13, LeMoyne College.

102. Albert W. Dent to Editor, 24 January 1972, box 5, folder 1, Albert W. and Ernestine Jessie C. Dent Papers, Amistad Research Center; *(Des Moines) Iowa Bystander,* 7 May 1942; *(Knoxville) East Tennessee News,* 7 May 1942; Mary E. Branch to Fred L. Brownlee, 23 November 1942, Huston-Tillotson; Lillian W. Voorhees, "A Program of Speech Education for Talladega College: The Report of a Type B. Project" (PhD diss., Teachers College, Columbia University, 1943), 6; Kimball and Pearsall, *Talladega Story,* 120; Hilda A. Davis to Ola Mae Hitt, 24 March 1948, Dean of Women Papers, TC/Adm. 8/4/6/2/1/9/2; Davis to Roy Cunningham, 3 February 1948, Dean of Women Papers, TC/Adm. 8/4/6/2/1/4/2; *Talladega Student* 27 (March 1950): 3.

103. *Talladega Student* 19 (November 1941): 10; Gallagher's statement on AMA Facts and Figures Form, 1942, AMAA, Addendum; LeMoyne Social Living Questionnaire, 19 March 1942, box 149, folder 15, LeMoyne-Owen College; *Missionary Herald* 140 (April 1944): 12.

104. Brownlee and Morton, *Shackled Still,* 27; Judson L. Cross to F. L. Brownlee, 25 October 1941, box 106, folder 21, Tougaloo College; *Crisis* 51 (August 1944): 260; LeMoyne enrollment figures, 1943–44, box 151, folder 1, LeMoyne-Owen College; *Talladegan* 63 (November 1945): 5.

105. Brownlee gave salary for top professors for 1944 as follows: Talladega, $2,850 with house; Dillard, $3,300 without house; LeMoyne, $2,400 without house; Tillotson, $2,400 without house; and Tougaloo, $2,100 without house. The lowest salary was $1,800 without housing at Tougaloo. F. L. Brownlee, "Proposed Field Budget for 1945–1946," box 326, General Secretary Correspondence; James T. Cater to George W. Crawford, 9 March 1945, James T. Cater Papers, TC/Adm. 4/12/2/7; Hollis F. Price to F. L. Brownlee, 22 December 1942, box 150, folder 5, LeMoyne-Owen College; F. L. Brownlee to Judson L. Cross, 19 April 1944, box 107, folder 7; Louis M. Hicks to Marguerite Dixon, 16 June 1942, box 106, folder 25, Tougaloo College; F. L. Brownlee to James Watson, 12 November 1943, box 324, General Secretary Correspondence.

106. Hollis Price to Leo Wolman, 1 August 1943, Hollis Price Family Papers; F. L. Brownlee to John A. Hanna, 26 July 1944, box 325, General Secretary Correspondence.

107. F. L. Brownlee to Warren Pickett, 26 March 1941, General Secretary Correspondence; Judson L. Cross to Brownlee, 21 March 1941, box 106, folder 16; Brownlee to Cross, 27 March 1941, box 106, folder 16; Brownlee to Cross, 23 April 1942, box 106, folder 24; Brownlee to Cross, 19 April 1944, box 107, folder 7, Tougaloo College; Mary E. Branch to Ruth A. Morton, 20 October 1940, Huston-Tillotson; *Missionary Herald* 142 (November 1946): 22–23.

108. The final $500,000 was transferred from the university's building fund. *Dillard Bulletin* 11 (February 1947): 4; Joe M. Richardson, "Albert W. Dent: A Black New Orleans Hospital and University Administrator," *Louisiana History* 38 (Summer 1996): 320–21.

109. Buell G. Gallagher, "A Memorandum, Submitted to the Presidents of Colleges gathered at Tuskegee Institute," 19 April 1943, to discuss a proposal for a United College Drive, TC/Fin. 6/2/1/1, Talladega College; F. L. Brownlee to Robert Patterson, 27 November 1944, box 325, General Secretary Correspondence; A. D. Beittel, Questionnaire for 1949 UNCF campaign, 20 October 1948, TC/Fin. 6/4/24/1, Talladega College; *Missionary Herald* 142 (June 1946): 37.

110. Freshman News Sheet (mimeograph), 1 (30 April 1947): 4; Talladega College Trustees' minutes, 2 December 1947, TC/Adm. 3/3/2/2; *Dillard Bulletin* 12 (February 1948): 3; Drewry and Doermann, *Stand and Prosper,* 75; William H. Jones, "Annual Report of the President of Tillotson College to the Board of Trustees," 5 May 1949, Huston-Tillotson; Shackles, *Reminiscences of Huston-Tillotson College,* 54.

111. Talladega College faculty meeting minutes, 14 October 1947, Records of the Faculty, TC/Adm. 7/3/6; Tougaloo Faculty to AMA executive committee, 18 October 1951, box 109, folder 14; William M. Bender to Philip M. Widenhouse, 28 December 1950, box 109, folder 20, Tougaloo College.

112. For discussion of the fate of Tougaloo, see: P. H. Easom to Samuel C. Kincheloe, 9 November 1951, box 3, folder 5; Easom to Kincheloe, 14 January 1952, box 3, folder 6; Harold C. Warren to Kincheloe, 30 May 1953, box 3, folder 10; Philip M. Widenhouse to Kincheloe, 1 November 1951, box 3, folder 5; Kincheloe to Widenhouse, 10 December 1951, box 3, folder 5; Kincheloe to Charlton L. Lee, 19 November 1953, box 3, folder 11, Samuel C. Kincheloe Papers; David G. Sansing, *Making Haste Slowly: The Troubled History of Higher Education in Mississippi* (Jackson, MS, 1990), 70, 122, 154; Hollis F. Price to F. L. Brownlee, 19 December 1944, 24 December 1944, and 14 April 1947, box 151, folders 5 and 11, LeMoyne-Owen College.

113. Anderson and Moss, *Dangerous Donations,* 218; Luker, *Social Gospel in Black and White,* 113; Jones and Richardson, *Talladega College,* 99–100; Margaret Washington [Mrs. B. T. W.] to E. C. Silsby, 24 January 1916, Margaret Montgomery Papers, box 8, Talladega College Archives; *AM* 69 (November 1908): 282; Maxine D. Jones, "Edwin Chalmers Silsby and Talladega College," 271–87.

114. *Missionary Herald* 139 (March 1943): 40; B. G. Gallagher to Cy W. Record, 16 October 1942, Buell G. Gallagher Papers, TC/Adm. 4/11/2/70/5; Gallagher, undated rough draft of Report to the Trustees of Talladega College on the Opening of the Seventy-Sixth Academic Year, Buell G. Gallagher Papers, TC/Adm. 4/11/2/96; *Talladegan* 58 (May 1941): 11; *Chicago Defender,* 20 February 1943.

115. Shackles, *Reminiscences of Huston-Tillotson College,* 24, 29; Mary E. Branch, "President's Annual Report for the Year 1942–43" (Brochure, Tillotson, 1943); *Crisis* 50 (February 1943): 58; *New Handbook of Texas,* 1:701; A. W. Dent to Edwin R. Embree, 18 September 1945, box 193, folder 1, Julius Rosenwald Fund Papers; Herman H. Long to A. W. Dent, 16 February 1945, box 1, folder 6, Race Relations Department, UCBHMA.

116. Fred L. Brownlee to W. A. Bender, 4 December 1946, box 108, folder 7; Bender to Brownlee, 17 December 1946, box 108, folder 7, Tougaloo College; Hollyday, *On the Heels of Freedom,* 146–47. For more detail on Tougaloo's civil rights activities, see: Clarice T. Campbell and Oscar A. Rogers Jr., *Mississippi: The View from Tougaloo* (Jackson, MS, 1979).

117. Brownlee thought joining a black ministerial association was a good idea. When white president Harold Warren went to Tougaloo in 1947, Brownlee suggested he do so as a means "to break over race lines." Helen P. Desort (for Brownlee) to Harold C. Warren, 23 July 1947, box 108, folder 16, Tougaloo College; A. D. Beittel to W. L. Baker, 8 March 1946, TC/Adm. 4/13/2/112; Beittel to J. L. Cross, 5 December 1946, TC/Adm. 4/14/2/127.

118. Beittel to R. F. Blackford, 7 February 1948 and 3 January 1950, TC/Adm. 4/13/2/113; Beittel to J. E. Folsom, 23 June 1947, TC/Adm. 4/13/2.62; Beittel to E. Persons, 21 July 1951, TC/Adm. 4/13/2/62; Beittel to E. Connor, 7 March 1947, TC/Adm. 4/13/2/123.

119. P. R. Adams to A. D. Beittel, 24 August 1949, TC/Adm. 1/13/2/5; Beittel to Mrs. J. C. Boyers, 18 April 1949, TC/Adm. 1/13/2/5; Jones and Richardson, *Talladega College,* 146.

120. Hollis F. Price, LeMoyne president who was in Texas canvassing for the UNCF in May 1948, said Truman's civil rights program was making collections difficult. Hollis F. Price to F. L. Brownlee, 17 May 1948, box 151, folder 13, LeMoyne-Owen College; S. B. Wilson to A. D. Beittel, 17 April 1948; Beittel to Wilson, 19 April 1948; Wilson to O. E. Maurer, 31 August 1948, TC/Adm. 4/13/1/120; *Talladega Daily Home,* 13 April 1948.

121. Beittel also tenaciously attacked segregation in professional education associations including the SACCS. In 1949 he presented his case at the SACSS meeting in Houston, Texas. In a speech that foreshadowed the 1954 Brown case, he said, "to insist on *separate* education is to make *equal* education impossible." Even worse than the flagrant differential in public funds for black and white schools, he added, was "the assumption of inferiority which underlies the 'separate but equal' doctrine." Several black presidents wrote thanking him. Jones and Richardson, *Talladega College,* 148–49.

122. *Talladega Student* 26 (May 1949): 15–16; A. D. Beittel to Arthur D. Shores, 18 February 1949, Adam D. Beittel Papers, TC/Adm. 4/13/2/74; Jones and Richardson, *Talladega College,* 146; Margaret H. Scott, "The Miracle of Dixie, Story of My Life in Alabama, Mississippi, and Kentucky" (typescript, 1977), Margaret H. Scott Papers.

123. Jones and Richardson, *Talladega College,* 153; Fred L. Brownlee, "Yesterday and Tomorrow," 8–9, 70–71; Harold C. Warren to F. L. Brownlee, 28 April 1950, box 109, folder 8, Tougaloo College; Walter R. Allen and Joseph O. Jewell, "A Backward Glance Forward: Past, Present, and Future Perspectives on Historically Black Colleges and Universities," *Review of Higher Education* 25 (Spring 2002): 249; Drewry and Doermann, *Stand and Prosper,* 114–15.

124. Tillotson became Huston-Tillotson in 1952, Tougaloo became Tougaloo-Southern in 1954, and LeMoyne joined with Owen to become LeMoyne-Owen in 1968.

125. Allen and Jewell, "A Backward Glance Forward," 242.

CHAPTER 7

1. Robert L. Carter to Herman H. Long, 6 December 1955, box 23, folder 13; Carter to Philip M. Widenhouse, 20 January 1956, box 23, folder 14, Race Relations Department, UCBHMA; *(New York) Herald Tribune,* 28 July 1954.

2. *AM* 78 (December 1924): 344; *AM* 83 (April 1929): 505; *Eighty-Fourth Annual Report of the AMA* (1930), 17.

3. *Eighty-Fifth Annual Report of the AMA* (1931), 13–14; *Crisis* 40 (August 1931): 271; F. L. Brownlee to Edgar B. Stern, 3 March 1931, box 191, folder 8, Julius Rosenwald Fund Papers; *AM* 86 (4 February 1932): 136; *Eighty-Ninth Annual Report of the AMA* (1935), 4–6; F. L. Brownlee to Dr. Frazier and the Unity Committee, 23 December 1936, General Secretary Correspondence.

4. In 1944, Brownlee and Truman Douglass of the Board of Home Missions visited the Prince George Hotel in New York City in an unsuccessful attempt to con-

vince the manager to desegregate. Brownlee wrote that they left the manager uncomfortable. "We did not give him 'a piece of our mind,' but rather talked to him in ways that leave anyone uncomfortable when he makes himself party to basic human injustice. I confess it also made me sad at heart, and Truman was astounded to find New York behind South Louis [Saint Louis], as he put it." F. L. Brownlee to Charles S. Johnson, 30 October 1944, box 238, Race Relations Department, AMAA, Addendum.

5. Brownlee, *Perplexing Realities,* 13–15; Louis M. Hicks to W. W. Alexander, 25 April 1941, box 237, folder 3; S. A. Moffat to F. L. Brownlee, 20 June 1939, box 237, folder 1, Race Relations Department, AMAA, Addendum; F. L. Brownlee to Hon. Roy E. Ayers, 8 October 1940, General Secretary Correspondence.

6. Brownlee, "Yesterday and Tomorrow"; Fred L. Brownlee, "The Department of Race Relations," typescript, April 1953, Race Relations Department, AMAA, Addendum.

7. Edwin R. Embree to F. L. Brownlee, 22 November 1939, box 163, folder 7, Julius Rosenwald Fund Papers; Charles S. Johnson, introduction of Ruth Morton at Race Relations Institute, 27 July 1949, Race Relations Department, UCBHMA; F. L. Brownlee, "Yesterday and Tomorrow."

8. Johnson's biographers have agreed with Brownlee; for example, see Patrick J. Gilpin and Marybeth Gasman, *Charles S. Johnson: Leadership beyond the Veil in the Age of Jim Crow* (Albany, NY, 2003), 77. Brownlee and Morton, *Shackled Still,* 3–4; Brownlee, "Yesterday and Tomorrow"; F. L. Brownlee to Albert Stauffer, 14 August 1942; Brownlee to George C. Vincent, 6 March 1941, General Secretary Correspondence; Brownlee to Irene L. Hofmeister, 5 October 1943, box 237, folder 9, Race Relations Department, AMAA, Addendum.

9. Among more prominent participants were Dr. Will W. Alexander, now president of the Julius Rosenwald Fund; Jessie Daniel Ames of the Commission on Interracial Cooperation; Edwin R. Embree; Dr. Ambrose Caliver of the U.S. Office of Education; Jackson Davis, associate director of the GEB; Lester Granger of the National Urban League; Arthur Spingarn and Walter White of the NAACP; Oswald Garrison Villard, former *Nation* editor who had issued the call for the convention which formed the NAACP; Dr. Channing H. Tobias, general secretary of the Negro Division, YMCA; and Dr. Charles S. Johnson.

10. Edwin R. Embree to Charles S. Johnson, 31 October 1941, box 163, folder 7; List of Persons Planning To Attend the Seminar on American Racialism on January 16, 1942, and Summary of the Proceedings of the Seminar on Racialism, 16 January 1942, box 163, folder 7, Julius Rosenwald Fund Papers; Brownlee, *New Day Ascending,* 246–50; John Egerton, *Speak Now against the Day: The Generation before the Civil Rights Movement in the South* (Chapel Hill, 1995), 48; Brownlee and Morton, *Shackled Still,* 15.

11. The AMA had long ago turned its black churches over to the Church Extension Division and now was to do the same with American Indian churches. It was also to give up white schools in the South and its Puerto Rican mission. Brownlee and

Morton, *Shackled Still*, 16; F. L. Brownlee to Mrs. F. B. Riggs, 7 August 1942, General Secretary Correspondence; Buell G. Gallagher to Edwin R. Embree, 24 January 1942, box 355, folder 2; Embree to Gallagher, 2 February 1942, box 355, folder 2; F. L. Brownlee to Embree, 30 April 1942, box 163, folder 10, Julius Rosenwald Fund Papers; AMA Division executive committee minutes, 26 January 1942, AMAA, Addendum.

12. Brownlee, *New Day Ascending*, 246; Brownlee and Morton, *Shackled Still*, 16; F. L. Brownlee to Charles S. Johnson, 10 November 1943, box 237, folder 11; Brownlee to Mabel H. Gray, 29 November 1944, box 238, Race Relations Department, AMAA, Addendum; Fred L. Brownlee, "A Century of Christian Action," typescript, 26 May 1946, Frederick L. Brownlee Papers.

13. Buell G. Gallagher, Talladega College president, told Edwin R. Embree that "everybody in our camp," including Brownlee, thought amalgamation might be the eventual answer to the racial question. He quoted Brownlee as saying, "When we get integration, then amalgamation will normally and naturally take care of itself." That is exactly what white southerners feared. Buell G. Gallagher to Edwin R. Embree, 20 November 1940, box 355, folder 1, Julius Rosenwald Fund Papers; Brownlee, *Seeking a Way*, 5; F. L. Brownlee, "Century of Christian Action"; Ferdinand Q. Blanchard to F. L. Brownlee, 20 January 1945, box 238, Race Relations Department, AMAA, Addendum.

14. F. L. Brownlee, Proposed Field Budget for 1945–46," box 326; Brownlee to H. H. Thayer, 18 December 1944, box 326; Brownlee to Claude A. Barnett, 8 October 1946, box 327, General Secretary Correspondence.

15. Patrick J. Gilpin, a Johnson biographer, suggests that the race relations program was really the brainchild of Embree, Johnson, and Will W. Alexander, who decided in 1942 to initiate a more active race relations program. During the same year, the AMA established a race relations division and by the end of the year, the AMA, Fisk, and the Rosenwald Fund had come together. Patrick J. Gilpin, "Charles S. Johnson: An Intellectual Biography" (PhD diss., Vanderbilt University, 1973), 489–92.

16. *Fisk News* 8 (November–December 1934): 17; Egerton, *Speak Now against the Day*, 91–92; F. L. Brownlee to Edwin R. Embree, 25 September 1942, box 163, folder 10; Embree to Brownlee, 28 September 1942, box 163, folder 10, Julius Rosenwald Fund Papers; Board of Home Missions executive committee minutes, 21–22 September 1942, 7–8 December 1942, AMAA, Addendum.

17. Richardson, *History of Fisk University*, 137–38; Richard Robbins, *Sidelines Activist: Charles S. Johnson and the Struggle for Civil Rights* (Jackson, MS, 1996), 31–32; *New York Times*, 28 October 1956; Ernest V. Burgess et al., "Charles Spurgeon Johnson: Social Scientist, Editor, and Educational Statesman," *Phylon* 17 (Fourth Quarter 1956): 317–25.

18. Robbins, *Sidelines Activist*, 33; *Opportunity* 25 (Winter, 1946): 26; Richardson, *History of Fisk University*, 138.

19. See Robbins, *Sidelines Activist*, 34–36, for a discussion of the dilemma of a black scholar dependent upon white philanthropy and friends for support. Robbins

claims that Johnson was "co-opted to lend his considerable influence to the movers and shakers in the making of public policy without being able to be a central participant in the ultimate decision-making process." M. R. Werner, *Julius Rosenwald: The Life of a Practical Humanitarian* (New York, 1939), 170–73; *Crisis* 22 (August 1921): 180.

20. Richardson, *History of Fisk University*, 138; Robbins, *Sidelines Activist*, 37; *Crisis* 35 (August 1928): 270; Nathan Irvin Huggins, *Harlem Renaissance* (New York, paperback, 1973), 29; James Weldon Johnson, *Along This Way: The Autobiography of James Weldon Johnson* (New York, 1938), 376.

21. When Hurston moved to New York she sought out Johnson, who took her and many other young writers under his wing. He encouraged her to stay in New York, helped her find a job, and often invited her to dinner. Mrs. Marie Johnson sometimes gave Hurston cab fare so she could accept the invitations. Robert E. Hemenway, *Zora Neale Hurston: A Literary Biography* (Urbana, IL, 1980), 9–10.

22. W. F. Ogburn to Thomas E. Jones, 31 August 1929; Charles S. Johnson to Thomas E. Jones, 16 October 1929, Faculty and Staff Letters, Fisk University; August Meier, "Black Sociologist in White America," *Social Forces* 56 (September 1977): 260–65.

23. Richardson, *History of Fisk University*, 137–41; Robbins, *Sidelines Activist*, 45; *New York Times*, 2 July 1927.

24. In 1936, Johnson said "it is not enough merely to wait watchfully for times slow motion to cure social ills. . . . There are steps that can be taken immediately to correct old ills." Gilpin and Gasman, *Charles S. Johnson*, 180, 71–72, 74, 77, 249, 254.

25. Egerton, *Speak Now against the Day*, 91–93, 285; Edgar T. Thompson, "Sociology and Sociological Research in the South," *Social Forces* 23 (March 1945): 364–65; D. D. Jones, "Cultural Obligations of the Faculty in a Negro Liberal Arts College," *Association of American Colleges Bulletin* 25 (March 1939): 67; John Knox, "Charles Spurgeon Johnson," *Advance* (September 1943): 13.

26. The staff in June 1943 consisted of: Johnson, director; Ira DeA. Reid, associate director; Horace Mann Bond, collaborator on special projects; Harold M. Kingsley, part-time common ground worker; Herman H. Long, common ground worker; Charles R. Lawrence Jr., research and editorial work; Frank. D. Dorsey, common ground worker; Eunice D. Dorsey, common ground worker; and Anne R. Wesley, secretary and librarian. Charles S. Johnson, Memorandum on the Race Relations Department, 23 June 1943, box 247, Race Relations Department, AMAA, Addendum.

27. Long was at the University of Michigan from 1939 to 1943. He completed his dissertation and earned the Ph.D. in 1949. Jones and Richardson, *Talladega College*, 187–88; J. C. James to Herman H. Long, 25 September 1972, box 5, folder 1; Herman H. Long, "Doorway to Freedom," speech to AMA, 15 February 1950, box 1, folder 3, Herman H. Long Papers, Amistad Research Center; *Crisis* 46, (June 1939): 178–80.

28. Robbins, *Sidelines Activist*, 46; Charles S. Johnson, General Statement by the

Director of the Race Relations Division of the American Missionary Association, 30 November 1943, box 1, folder 1, Race Relations Department, UCBHMA.

29. Burgess et al., "Charles Spurgeon Johnson," 322; Robbins, *Sidelines Activist*, x, 77; Egerton, *Speak Now against the Day*, 284–86.

30. Edwin Embree, president of the Rosenwald Fund, once said of Johnson, "His Colored friends scold him for being a calm student rather than a rabid reformer. . . . White people get mad at him at his presumption in understanding them and their customs better than they do." Embree quoted in Dykeman and Stokely, *Seeds of Southern Change*, 186; Robbins, *Sidelines Activist*, x.

31. Charles R. Lawrence Jr., "Bridges of Understanding, Summary of the Virginia Institute of Race Relations," 16 March 1945, box 82, folder 18, Race Relations Department, UCBHMA; Robbins, *Sidelines Activist*, 132–34, 180; Gilpin and Gasman, *Charles S. Johnson*, 144, 149; Frank Persons to Charles S. Johnson, 29 December 1944, box 238, Race Relations Department, AMAA, Addendum.

32. Cyrik K. Glyn to F. L. Brownlee, 21 January 1944, box 237, folder 15; Charles S. Johnson to Paul Davies, 28 January 1944, box 237, folder 15; Johnson to Brownlee, 19 October 1944, box 238 [no folder number], Race Relations Department, AMAA, Addendum.

33. Nicholas Lemann, *The Promised Land: The Great Black Migration and How It Changed America* (New York, 1991), 70; Chicago *Daily Tribune*, 23 June 1943, 1–3; Charles S. Johnson, "Memorandum on the Race Relations Program of the American Missionary Association," 23 June 1943, box 247, Race Relations Department, AMAA, Addendum; Kari Frederickson, *The Dixiecrat Revolt and the End of the Solid South, 1932–1968* (Chapel Hill, 2001), 34; Fred L. Brownlee to Henry C. McDowell, 18 June 1943, box 137, folder 14, Lincoln Academy, AMAA, Addendum.

34. Charles S. Johnson, "Memorandum on the Race Relations Program"; Brownlee, *Seeking a Way*, 26–29; F. L. Brownlee to R. J. Cunningham, 6 October 1943, box 237; Brownlee to Margaret C. McCulloch, 7 October 1943, box 237, Race Relations Department, AMAA, Addendum; "The Race Relations Program of the American Missionary Association," undated transcript [1945], box 13, folder 5, Race Relations Department, UCBHMA.

35. Other common ground workers included Charles Lawrence Jr., who went to Ypsilanti, Michigan, in 1944 at the request of the local Council of Social Agencies which had been dealing with problems surrounding a black housing project, and tension between black and white workers at the Ford Bomber Plant. Brownlee, *Seeking a Way*, 28; F. L. Brownlee to Charles S. Johnson, 23 October 1944, box 238; Johnson to Brownlee, 23 October 1944, box 238; Brownlee to Paul A. Davis, 3 December 1946, box 239; Hillary Bissell to Galen Weaver, 1 July 1949, box 240, Race Relations Department, AMAA, Addendum.

36. Warren E. Bow to Charles S. Johnson, 28 November 1944, box 1, folder 1; "Race Relations Program of the American Missionary Association"; Grace C. Jones to Herman Long, 15 January 1945, box 1, folder 1; Grace C. Jones, notes, 19 January 1945, box 1, folder 6, Race Relations Department, UCBHMA; Grace C. Jones to

Philip Widenhouse, 4 January 1952, box 241, Race Relations Department, AMAA, Addendum.

37. L. Maynard Catchings's report for 1946–47 indicated that common ground workers were varying from their original purpose. Catchings was hired in January 1945 as a common ground worker and field representative for the department. During 1946–47 he investigated and reported on a racial disturbance in Athens, Alabama; worked on the self-surveys in Pittsburgh and Minneapolis; assisted in planning and served as coordinator of activities for Youth Institute on Race Relations at Fisk in July 1947; participated in the Annual Race Relations Institute; served as leader for a clinic on Church and Race at the Annual Institute; and cooperated on several research projects. L. Maynard Catchings to Charles S. Johnson, 25 August 1947, box 239, Race Relations Department, AMAA, Addendum.

38. In a 1958 biographical note, Long said he "developed, supervised and conducted community self-survey projects in intergroup relations" for San Francisco, Minneapolis, and several other cities. Herman H. Long, Brief Biographical Note, 7 October 1958, box 24, folder 20, Race Relations Department, UCBHMA.

39. Raymond Bernard, "Protestant Work in Race Relations," *Interracial Review* 27 (January 1954): 6; Minutes of the advisory committee of the Race Relations Department, 1 July 1954, box 243; Herman H. Long to F. L. Brownlee, 8 October 1948, box 239, Race Relations Department, AMAA, Addendum.

40. For an excellent description of the self-survey technique, see: Race Relations Department, *Human Relations in Action,* an unnumbered twelve-page pamphlet published in 1948; Herman H. Long, "Community Research and Intergroup Adjustment," speech at Fisk University, April 1955, box 1, folder 1, Herman H. Long Papers.

41. Race Relations Department, *Human Relations in Action; Missionary Herald* 142 (June 1946): 34–35; Herman H. Long, "Ten Year Perspective on Our Work in Race Relations," 16 June 1953, box 245, Race Relations Department, AMAA, Addendum.

42. Charles S. Johnson to Sponsoring Committee, Pittsburgh Survey, 29 October 1945, box 95, folder 1, Race Relations Department, UCBHMA. Accompanying Long were Grace C. Jones, L. Maynard Catchings, John Hope II, and Charles R. Lawrence.

43. Charles S. Johnson to Sponsoring Committee, Pittsburgh Survey, 29 October 1945, box 95, folder 1, Race Relations Department, UCBHMA; Race Relations Department, *Human Relations in Action.*

44. Humphrey was elected to a one-year term on the advisory board in 1949, and reelected to a three-year term in 1950. Herman H. Long to F. L. Brownlee, 4 January 1950, box 240; Long to Gladys Williams, 20 July 1950, box 240; Long to Philip Widenhouse, 24 March 1952, box 241, Race Relations Department, AMAA, Addendum.

45. The October 1951 issue of *Women's Home Companion* published "How Minneapolis Beat the Bigots," which described the survey and credited the department

with bringing positive change. Mrs. Zoe M. MacCorquodale to Herman H. Long, 26 February 1952, box 10, folder 4; Meeting of the Steering Committee of the Minneapolis Self-Survey, 17 March 1947, box 14, folder 17, Race Relations Department, UCBHMA; *Missionary Herald* 143 (October 1947): 61; *Minneapolis Star,* 30 November 1949, 1–2; Race Relations Department, *Human Relations in Action.*

46. Although Long was the supervisor of the project, John Hope II and Galen Weaver did much of the groundwork and guided volunteer workers. Baltimore Commission on Human Relations, "An American City in Transition: The Baltimore Community Self-Survey in Intergroup Relations," unpublished 264-page report, Race Relations Department, AMAA, Addendum.

47. *(Baltimore) Afro-American,* 23 January 1954; *(Baltimore) Evening Sun,* 2 December 1953, 61; William C. Rogers to Herman H. Long, 1 August 1953, box 1, folder 6, Herman H. Long Papers; AMA division committee minutes, 21 April 1954, box 363, General Secretary Correspondence; Irving Gitlin to Herman H. Long, 8 December 1954, box 98, folder 8, Race Relations Department, UCBHMA; Herman H. Long to Philip Widenhouse, 16 September 1954, box 241; Widenhouse to Long, 23 March 1955, box 241, Race Relations Department, AMAA, Addendum.

48. F. L. Brownlee, Proposed Field Budget for 1945–46, box 326, General Secretary Correspondence; Brownlee, "Yesterday and Tomorrow"; Charles S. Johnson to F. L. Brownlee, 27 April 1944, box 238, Race Relations Department, AMAA Addendum; Ruth Morton to Earnest A. Smith, 25 July 1944, box 13, folder 10, Lincoln School; Robbins, *Sidelines Activist,* 79; Herman H. Long, "New Directions in Race Relations," *Classmate* [periodical of the General Board of Education, Methodist Church] 57 (April 1950): 8–10; Gilpin, "Charles S. Johnson: An Intellectual Biography," 533.

49. Gilpin and Gasman, *Charles S. Johnson,* 187–88; Gilpin, "Charles S. Johnson: An Intellectual Biography," 528–37; *Pittsburgh Courier,* 12 July 1947; Charles S. Johnson to Gerald W. Johnson, 30 April 1947, box 38, folder 5, Race Relations Department, UCBHMA; Egerton, *Speak Now against the Day,* 285.

50. *Nashville Banner,* 30 July 1945, 1–2; Benjamin J. Davis telegram to Johnson, quoted in *New York Sun,* 12 July 1947, and *(Nashville) Tennessean,* 12 July 1947.

51. A few of the many lecturers in 1948 were Will W. Alexander; Gordon W. Allport, of the Harvard department of psychology; psychologist Kenneth Clark; Edwin R. Embree; Lester Granger, executive secretary of the National Urban League; Charles H. Houston, NAACP legal counsel; Marie Jahoda of the American Jewish Committee; A. A. Livermore, executive director of the American Council on Race Relations; George S. Mitchell, regional director of the CIO political action committee; Ashley M. F. Montague, Harvard anthropologist and author of *Man's Most Dangerous Myth: The Fallacy of Race;* Henry Lee Moon of the CIO political action committee; Gene Wetfish of the Columbia University department of anthropology; Robert K. Carr, executive secretary of Truman's Committee on Civil Rights; and A. Abbot Rosen, chief of civil rights section of the United States Department of

Justice. List of lecturers and consultants taken from announcement of Race Relations Institute, 1948. Topics covered came from Announcement of The Fourth Annual Institute of Race Relations, July 1st to 19th, Race Relations Department, UCBHMA.

52. *New York Times,* 30 June 1948, 3 July 1951; *Christian Science Monitor,* 17 July 1948; *(Chicago) Daily News,* 8 July 1947; Mrs. Opal G. Gruner to Herman H. Long, 11 November 1954, box 23, folder 1, Race Relations Department, UCBHMA; Thurgood Marshall quoted in *(Nashville) Tennessean,* 7 July 1950; Charles S. Johnson, undated 1946 Summary of the Third Annual Institute of Race Relations, Race Relations Department, UCBHMA; Herman H. Long, "Ten Year Perspective on Our Work in Race Relations"; "Current: An Information Bulletin to the Constituency of the Race Relations Department of the American Missionary Association" 1 (January 1950), mimeograph copy, box 13, folder 26, Race Relations Department, UCBHMA; Charles S. Johnson to Samuel C. Kincheloe, 30 June 1953, box 3, folder 10, Samuel C. Kincheloe Papers.

53. *Christian Science Monitor,* 19 July 1948; Long, "Ten Year Perspective on Our Work in Race Relations."

54. *(Chicago Daily) News,* 8 July 1947; *(Detroit) Free Press,* 11 July 1947; Paul M. Clanton to Herman H. Long, 14 March 1949, box 239, Race Relations Department, AMAA, Addendum.

55. Hollis F. Price to Albert W. Dent, 11 August 1945, box 8, folder 35, Charles S. Johnson Papers, microfilm, Amistad Research Center; *Christian Science Monitor,* 17 July 1947.

56. Brownlee, "A Century of Christian Action"; Egerton, *Speak Now against the Day,* 354, 526–27; *(Chicago) Daily News,* 8 July 1947; *Christian Science Monitor,* 8 July 1950.

57. William H. Grayson to Charles S. Johnson, 4 November 1946, 11 April 1947, box 82, folder 1; Herman H. Long to Charles S. Johnson, 13 February 1945, box 82, folder 10, Race Relations Department, UCBHMA; *(Baltimore) Evening Sun,* 16 January 1947, 17 January 1947.

58. Margaret McCulloch spent most of her adult life trying to improve race relations. While professor of history at LeMoyne College, she lived in the community rather than on campus. In both Memphis and later Nashville, she selected housing that joined black and white neighborhoods and tried to bring the races together. After resigning from LeMoyne in 1940, she studied philosophy at the University of Virginia for a year and moved to Nashville in 1941 where she worked in a black community center and as volunteer race relations worker. In 1943, she joined the Race Relations Department. McCulloch returned to LeMoyne in 1946. Margaret McCulloch to Dear Warren and Rook, 14 March 1942, 28 October 1944, box 1, folder 5; McCulloch to Dear Mother, 2 July 1943, box 1, folder 5, Margaret McCulloch Papers.

59. *(Nashville) Tennessean,* 23 June 1948; *New York Times,* 28 June 1949; Race Relations Department, "Implementing Civil Rights: Summary Report," Sixth An-

nual Institute of Race Relations, 27 June–9 July 1949, Race Relations Department, AMAA, Addendum; Charles S. Johnson, introduction at Race Relations Institute, 1 July 1947, box 38, folder 39, Race Relations Department, UCBHMA.

60. Irving Goldaber to Ruth Morton, 27 July 1949; Morton to Goldaber, 28 July 1949, Race Relations Department, AMAA, Addendum; Participants of the Race Relations Institute 1950, box 44, folder 9, Race Relations Department, UCBHMA; Bernard Crick, "To Go South Is to Be Surprised," *Christian Science Monitor,* 8 September 1953; Herman H. Long to Howard Sprague, 1955, box 51, folder 24; Long to Philip Widenhouse, 20 October 1955, box 51, folder 24.

61. Robbins, *Sidelines Activist,* 148, 190; June Shagaloff [Field Secretary of NAACP] to Herman H. Long, 22 July 1953, box 23, folder 18, Race Relations Department, UCBHMA; *New York Times,* 11 July 1954; AMA division committee minutes, 23 June 1954, Records of the Southern Delegation at the General Council, 28 June 1954, box 245, AMAA, Addendum.

62. *New York Times,* 11 July 1954; AMA division committee minutes, 21 April 1954, box 363, General Secretary Correspondence; Herman H. Long to Philip Widenhouse, 28 July 1954, box 241, Race Relations Department, AMAA, Addendum; *Nashville Banner,* 9 July 1954; Alvin M. Rucker, "A New Approach to Equal Economic Opportunity," speech to Race Relations Institute, 9 July 1954, box 50, folder 31, Race Relations Department, UCBHMA; James P. Mitchell speech, 28 June 1955, box 251, Race Relations Department, AMAA, Addendum.

63. Charles S. Johnson, "Statesmanship in a National Crisis," opening statement at annual Race Relations Institute, 3 July 1956, box 52, folder 8; Herman H. Long to Philip Widenhouse, February 1956, box 51, folder 2; M. L. Nelson to Long, 11 March 1956, box 2, folder 11, Race Relations Department, UCBHMA; Gilpin and Gasman, *Charles S. Johnson,* 250.

64. Herman H. Long to Z. Alexander Looby, 8 April 1952, box 117, folder 1; *Paul Hayes and Herman Long v. Edwin Crutcher et al. Consisting of the Board of Park Commissioners of the City of Nashville, Tenn.,* Civil Action 1344, box 117, folder 2; C. L. Dinkins to Long, 1 December 1952, box 23, folder 11; Long to Station WMAK, 19 February 1953, box 48, folder 6; Long to Avon Williams, 2 September 1955, box 23, folder 19, Race Relations Department, UCBHMA; *(Nashville) Tennessean,* 3 February 1954.

65. Herman Long to Philip Widenhouse, 14 June 1955, box 241, Race Relations Department, AMAA, Addendum; Herman H. Long to Mrs. Sarah R. Murdy, 4 March 1957, box 3, folder 1; Long to William E. Vickery, 21 February 1958, box 26, folder 7, Race Relations Department, UCBHMA; Peter M. Bergman, *The Chronological History of the Negro in America* (New York, 1969), 545–46; Egerton, *Speak Now against the Day,* 620; Robbins, *Sidelines Activist,* 3.

66. Robbins, *Sidelines Activist,* 28; Gilpin and Gasman, *Charles S. Johnson,* 10, 31, 141.

67. Long was a treasured speaker for church groups. In 1954 he spent a week with the Connecticut Congregational Christian Conference in connection with their School of Churchmanship for Laymen, and he nearly mesmerized them. The State

Layman's Committee voted unanimously to bring him back the next year. *New York Times*, 11 July 1954; Craig G. Whitsitt to Philip M. Widenhouse, 17 March 1954, 14 March 1955, box 241, Race Relations Department, AMAA, Addendum.

68. Helen E. Amerman to Herman H. Long, 2 March 1954, 2 December 1954, box 24, folder 17; Long to Frances Levenson, 18 February 1955, box 25, folder 14; Long to Dr. Herbert L. Seamans, 24 October 1952, box 26, folder 2; T. H. McDowell to Long, 15 December 1952, box 25, folder 3; Long to Dr. Dumont F. Kenny, 24 August 1954, box 26, folder 5; Long to Sterling Brown, 14 November 1954, box 26, folder 5; Long to A. D. Henderson, 29 March 1956, box 26, folder 6; Anne Braden to Long, 3 January 1962, box 30, folder 12; Long to Lee White, 5 January 1962, box 30, folder 12; F. D. Patterson to Long, 3 August 1956, box 20, folder 18; Myles Horton to Long, 17 January 1957, box 21, folder 1; Long to Horton, 14 February 1957, box 21, folder 1, Race Relations Department, UCBHMA; Egerton, *Speak Now against the Day*, 614; *Christian Science Monitor*, 17 November 1954.

69. Herman H. Long to L. R. Bruce, 10 August 1957, box 33, folder 5; Long to Pauline Gates, 18 April 1957, box 23, folder 8; Herman H. Long, "Summary of the 15th Annual Race Relations Institute Discussion," summer 1958, box 2, folder 3; Race Relations Institute participants to Honorable Dwight D. Eisenhower, 11 July 1958, box 54, folder 5, Race Relations Department, UCBHMA; Herman H. Long, "Human Rights in the Great Society," keynote address at institute, 28 June 1965, box 4, folder 6a, Herman H. Long Papers; *Nashville Banner*, 27 June 1966; *Chattanooga Times*, 28 June 1966; AMA Division of Higher Education committee minutes, 29 October 1968, box 364, General Secretary Correspondence.

70. Katrina Marie Sanders has said the institutes were "not in keeping with the overall African American ideology" of the 1940s, 1950s, and 1960s because the institute "held itself to observing and discussing the prevalent racial issues of the day" rather than encouraging blacks actively to seek racial equality through direct action. Much of her criticism applies to the early period when there was limited direct action nationwide, and ignores later years when Long and others encouraged sit-ins, including those of Fisk students in Nashville. Many institute participants engaged in direct action in their communities before the sit-ins became popular in the 1960s. Katrina Marie Sanders, "Building Racial Tolerance through Education: The Fisk University Race Relations Institute, 1944–1969" (Ph.D. diss., University of Illinois, 1997), 224–27.

71. Gilpin and Gasman write that the institutes "gave Johnson a public forum while legitimating his position as a spokesman on the eve of the demise of statutory Jim Crow." Gilpin and Gasman, *Charles S. Johnson*, 200. Johnson statement in Race Relations Department advisory council minutes, 1 July 1950, box 243, Race Relations Department, AMAA, Addendum; Herman H. Long to Mary Evarts, 13 July 1960, box 4, folder 3; Long to Kelly Miller Smith, 13 July 1960, box 4, folder 3, Race Relations Department, UCBHMA.

72. List of sales of *People v. Property*, 29 October–31 December 1947, box 11, folder 8; Summary of Lectures, Race Relations Institute, 3–21 July 1944, Race Re-

lations Department, UCBHMA; *New York Times,* 10 December 1947; Robbins, *Sidelines Activist,* 119; Herman H. Long to Charles H. Houston, 20 November 1947, 6 December 1947; Houston to Long, 20 November 1947, 22 November 1947, 8 December 1947; Long to Susan Brandeis, 17 December 1947; Houston to Long, 19 January 1948; Houston telegram to Charles S. Johnson, 3 May 1948, box 119, folders 1, 2, 3, 6, Race Relations Department; undated news release, box 119, folder 11; Charles S. Johnson, "The Sociological Foundations of Church Action in Race Relations," undated typescript, box 13, folder 30, Race Relations Department, UCBHMA; Stephen Grant Meyer, *As Long as They Don't Move Next Door: Segregation and Racial Conflict in American Neighborhoods* (Lanham, MD, 2000), 92–95.

73. *New York Times* 6 June 1950, 7 June 1950, 13 November 1950; *In the Supreme Court of the United States, October Term 1949, Elmer W. Henderson, Appellant v. The United States of America, Interstate Commerce Commission and the Southern Railroad Company. On Appeal from the United States District Court for the District of Maryland* (Washington, DC, 1949), ii–5; Herman H. Long to Galen R. Weaver, 31 October 1949, box 240, Race Relations Department advisory committee minutes, 1 July 1950, box 243, Race Relations Department, AMAA, Addendum.

74. Herman H. Long, *Segregation in Interstate Railway Coach Travel* (Nashville, 1953), 13; Herman H. Long, Report to Philip Widenhouse, "Some Aspects of Our Race Relations Work during the Biennium," February 1956, box 51, folder 2, Race Relations Department, UCBHMA.

75. Herman H. Long to Honorable Hubert H. Humphrey, 17 May 1949, box 132, folder 1; Long to Honorable Estes Kefauver, 9 February 1953, box 132, folder 2; Kefauver to Long, 25 February 1953, box 132, folder 3; Long to Honorable Alvin R. Bush, 5 March 1953, box 132, folder 4; Hugo L. Black to Long, 13 March 1953, box 132, folder 4; Long to Dr. Max M. Kapelman, 20 February 1953, box 132, folder 3, Race Relations Department, UCBHMA.

76. Herman H. Long to Margaret McCulloch, 20 February 1953, box 10, folder 16; Phineas Indritz to Long, 10 December 1953, box 132, folder 5; Long to Indritz, 15 December 1953, box 132, folder 5; Indritz to Long, 2 July 1954, box 132, folder 6; Long to Congressman Charles Wolverton, 6 May 1954, box 132, folder 6; Testimony of Dr. Herman Long before the Committee on Interstate and Foreign Commerce, Congress of the United States, House Public Hearings, May 12, 13, 14, 1954, reprint from *Congressional Record,* 83rd Cong., 2nd Sess., 1954, 1–3, Race Relations Department, UCBHMA.

77. Thurgood Marshall to Herman H. Long, 26 September 1952, box 132, folder 1; Long to Marshall, 1 October 1952, 14 October 1952, box 132, folder 1; Robert L. Carter to Long, 24 February 1953, box 132, folder 3; Carter to Long, 22 June 1954, 22 July 1954, box 132, folder 6; Long to Carter, 9 July 1954, box 132, folder 6; Walter White to Long, 23 March 1953, box 131, folder 4; Long, Report to Philip Widenhouse, "Some Aspects of Our Race Relations Work during the Biennium"; Long to Louise Young, 3 March 1959, box 132, folder 6, Race Relations Department, UCBHMA; Interstate Commerce Commission, no. 31423, *NAACP et al. v. St. Louis–*

San Francisco Railway Company, et al., 21 December 1953, box 1, folder 6, Herman H. Long Papers; AMA division committee minutes, 6 December 1955, box 363, General Secretary Correspondence.

78. Herman H. Long to Philip Widenhouse, 30 November 1955, box 241, Race Relations Department, AMAA, Addendum; Walter Washington to Herman H. Long, 8 May 1956, box 132, folder 6, Race Relations Department, UCBHMA.

79. Edmonia W. Grant to Thomas Anderson, 27 November 1944, box 238; F. L. Brownlee to Henry S. Leiper, 12 March 1945, box 239; Charles S. Johnson to Andrew McCracken, 19 March 1945, box 238; Long, "Ten Year Perspective on Our Work in Race Relations"; *New York Times,* 2 February 1945; Herman H. Long to Grace C. Jones, 9 March 1945, box 1, folder 6, Race Relations Department, UCBHMA.

80. Margaret C. McCulloch to Dear Mother, 2 July 1943, box 1, folder 5, Margaret C. McCulloch Papers; Margaret C. McCulloch to Drs. Redd, Valien, and Long, 25 April 1957, box 10, folder 16; Herman H. Long to Patricia Herron, 10 September 1953, box 8, folder 6; Hattie M. Perry to Margaret McCulloch, 23 February 1955, box 10, folder 16; Hunter O'Dell to Herman H. Long, 22 August 1959, box 56, folder 16, Race Relations Department, UCBHMA.

81. Leroy Davis, *A Clashing of the Soul: John Hope and the Dilemma of African American Leadership and Black Higher Education in the Early Twentieth Century* (Athens, GA, 1998), 200–201, 237, 317–18; Race Relations Department, *Human Relations in Action;* Race Relations Department advisory committee minutes, 12 February 1950, Race Relations Department, AMAA, Addendum.

82. Arthur Chapin to Charles S. Johnson, 22 April 1948, box 8, folder 2, UCBHMA; Race Relations Department advisory committee minutes, 1 July 1950, box 243, Race Relations Department, AMAA, Addendum; Bergman, *Chronological History of the Negro,* 500–501, 505. For a detailed account of the causes of and participants in the Detroit riot, see: Dominic J. Capeci Jr. and Martha Wilkerson, *Layered Violence: The Detroit Rioters of 1943* (Jackson, MS, 1991).

83. *New York Times,* 4 July 1950; Herman H. Long to Philip Widenhouse, 10 November 1950, box 240; 4 March 1952, box 241; Race Relations Department advisory committee minutes, 27–28 January 1951, box 243, Race Relations Department, AMAA, Addendum.

84. John Hope II, "The Problem of Unemployment as It Relates to Negroes," 18 December 1959, box 246, Race Relations Department, AMAA, Addendum; *New York Times,* 16 January 1962; Herman H. Long, Testimony before the Special Subcommittee on Labor, U.S. House of Representatives, 15 January 1962, box 3, folder 3; Long to John Henrik Clarke, 26 January 1962, box 3, folder 4; Long to Anne Braden, 2 March 1962, box 30, folder 12, Race Relations Department, UCBHMA; Bergman, *Chronological History of the Negro,* 552, 554.

85. Race Relations Department staff meeting minutes, 13 December 1944, box 14, folder 15; Ruth A. Morton to Herman H. Long, 8 August 1947, box 1, folder 9, Race Relations Department, UCBHMA.

86. Actually the AMA and the church's Council for Social Action jointly em-

ployed Weaver. The AMA contributed $7,500 annually. Galen R. Weaver to Lemuel A. Peterson, 9 October 1946, box 239; Ray Gibbons to Weaver, 1 May 1946, box 239; Ralph H. Rouse to F. L. Brownlee, 10 July 1947, box 239, Race Relations Department, AMAA, Addendum.

87. F. L. Brownlee Memorandum, 8 July 1948, box 239; Brownlee to Herman H. Long, 1 September 1948, box 239; F. L. Brownlee to Will Frazier, and Frazier handwritten note on Brownlee's letter, 19 May 1948, box 239; Galen R. Weaver, "Report of the Religion and Race Phases of Department of Race Relations," 15 January 1951, box 244; Race Relations Department advisory committee minutes, 12 February 1950, box 243, Race Relations Department, AMAA, Addendum.

88. An undated memorandum complained that the department did not work directly with the churches, it did not have "daily religious periods or any noticeable religious emphasis," it subordinated basic Bible teaching, and its literature did not indicate affiliation with the church. In 1951 John Ives, who had been chairman of the Committee on Church and Race and had been added to the department advisory committee, still had problems with the lack of emphasis on religion and church. Unsigned, undated memorandum, [1950], box 240; Philip M. Widenhouse to Herman H. Long, 6 June 1951, box 240, Race Relations Department, AMAA, Addendum.

89. Roger G. Mastrude to Charles S. Johnson and Herman H. Long, 22 January 1948, box 1, folder 10, Race Relations Department, UCBHMA; Board of Home Missions executive committee minutes, 28–29 September 1948, box 244; Committee on Church and Race minutes, 21 April 1948, box 243; Race Relations Department advisory committee minutes, 12 February 1950, box 243, Race Relations Department, AMAA, Addendum; F. L. Brownlee to Charles S. Johnson, 1950, box 29, folder 10, Charles S. Johnson Papers; Herman H. Long, *Fellowship for Whom: A Study of Racial Inclusiveness in Congregational Christian Churches* (New York, 1958), 2; Reports of the Evaluations Committee, Race Relations Department, American Missionary Association Division, Board of Home Missions, Congregational and Christian Churches, 20–22 June 1956, box 246, Race Relations Department, AMAA, Addendum; Wesley A. Hotchkiss to Herman H. Long, 19 September 1960, box 4, folder 3, Race Relations Department, UCBHMA.

90. Beulah T. Whitby to Herman H. Long, 17 February 1959, box 3, folder 10; Helen Fuller to Long, 19 February 1959, box 3, folder 10; C. C. Furnas to Herman H. Long, 13 November 1959, box 3, folder 13; James A. Dombrowski to Long, 22 July 1959, box 20, folder 8; James C. Evans to Long, 14 January 1960, box 4, folder 1; Evans to Harold Fleming, 18 January 1960, box 4, folder 1; Long to T. K. Lawless, 5 February 1959, box 30, folder 10; Long to Fowler McCormick, 5 February 1959, box 30, folder 10; Long to Mayor Thomas L. Cummings, 8 August 1949, box 25, folder 2; Harland Randolph and Timothy Jenkins to Long, 5 July 1961, box 4, folder 12; Long to Esther Stamats, 20 December 1960, box 4, folder 5; Emma Wheeler to Long, 20 February 1961, box 4, folder 7, Race Relations Department, UCBHMA.

91. Herman H. Long to George Schermer, 2 July 1959, box 3, folder 12; Long to

James E. Allen, 23 January 1964, box 3, folder 11; Long to Rufus A. Clement, 1 July 1958, 2 July 1958, box 2, folder 3, Herman H. Long Papers.

92. Duke University attempted to secure the AMA archives for its library, but the AMA concluded that they should be located at a black college and deposited them at Fisk. R. H. Woody to F. L. Brownlee, 1 March 1944, box 234; Brownlee to Woody, 19 April 1944, box 234; Board of Home Missions executive committee minutes, 11–12 April 1944, box 234, General Secretary Correspondence.

93. In his proposal for the Amistad Research Center, Johnson said it would have the following functions: to conduct research and surveys on race relations in the tradition of the earlier department; to house and superintend the AMA archives and continue collections; to conduct a publishing program; and to conduct consultations, conferences, and other meetings to assist in integration. Clifton H. Johnson, "The Amistad Center," undated proposal in box 364, General Secretary Correspondence; Clifton H. Johnson, "A Report to the Division of Higher Education and the American Missionary Association," 30 January 1967, box 247; announcement, "Research Center Established in Nashville," 26 September 1966, box 241, Race Relations Department, AMAA, Addendum; Division of Higher Education and AMA committee minutes, 30 January 1967, box 364, General Secretary Correspondence.

CHAPTER 8

1. Probably the clearest discussion of the relationship between the AMA and the Board of Home Missions and later the United Church Board for Homeland Ministries is BHM treasurer and executive vice president Howard E. Spragg's interviews with Clifton H. Johnson. Howard E. Spragg interviews with Clifton H. Johnson, 21 October 1987 and 28 December 1989, Clifton H. Johnson Papers, Amistad Research Center.

2. A Guide to the Arrangement of the American Missionary Association Archives, Addendum, Records 1858–1991, Amistad Research Center.

3. The tension between Brownlee, who was accustomed to running the AMA, and the powerful treasurer Frazier, both strong-willed and accustomed to having their way, was sometimes intense. Brownlee claimed that Frazier tried for years to remove him, and Brownlee privately strongly condemned Frazier. Fred L. Brownlee to Charles S. Johnson, 1950, box 29, folder 10, Charles S. Johnson Papers; Howard E. Spragg interview, 28 September 1989, 17; Howard E. Spragg interview, 21 October 1987, 11, 17, Clifton H. Johnson Papers, Amistad Research Center.

4. In 1954 the AMA had assets of $13 million in addition to the $5,400,000 Hall Fund and the $1,500,000 Hand Fund. Spragg said in later years the church funds going to the AMA were a pittance, in some years no more than $25,000. Statement of AMA assets written on Model Foundations Description, 1955, box 332, General Secretary Correspondence; Howard E. Spragg interview, 28 September 1928, 17–18, Clifton H. Johnson Papers.

5. Howard E. Spragg quoted Truman Douglass saying that it would be unwise

to appoint an "AMA black" or "an old time AMA" person. Douglass was not opposed to black leadership. He simply wanted an executive who had no ties to the AMA and would be more cooperative with the BHM. Blacks saw the AMA as their organization and worried about loss of independence. Howard E. Spragg interview, 28 September 1989, 18, Clifton H. Johnson Papers; Philip M. Widenhouse, undated curriculum vita, box 343; undated biographical sketch of Widenhouse, box 332; Joseph A. French to Philip Widenhouse, 25 January 1951, 4 February 1951, box 329; Truman B. Douglass to Corporate Members of the Board of Home Missions, 2 May 1951, box 329, General Secretary Correspondence.

6. Spragg said, "Phil was supposed to be cooperative, but humans being what they are, Phil kept really wanting to carry forward some of the independence of the AMA." His independence created tension with Douglass. Howard E. Spragg interview, 28 September 1989, 18, Clifton H. Johnson Papers.

7. AMA division committee minutes, 3 April 1956, box 363; Division of Higher Education and AMA minutes, 19 June 1956, 29 April 1959, box 363, General Secretary Correspondence; Howard E. Spragg interview, 28 September 1989, 16–18, Clifton H. Johnson Papers; Clifton H. Johnson interview with Wesley A. Hotchkiss, 11 November 1992, box 39, folder 8, Clifton H. Johnson Papers.

8. Hotchkiss was succeeded in 1983 by acting general secretary Veryln Baker; and in 1984 Nanette Roberts, an efficient lobbyist for AMA needs, became general secretary. She was succeeded by Theodore Erickson in 1987. In 1989 Rev. B. Ann Eickhorn and Rev. L. William Eickhorn became co-secretaries. Division of Higher Education and AMAA minutes, 8 September 1958, box 363, General Secretary Correspondence; Guide to the Arrangement of the American Missionary Association Archive, Addendum, Records 1858–1991, Amistad Research Center; Howard E. Spragg interview, 28 September 1989, 18, Clifton H. Johnson Papers.

9. Truman Douglass to general secretaries of the Board of Home Missions, 20 October 1961, box 333, General Secretary Correspondence; A. Knighton Stanley, *The Children Is Crying: Congregationalism among Black People* (New York, 1979), ix; Howard E. Spragg interview, 28 September 1989, 10, Clifton H. Johnson Papers.

10. Howard E. Spragg interview, 21 October 1987, 40–43; Howard E. Spragg interview, 28 September 1989, 24–25, Clifton H. Johnson Papers.

11. The 1967 appropriations was as follows: Dillard, $72,000; Fisk, $13,000; Huston-Tillotson, $62,500; LeMoyne, $61,800; Talladega, $61,800; Tougaloo, $97,000, for repairs and renewals $71,567, and capital fund, $65,000 for a total of $504,667 to the colleges. Division of Higher Education and AMA committee minutes, 25 October 1966, box 364, General Secretary Correspondence.

12. Carl Braden, who had been accused of being a Communist and had been called before the House Un-American Activities Committee, spent time at Tougaloo in 1962. He traveled through Mississippi with Bob Moses. Braden said Tougaloo "was made available to the student movement for workshops and seminars." He discussed adult education workshops with President Beittel, who was interested and promised to help in any way he could. Carl Braden, Confidential Report on a Field

Trip through Mississippi, 13–19 July 1962, 23 July 1962, Race Relations Department, UCBHMA.

13. For a discussion of Tougaloo and civil rights, see: Clarice T. Campbell and Oscar A. Rogers Jr., *Mississippi: The View from Tougaloo* (Jackson, MS, 1979); Barron C. Ricketts to Philip M. Widenhouse, 27 August 1955; Harold C. Warren to Samuel C. Kincheloe, box 4, folders 2, 4, 5, Samuel C. Kincheloe Papers; Clifton H. Johnson interview with Wesley A. Hotchkiss, 11 November 1992, box 39, folder 8, Clifton H. Johnson Papers.

14. Bryant Drake to H. C. Noble, 21 June 1960, box 333, Division of Higher Education and AMA committee minutes, 3 January 1960, 2 July 1960, and 3 July 1960, box 363; Division of Higher Education and AMA committee minutes, 27 May 1964, 3 January 1966, and 2 February 1966, box 364; Jones and Richardson, *Talladega College,* 180; Howard E. Spragg interview, 28 September 1989, 5, Clifton H. Johnson Papers.

15. Howard E. Spragg interview, 21 October 1987, 21, Clifton H. Johnson Papers; Jones and Richardson, *Talladega College,* 194–97; Drewry and Doermann, *Stand and Prosper,* 106–7; M. Christopher Brown II and Kassie Freeman, *Black Colleges: New Perspectives on Policy and Practice* (Westport, CT, 2004), 70–80.

16. G. H. Gessert, "A Financial Analysis of Talladega College Covering Ten Year Period from 1963–64 to 1972–73," TC/Adm. 4/15/4/29; Herman H. Long, "Memo to President of the Six AMA Colleges and Member of the Presidents' Council, 16 July 1971," TC/Adm. 8/7/2/3B; H. Long to F. D. Montgomery, 2 February 1973, TC/Adm. 8/7/2/4B; Jones and Richardson, *Talladega College,* 195; *United Church News,* June–July 2006, A7.

17. Wesley A. Hotchkiss to Albert W. Dent, 9 January 1981, box 6, folder 8; Clifton H. Johnson to Dent, 5 May 1981, box 6, folder 8, Albert W. and Ernestine Jessie C. Dent Family Papers; Howard E. Spragg interview, 28 September 1989, 24, Clifton H. Johnson Papers; Clifton H. Johnson e-mail to Joe M. Richardson, 19 April 2006.

18. Nanette M. Roberts to Samuel DuBois Cook, 10 April 1985, box 89, Dillard University, AMAA, Addendum.

19. Howard E. Spragg, who became BHM treasurer, claimed that the BHM legally could have taken over the AMA legacies anytime after 1937 if it chose to since it had power of attorney and agency for all the divisions including the AMA. It could be the successor corporation, and legacies made to the AMA could be legally held by the successor corporation as long as they were being used in accordance with AMA principles. Howard E. Spragg interview, 28 September 1989, 9, 15, 16, Clifton H. Johnson Papers; A Guide to the Arrangement of the American Missionary Association Archives, Addendum, Records 1858–1991, Amistad Research Center, Nanette M. Roberts to Samuel DuBois Cook, 2 February 1983, box 89, folder 22, Dillard University.

Index